Ending Poverty in South Asia

Ending Poverty in South Asia
Ideas That Work

Edited by
Deepa Narayan
Elena Glinskaya

THE WORLD BANK
Washington, DC

Contents

Foreword

The last two decades saw substantial change in the countries of South Asia. All countries of the subcontinent experienced more rapid growth than in the earlier decades and also saw a definite reduction in the incidence of poverty, resulting in the improvement of the lives of hundreds of millions of poor people. The extent of improvement in growth performance varied across countries and different factors were involved in different countries, but a common element was the adoption of broad based economic reforms involving rethinking of earlier approaches to development. The reforms in South Asia were notable in that they were homegrown, gradual, and accompanied by continual redesign and fine tuning.

Greater openness of economic policies was one common factor in the reforms in the countries of South Asia and it was accompanied by openness to new ideas. One of the new elements was a willingness to create space for innovations, fresh thinking and experimentation, with greater scope for decentralized initiative. This allowed visionary individuals from all segments—civil society, government, and the private sector—to undertake experiments designed to help poor people improve their lives. This book is about twelve such experiments in India, Pakistan, Bangladesh, and Afghanistan. We have always had visionaries in South Asia. Some of their visions have been translated into action. But never before have so many of these innovations been 'scaled up', to benefit whole communities, districts, states, and even countries. What they did and how they did it is the subject of this book.

The book offers no pre-cooked blueprint for replication. Rather, it offers readers a look at what has worked in practice and suggests a framework for distilling the common elements across these case studies. The lessons are complex, and applying them will undoubtedly require redesign and fine-tuning to fit the initiatives to the local context. What is important, however, is that the experience of the last two decades shows us that reforms and scaling-up innovations can work in South Asia—and if these examples can be strengthened and expanded in the coming decades, we may realize our dream of a subcontinent free of poverty.

March 2006   MONTEK SINGH AHLUWALIA
New Delhi

Acknowledgments

The case studies in this book were developed as part of a year-long learning process initiated by the World Bank in 2003–4 to examine large scale poverty reduction programs in a wide range of developing countries around the world. The process was inspired by Jim Wolfensohn, then president, led by Frannie Léautier, vice president of the World Bank Institute, and managed by Blanca Moreno-Dodson and Michele de Nevers under the guidance of a steering committee made up of several World Bank vice presidents and then-chief economist Nick Stern. Without their efforts and guidance, none of the case studies would have been prepared.

The learning process culminated in a workshop in Shanghai in May 2004, hosted by the Chinese government, with additional financing from donors, foundations, and the private sector. At the workshop, 105 case studies with policy implications were discussed by policy makers, practitioners, civil society representatives, and academicians from 83 countries around the world.

This volume presents 12 of the case studies from South Asia. Deepa Narayan, one of the editors, coordinated all the case studies from India, under the helpful guidance of Michael Carter, former country director for India, Gobind Nankani and Danny Leipziger, former and current vice presidents for the Poverty Reduction and Economic Management network (PREM) at World Bank headquarters, and John Page, who was then director of the Poverty Reduction Group. Elena Glinskaya, the other editor, coordinated the remaining case studies from South Asia, under the overall direction of Praful Patel, vice president for the South Asia Region, Shantayanan Devarajan, chief economist for the South Asia Region, and Sadiq Ahmed, South Asia PREM director.

Thanks are due to Luca Barbone, director of the Poverty Reduction Group, and Shantayanan Devarajan, chief economist for the South Asia Region, who supported the additional work needed to turn the original case studies into this book. We also thank all the authors of the case studies for updating and revising the workshop papers for publication, and their organizations for providing additional information for finalizing the case studies. We acknowledge the invaluable contribution of the Poverty Reduction Group staff based in India, who provided research assistance and helped coordinate the work of authors, editors, and the publisher; the team included Sunila Andrews, Kaushik Barua, Molly Kinder, Divya Nambiar, and Soumya Kapoor at different stages of the production process. We are deeply grateful to Cathy Sunshine for her editing skills.

Finally, our most profound gratitude and admiration are due to the visionary individuals and their dedicated associates whose work is reported here. We hope their example will provide both inspiration and guidance to all those seeking to end poverty and destitution in South Asia.

October 2006   DEEPA NARAYAN

                                                               ELENA GLINSKAYA

Contributors

SWAMINATHAN S. ANKLESARIA AIYAR is consulting editor of the *Economic Times* of India and a consultant to the World Bank, based in New Delhi and Washington, DC. He was previously editor of the *Economic Times* (1992–94) and the *Financial Express* (1988–90), and has served as India correspondent for the *Economist*. His work for the World Bank and the Asian Development Bank has focused on topics such as community-driven development, the Heavily Indebted Poor Countries initiative, industrial liberalization, and the impact of reforms on poverty in India. He is the author of *Towards Globalisation: The Case for Foreign Investment* (Sangam Books, 1992).

KUTTAYAN ANNAMALAI works as a management consultant for Deloitte Consulting LLP, based in Dallas, Texas. His consulting experiences include developing customer and market strategies and creating operational process improvement for clients across several industries, including retail, telecommunications, technology, and financial services. His research interests center on exploring innovative business models that catalyse rural transformations in emerging economies. He is a contributor to *The Fortune at the Bottom of the Pyramid: Eradicating Poverty through Profits*, edited by C.K. Prahalad (Wharton School Publishing, 2005).

RASHID BAJWA has been the chief executive of Pakistan's National Rural Support Programme since 1994. A medical doctor, he was previously a member of the civil service of Pakistan.

SUBHASH BHATNAGAR is an adjunct professor at the Indian Institute of Management, Ahmedabad. He also serves as an e-government adviser for the World Bank and was part of the World Bank team during the early implementation of the Bhoomi land registration project. His principal interest is the use of information and communication technology for governance and rural development. He has published eight books, including

Information and Communication Technology in Development: Cases from India (with R. Schware, Sage India, 2000) and *E-Government: From Vision to Implementation* (Sage India, 2004). He is a fellow of the Computer Society of India.

JOHN BLAXALL is a development economist who spent most of his career at the World Bank, focusing on low-cost water and sanitation in Asia and Africa and on helping poor communities to identify and solve their own problems. He currently lives in New Delhi and has undertaken volunteer and consulting assignments.

RAJEEV CHAWLA is a member of the Indian Administrative Service and is currently the secretary of e-governance in the state government of Karnataka. As additional secretary in the Department of Revenue in Karnataka, he was responsible for implementation of the Bhoomi land registration project from its inception to the current level of development.

SHANTAYANAN DEVARAJAN is chief economist of the South Asia Region of the World Bank. Since 1991, he has been the Bank's research manager for public economics, chief economist of the Human Development Network, and director of *World Development Report 2004*. Before joining the World Bank he was on the faculty of Harvard University's John F. Kennedy School of Government. His research covers public economics, trade policy, natural resources and the environment, and general-equilibrium modelling.

ELENA GLINSKAYA is a senior economist in the Poverty Reduction and Economic Management Unit in the South Asia Vice Presidency of the World Bank. She has published in a number of areas, including poverty, education, and the labour market in developing and transition countries. Her current projects include work on remittances, poverty and inequality in Nepal, poverty monitoring in the Indian states of Orissa and Uttar Pradesh, and employment and pay issues in the formal and informal sectors in India.

NAOMI HOSSAIN, a political sociologist, is senior research fellow in the Research and Evaluation Division of BRAC in Bangladesh. She is currently coordinating research on the impact of village governance arrangements on the extremely poor. Her other research interests include the politics of poverty and social policy and relations between aid donors and recipients. She is the author of *Elite Perceptions of Poverty in Bangladesh* (University Press Limited, 2005).

RAVI KANBUR is T.H. Lee Professor of World Affairs, international professor of applied economics and management, and professor of economics at

Cornell University. He has served on the staff of the World Bank as economic adviser, senior economic adviser, resident representative in Ghana, chief economist of the Africa Region, and principal adviser to the chief economist of the World Bank. The author of over 100 publications, he received the Quality of Research Discovery Award from the American Agricultural Economics Association and an honorary professorship at the University of Warwick.

VERGHESE KURIEN is recognized as the 'father of India's milk revolution'. Trained as a mechanical engineer, he helped form India's first dairy cooperative and then led development of the nationwide dairy cooperative movement. He is a founder of the National Cooperative Dairy Federation of India, the Gujarat Cooperative Milk Marketing Federation, and the Institute of Rural Management, Anand. His organizational positions have included, among others, founder-chairman of the National Dairy Development Board and chairman of the board of governors of the Institute of Agriculture, Anand. He has received numerous awards, including the 1989 World Food Prize and India's Padma Vibhushan and Magsaysay awards.

ABDUL MALIK, an economist, has been with the Aga Khan Rural Support Programme in Pakistan since 1998. He has worked extensively on poverty and livelihood issues and is co-author of several papers on this subject.

AADIL MANSOOR began his career as an economist in 1999 with the National Rural Support Programme in Pakistan. He went on to work for the Aga Khan Rural Support Programme and the Rural Support Programmes Network, where he is currently the grants program manager for a US-funded project that supports innovative development partnerships at the district level.

ABI MASEFIELD is a consultant to the World Bank on social protection, vulnerability, and rural development policy in Afghanistan. She was previously employed by the United Nations, and then directly by the government of Afghanistan as a policy adviser to the Ministry for Rural Rehabilitation and Development, based in Kabul. She has also worked in Ethiopia, India, Sri Lanka, Kenya, Somalia, Sudan, and South Africa as a consultant to the UK Department for International Development and other international agencies.

DEEPA NARAYAN is Senior Adviser in the Poverty Reduction and Economic Management Network of the World Bank, based in New Delhi. She led a multicountry research initiative to understand poverty from the perspective of poor people, and is the lead author of the three-volume series *Voices of the Poor* (Oxford University Press, 2000–2). Her recent publications include the edited volumes *Empowerment and Poverty Reduction: A Sourcebook* (World Bank, 2002) and *Measuring Empowerment: Cross-Disciplinary Perspectives* (World Bank, 2005). She is currently leading a 15-country study aimed at understanding how people create wealth to move out of poverty.

SAMUEL PAUL is founder and chairperson of the Public Affairs Centre in Bangalore, India. He spearheaded development of the citizens' report card as an accountability tool, an experience described in his book *Holding the State to Account: Citizen Monitoring in Action* (Books for Change, 2002). A former director and professor of economics at the Indian Institute of Management, Ahmedabad, he has served as adviser to the Indian government and to the United Nations, the World Bank, and the International Labour Organisation. His many awards include the Indian government's Padma Shri award in 2004.

M. MUJTABA PIRACHA is an economist and a member of the civil service of Pakistan. He took leave from government service to work for the Aga Khan Rural Support Programme and the Rural Support Programmes Network from 2002 until 2005. He presently works as a consultant for a national education sector project funded by the US Agency for International Development.

K. RAJU is a member of the Indian Administrative Service, 1981 batch. Based in Hyderabad, he currently serves in the state government of Andhra Pradesh as principal secretary for rural development. As national project coordinator for the South Asia Poverty Alleviation Programme, supported by the United Nations Development Programme, he has helped to demonstrate a sustainable model of social mobilization and community empowerment for poverty reduction across the state of Andhra Pradesh.

VIMALA RAMACHANDRAN is director of the Educational Resource Unit, a research and consulting group in India, where she works on elementary education, girls' education, and women's empowerment issues. She was the first national project director of Mahila Samakhya (1988–93), a government of India program for women's education and empowerment. Her books include *Snakes and Ladders: Factors Influencing Successful Primary School Completion for Children in Poverty Contexts* (World Bank, 2004) and *Gender and Equity in Primary Education: Hierarchies of Access* (Sage Publications, 2004).

SACHIN RAO is a senior researcher-analyst at the Centre for Civil Society in New Delhi. His primary area of interest is the development of ecosystems that encourage large and small entrepreneurs to develop commercial solutions to problems of social development.

STEPHEN F. RASMUSSEN was chief executive of the Aga Khan Rural Support Programme in Pakistan from 1994 to 2003 and went on to become chief executive of the Pakistan Microfinance Network. Based in Islamabad, he is currently a lead specialist in the Finance and Private Sector Development Unit of the World Bank and the regional resource person for microfinance. He has worked as a consultant on health care, rural development, microfinance, and enterprise development in Pakistan, Afghanistan, Kenya, Tajikistan, Kyrgyzstan, and other countries.

SAMEER VYAS is managing director of the New Tirupur Area Development Corporation Limited in Chennai, India. He was appointed to the Indian Administrative Services in 1977 and has held various positions in the state government of Tamil Nadu as well as the central government. He was appointed in 1995 as director of the Department of Economic Affairs in the Ministry of Finance, and subsequently as private secretary to the union minister for finance. In 1996 he was appointed as an adviser to the executive director of the World Bank for India, Bangladesh, Sri Lanka, and Bhutan.

HASSAN ZAMAN is a senior economist on the South Asia Poverty Reduction and Economic Management team at the World Bank. He has worked on structural reform issues in his capacity as the Bank's country economist in Malawi and Nepal and on microfinance issues in Bangladesh and Pakistan. He is the principal author of a World Bank report titled *Economics and Governance of NGOs in Bangladesh* (2005). Prior to joining the World Bank in 1998, he was a senior researcher at BRAC, the largest non-governmental organization in Bangladesh.

Abbreviations

AKRSP	Aga Khan Rural Support Programme
AREU	Afghanistan Research and Evaluation Unit
ARTF	Afghanistan Reconstruction Trust Fund
ASA	Association for Social Advancement
BATF	Bangalore Agenda Task Force
BDA	Bangalore Development Authority
BESCOM	Bangalore Electricity Company
BMP	Bangalore Municipal Corporation
BMTC	Bangalore Metropolitan Transport Corporation
BMZ	Federal Ministry for Economic Cooperation and Development (Germany)
BOT	build, operate, and transfer
BRSP	Balochistan Rural Support Programme
BSNL	Bharat Sanchar Nigam Limited (telecommunications)
BWSSB	Bangalore Water Supply and Sewerage Board
CAMPE	Campaign for Popular Education
CDC	community development council
C-DoT	Centre for Development of Telematics
CDP	community development plan
DNFE	Directorate of Non-Formal Education
DPEP	District Primary Education Project
DWCRA	Development of Women and Children in Rural Areas
EEC	European Economic Community
EGS	Education Guarantee Scheme
FFE	Food for Education
FP	facilitating partner
FSS	Female Secondary Stipends

GBTI	Ghazi Barotha Taraqiati Idara
GCMMF	Gujarat Cooperative Milk Marketing Federation
GDP	gross domestic product
GER	gross enrolment ratio
gm	grams
GTZ	German Agency for Technical Cooperation
hh	households
IBD	International Business Division (of ITC)
IDA	International Development Association (of the World Bank)
IDC	Indian Dairy Corporation
IL&FS	Infrastructure Leasing & Financial Services Limited
IT	information technology
JPMU	joint programme management unit
kbps	kilobits per second
KfW	Kreditanstalt für Wiederaufbau (Official Development Bank, Germany)
kg	kilograms
LSA	Lok Sampark Abhiyan (house-to-house survey of school participation)
LSP	Livelihood and Social Protection Programme
metric ton	1,000 kilograms
MFI	microfinance institution
MMS	mahila mandal samakhya (subdistrict-level women's federation)
MRRD	Ministry of Rural Rehabilitation and Development
mt	metric ton (1,000 kilograms)
NABARD	National Bank for Agricultural and Rural Development
NAC	Northern Areas and Chitral
NDDB	National Dairy Development Board
NEEP	National Emergency Employment Programme
NGO	non-governmental organization
NIC	National Informatics Centre
NPP	National Priority Programme
NRSP	National Rural Support Programme

NSP	National Solidarity Programme
NTADCL	New Tirupur Area Development Corporation Limited
NWFP	North-West Frontier Province
OF	Operation Flood
PAC	Public Affairs Centre
PESP	Primary Education Stipend Project
PKSF	Palli Karma-Sahayak Foundation
PPAF	Pakistan Poverty Alleviation Fund
PRSP	Punjab Rural Support Programme
PTA	parent–teacher association
RBI	Reserve Bank of India
RGSM	Rajiv Gandhi Shiksha Mission (Rajiv Gandhi Education Mission)
Rs	rupees
RSP	Rural Support Programme
RTC	Record of Rights, Tenancy and Crops
RTO	Road Transport Authority
SAPAP	South Asia Poverty Alleviation Programme
SERP	Society for Elimination of Rural Poverty
SEWA	Self-Employed Women's Association
SHG	self-help group
SNF	solids-not-fat
SRSO	Sindh Rural Support Organization
SRSP	Sarhad Rural Support Programme
TNRDC	Tamil Nadu Road Development Company Limited
TNUDF	Tamil Nadu Urban Development Fund
TNUDP	Tamil Nadu Urban Development Project
TNUIFSL	Tamil Nadu Urban Infrastructure Financial Services Limited
TWIC	Tamil Nadu Water Investment Company Limited
ULB	urban local body
UNDP	United Nations Development Programme
UNICEF	United Nations Children's Fund
UPS	uninterrupted power supply
USAID	US Agency for International Development

VO	village organization
VSAT	very small aperture terminal
WAPDA	Water and Power Development Authority
WSPF	Water and Sanitation Pooled Fund
WTO	World Trade Organization

Note: All dollar amounts are US dollars.

Tables, Boxes, Figures

Tables

Boxes

Figures

1

Overview and Lessons Learned

Deepa Narayan and *Elena Glinskaya*

One ordinary person; one extraordinary dissatisfaction. Questions without answers. A young woman lawyer in Ahmedabad, India, wonders how forming a union could benefit poor women who work at home or as vendors on the streets. An anthropologist-turned-finance-minister in Afghanistan asks where to start in rebuilding a war-ruined country where government structures barely exist. An economist in Bangladesh ponders whether poor people would be able to manage loans. A government official in Andhra Pradesh, India, considers how government action could unleash the power of the poorest, illiterate women to help themselves. The CEO of a large private company imagines that creating wealth for millions of farmers in rural Madhya Pradesh, India, might also be profitable.

The development record shows that individuals can make a difference in fighting poverty when ways are found to institutionalize creative ideas and apply them on a scale extending beyond pilot projects. This book recounts 12 such cases from a range of countries and sectors in the South Asia region, with a focus on how these programmes scaled up and on the potential for applying lessons in other settings.

Across South Asia, thoughtful actions by visionary individuals and organizations from civil society, government, and the private sector are helping poor people improve their lives. These development successes have occurred in less than optimal settings, often under appalling conditions of weak governance, widespread corruption, minimal infrastructure, deep-rooted social divisions, and poorly functioning judicial systems. In each case, creative individuals saw possibilities where others saw only hopelessness. They imagined a way forward that took into account local realities and built on local strengths. They were willing to experiment and ignore the sceptics, until the sceptics became supporters and then often partners working to bring about change on a large scale.

While achieving high levels of growth is critical, growth alone does not necessarily translate into better lives for the millions of poor women, men, and children in South Asia. Growth alone does not increase the chances of survival of a poor girl infant or her mother. But growth can be an important factor in their survival and rising prosperity if other changes also occur—if health services improve, or if the mother obtains credit to start a small business, or receives a scholarship to send her daughter to school, or joins a union that provides her with insurance and health care.

This book has an ambitious title, because without a burning ambition to end poverty, poverty will not end. The achievements documented would not have been possible if someone had not been determined to alter the status quo. These case studies do not offer a blueprint or model for poverty reduction; there is no single model. Nor do they cover every issue that is important. But they suggest the range of ideas that can be successful and the underlying principles that cut across these diverse initiatives. All the programmes tap the imagination and ingenuity of the South Asian people—in government offices, in civil society organizations, in the private sector, and in the villages and urban neighbourhoods. All seek to empower poor people to access the economic opportunities and basic services so necessary to human dignity.

This opening chapter is divided into four sections. The first section sketches the broad economic and human development context for the South Asia region, focusing on India, Pakistan, Bangladesh, and Afghanistan, the country settings for the 12 case studies. The second section outlines the conceptual framework, discussing the investment climate, empowerment, and the process of change. The third section provides a brief guide to the case studies, and the final section distils four key lessons learned from these experiences.

THE REGIONAL CONTEXT

South Asia used to make headlines as home to the largest number of the world's poor.[1] While the region still has close to one-quarter of all humanity and almost 40 per cent of the world's poor people,[2] the dynamic economies of South Asia are increasingly in the news for more positive reasons.

The spectacular success of India, fast becoming a global centre for information technology (IT), stands out. Cross-border IT services grew astoundingly during the 1990s, from $1 billion, or 0.3 per cent of gross domestic product (GDP), to $9.6 billion, or 2 per cent of GDP. IT-enabled services such as back office operations, remote maintenance, accounting, public call centres, medical transcription, insurance claims processing, and data entry are expanding rapidly. Other sectors of the economy such as textiles have also done very well in the past two decades. The impact has been felt across the country. Not only are the IT-savvy and entrepreneurial few reaping benefits, but there has also been substantial growth and poverty reduction overall in India.

On the whole, the 1990s was a good decade for South Asia. GDP growth averaged 5.4 per cent per year for the region, ranging from a low of 3.6 to a high of 5.9 per cent per year in individual countries (Table 1.1). This strong performance came during a decade when growth in developing countries elsewhere in the world slowed considerably.

TABLE 1.1 Growth of GDP, 1980–2003

Country or region	1980–90	1990–2003
Bangladesh	3.7	4.9
India	5.7	5.9
Nepal	4.6	4.6
Pakistan	6.3	3.6
Sri Lanka	4.0	4.7
South Asia average	5.5	5.4
East Asia and Pacific average	7.9	7.6
Low-income countries (world)	4.7	4.7
Middle-income countries (world)	2.9	3.5

Source: World Development Indicators 2005.

Economic growth in South Asia has brought with it declines in income poverty rates. These now range from 50 per cent in Bangladesh to 25 per cent in Sri Lanka based on national poverty lines, and from 36 per cent to 6.6 per cent respectively based on the $1 a day international poverty line (Figure 1.1). If these trends continue, South Asia will be one of the few regions to actually meet the Millennium Development Goal of halving poverty by 2015.

But there is still a long way to go. Deep human deprivation persists in the region, especially for excluded social groups and children. In order to significantly reduce poverty and improve human development outcomes, South Asian countries face a twin challenge: they must ensure both that

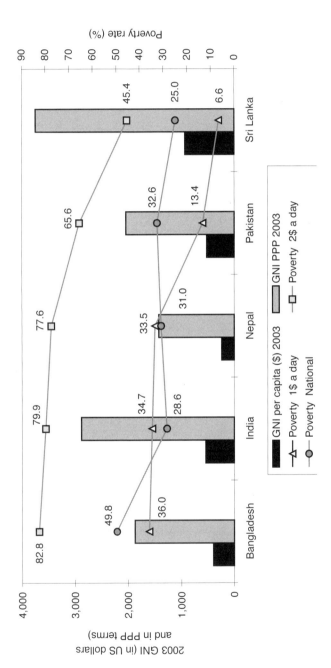

FIGURE 1.1 Per Capita Income and Poverty Rates

Sources: GNI, $1 and $2 a day rates: *World Development Indicators 2005*. National poverty rates: national governments and World Bank data (most recent estimates).

TABLE 1.2 Selected Social Indicators, 1990–2003

Country or region	Child malnutrition (weight for age)		Ratio of female to male in primary and secondary school		Child mortality (under 5 mortality rate per 1,000)		Maternal mortality (per 100,000)	Life expectancy (years)		Access to improved water (%)		Primary completion rate (2000–3)		Total fertility rate (births per woman)	
	1990/ 91	2002/ 03	1990/ 91	2002/ 03	1990/ 91	2002/ 03	2000	1990/ 91	2002/ 03	1990/ 91	2002/ 03	male	female	1990/ 91	2002/ 03
Bangladesh	68	52	77	107	144	69	380	55	62	71	75	71	76	4.1	2.9
India	53	—	70	80	123	87	540	59	63	68	86	85	77	3.8	2.9
Nepal	—	48	57	83	145	82	740	54	60	69	84	84	72	5.3	4.1
Pakistan	40	35	47	71	138	98	500	59	64	83	90	—	—	5.8	4.5
Sri Lanka	38	33	102	103	32	15	92	70	74	68	78	118	108	2.5	2.0
South Asia average	—	48.4	71	83	130	92	567	58	63	70	84	85	77	4.1	3.1
East Asia and Pacific average	—	14.7	89	97	59	41	116	67	70	71	78	98	95	2.4	2.1
Low-income countries (world)	—	43.7	74	84	149	123	689	56	58	64	75	76	66	4.7	3.7
Middle-income countries (world)	—	11.1	91	98	55	37	115	68	70	77	83	96	94	2.6	2.1

Source: World Development Indicators 2005.
Note: — Nor available.

their growth rates accelerate to 7–8 per cent per year over the next decade and that the benefits of faster growth are shared more broadly across their populations.

India

India, the world's second-largest country after China, dominates the economy of South Asia, accounting for three-quarters of the region's total population. Its annual GDP is now more than half a trillion dollars. In purchasing power parity terms, India is the fourth-largest economy in the world, after the United States, China, and Japan. India's economy performed well during the 1980s and 1990s, with the growth rate accelerating from 3.5 per cent per year earlier to nearly 6 per cent annually over these two decades.

Income poverty in the country also appears to have declined quite significantly over the same period.[3] Survey estimates indicate that the share of the population living below the poverty line fell from nearly 50 per cent in the early 1980s to a little over one-quarter in 1999/2000 (26 per cent according to official government of India estimates, 29 per cent according to alternative estimates).[4] Internationally comparable poverty estimates also show a decline in the proportion of people living on less than $1 a day in India, from 46 per cent in the early 1990s to 34.7 per cent in 1999/2000. Most of the reduction in income poverty has been driven by economic growth, a result of increases in average consumption per capita (Deaton and Drèze 2002). These averages hide great variation between states, however.

The overall investment climate in India improved during the 1980s and 1990s. Previously, the economy had been characterized by extensive government regulation of private sector activity through price controls and investment licensing—the infamous 'License Raj' regime, under which local firms enjoyed a high level of tariff protection combined with quantity restrictions on imports.[5] This system underwent extensive overhaul through a number of key economic reforms that started in the 1980s and continued in the 1990s. The country's trade policy and the exchange rate regime were liberalized, and capital markets were reformed. Perhaps the single most important change was the recognition of the private sector as the leading engine for growth, abandoning the earlier tilt in favour of a dominant role for the public sector (Ahluwalia 2005). While private sector investments were 55 per cent of total investments in India in 1980s, they increased to 65 per cent by the middle of the 1990s, and to 71 per cent in early 2000 (World Bank 2003a).

While the countrywide investment climate has improved, there are persistent impediments to faster growth and job creation, particularly in the lagging states. In India, starting a new business requires 10 permits compared with six in China; the median time required to secure these permits is 90 days, compared with 30 days in China (World Bank 2005a). Complaints of delays, corruption, and harassment in these interactions are common. A recent survey by the World Bank and the Confederation of Indian Industry found the share of firms in India making irregular payments to be almost twice that in Malaysia (World Bank/CII 2002).[6] It has been estimated that the potential gains from removing key investment constraints (inefficiencies in labour, capital, and land markets, as well as bottlenecks in infrastructure, especially in power) could add 2–4 per cent to annual GDP growth (McKinsey Global Institute 2001). Importantly, thousands of India's poor make their living as microentrepreneurs—as self-employed farmers, street vendors, and home-based workers. They face many of the same constraints as larger firms, including insecure property rights, limited access to finance, insufficient public services, and, often, corruption (World Bank 2003a).

While the manufacturing and services sectors of the Indian economy performed well during the 1980s and 1990s, agricultural output expanded relatively slowly. Agriculture contributes only about a quarter of total GDP today, but its importance to the economic, social, and political fabric of India is far greater than this number suggests. About three-quarters of India's poor people continue to live in rural areas, and a large proportion of them depend on agriculture for employment.

Over the past three decades, the Indian government's agricultural policy has relied on subsidizing key inputs (fertilizer, water, and power) to promote more rapid growth in grain production, thereby ensuring food security for the population. The government also uses output subsidies. Nonetheless, factor productivity in agriculture has declined over the past two decades. Public investment in agricultural infrastructure has been quite limited during this time, and the minimum support price at which the government guarantees purchase of food grains from selected farmers has given farmers little incentive to diversify. Furthermore, productivity increases induced earlier by the green revolution across India, especially in Punjab, Haryana, Andhra Pradesh, and western Uttar Pradesh, have by now subsided. It is now well accepted that wasteful public subsidies have crowded out productivity-enhancing public investments, while the remaining restrictions on domestic trade have not allowed farmers to realize the true potential of the agricultural sector (Ahluwalia 2005).

Land is a supremely important asset in rural India. When asked what it means to be poor, poor people often equate landlessness with poverty (Narayan, Patel, et al. 2000). There has been some improvement in India with regard to the distribution of this asset, as patterns of land ownership have become somewhat less skewed since the 1970s. An increasing share of land is now owned by marginal to medium farmers. The increase in the rate of landlessness has also been arrested, with the proportion of landless remaining at around 11 per cent in the 1990s despite the pressure of population growth (World Bank 2003a). Driving forces include the government's land policies, which have focused on abolishing intermediaries between the state and cultivators, imposing land ownership ceilings, and distributing surplus lands to the landless. There are encouraging signs of innovative programmes in land registration.

One weakness of India's growth record over the past decade has been its inability to generate jobs commensurate with the aspirations of the population. Even as output growth accelerated in the 1990s, employment growth fell to less than half that witnessed in the preceding decade. Employment increases of about 1 per cent per year from 1994 to 2000 earned this period the epithet of 'a decade of jobless growth' (Bhattacharya and Sakthivel 2004).

Desirable jobs in India are ones in the formal or 'organized' sectors of the economy because these typically provide higher wages and job security. Yet the organized industry and services sectors account for only about 27 million jobs overall, of which just 7 million are in manufacturing and 17 million are in services. The total labour force in the country is around 406 million people. While about 1 million workers are moving out of agriculture every year, the organized service sector generated only 76,000 new jobs annually over the past decade. Organized manufacturing created 350,000 new jobs between 1993/94 and 1999/2000. Total manufacturing employment (both organized and unorganized) in India grew at about 2 per cent per year during the 1994–2000 period, with the unorganized sector of accounting for the bulk of this growth.[7]

The quality of state institutions helps to explain differences in outcomes across states in India. Differences in governance and the performance of public sector institutions are very much in the forefront of policy debate in India today—not just in the context of the overall management of public resources, but also in relation to the delivery of public services. On the one hand, the overall consolidated (i.e., central and state combined) fiscal deficit in India has averaged more than 9 per cent of GDP over the last six years, with the overall debt stock rising to almost 90 per cent of GDP. On the other hand, despite this rapid rise in public expenditures, clear shortcomings are evident in the access to services delivered by public institutions (World Bank 2003a).

As one indication, recent estimates of absentee rates for teachers and medical providers are high, and the problem is generally much worse in poorer states (Table 1.3). Surprise visits to schools in Bihar indicated that as many as 39 per cent of the teachers were not present—and for medical practitioners, the rate was 58 per cent. It is therefore not so surprising that increases in government expenditures on education, health, and social safety nets during the 1990s did not always yield commensurate improvements in services or in outcomes. For example, national child mortality declined by only 25 per cent in the 1990s and now stands at 87 children per 1,000. By comparison, child mortality in Bangladesh declined by almost 50 per cent during the same period and now stands at 69 children per 1,000 (Table 1.2).

TABLE 1.3 Absentee Rates from Primary Facilities in Different States, 2003

(per cent)

State	Primary school teachers	Primary health care workers
Andhra Pradesh	26	—
Assam	34	58
Uttar Pradesh	26	42
Bihar	39	58
Uttaranchal	33	45
Rajasthan	24	39
Karnataka	20	43
West Bengal	23	43
Gujarat	15	52
Haryana	24	35
Kerala	23	—
Punjab	37	—
Tamil Nadu	21	—
Orissa	23	35

Source: World Development Report 2004.

Another area in India where inefficiencies constrain faster poverty reduction is the financial system. Although there is a wide network of rural banks in India, very few poor households have access to financing from formal sources—only 21 per cent, according to a 2003 survey on rural access to finance (P. Basu 2005). Moneylenders and other informal sources of credit remain an important source of financing for the poor—the study found that 48 per cent of landless and marginal farmers had borrowed from an informal source at least once in the preceding 12 months, at rates of interest averaging close to 50 per cent per year. A key factor constraining improved access to rural credit is inefficiencies in formal rural financial institutions.

Bangladesh

Bangladesh averaged 5 per cent GDP growth per year during the 1990s, growth only slightly lower than that of India. This helped reduce poverty from about 70 per cent in the 1970s to 50 per cent by early 2000. In contrast to India, growth in Bangladesh has been led by manufacturing (the ready-made garment sector in particular) and agriculture. Total factor productivity in agriculture increased by 1 per cent per year over this period, fuelled by improvements in rice productivity and growth of the fisheries subsector. The government's policy of agricultural liberalization, focused mainly on input markets, has paid off well. Similarly, progress with industrial deregulation, which gained momentum during the 1980s, has greatly benefited the ready-made garments industry, as did the policy of significant liberalization in trade policy in the early 1990s.

Despite these advances, the country is paying a high price for its public service inefficiencies, poor governance, and corruption. Their cost is estimated at about 2–3 percentage points of GDP growth forgone annually (Rahman, Kisunko, and Kapoor 2000).

More so than in other countries of the region, good human development policies in Bangladesh have been complemented by public–private partnerships. This policy stance has been a key factor in Bangladesh's success in expanding the delivery of primary and secondary education and basic health care.[8] In fact, many have asked how Bangladesh managed to achieve these successes while corruption remains so prevalent. The answer is that the government has actively pursued a policy of public financing coupled with private provision, forging partnerships with local communities and non-governmental organizations (NGOs). This has allowed it to alleviate the 'capacity deficit' and to tap into the creative potential of the poor. An added value of greater community involvement in the social sectors is that it ensures a minimum level of accountability (World Bank 2003c).

Bangladesh offers the best example in South Asia of how to provide access to finance for the poor. Today approximately 14 million poor households can tap formal financial sources. Access to finance has important advantages for the poor, allowing both consumption smoothing and investment in productive activities. Bangladesh's success in this area is credited to sound macroeconomic management that provides an enabling environment for microcredit: single-digit inflation, market-determined interest rates, a low external debt servicing ratio, and public expenditure focused on human development activities and expansion of physical infrastructure, especially the road network (World Bank 2003c).

Unlike elsewhere in South Asia, the state in Bangladesh, has 'made space' for social entrepreneurs to provide services where the state cannot. As a result, not only have microcredit institutions provided informal loans to rural households, they have also raised social awareness among the weaker sections of society and helped boost the decision-making capacity of women, who are often their main clients.

Pakistan

The experience of Pakistan differs from that of either India or Bangladesh. While Pakistan had the highest growth rate in South Asia (over 6 per cent) during the 1970s and 1980s, it became the slowest-growing country of the region during the 1990s as the growth rate faltered to less than 4 per cent per year. High fiscal deficits averaging 6 per cent of GDP fed into mounting debt, rising interest spending, and high defence expenditures, forcing the government to cut sharply into development spending. The incidence of poverty declined rapidly from 46 per cent in the mid-1980s to 34 per cent in the mid-1990s, but has largely stagnated since. While economic reforms pursued by the government since the late 1990s have helped boost the growth rate in recent years, it is too early to assess their impact in reducing poverty (the last household survey used to compute official poverty estimates for Pakistan was conducted in 2001).

One of the worst gaps is caused by Pakistan's underinvestment in people. The country underperforms (in terms of both expenditures as well as outcomes) other countries with similar per capita income on just about all major social indicators—in education, health, nutrition, and population growth rates (Table 1.2). This phenomenon is known as the 'social gap'. The discrepancies are especially large for women, so that a gender gap reinforces the persistent social gap (World Bank 2002).

Afghanistan

As Afghanistan emerges from two decades of conflict, the new authorities face a largely defunct government and financial institutions, weak administrative capacity, and depleted stocks of physical infrastructure. The country suffered significant damage during the extended period of conflict, especially to the power system, roads, and telecommunications, and to the stock of private housing. Traditional irrigation systems were destroyed or eroded by lack of maintenance. Agricultural production collapsed, livestock herds were depleted, and industries shut down. Most skilled professionals fled the country.

By the end of 2001, government services, including health care and education, had essentially stopped functioning. The result was a dramatic decline in social indicators, particularly for women and children. Infant and under-five mortality as well as maternal mortality rates were estimated to be among the highest in the world, and malnutrition affected about half of all children under age 5. The average life expectancy for an Afghan national was estimated to be little more than 40 years.

While tackling the monumental task of rebuilding the state, the Afghan government has also introduced various programmes to provide a basic safety net and reduce poverty in the country. The largest of these is the National Emergency Employment Programme, which is a cash-for-work programme to rehabilitate rural infrastructure. The National Solidarity Programme provides block grants for small community-managed reconstruction and development projects in rural areas.

In sum, the countries of South Asia have made significant advances in recent years, and several have experienced more rapid growth than many observers would have thought possible 20 to 30 years ago. Remarkable, too, has been the overall improvement in living standards in the last few decades. But enormous challenges remain, with the nature of these challenges varying from country to country. All the region's countries face the need to further reduce poverty, to overcome gender exclusion, to enrol more boys and girls in school, to improve the quality of education, and to reduce malnutrition and maternal mortality. There are many questions about the best ways to formulate and implement policies to achieve these goals. The cases described in this volume put a spotlight on some of the most successful initiatives pursued in the region and provide ideas for scaling up similar programmes in other parts of the world.

STRATEGIC FRAMEWORK

There is a growing consensus that a broad strategy for poverty reduction must rest on two pillars: improvements in the investment climate, so that people have access to markets and want to invest their resources to reap future benefits; and empowerment of poor women and men, so that they can participate in markets, governance, and society on their terms. Both concepts can be applied at the macro or national level as well as at the micro or local level. There is also a realization that the process through which decisions are made and implemented matters at all levels.

Investment Climate

As people make decisions whether to invest or consume their income, they take into account many aspects of the investment climate. Property rights are one important factor. A small farmer will not plant fruit trees that reach maturity in 10 years unless she is sure that her right to her land is secure for her lifetime. It is not rational for a farmer to invest in building a house or a small dam or to engage in land conservation if he feels that his land could be taken from him at any time.

Access to markets is another critical component of the investment climate. There is little incentive to produce if transporting the product to market costs so much and takes so long that production is no longer profitable or competitive. Equally important to small firms and microentrepreneurs is the quality of local infrastructure, including electricity, water, roads, transport, and telephones, and of local governance, including freedom from harassment by the police and government officials.

At the national level, large domestic and foreign investors weigh similar issues when deciding whether to invest capital in the country. Are their property rights secure? Will their investments be safe? Is the policy and regulatory environment stable and predictable?

Empowerment

Empowerment is about expanding women's and men's freedom of choice and action to shape their own lives. People are empowered when they gain control and influence over resources and decisions—control that typically is curtailed sharply for the poor because of their powerlessness. More powerful groups with finance, education, and social and political connections capture resources disproportionately and continue to shape institutions in their image, while the poor remain excluded.

Empowerment and improved development outcomes are a product of the interaction between the opportunity structure (rules, norms, behaviours) and the agency of poor and excluded groups (Narayan 2005; Petesch, Smulovitz, and Walton 2005; World Bank 2004, 2005c). Empowerment therefore involves both changing the opportunity structure through changes in institutions and increasing the agency of poor people to take action on their own behalf. Empowerment is the expansion of assets and capabilities of poor people to participate in, negotiate with, influence, control, and hold accountable the institutions that affect their lives.

Figure 1.2 outlines a framework for understanding empowerment in terms of the relationship between institutions of the state, market, and civil society—the more powerful actors—and poor people. It also points to possible intervention points.

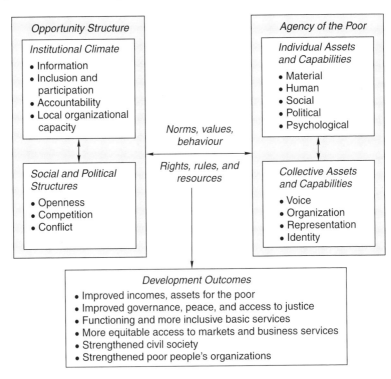

FIGURE 1.2 Overview of the Empowerment Framework

Four elements have been found to be consistently important in changing the institutional climate, power relations, and the incentives of actors engaged in unequal power relationships. They are access to information, mechanisms of inclusion and participation, social accountability, and local organizational capacity. Change can also come about through direct intervention in social and political structures, for example, by legislating that one-third of the seats in local governments and national parliaments should be reserved for women. These changes require national consensus and debate and are more difficult than carefully designed changes in the institutional climate governing relations between poor people and other actors.

Agency of poor people has both individual and collective aspects. Individual agency depends on assets such as health, education, and finance, as well as psychological dimensions of self-confidence and aspiration. Collective agency comes from poor people's own organizations, which enable their voices to be heard, their identity and dignity to be asserted, and their interests to be represented.

Process of Change

Much is known in general terms about what it takes to achieve successful outcomes in government, in the private sector, and in civil society. Even so, most programmes experience problems in implementation. A big issue is how to align incentives for different actors so that they behave in ways that lead to desirable outcomes for poor people. Incentives are not only financial; poor people and other actors make calculations based on cultural, social, political, and legal factors as well. When enforcement mechanisms are weak, laws and formal rules about punishing corruption fail to deter bribe-taking and other forms of harassment. When safety of girls is an issue, even a policy of free education will not induce poor parents to send their daughters to co-educational schools. A decision to change (or not change) national policy is often based on political calculations by state and national leaders rather than on strictly technical grounds.

To generate learning about change processes across countries, the World Bank organized the Shanghai Conference on Scaling Up Poverty Reduction in 2004. Development actors from around the world—practitioners, academics, government officials, private sector leaders, and civil society representatives—shared their experiences with poverty reduction initiatives, focusing especially on how successful programmes have scaled up. More than 100 case studies were developed for the conference, each examining the role of four key factors affecting implementation: leadership and political economy of change, institutional innovation, learning and experimentation, and the role of external catalysts (including external agencies).[9]

GUIDE TO THE CASE STUDIES

This book presents 12 of these case studies from South Asia. All of the initiatives profiled have been widely recognized as successful either in empowering poor women and men or in contributing to an improved investment climate. All underscore the importance of leadership, institutional innovations, learning and experimentation, and involvement of external catalysts. None of the efforts have proceeded without problems, and none are perfect examples. But all represent creative experiments that have attained a significant degree of success and that have scaled up from modest beginnings to achieve wider impact.

India's Milk Revolution

The book starts with the story of the Indian dairy development programme known as Operation Flood. Cooperatives in South Asia have a long and chequered history; many have been discredited because of elite capture, declining returns, and lack of accountability to their members. Yet India today is home to one of the most successful cooperative ventures in the world, the Anand pattern dairy cooperatives, which have transformed India from a net importer to the world's largest producer of milk and a milk exporter.

The initiative began with a small farmer cooperative in Anand, Gujarat, that was created to break up the monopolistic practices of exploitative middlemen. Building on this pattern, the Operation Flood programme implemented by the National Dairy Development Board has transformed the Indian dairy industry in just over three decades. Producers, mostly small farmers with one or two cows, are organized into more than 100,000 village-level dairy cooperative societies. These are grouped into district-level unions, which in turn are joined in state-level marketing federations. The entire federated structure is governed democratically by the farmer-members, supported by professional managers.

By 2003–4, the dairy cooperative movement involved nearly 12 million farmers. Their farms supplied almost 15 million litres of milk per day to over 750 towns and cities across India, with an annual value of Rs 880 billion. Among other innovations, Operation Flood marked the first creative use of food aid from developed countries to 'prime the pump' for a domestic dairy industry rather than depressing prices for local producers.

The Self-Employed Women's Association

Labour unions have long been an important channel to protect labour rights. But in developing countries, most poor people work in the unorganized informal economy and hence are unprotected by labour unions or labour laws. In India, an estimated 93 per cent of workers are in the informal sector. In 1972 Ela Bhatt, a lawyer who had represented unionized textile workers in Ahmedabad, turned her attention to the plight of informal women workers—day labourers, street vendors, head loaders, and home workers, among others. The conventional wisdom said such workers were not 'workers' and thus could not be organized. Against great odds, the Self-Employed Women's Association, known as SEWA, established and registered itself as India's and the world's first labour union representing informal and self-employed women workers.

Today SEWA has nearly three-quarters of a million members in urban and rural areas of Gujarat and six other states. Casting itself as a movement rather than an organization, SEWA aims to help women in more than 70 occupations seek secure employment and self-reliance. It fights for its members, seeking fairer wages and benefits and developing alternative employment in rural areas to drive farm wages up. In addition, some 86 cooperatives under the SEWA umbrella provide training and marketing assistance to members, and SEWA Bank offers microloans. SEWA's responsiveness to its members' needs has led it to provide health and life insurance, disaster relief, and a range of training and research activities in watershed management, forestry, childcare, literacy, and adult education, to name a few. Chapter 3 documents SEWA's growth and profiles three members whose lives have changed for the better.

Self-Help Groups in Andhra Pradesh

When discrimination is embedded in social and economic institutions and the poor are conditioned to expect a life of poverty, change becomes extremely difficult. In India, improving the lives of Dalit women is a particularly daunting task. Considered untouchable, these mostly illiterate women live on the fringes of society, eking out a living on seasonal wage labour. They are frequently beaten by their husbands, and their children often end up as bonded labour. Chapter 4 traces the history and achievements of the women's self-help movement in Andhra Pradesh, which reaches out to these women and others among the poorest of the poor.

The movement began on a small scale in 1996, organizing groups of 10–15 women who would start saving money together and then seek links to banks. Building on early efforts by the government and NGOs, a government-created independent society called Velugu (and recently renamed Indira Kranti Patham) fostered the spread of the self-help groups. Today Andhra Pradesh has over 600,000 groups, half of all self-help groups in the country. The groups are federated at the village, subdistrict, and district levels, with plans for a presence at the state level.

Responding to women's needs, the programme focuses on social mobilization through group formation and economic empowerment. Members with successful repayment records may take repeated loans. As the women have gained experience and strength in numbers, they have taken up large-scale economic activities including the procurement of maize, neem, and other agricultural commodities. By eliminating the role of exploitative middlemen, the women traders realize 20–30 per cent greater returns.

Pakistan's Rural Support Programmes

Chapter 5 turns to Pakistan, where persistent poverty and inadequate service delivery spurred a quest for community-driven solutions not dependent on government. The nationwide spread of Rural Support Programmes, or RSPs, began in 1982 in the remote and mountainous Northern Areas. The Aga Khan Rural Support Programme organized community groups and helped them identify their priority needs. It built assets and capabilities of rural households, both filling gaps in service provision and improving the effectiveness of services provided by government and the private sector. In the 1980s the average income in the Northern Areas was less than one-third the national average. But in the 1990s, even as the national economy slowed, per capita income in the Northern Areas grew by 84 per cent. Health and education outcomes improved significantly.

Encouraged by this apparent success, the government supported replication of the RSP approach in other parts of Pakistan. By 2005 there were 10 Rural Support Programmes active in more than 70 districts, engaging more than 72,000 community organizations. The movement affects almost 1.2 million members and their households, perhaps 8 million people overall. Each RSP is an autonomous organization that develops programmes tailored to local needs. The twin principles of cooperation with and autonomy from government have been key to the successful expansion of the RSPs.

Community-Driven Development in Afghanistan

After a quarter century of conflict, Afghanistan is one of the poorest countries in the world. Its social indicators in 2001 ranked at or near the bottom among developing countries, and over 25 per cent of its population was displaced within the region. How to go about poverty reduction and nation building in such a fragile and devastated situation?

Experience suggests that projects planned and managed by communities typically show higher rates of return and are more sustainable than those planned and managed by government agencies or development partners. The two programmes profiled in chapter 6, Afghanistan's National Solidarity Programme (NSP) and National Emergency Employment Programme (NEEP), were developed on these principles. NSP makes block grants to support small-scale reconstruction and development projects in communities across Afghanistan. Communities make decisions and control resources throughout the project cycle, working through elected village councils. NEEP builds new infrastructure such as roads and irrigation systems, employing local people on a cash-for-work basis. Both programmes not only transfer resources to communities but also help to strengthen fledgling institutions in the ravaged country—community development councils in the case of NSP, and public administration and private sector enterprises in the case of NEEP.

It is too early to know whether these efforts will have a lasting impact in Afghanistan, where sustainable poverty reduction will depend on complex political and economic dynamics. But some outcomes are already evident. By 2005, about 10,000 community development councils had been established in all 34 provinces of the country, and were being managed by 278,000 elected representatives. Working with the councils, NSP had supplied safe drinking water to 2,000 communities and connected another 2,000 to district centres with rural access roads. NEEP had generated an estimated 11.2 million labour-days, benefiting some 375,000 households. Through the programme, local people have built or rehabilitated about 6,000 kilometres of access roads, 11,000 metres of bridges and culverts, and 187 irrigation schemes.

The Bangladesh Microfinance Experience

Chapter 7 describes the evolution of the microfinance industry in Bangladesh over three decades. The sheer scale of microfinance access in Bangladesh, where more than one in three households in the country now have access to credit, has led to considerable interest in how this growth took place. Most of the approximately 1,200 microfinance institutions (MFIs) in Bangladesh are non-governmental organizations. The industry is dominated by four large MFIs—Grameen Bank, BRAC, ASA, and Proshika—that serve almost 87 per cent of borrowers. These four institutions combined have approximately $950 million in outstanding loans and $470 million in savings.

In addition to providing access to microcredit, MFIs provide non-credit services such as training, business development services, and social messages on education, health, and civic rights. Numerous countries have attempted to replicate the success of Bangladesh's Grameen Bank, but for various reasons (lack of funds, weak management capacity, and regulatory hassles, among others) several of these Grameen replications are struggling to achieve scale or are underperforming financially. By examining the innovative ideas and practical experiences that contributed to scaling up microfinance in Bangladesh, practitioners hope to determine which ones are unique to that country and which can be replicated elsewhere.

Computerizing Land Records in Karnataka

Two case studies involve the use of information technology to correct government failure and market failure without the organization of citizens or poor people into groups. The computer, embedded in cleverly designed systems, becomes the aggregator of demand.

Chapter 8 describes India's only successful computerization of land records, under the project known as Bhoomi. Land records are of critical importance to farmers, who need them to access bank loans and other services. As of 2005, 20 million land records of 6.7 million farmers in the state of Karnataka had been computerized, bringing increased transparency and accountability in the maintenance of these records. This replaced an archaic system in which farmers depended on the whims and availability of 9,000 village accountants, who usually demanded hefty bribes to process records manually. Today a printed copy of a land record can be obtained for a fee of Rs 15 from kiosks located in 177 taluk offices. Public use of the kiosks is steadily increasing.

A key reason for success was that as computerization capability was developed, the manual system was phased out to create an incentive to make the new system work. The process involved extensive participatory meetings at the district and subdistrict levels. Village accountants, who had the most to lose and thus the greatest reason to resist change, were offered training to become computer-proficient. Despite some limitations in access related to gender and other factors, Bhoomi has had an unmistakably positive impact in terms of improved service delivery and reduced corruption, and has helped to increase coverage of crop insurance.

India's E-choupals

Chapter 9 tells the story of a private sector initiative that is helping to transform the face of rural India. ITC, a private for-profit company, began an initiative in 2000 intended to transform the agrarian marketing system and re-engineer the supply chain. The company places computers, called e-choupals, in the homes of village farmers who are trained to operate them. Farmers from the surrounding area can use the computer free of charge to learn the prices of crops and make decisions about where and when to sell. Farmers are not obliged to sell to ITC, but if they do, they can take their crop to a company procurement centre where they are treated fairly and with respect. The system thus bypasses the traditional but inefficient market yards, where farmers face much less advantageous terms of sale.

Scaling up rapidly, the company has set up 5,200 e-choupals in more than 31,000 farming villages across six states, with plans to cover 100,000 villages by 2010. Initially targeting the soybean crop, the scheme has expanded to take in coffee, wheat, rice, pulses, and shrimp. The network of e-choupals is profitable both for ITC and for the 3.1 million farmers who have access to the system. Farmers typically receive about 2.5 per cent more for their soy than they would get at the market yards, while ITC benefits from net procurement costs that are about 2.5 per cent lower than it would otherwise pay. In the areas where e-choupals are functioning, 50–90 per cent more farmers are planting soy, but the volume of soy marketed through traditional channels has dropped by 50 per cent. By making procurement more efficient and providing information at low cost, ITC has hit upon a profitable venture that benefits rural communities as well.

Community Schools in Madhya Pradesh

Throughout most of India, universal primary education remains an elusive goal. But one state, Madhya Pradesh, has experimented with a radical approach so as to not lose another generation of children to illiteracy. A statewide house-to-house survey showed that lack of access to schools within walking distance prevented many village parents from educating their children. Under the Education Guarantee Scheme launched in 1997 with the strong support of the state chief minister, the government committed itself to provide a school to any village within 90 days of a written request. The village recruits a teacher candidate locally, who is then trained and paid a salary by the government. Each school is managed by an elected village education committee; parent–teacher associations monitor teacher performance and student attendance and provide the all-important midday meal.

This bottom-up, demand-driven approach to universalizing education has already shown impressive results. Between 1997 and 2000, over 26,000 schools were opened for 1.2 million children, mostly from poor and disadvantaged communities. Enrolment rates have surged. In less than a decade, Madhya Pradesh has cut the number of out-of-school students by more than two-thirds and has virtually eliminated enrolment disparities by gender.

Educating Girls and the Poor in Bangladesh

Neighbouring Bangladesh also boasts dramatic successes in expanding access to primary education, even though average incomes in Bangladesh are lower than in India. It has done so with a unique combination of centralized education planning and plural provision, with many schools run by NGOs. Adding a million new school places each year between 1990 and 1995, the country now has 18 million primary school seats, theoretically sufficient for the entire school-aged population. While expanding supply, the government also offered carefully crafted incentives to boost the demand for education among historically underserved groups such as girls and the poor. As a result, the gender gap in primary education has been eliminated.

Chapter 11 analyses the driving factors behind this remarkable expansion. The crucial ingredient was political will at the centre, rooted in consensus among the national elite on the vital role of education in poverty reduction and economic development. Key factors in raising resources for the effort were the convergence of donor and government interest in primary education and policies encouraging community and private involvement. Although the relationship between NGOs and the government has occasionally been tense, the NGO schools have been instrumental in reaching out to girls and the poor. Despite the overall success of the expansion effort, problems of quality and pockets of exclusion persist, and Bangladesh is now embarking on reforms to address these issues.

Partnerships for Infrastructure in Tamil Nadu

While India has posted high growth rates in recent years, they would be even higher were it not for the crumbling urban infrastructure, poorly functioning road system, and isolation of villages by lack of roads and transport. In addition, not a single city in the country has safe drinking water available 24 hours a day or sanitation services for all its residents. Conditions in the urban slums are deplorable. In response, two initiatives have emerged, one that mobilizes private sector investment for infrastructure and another that taps the power of civil society to demand improved public services for citizens. Both experiences are from India's southern states, which have relatively healthy economies.

Chapter 12 focuses on Tamil Nadu, one of the most urbanized states in India. The urban local bodies that are responsible for providing basic services face severe financial and managerial constraints, so the quality of services in Tamil Nadu's cities is poor. In the mid-1990s, the state government undertook administrative and fiscal reforms to create space for demand-driven initiatives in partnership with the private sector. Three new autonomous institutions were created: the Tamil Nadu Water Investment Company, the Tamil Nadu Urban Infrastructure Financial Services, and the Tamil Nadu Road Development Company.

Under the public–private partnership framework, these ventures have developed an array of projects, including a $220 million water and sanitation project in Tirupur and an underground sewerage project at Alandur. They have built toll roads like the Madurai Inner Ring Road and the East Coast Road that are cost-effective and spur new business activities. The success of the public–private model in Tamil Nadu reflects the positive investment climate in the state and the demand-driven nature of the projects. It also stems from the nature of the partnerships themselves, which provide for viable risk sharing, transparency mechanisms, and an effective system of checks and balances.

Bangalore's Citizen Report Cards

In neighbouring Karnataka, the industrial city of Bangalore also experienced crumbling infrastructure and lagging basic services as the city's population swelled in the 1990s. Determined to hold the government accountable, a small group of concerned citizens led by Sam Paul devised a system known as the 'citizen report card' to spotlight the poor quality of public service provision and demand change. Based on feedback from users of the services, the report card grades each city agency on the quality of services provided. The results obtained from a series of three report cards in 1994, 1999, and 2003 were widely publicized in the Bangalore press.

The first report card revealed widespread dissatisfaction with services and caused some embarrassment among the government providers. Pressure from civil society groups, especially the newly created Public Affairs Centre, spurred the agencies to work on improving their performance. The second report card showed limited progress. Soon after, the new chief minister of Karnataka state announced the creation of a public–private task force to improve city services with greater public participation. Agency leaders were generally responsive and made reforms. By 2003, the third report card showed a significant improvement in public satisfaction with the city's service providers. As discussed in chapter 13, the success of the Bangalore experiment rested on two pillars: the pressure of civil society demands for improvements, and high-level political commitment that encouraged a response from state agencies.

A Framework for Analysis

The final chapter proposes an analytical framework for considering how to achieve poverty reduction by expanding interventions that are known to work well on a small scale. The authors use the concepts of market failure, government failure, and civil society failure to identify the gaps that scaling up must fill, as well as the constraints that such efforts will face. The framework derives from the understandings that emerge from the case studies but also helps to better interpret their findings. Although it is based on the South Asia experiences described in this volume, the framework has broad applicability throughout the developing world.

BROAD LESSONS FOR POVERTY REDUCTION PROGRAMMES

There are many lessons that emerge from these 12 case studies. Four lessons highlighted here link back to the conceptual framework on empowerment and improving the investment climate for the poor.

Invest in the Collective Agency of the Poor

The first lesson is that investment in the collective agency of poor women and men is essential to reach the poor. In socially stratified countries, poor people are poor because they lack the social and political connections, organization, education, and assets needed to take advantage of economic opportunity. Nobody is accountable to them. This is even more true for the poorest of the poor. Thus many of the programmes described in this book, even those focused on individuals, start by building the organizational structures and collective agency of poor women and men through producer cooperatives, self-help groups, savings groups, or other such structures.

The assumption, common in economic analysis that individuals move out of poverty through their individual efforts does not take into account social and cultural norms and constraints that are imposed by powerful social groups and internalized by the powerless. Entire social categories of poor people are barred from social or economic mobility because of institutionalized inequality. The Indian caste system, for example, has remained in place because its hierarchical rules are practised and internalized not just by the higher caste but also by the lower castes. Everywhere, people's life chances are affected not only by their individual efforts but also by the social categories they are born into (Béteille 1977; Tilly 1999; Loury 2002; Narayan, Chambers, et al. 2000; Gupta 2000; Narayan and Petesch 2002; Rao and Walton 2004; World Bank 2005c).

It is striking to note that nine of the 12 case studies focus on investing in agency by creating solidarity groups of the poor, despite the fact that this was never a criterion for selection of the case studies. These groups have adopted various practices to affirm their new identity and their rejection of age-old discrimination. In Andhra Pradesh, India, groups of disenfranchised women collectively take symbolic action to reject the concept of untouchability, such as by drinking water from the public well from which they were traditionally barred by the higher castes. In Gujarat, members of the Self-Employed Women's Association address foreign dignitaries by their names and add the traditional suffixes meaning 'brother' and 'sister' to establish equality between the members and the foreign visitors. Group solidarity is often reinforced by collective prayers and songs before meetings begin. Members of such groups across different countries report loss of fear as their biggest gain.

Discrimination by gender is marked throughout the South Asia region, and poor women face the most severe forms of social exclusion. Unless special efforts are made to reach women, they will continue to be marginalized even in programmes that succeed in helping poor men. Some programmes focus exclusively on women in order to break through culturally imposed constraints on women's agency. Others that serve both women and men have had to build special outreach to women into their programme design. In India, where milch cattle are tended mainly by women, the Operation Flood dairy development programme had to start special women's empowerment and training activities to ensure the inclusion of women in the cooperatives. The programme gives special incentives to encourage participation of women in governance of the cooperatives and has trained local women as dairy resource persons in the villages. The number of women who are members of dairy cooperatives rose from 0.62 million in 1986–87 to 2.47 million in 2001–02—still only 20 per cent of total members.

Change the Opportunity Structure

Participation of poor people in markets on a large scale requires changes in the opportunity structure. This in turn means changing the institutional climate of the state, private sector, and civil society actors that interact with poor people. It is usually easier to change the institutional climate of organizations than to intervene directly in deeply embedded social and political structures such as caste relations, interethnic relations, or national constitutions.

Poor people increase their incomes when their social organizations are leveraged to access or create new economic opportunities that are *linked to their livelihoods*. Pervasive inequality is a barrier to this process, and often the efforts of support agencies are too scattered to enable poor producers to effectively gain a market share large enough to change their bargaining power in markets. Furthermore, as long as the focus of poor people's groups is on the production and sale of raw commodities, their margins and hence their returns will remain low. Enterprises higher up the value chain have higher profit margins.

The women's self-help groups in Andhra Pradesh, the producer cooperatives of SEWA, and the Operation Flood dairy cooperatives all seek to leverage social capital into economic gains for their members, but they have had markedly different results. The Andhra Pradesh programme has a three-tiered approach in which individual groups at the village level form village organizations that then send representatives to subdistrict bodies, which manage finances and have decision-making authority. These then federate into district entities. It is this federated structure that enables the women to leverage their numbers very quickly.

The programme decided to shift its focus to work on activities higher up in the agribusiness value chain so as to capture greater returns for the members. Instead of losing profits to middlemen, the women have become procurement agents for a number of agricultural commodities. Andhra Pradesh is one of the largest producers of neem (margosa), a tree crop. In one part of the state, women's groups buying neem fruit from their members as well as from other farmers captured 90 per cent of the neem market in the state within two years. Women received training from the largest wholesaler in quality control, and the project provided weighing scales and moisture measurement instruments to women's village organizations. Similarly, the women's groups are rapidly becoming important procurers of maize, managing new decentralized procurement centres for the government-run state marketing federation that procures grains for the Food Corporation of India. As a result of their activities, prices that maize traders pay to all farmers have gone up in these areas.

SEWA has been less successful in capturing large market shares for its members, although its members are clearly better off in many ways because of their mutual solidarity. The sheer range and diversity of SEWA's economic activities, now numbering over 70, means that its efforts are diluted. The movement has a mistrust of the private sector, reflecting its union origins as well as Gandhian principles of self-reliance. The top management has a deep moral commitment to rural women, values rooted in social work rather than in business. SEWA members have yet to gain significant bargaining power in markets. Recently, SEWA has started experimenting with the private sector, including marketing women's embroidery and other textile products through large private sector retail shops and entering partnerships with ITC, Hindustan Lever, and other firms as distribution and procurement channels.

Unlike the women's movement in Andhra Pradesh or SEWA, Operation Flood started with a single purpose: to enable small dairy producers to receive a higher share of the consumer's rupee for every litre of milk sold. This required the cooperative movement to understand the producers' needs and desires, analyse the markets, and move up the value chain by integrating production, procurement, processing, and market operations. The cooperatives employ professional managers who can be hired and fired by the farmer-controlled board. Key features include spot payment to farmers for milk procured, transparent and fair terms, smart use of technology, and a strong market orientation. The large numbers of farmers involved, together with Dr Kurien's strategic vision and growing political clout, ensured that the government would support the scaling up of the cooperative dairy movement. This support included major financing over two decades through grants and loans from several donors, including the European Union and the World Bank.

Poor people can also access markets on fairer terms if interventions truly level the playing field so that self-inclusion is possible through individual action. Interventions that enable poor people to take advantage of opportunity can include providing access to information, increasing transparency, breaking the monopolistic power of traders or officials, ensuring accountability, and keeping transaction costs low.

Two of the programmes studied, e-choupals and the Bhoomi land registration system, use the power of information technology to reach large numbers of farmers. Both have scaled up quickly rather than over decades. Use of computers aggregates demand and reduces transaction costs. It also increases transparency and removes opportunities for corruption by reducing the discretion of providers or buyers. Access to information is embedded in a delivery design that is culturally appropriate and fine-tuned to existing local realities. Neither of these initiatives focuses exclusively on the poor or women, and while both groups participate in the programmes, the extent of their participation remains quite limited. There is more evidence of poor farmers and women farmers participating in Bhoomi than in the e-choupal system. When economic initiatives are not specifically targeted to the poor, the involvement of the middle class creates support for rapid expansion. However without special design features and outreach, socially excluded groups will remain excluded.

Involve Civil Society, Government, and the Private Sector

Successful programmes can be implemented by civil society organizations, government agencies, or private sector entities—or by partnerships between them. There has been much polarized debate on the merits of these three sectors as implementers. The case studies suggest that innovative ideas can come from within any sector of society, but their implementation usually requires synergies among two or all three sectors. In India, government agencies took the initiative in the design and implementation of Bhoomi, in the promotion of community-based education in Madhya Pradesh, and in the formation of self-help groups in Andhra Pradesh. Similarly, in Afghanistan, the National Solidarity Programme was a government creation. The microfinance revolution in Bangladesh was initiated by civil society, as were the citizen report cards in Bangalore. India's e-choupals were an innovation of the private sector.

All the multisectoral programmes that involve organizing poor people into groups, cooperatives, or federations that function well over time have been implemented by civil society groups and supported by government without interference in the programmes' internal policies. Government-created entities such as the one that promotes self-help groups in Andhra

Pradesh have functional autonomy. Government administrators on deputation work like NGOs in orientation and outreach, but can leverage their high connections within government. Scaling up these programmes requires massive financing, which must usually be provided by government and external donors. The community-driven rural programmes in Pakistan, the village-based programmes in Afghanistan, and the NGO schools in Bangladesh all depend on government and donors for financing.

Single-sector programmes that can be standardized over time and depend less on community capacity to organize and implement can be successfully carried out by government. Still, these programmes work best when service providers are made accountable to local community groups, as in educational expansion in Madhya Pradesh, or when civil society groups organize to demand accountability, as in Bangalore.

Two kinds of relationships have emerged between governments and civil society groups. In the first type, projects are financed by government but implemented by autonomous civil society groups, free of government interference. Examples include the Rural Support Programmes in Pakistan, the National Solidarity Programme implemented by 22 civil society partners in Afghanistan, and Operation Flood in India, for which the government created the National Dairy Development Board as an autonomous body. The second type of relationship involves a hands-off stance by government that allows multiple civil society providers to experiment and to scale up their efforts without interference. This dynamic is seen in the development of the primary education and microfinance sectors in Bangladesh.

The private sector is driven by the profit motive, and the challenge is to combine this with a value orientation to provision of services that benefit citizens and include the poor. Two approaches have emerged. In the first, innovations are designed, driven, and financed by the private sector without any policy changes in the investment climate, as happened with ITC's e-choupals. Policy changes follow rather than precede change. The second approach centres on public-private partnerships. This is the approach adopted in Tamil Nadu for the provision of urban infrastructure; that effort required changes in the regulatory framework and new institutions such as the Tamil Nadu Water Investment Company, a government–private joint venture. The government bears the regulatory and policy risks and the private entity bears the commercial risks, with projects developed based on demand. Both of these approaches benefit all citizens, not just the poor.

Follow Principles, Not Models

The final lesson is that there are no models or blueprints, only common principles that have been shown to underlie successful efforts and that can serve as a guide for the future. The search for models has led to an inordinate waste of development resources, while the poor remain poor. The experiences documented in this book confirm that there is no single model by which development efforts can reach and empower poor people, but there are common principles that cut across the activities described. The principles sketched briefly below can serve as guides in developing both policies and programmes that benefit poor people and other citizens on a large scale.

Successful programmes focus on knowing their clients. The most effective programmes had a strong focus on their 'core group' of clients, citizens, partners, producers, customers, or suppliers. Programmes that address priority needs defined by poor people themselves are much more likely to generate interest, support, short-term sacrifices, and risk-taking than programmes that simply assume the needs of 'beneficiaries'. Programmes that work well and scale up rapidly all remain connected to their clients through backward and forward linkages and know their clients' characteristics, preferences, habits, values, and strengths. The behaviour of clients is key because ultimately they are the ones who decide whether to participate or not, and whether to use and pay for services provided.

In the 12 cases studied, this demand orientation was achieved in a variety of ways: through poor people managing and designing their own programmes, or through use of fieldworkers, information technology, management feedback loops, or formal management information systems. SEWA relies on fieldworkers for monitoring and also maintains direct and frequent contact with its members. ITC, a private company, does continuous research and monitors the behaviour of farmers, working closely with sanchalaks who know their villages. Bhoomi works through participatory meetings with district-level workers and field visits to kiosks. The Education Guarantee Scheme in Madhya Pradesh relies on parent–teacher associations and gram panchayats. The microfinance groups in Bangladesh and the self-help groups in Andhra Pradesh collect behavioural information through weekly meetings; this information is then aggregated upward to managers at different levels.

Star trek: leaders, visionaries, and champions are needed to get started and inspire. Every successful large-scale programme was initially led by tenacious individuals who did not start off as 'stars' but who became stars in the process of starting, nurturing, and spreading something that worked. In the Indian cases, the government-initiated reforms were led by exceptionally talented and tenacious officers of the Indian Administrative Service, working from within the government machinery—K. Raju and Vijay Kumar in Andhra Pradesh, Rajeev Chawla in Karnataka, R. Gopalakrishnan and Amita Sharma in Madhya Pradesh. While providing leadership, they paid attention to the need for systems change to mobilize hundreds of thousands of people. In each case this involved extensive travel to rural areas to share the vision of change, to explain the rules of the game to those affected, to inspire and to cajole. In some cases the first generation of programme leadership has now passed the torch to others.

Other leaders have come from civil society and over time have become folk heroes. They include Akhter Hameed Khan and Shoaib Sultan Khan in Pakistan, Faisal Abad and Muhammad Yunus in Bangladesh, and Verghese Kurien and Ela Bhatt in India. All these individuals were associated with their programmes for decades. From the private sector, Nandan Nilekani of Infosys and S. Sivakumar of ITC are recognized for their role in bringing about positive societal change while at the same time managing companies for profit.

Many programmes have also had the support of strategically placed politicians, from state chief ministers to national prime ministers. The Bangalore Agenda Task Force was promoted by S.M. Krishna, then the state chief minister; the Andhra Pradesh self-help movement by then chief minister Chandrababu Naidu; the Madhya Pradesh education expansion by then chief minister Digvijay Singh. In Pakistan, successive prime ministers supported the spread of the RSP approach. In Bangladesh, the sweeping reform to expand basic education cut across political parties and was supported by the national elite. In Afghanistan, community-based approaches were championed by then finance minister Ashraf Ghani.

Rules and incentives are key. Even though change is initiated by leaders, programmes achieve success on a large scale when systems, processes, and products continuously support the needs of poor people, using feedback mechanisms to adjust and evolve. Human beings, particularly poor women and men, do careful cost-benefit analyses when making choices about how to deploy their limited resources. These calculations are based not only on economic circumstances but also on social, political, and cultural considerations that have long-term economic consequences. For behavioural change to occur, these calculations must change for large numbers of poor people. This change can be induced by the policy regime and the rules, incentives, norms, and behaviours of the frontline workers who are in contact with poor people.

The management style can be participatory or based on command and control; either can be successful provided that rules and incentives are aligned within the management system to deliver results. Thus, the Andhra Pradesh programme promotes accountability to the poor by giving self-help groups the right to hire and fire the workers who support them. Candidates are required to spend a month-long trial period in the villages and are hired as coordinators only if the community of poor Dalit women approves their skills and behaviour. To signal the power of the women's groups, the programme has the groups pay the community coordinator directly, initially out of project funds; over time, the women's groups themselves finance the salary of the coordinator.

Bangladesh's scholarship programme for secondary education of girls makes direct deposit of funds to a passbook account opened in the girl's name. The programme is monitored by parent associations and supported by opinion leaders, including religious leaders. This combination of factors has tipped the cost-benefit analysis that thousands of parents do, inducing them to switch from keeping their daughters at home to sending them to school.

In Tamil Nadu, changes in the regulatory framework have encouraged a flow of private funds to infrastructure ventures. And in Madhya Pradesh and other Indian states, getting the incentives right for all the key actors, particularly the farmers, has resulted in the high use and rapid spread of e-choupals—without any change in government policy.

A culture of participation or innovation fosters success. An organizational climate that supports broad-based participation or encourages and rewards innovation at all levels is needed to generate a vibrant system that does not collapse over time under the weight of its own success. Participatory processes may be more critical in early phases of a programme, to develop appropriate design features and incentives which can then become standardized with experience. This approach works best when the overall goals and vision are shared and objectives are clear.

Some of the programmes profiled such as the Pakistan RSPs, SEWA, and the self-help groups in Andhra Pradesh have a strong culture of participatory development and management. This culture is particularly striking in SEWA, where village women are members of the executive board and constitute the decision-making body. Operation Flood draws a clear distinction between the farmer-members who make decisions for the cooperatives and the professional managers who are responsible for innovation, marketing, and new products, with accountability to the members. In Madhya Pradesh, the community has to apply for a school through the gram panchayat; once a school is built, community members make contributions, identify a teacher candidate, and monitor teacher performance and student attendance.

Even where participatory culture is weak, a programme can still be successful if it achieves a fit with the demands of poor people and encourages innovation at all levels. Toward this end, frontline workers may give feedback to management, or managers may stay directly in touch with realities in the field. Business administration specialists supporting the e-choupal programme spend time in the villages, riding along on trucks that buy and sell agricultural commodities, in order to understand the situation on the ground. The Bhoomi programme retrains village accountants to use computers, using positive incentives such as 'nobody fails'; those who do not score high on computer exams are not thrown out but are coached until their scores improve.

The poor benefit faster when energies of the middle class and the private sector are harnessed to improve basic infrastructure and services. Targeted programmes only for poor people are difficult to implement and are susceptible to elite capture and corruption, particularly when the poor lack the capacity to organize, monitor, and demand their rights. When improvements in services benefit all citizens, poor people may benefit as well, but special design features are usually needed to ensure their inclusion. Infrastructure improvements benefit all, although provisioning of slums or small towns requires design adaptation. Quick access to land records through computerized kiosks benefits all farmers, including marginal farmers.

When the elite or middle-class people, acting either as citizens or through civil society organizations, get involved in monitoring government-financed programmes or linking these programmes to poor people, the programmes are more likely to reach the poor. They are also more likely to become politically sustainable. The Rural Support Programmes in Pakistan, the self-help groups in Andhra Pradesh, and the microfinance and educational expansion efforts in Bangladesh are all examples. The Bangalore Agenda Task Force, with strong civil society participation, helped achieve dramatic improvements in services within two years.

Private sector involvement can help drive rapid expansion, but steps must be taken to ensure the inclusion of the poor and fit with their needs. The e-choupal scheme, a creation of the private sector, expanded to cover 31,000 villages in less than five years, but only 10 per cent of the farmers using the kiosks are poor. To reach poor women, ITC is now setting up partnerships with poor women's organizations. The further expansion of Bhoomi to the village level will likely happen with private sector participation, both in running the kiosks and in using them to buy and sell to farmers.

Intangibles are critical: values, ethics, trust, self-esteem, self-confidence.
Development requires a mindset that is guided by core values and ethics.
Leaders at all levels of these successful programmes are determined to make
a difference in their environment for the greater good—not only to reap
profits for themselves or for their companies.

Development also depends upon self-confidence, pride, and a belief
that 'I can make a difference, I can achieve my goals.' Only people who
believe this take action. Government functionaries or civil society activists
involved in these programmes may work 16-hour days, day after day, not
for money but because they feel their work will make life easier for poor
people. A panchayat member in Madhya Pradesh feels deeply rewarded in
actually seeing poor girls going to school. A chief minister in Karnataka
personally signs letters to signal his support of the Bhoomi programme from
his sickbed in the hospital.

It is these intangibles—values, self-confidence, self-esteem, and networks
of trust—that will be the biggest contributor to further development and
poverty reduction on a large scale.

References

Ahluwalia, M., 2005, 'Lessons from India's Economic Reforms,' T. Besley and
    N.R. Zagha (eds), *Development Challenges in the 1990s: Leading Policymakers
    Speak from Experience*, Washington, DC: World Bank; New York: Oxford
    University Press.

Basu, P., 2005, 'A Financial System for India's Poor,' *Economic and Political Weekly*
    (Mumbai), 10 September.

Béteille, A., 1977, *Inequality Among Men*, Oxford: Basil Blackwell.

Bhattacharya, B.B. and S. Sakthivel, 2004, 'Economics Reforms and Jobless Growth
    in India in the 1990s,' Working Paper E/245/2004, Institute of Economic
    Growth, New Delhi.

Deaton, A. and J. Drèze, 2002, 'Poverty and Inequality in India: A Re-examination,'
    Economic and Political Weekly (Mumbai), September 7.

Deaton, A. and V. Kozel, 2005, *The Great Indian Poverty Debate*, New Delhi:
    Macmillan.

Gupta, D., 2000, *Social Stratification*, New Delhi: Oxford University Press.

Kurien, V., 2005, *I Too Had a Dream*, New Delhi: Roli Books.

Loury, G.C., 2002, *The Anatomy of Racial Inequality*, Cambridge, MA: Harvard
    University Press.

McKinsey Global Institute, 2001, 'India: The Growth Imperative: Understanding
    the Barriers to Rapid Growth and Employment Creation,' New Delhi.

Moreno-Dodson, B. (ed.), 2005. *Reducing Poverty on a Global Scale: Learning and Innovating for Development: Findings from the Shanghai Global Learning Initiative*, Washington, DC: World Bank.

Narayan, D. (ed.), 2005, *Measuring Empowerment: Cross-Disciplinary Perspectives*, Washington, DC: World Bank.

Narayan, D., R. Chambers, M.K. Shah and P. Petesch, 2000, *Voices of the Poor: Crying Out for Change*, Washington, DC: World Bank; New York: Oxford University Press.

Narayan, D., with R. Patel, K. Schafft, A. Rademacher, and S. Koch-Schulte, 2000, *Voices of the Poor: Can Anyone Hear Us?* Washington, DC: World Bank; New York: Oxford University Press.

Narayan, D. and P. Petesch (eds), 2002, *Voices of the Poor: From Many Lands*, Washington, DC: World Bank; New York: Oxford University Press.

Petesch, P., C. Smulovitz and M. Walton, 2005, 'Evaluating Empowerment: A Framework with Cases from Latin America,' D. Narayan (ed.), *Measuring Empowerment*, 39–67. Washington, DC: World Bank.

Planning Commission, 2001, 'Report of the Task Force on Employment Opportunities,' Planning Commission, Government of India, New Delhi.

Rahman A., G. Kisunko and K. Kapoor, 2000, 'Estimating the Effects of Corruption: Implications for Bangladesh,' Working Paper 2479, World Bank, Washington, DC.

Rao, V. and M. Walton (eds), 2004, *Culture and Public Action*, Stanford, CA: Stanford University Press.

Tilly, C., 1999, *Durable Inequality*, Berkeley: University of California Press.

World Bank, 2002, *Pakistan Poverty Assessment*, Washington, DC: World Bank.

———, 2003a. *India: Sustaining Reform, Reducing Poverty*, Development Policy Review, World Bank, Washington, DC.

———, 2003b. *World Development Report 2004: Making Services Work for Poor People*, New York: Oxford University Press.

———, 2003c. *Bangladesh Public Expenditure Review*, Washington, DC: World Bank.

———, 2004. *World Development Report 2005: A Better Investment Climate for Everyone*, New York: Oxford University Press.

———, 2005a, *Doing Business in 2004: Understanding Regulation*, Washington, DC: World Bank; New York: Oxford University Press.

———, 2005b, *World Development Indicators 2005*, Washington, DC: World Bank.

———, 2005c, *World Development Report 2006: Equity and Development*, New York: Oxford University Press.

World Bank/CII, 2002, *Improving India's Investment Climate*, Washington, DC: World Bank; New Delhi: Confederation of Indian Industry.

World Economic Forum, 2003, *The Global Competitiveness Report 2002–2003*, New York: Oxford University Press.

Notes

1 The South Asia region comprises India, Bangladesh, Pakistan, Sri Lanka, Nepal, Afghanistan, Bhutan, and Maldives. Reliable data for the latter three countries are scarce, so these countries typically are not included in analyses of consumption poverty or human development outcomes in the region.

2 Based on the $1 a day threshold. See *World Development Indicators 2005* (World Bank 2005b).

3 India's definition of poverty equates it with income or expenditure levels. The Indian government's Planning Commission defines the national poverty line as the level of per capita consumer expenditure sufficient to provide an average daily intake of 2,400 calories per person in rural areas and 2,100 calories per person in urban areas, plus a small allocation for basic non-food items. The national poverty lines for the other South Asian countries are computed using similar methods, though the average daily caloric intake used varies across countries.

4 There is a lively debate under way in India regarding the extent to which poverty rates in the country fell during the 1990s. For more details, see Deaton and Kozel (2005).

5 The License Raj was so called because producers had to obtain a license from the central and/or state government to produce certain products. As late as 1990, some 800 items were reserved for exclusive production in the small-scale industry sector. This meant that investment in plant and machinery in any individual small industry unit could not exceed a specified monetary ceiling.

6 According to the *Global Competitiveness Report* (World Economic Forum 2003), India ranks 73rd of 75 countries. China ranks 23rd.

7 Estimates based on the National Sample Surveys in India (Planning Commission 2001).

8 In health, good results have come from an emphasis on child immunization and control of communicable diseases, progress in regulating the pharmaceutical industry and drug imports, and improvements in public safety related to drug use. In education, emphasis on sending girls to school has closed the gender gap at the primary level. Other successes include Bangladesh's population control programme, which combined education, social marketing of population control materials, and technical advice from family health workers with an effective delivery system, resulting in a sharp decline in fertility.

9 For more information on the Shanghai conference, see Moreno-Dodson (2005).

2

India's Milk Revolution
Investing in Rural Producer Organizations

Verghese Kurien

Over the last quarter century, the Indian dairy industry has progressed from a situation of scarcity to one of plenty, as India has become the world's largest milk producer. What began as an innovative local solution to the widespread exploitation of India's milk producers by rapacious middlemen became a large national programme, transforming the livelihoods of some 12 million rural families.

The seeds of what would eventually become India's 'white revolution' were planted in the state of Gujarat in the 1940s. There a small group of farmers were organized into a dairy cooperative in an effort to retain a greater percentage of their milk's profit. With the assistance of professional managers, the cooperative developed a business model based on farmer control over the entire value chain: production, procurement, processing, and marketing of milk and milk products. By cutting out the need for intermediaries in the procurement and sale of milk, the cooperative enabled the farmers to enjoy the fruits of their labour instead of surrendering most of the profit to corrupt and exploitative middlemen. The fledgling cooperative soon proved a success and was replicated across the state, eventually growing into a multimillion-rupee dairy industry.

Beginning in 1970, the National Dairy Development Board (NDDB) replicated the village cooperatives all over India through the Operation Flood programme. Between 1970 and 1996, Operation Flood developed a self-sustaining network of some 34,500 cooperatives, covering 3.63 million producers. In each state, the network features:

- Decentralized milk *production* by the small milk producers
- Milk *procurement* by the village-level dairy cooperative societies

- Centralized milk *processing* by the district-level unions
- *Marketing* of milk and milk products by the state-level federation.

The results are extraordinary. Total milk production has grown 400 per cent, from 21.2 million metric tons in 1968–69 to 88.1 million metric tons in 2003–04. Customers, too, have benefited. Milk consumption in India has more than doubled, from 112 to 231 grams per day in the same period. The cooperatives alone supply milk to consumers in over 750 towns and cities across India.

The programme has also had an important impact on the millions of landless, marginal, and small farmers engaged in milk production who make up the bulk of cooperative membership. Because it is low-capital-intensity, has a short operating cycle, and offers steady returns, dairying has become a preferred activity among small rural producers. It currently engages some 70 million Indian households. Operation Flood has provided an economic boost to small farmers participating in the programme by increasing their level of employment and income and the average prices they receive for their milk.

This chapter documents India's experience with dairy cooperatives and explores the model as an instrument for rural development and employment generation. It tracks the history of the Operation Flood programme, looks at the sequence of events that led to its scaling up, examines its major achievements, and finally highlights the factors that underpinned the programme's many successes.

Box 2.1 Achievements of Dairy Cooperatives in India, 2003–04

Reach

- The dairy cooperative network is owned by nearly 12 million farmer members.
- These producers are grouped in more than 108,500 village-level dairy cooperative societies.
- The societies are grouped in 170 district-level unions spanning 338 districts.
- The unions make up 22 state-level marketing federations.

Milk production

- India's milk production increased from 21.2 million metric tons in 1968–69 to 88.1 million metric tons in 2003–04.

(Contd)

Box 2.1 (Contd)

- Per capita availability of milk increased from 112 grams per day in 1968–69 to 231 grams per day in 2003–04.
- India's 3.8 per cent annual growth of milk production surpasses the 2 per cent growth in population; the net increase in availability is around 2 per cent per year.

Marketing

- In 2003–04, average daily cooperative milk marketing stood at 14.87 million litres; annual growth has averaged about 4.2 per cent compounded over the last five years.
- Dairy cooperatives now market milk in about 200 cities, including the large metropolitan areas of Kolkata, Chennai, Delhi, and Mumbai, and in some 550 smaller towns.
- During the last decade, the daily milk supply has increased from 17.5 to 52.0 litres per 1,000 urban consumers.

Innovation

- Bulk vending saves money and conserves the environment.
- Milk travels as far as 2,200 kilometres to areas of shortage, carried by rail and road milk tankers.
- India produces 95 per cent of its own dairy equipment, saving valuable foreign exchange.

Macro impact

- The annual value of India's milk production amounts to about Rs 880 billion.
- Dairy cooperatives generate employment opportunities for about 12 million farm families.

Source: NDDB 2005.

HISTORICAL BACKGROUND

Cattle play a significant role in the economic life of rural India. They have remained the keystone of Indian farming since time immemorial as draught and milch stock. Their utility for the rural community is so high that they are considered to embody divinity. The Atharva Veda says: 'Welfare be to our mother and father; welfare be to our cows.' The Royal Commission on Agriculture noted:

The cow and the working bullock carry on their patient backs the whole structure of Indian agriculture. In the actual life of the people and in the rural economy of the country, the relative importance of bovine animals is indeed much more marked than the figures of the total numbers of cattle suggest (quoted in Khurody 1974: 4).

Promotion of dairying in India has two main purposes: (a) to supply an adequate quantity of milk at a reasonable price to urban consumers, and (b) to provide a viable occupation to the unemployed rural poor so as to raise their income-earning capacities.

In pre-independence India, public and private agencies dominated the dairy industry, although government policy did not favour any one organizational form (Singh and Singh 1998). Early efforts to organize dairying along cooperative lines were made after the enactment of the Cooperative Societies Act of 1912. The Government of India subsequently took some steps to improve the quality of milch animals and their productivity through the Key Village Scheme, launched under the First Five-Year Plan (1951–56), and the Intensive Cattle Development Plan, launched under the Third Five-Year plan (1961–66). However, in the absence of a stable and remunerative market for milk, production remained more or less stagnant. During the two decades between 1951 and 1970, milk production grew by barely 1 per cent per year, while per capita milk availability declined by an equivalent amount.

During the 1960s, various state governments tried different strategies to develop dairying, including establishing dairies run by their own departments, setting up cattle colonies in urban areas, and organizing milk schemes. Almost invariably, dairy processing plants were built in cities rather than in the milksheds where milk was produced. This urban orientation to milk production led to the establishment of cattle colonies in Bombay, Calcutta, and Madras. Their main aim was to meet the demand for milk and milk products in big cities through improvements in milk collection, processing, and distribution.

Unfolding the Vision of Sardar

Because the government projects did not create an organized system for procurement of milk, unscrupulous contractors and middlemen exploited milk producers. The establishment of the Kaira District Cooperative Milk Producers' Union Ltd (Gujarat), now known as Amul, was in response to this problem.

Polson Dairy, a private dairy established in Anand, Gujarat in 1929, procured milk from producers in Kaira district through middlemen, processed it, and then sent it to Mumbai, mainly to what was then called the Bombay Milk Supply Scheme. Mumbai was a good market for milk, and Polson profited immensely. In the mid-1940s, when the milk producers in Kaira district asked for a share in the profits, they were denied even a modest increase in the price they were receiving for their milk. The producers went on strike, refusing to supply milk to Polson. The Kaira milk cooperatives began as a response to this exploitation.

The first dairy cooperative was the outcome of a farmers' meeting in Samarkha village, Kaira district, on January 4, 1946. The meeting was called by Morarji Desai on the advice of Sardar Vallabhbhai Patel (both men were Congress party leaders from Gujarat who spearheaded India's freedom movement under the leadership of Gandhi). It was Sardar's vision to organize milk farmers and have them gain control over procurement, processing, and marketing by entrusting the task of managing these to qualified professionals, thereby eliminating the middlemen. Sardar Vallabhbhai Patel assigned Tribhuvandas Patel, a local Congress leader, the task of 'making the Kaira farmers happy and organiz[ing] them into a cooperative unit.' This led to the formation of the Kaira District Cooperative Milk Producers' Union, and Tribhuvandas served as elected chairman of the cooperative for the first 25 years. The cooperative, popularly known now by its products' brand name, Amul, successfully competed with the private Polson Dairy.

I began working with milk farmers in Kaira in 1949. I had just returned to India from Michigan State University and was posted as a dairy engineer at the government milk creamery in Anand. Fed up with the lack of challenges at the creamery, I volunteered to help Tribhuvandas Patel, then chairman of the Kaira cooperative union, set up a milk processing plant. At the time, the union consisted of only two village milk cooperatives, representing a handful of farmers.

The Kaira union began with a clear goal: to ensure that its producer members received the highest possible share of the consumer's rupee. This goal defined the union's direction. The focus was on production by the masses, not mass production. The secret of the union was in combining the wisdom of farmers with the skills and knowledge of professional managers. The partnership was based on a relationship of mutual trust, faith, and respect. The professionals, who had skills and education, had to recognize that the illiterate milk farmers had wisdom passed on to them through generations of tradition. For their part, the farmers had to appreciate that in order to survive in a highly competitive local and global marketplace, an economic organization like a cooperative must have committed professionals of the highest quality and integrity.

By the early 1960s the modest experiment in Kaira was being widely recognized as a success. The basic constituent unit of the model was the milk producers' cooperative society at the village level. Membership in these societies was open to all who needed their services. Decisions were taken on the basis of one member exercising one vote. No privilege accrued to capital, and the economic returns, whether profit or loss, were divided among the members in proportion to the amount of milk they supplied to the cooperative.

Farmers from all parts of Gujarat started visiting Kaira to learn from Amul's success. They went back to their own districts and started their own cooperatives on the same pattern, in districts such as Mehsana, Surat, Valsad, Bharuch, Sabarkantha, Banaskantha, Baroda, Ahmedabad, Panchmahals, and Rajkot. In each district, the cooperatives in villages formed a district-level cooperative milk producers' union that processed milk into various milk products. The core feature of the model, which came to be known as the Anand Pattern, remained the same—farmer control over procurement, processing, and marketing of milk and milk products.

After years of struggle, the cooperatives began to produce dramatic results. The Gujarat Cooperative Milk Marketing Federation (GCMMF) was established in 1973 to jointly market the products of the dairy cooperative unions of Gujarat. Today, the GCMMF sells Amul brand products not only in India but also overseas. In 2002–03 the GCMMF's turnover exceeded Rs 27,000 million, making it the largest food company in India. What started as a fledgling cooperative became a multimillion-rupee dairy industry.

SCALING UP: THE OPERATION FLOOD PROGRAMME

The struggles and achievements of Anand Pattern dairy cooperatives in Gujarat caught the attention of the Government of India. In October 1964, on the occasion of the inauguration of Amul's cattle feed plant, the prime minister of India, Lal Bahadur Shastri, spent a night as the guest of a village milk cooperative society near Anand. Impressed by the socio-economic changes brought about by the milk cooperatives, he expressed the desire for a national organization to replicate the Anand Pattern dairy cooperatives throughout the country. As a result, in 1965 the National Dairy Development Board was established with headquarters at Anand. The mandate of the NDDB was to replicate Anand Pattern dairy cooperatives in other parts of the country.

Using Aid for Self-Reliance

The proposal to establish a national network of milk cooperatives sought to make innovative use of the abundant stock of milk products donated by the countries of the European Economic Community (EEC) in the late 1960s. The worldwide glut of milk products during this period offered such an opportunity; moreover, it was a chance that was unlikely to come again, because the developed countries would not likely repeat the costly error of producing such large dairy surpluses. The challenge was to use the European surpluses as an investment in the modernization of India's dairy industry while averting a less desirable outcome, namely that massive exports of low-cost dairy products to India would sound the death-knell for India's struggling dairy industry.

Through the World Food Programme, an agency of the United Nations Food and Agriculture Organization, food aid in the form of milk powder and butter oil was obtained from the EEC countries. It was used in three strategic ways. First, the donated milk powder was reconstituted in order to provide enough liquid milk to enable liquid milk schemes in the major cities to obtain a commanding share of their markets. Second, funds realized from the sale of donated products were used to resettle city-kept milch cattle and permit their progeny to multiply, so as to increase organized milk production, procurement, and processing. Third, the entire operation was directed towards stabilizing the position of major liquid milk schemes in their markets. It was the first time in the history of economic development that food aid had been used as a buffer stock to stabilize market fluctuations as well as to 'prime the pump' of markets that would later be supplied by domestic production. The overriding objective of this aid was the elimination of the need for aid. The project came to be referred to as the 'billion-litre idea' and was formally named Operation Flood (OF).

During its initial stages, NDDB was assisted financially by the Government of India, by the Danish government, and by Amul. It also received teaching material and equipment from UNICEF, the United Nations Children's Fund. In 1969, when the Government of India approved the OF programme and its financing through the monetization of donated commodities, it was found that the statutes under which NDDB was registered did not provide for handling of government funds. Therefore, in 1970 the government established a public sector company, the Indian Dairy Corporation (IDC).

The IDC was given responsibility for receiving the project's donated commodities, testing their quality, storing them, transferring them to user dairies, and receiving the dairies' payments. Thus, it served as a finance-cum-promotion entity, while the entire OF technical support was provided by NDDB. To avoid any duplication in their activities or overlap of functions, the IDC and NDDB were eventually merged into a newly constituted NDDB by an act of Parliament in 1987. The act designated the NDDB as an institution of national importance and accorded it the same autonomy of operation that it had enjoyed and that had been a major factor in its success.

Three Phases of Implementation

The Operation Flood programme was implemented in three phases between 1970 and 1996. Working through the state governments, the programme created the three-tier structure of Anand Pattern dairy cooperatives all over India.

Phase I of OF (1970–81) was financed by Rs 1,165.5 million generated from the sale of 126,000 metric tons of skim milk powder and 42,000 metric tons of butter oil donated to India by the EEC countries through the World Food Programme. As founder-chairman of the NDDB, I finalized the plans and negotiated the details of EEC assistance. The funds were disbursed as 30 per cent grant and 70 per cent loan to the implementing agencies nominated by the participating state governments (Singh and Singh 1998: 8).

During the first phase, the initial thrust was to set up dairy cooperatives in India's 18 best milksheds and link them with the four main cities of Mumbai, Calcutta, Delhi, and Madras, in which a commanding share of the milk market was to be captured. The goal was eventually to cover 39 milksheds. This phase involved organizing dairy cooperatives at the village level; creating the physical and institutional infrastructure for milk procurement, processing, marketing, and production enhancement services at the district union level; and establishing dairies in India's major metropolitan centres. Thus the first phase of OF not only laid the foundation for India's modern dairy industry but also established the possibility of successfully replicating a robust design concept.

Phase II, launched while Phase I was still under way, was implemented during 1979–85. It covered some 136 milksheds linked to over 290 urban markets. Using seed capital raised from the sale of 186,000 metric tons of milk powder and 76,000 metric tons of butter oil from the EEC, together with a World Bank loan of $150 million, OF created a self-sustaining system of 34,500 village cooperatives covering 3.63 million milk producers. Milk drying capacity for powder production rose from 261 metric tons per day in the pre-project year to 507.5 metric tons in 1985, mainly on account of the dairies set up under the OF programme. The EEC gifts thus helped to promote self-reliance. A World Bank audit showed that of the Rs 2,000 million it invested in Operation Flood Phase II, the net return to the rural economy was a massive Rs 240,000 million per year over a period of 10 years (Candler and Kumar 1998).

Phase III, implemented during 1985–96, ensured that the cooperative institutions would become self-sustaining. With an investment of Rs 13,031 million (including Rs 10,954 million from the World Bank and Rs 2,077 million from NDDB's own internal resources) plus commodity assistance from the EEC, the programme achieved substantial expansion of the dairy processing and marketing facilities, an extended milk procurement infrastructure, increased outreach of production enhancement activities, and professionalization of management in the dairy institutions (Singh and Singh 1998: 10). The cooperatives created facilities to provide their producer members with better cattle feed, veterinary first aid and health care services, and breed improvement technologies such as artificial insemination. They also disseminated techniques for hygienic milk production and modern animal husbandry management.

Scaling up mammoth programmes like Operation Flood requires a meticulous process of planning and implementation. Because the Anand model evolved under socio-economic and agro-ecological factors that were specific to the Anand region, doubts were expressed regarding the feasibility of replicating the model in other regions. However, genuine Anand Pattern cooperatives have succeeded in all of the country's socio-economic and agro-ecological environments.

Learning and Innovation

A key factor in this achievement has been the use of teams to promote learning and innovation in stages. Korten (1980: 480–81) explained the learning process involved in Operation Flood:

Along with the farmers, Kurien learned how the problems of milk production and marketing within a village co-operative framework could be overcome. As they learned, other co-operatives were formed and brought within the organizational umbrella. Gradually methods were refined, and the organization that was eventually to become the NDDB grew—from the bottom up—adding new layers and branches as it grew ... Appropriate management systems to meet the demands of the program were worked out through experience. The values of integrity, service, and commitment to the poorest member producers were deeply imbedded in its emerging structures. Management staff was hired fresh from school, trained through experience on the job, indoctrinated in the values of the program, and advanced rapidly as the program grew.

In each replication effort, the overall process can be broken down into three stages, each with its own learning requirements. The three stages as represented here are a simplified abstraction of what in reality has sometimes been a disorderly and largely intuitive process. Yet the abstraction helps to explicate an alternative to the blueprint approach to programming.

Stage 1: Learning to be effective

One or more 'spearhead teams' of highly qualified personnel are sent to one or several villages that constitute their learning laboratory or pilot site. Here the teams develop a familiarity with the problem in question from the beneficiaries' perspective and try out some promising approaches to addressing jointly identified needs. They may be supported by a variety of external resource persons with expertise in the social, managerial, and related technical sciences. In this process of exploration and experimentation, errors will be common, and the resource inputs will be high relative to results. It is assumed that rapid adaptive action will be taken as errors in initial assumptions are identified.

Stage 2: Learning to be efficient

As insights are gained into what to do, attention is redirected to learning how to do it more efficiently, eliminating activities that are relatively non-productive and working out simplified problem-solving routines so that less-skilled people are able to handle critical activities. Local teams (leaders as well as professionals) are identified, and training and education is provided to enable them to take over and run the organizations once established. New learning laboratory sites may be selectively established to test and further refine such methods, simultaneously giving additional personnel experience in their application.

Stage 3: Learning to expand

The last learning stage involves the phased development of a network of supporting organizations. Each organization has a specialized function that can substantially and synergistically contribute to the overall purpose and help to carry out the activities on a larger scale. This requires building into the organization the supporting skills, management systems, structures, and values required.

The spearhead teams thus organize milk producers and assist in building institutions that the producers own and control. As soon as feasible, 'handholding' support is withdrawn. This approach has contributed to the successful scaling up of the programme.

A Key Breakthrough: Using the SNF Surplus

If there was one technological breakthrough that revolutionized India's organized dairy industry, it was the making of skim milk powder out of buffalo milk. The man who made this possible, and who had the foresight to defy the prevailing technical wisdom, was H. M. Dalaya. While the Kaira District Cooperative Milk Producers' Union is usually associated with its founder, Tribhuvandas Patel, it was Dalaya who provided the real technical backbone to the Amul organization.

Liquid milk contains water, milkfat, and non-fat solids, known in the dairy industry as solids-not-fat (SNF). Buffalo milk, with 7–10 per cent fat and 9–9.5 per cent SNF, has a relatively high fat content (ordinary cow milk contains 2.5–5 per cent fat).

In the Indian subsistence dairy system, conversion of surplus milk into ghee (clarified butter) was the most popular mode of conserving and marketing milk. Until the mid-1960s, over half of the Indian buffalo milk output was converted into ghee at the household level. The buttermilk produced as a by-product also had an important place in the traditional Indian diet, but little economic value. Between 10 and 13 kilograms of buffalo milk would yield a kilogram of ghee plus some 25–30 litres of buttermilk that had to be used within 6–12 hours, especially in summer. Even if only 10 kilograms of ghee were made daily in a village, 250–300 litres of buttermilk would be available for consumers in the village every day. Possibly because of this overproduction, traditionally there has been no market for buttermilk in Indian villages.

In converting buffalo milk into ghee, therefore, the farmer would put much less than the true economic value on the milk proteins separated as buttermilk. As a result, if a producer could sell milk with 7 per cent fat at, say, Rs 2 per kilogram, he would not convert it into ghee unless the price of ghee was at least Rs 26 per kilogram. From the 1950s through the early 1970s, ghee prices prevailing in Indian markets included not only the value of the milkfat but also some of the unrealized value of the non-fat solids (Shah 1996).

The development of new technology to produce skim milk powder from buffalo milk allowed the Indian dairy cooperatives to benefit from the SNF surplus. This in turn made it possible to offer much higher prices to the members than the farmers had received from traditional operators. With access to a modern powder plant, an operator buying 13 kilograms of buffalo milk with 7 per cent fat and 9.5 per cent SNF can obtain about 1 kilogram of ghee and 1.35 kilograms of powder. If he sells the ghee at the Indian market price, which already includes some of the value of the SNF, and also sells the powder, effectively he is paid for the SNF twice. He incurs some additional cost in using an energy-intensive drying technology, so the net SNF surplus is the value of the milk powder output less the incremental drying cost. Ability to utilize this surplus gives operators with access to a powder plant a unique and powerful competitive advantage over the traditional milk traders (Shah 1996).

RESULTS AND IMPACT

Over the last 30 years or so, the growth of the Indian dairy industry has made India the largest producer of milk in the world. The credit for this should go mainly to the Operation Flood programme.

The programme's impact can be assessed using various criteria. Some of the more salient are (a) achievements of Anand pattern dairy cooperatives on some important parameters, (b) growth of women's dairy cooperatives, (c) increase in milk production and milk availability, (d) product and market leadership of dairy cooperatives, and (e) impact at the micro level.

Achievements on Key Parameters

Table 2.1 presents selected data on the growth of dairy cooperatives during the three OF phases and afterward. It is heartening to note that the momentum of growth has been maintained during the post-OF period, indicating that the programme laid a solid foundation.

Total investments at the end of Phase III were estimated at Rs 16,968 million. The World Bank investment in the five projects was $500 million nominal, which converts after compounding at 10 per cent and allowance for inflation to $1.9 billion (in 1996 dollars). By 1996, the higher growth rate associated with the Operation Flood period (especially the associated policy changes) was resulting in an extra 43 million metric tons of milk per year. Since the start of the faster growth trend, and using a 10 per cent rate to compound its value to 1996, the total increment was 1,086 million metric tons.

TABLE 2.1 Key Features and Achievements of Operation Flood, 1970–2002

Indicator	OF phases			Post-OF
	Phase I	Phase II	Phase III	
Date started	July 1970	October 1979	April 1985	April 1996
Date concluded	March 1981	March 1985	March 1996	March 2002
Investments (Rs million)	1,165	2,772	13,031	0
No. of federations/apex milk unions operating	10	18	22	22
No. of milksheds covered	39	136	170	170
No. of dairy cooperative societies operating (thousands)	13.3	34.5	72.5	74.3
No. of members (millions)	1.75	3.63	9.26	11.06
Average milk procurement (million kg/day)	2.56	5.78	10.99	17.60
Liquid milk marketing (million litres/day)	2.79	5.01	10.02	12.67
Processing capacity				
Rural dairies (million litres/day)	3.59	8.78	18.09	26.47[a]
Metro dairies (million litres/day)	2.9	3.5	3.88	—
Milk drying capacity (mt/day)	261.0	507.5	842.0	990.0[a]

(Contd)

Table 2.1 (Contd)

Indicator	OF phases			Post-OF
	Phase I	Phase II	Phase III	
Technical inputs				
No. of artificial insemination centres (thousands)	4.9	7.5	16.8	22.0
No. of artificial inseminations done (million/year)	0.82	1.33	3.94	–6.00
Cattle feed capacity (thousand mt/day)	1.7	3.3	4.9	5.2[a]

Sources: Gupta 1997; NDDB 2001–02; NDDB quarterly and monthly progress reports on Operation Flood for 1996 as quoted in Singh (1999: 205).

Notes: – Not available;
    a. For 1997–98.

If even 0.56 per cent of the observed increase in milk production was due to World Bank investments, the projects would have an economic rate of return of 10 per cent. If all investments (from the World Food Programme, EEC, and Government of India) are taken into account, at most 2 per cent of the increased production would need to be attributable to the project to yield an economic rate of return of 10 per cent (Candler and Kumar 1998: 38). And if most of the increased growth is attributed to OF, the return is phenomenal. This is due in part to the fact that OF has encouraged members to invest in biological assets—milch animals—that periodically reproduce themselves without major reinvestment and continue to yield regular benefits, utilizing crop residues that otherwise do not have much economic value.

Women's Dairy Cooperatives

Milch cattle in India are tended mainly by women. Amul realized this and built in women's empowerment activities as an important component of its dairy development programme. In the early phases of OF, the strategy was to train women in modern animal husbandry practices, and a large number of training programmes were specifically organized for them. Special incentives were given to all 'women's dairy cooperative societies' in order to encourage participation of women in governance of the cooperatives. More recently, NDDB launched a Women's Dairy Cooperative Leadership Programme to further strengthen efforts to empower women. The main objective is to train and position local women as resource persons in the villages. According to NDDB's annual report for 2001–02, the number of district unions covered under the women's leadership programme increased to 50 in 2002, with 2,062 cooperatives and 90,000 participants. The number of women who are members of dairy cooperatives is even more impressive, increasing from 0.62 million in 1986–87 to 2.47 million in 2001–02 (Figure 2.1).

Impact on Milk Production and Milk Availability

Milk production in 1968–69, just before the launch of Operation Flood, was only 21.2 million metric tons. It increased to 31.6 million metric tons by 1980–81, 53.9 million by 1990–91, and 84.6 million by 2001–02 (Figure 2.2). The increase in milk production was slow to start with: the annual growth rate was just 4.08 per cent during the first phase of Operation Flood. It was much higher, at 7.85 per cent, during the second phase, and production continued to grow at 5.05 per cent per year during the third phase.

Ending Poverty in South Asia

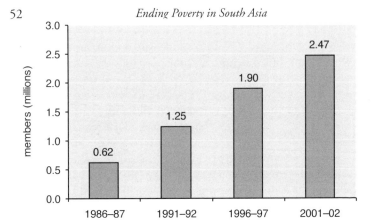

Source: NDDB 2001–02.

FIGURE 2.1 Women Members of Dairy Cooperatives in India, 1986–2002

As a result of the substantial increase in milk production, milk consumption in India rose from a low of 112 grams per day in 1968–69 to over 226 grams per day in 2002 (Figure 2.3). These substantial increases in milk production and milk availability have resulted in the stabilization of milk prices in the country. India's towns and cities receive an adequate supply of hygienic milk, and the small farmers and landless labourers who make up the majority of dairy cooperative members now have a regular source of income.

Though official statistics show a substantial increase in milk production beginning in the 1970s under the OF programme, several scholars have challenged the accuracy of these data. Mergos and Alderman (1987) assessed the impact of Operation Flood in two World Bank-funded dairy development projects, one each in Madhya Pradesh and Karnataka. They found that milk production had increased at the average incremental rate of about 7 per cent per year in the project areas under OF, while in non-OF areas the increase was smaller. In a more recent study based on the available theoretical and empirical evidence, Mergos (1997) examined the increase in milk production and the direct impact of OF on milk production. The study acknowledged that the impact had been modest and indicated that 25–50 per cent of the increase in procurement by OF was likely due to producers switching from small private vendors to cooperatives. It also asserted that the milk production increase in the country was real and that no evidence was available to show otherwise.

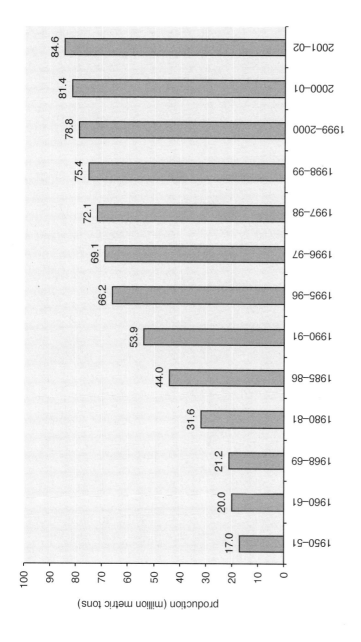

Son

Note: Estimates for 1999–2002 are provisional.

FIGURE 2.2 Estimated Milk Production in India, 1950–2002

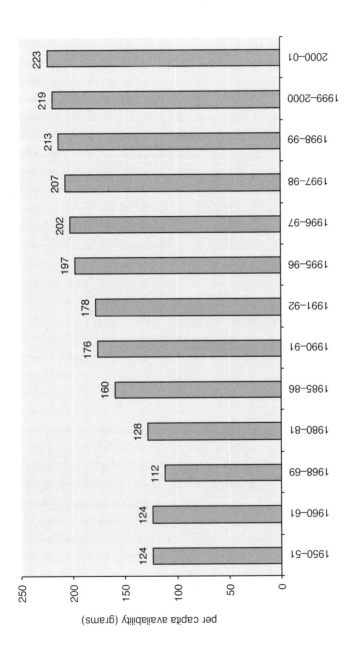

Source: Government of India 2002.
Note: Estimates for 1999–2002 are provisional.

FIGURE 2.3 Estimated Per Capita Milk Availability in India, 1950–2002

Kumar (1997: 34), reviewing the literature on OF, particularly in the post-1987 period, observed that the programme had generated a voluminous and controversial literature. He noted that much of the evidence was either anecdotal or was based on area-specific case studies. Lack of empirical data and scientific rigour continues to be a serious limitation of the available evidence on OF programme effects. Critics have even questioned the accuracy of official estimates of milk production. But there is sufficient evidence to show substantial growth in the dairy sector. A wider marketing network and increased per capita availability of milk, despite the steep increase in population, are indicators of this growth.

Product and Market Leadership of Dairy Cooperatives

As of 2004, milk was processed and marketed by 170 district-level unions, federated into 22 state-level marketing federations. Over the years, brands created by the cooperatives have become known for quality and value. Among the brands that have earned consumer confidence are Amul (in Gujarat), Vijaya (Andhra Pradesh), Verka (Punjab), Saras (Rajasthan), Nandini (Karnataka), Milma (Kerala), and Gokul (Kolhapur). Each has become a market leader in its state of origin and also has significant presence in other states. The Gujarat Cooperative Milk Marketing Federation, as mentioned earlier, is the largest food company in India. The market shares of some GCMMF products are shown in Table 2.2. The success of GCMMF proves that cooperatives can successfully compete with multinational companies.

Impact of Milk Cooperatives at the Village Level

A number of scholars have recently attempted to study the impact of milk cooperatives on milk production, milk prices, income, and employment, and have compared milk cooperatives with private traders and dairies. Impact evaluation has mostly been done using the 'with and without' approach, and the impact was found to be positive in almost all the cases studied (Singh and Singh 1998). For example, Singh and Das (1984) studied OF's Phase I in three selected milksheds (Bikaner in Rajasthan, Periyar in Tamil Nadu, and Sabarkantha in Gujarat) during June–September 1980. They observed that the average milk yield per milch animal, average milk production per household, average price received by milk producers, level of employment in dairying, and per capita daily intake of calories and protein from milk and milk products were all substantially higher in the cooperative villages than in control villages (Table 2.3).

TABLE 2.2 Market Shares of Selected GCMMF Products, 2002–03

Category	Brand name	All-India market share (%)	All-India industry rank	Competitor
Infant milk food	Amulspray	65	1	Nestlé
Dairy whitener	Amulya Dairy Whitener	60	1	Nestlé, Britannia
Whole milk powder	Amul Whole Milk Powder	80	1	Nestlé
Skim milk powder	Sagar Skimmed Milk Powder	50	1	Anik
Butter	Amul Butter	80	1	Nestlé, Britannia
Bread spread	Amul Lite	80	1	Nutralite
Cheese	Amul Cheese	60	1	Britannia
Cheese spread	Amul Cheese Spread	80	1	Britannia
Mozzarella cheese	Amul Pizza Cheese	70	1	Britannia
Emmental cheese	Amul Emmental Cheese	80	1	Imported
Fresh milk	Amul (A'bad)	60	1	Britannia
UHT milk	Amul Taaza	60	1	Nestlé
Fresh curd	Masti Dahi	75	1	Nestlé
Pure ghee	Amul Pure Ghee	25	1	Nestlé
Ice cream	Amul Ice Cream	40	1	Hindustan Lever, Vadilal
Condensed milk	Mithai Mate	55	1	Nestlé
Ethnic sweets	Shrikhand	50	1	Warana

Source: Personal communication from B.M. Vyas, Managing Director, GCMMF.

TABLE 2.3 Village-Level Impact of Operation Flood Phase I in Bikaner, Periyar, and Sabarkantha Milksheds, 1980

Indicator	Bikaner		Periyar		Sabarkantha	
	Coop. villages	Control villages	Coop. villages	Control villages	Coop. villages	Control villages
Average milk production (litres/hh, May 1980)	190.96	134.17	121.36	90.89	89.63	43.14
Average milk production (litres/hh/milch animal in milk, May 1980)	109.02	69.21	69.74	62.24	79.31	53.25
Average price realized[a] (Rs/litre, May 1980)	1.36	1.14	2.02	1.52	1.76	1.96
Gross revenue from milk and milk products (Rs/hh, May 1980)	142.99	14.24	220.77	84.80	102.16	29.54
Gross revenue per milch animal in milk (Rs/hh, May 1980)	81.71	7.34	126.87	58.08	90.40	36.47
Average annual income from milk (Rs/hh, May 1980)[b]						
Landless households	428.78 (3.43)	938.40 (2.47)	32.41 (2.38)	49.40 (6.43)	557.79 (11.51)	370.75 (11.72)
Landed households	1,672.61 (96.57)	1,596.59 (97.53)	543.37 (97.62)	253.51 (93.57)	1,619.97 (88.48)	788.74 (88.28)

(Contd)

Table 2.3 (Contd)

Indicator	Bikaner		Periyar		Sabarkantha	
	Coop. villages	Control villages	Coop. villages	Control villages	Coop. villages	Control villages
Employment from dairying[c] (days/hh/year, 1979–80)						
Landless households	76.84 (67.57)	190.10 (53.28)	79.28 (11.38)	40.04 (5.03)	66.54 (14.62)	38.97 (19.91)
Landed households	169.84 (32.47)	100.60 (26.06)	180.36 (35.32)	155.91 (32.13)	169.21 (38.26)	156.20 (36.40)
Calorie intake from milk and milk products (cal/capita/day)	460	255	107	94	154	97
Protein intake from milk and milk products (gm/capita/day)	9	6	4	4	5	4

Source: Singh and Das 1984.
Notes: a. Implicit value of milk in terms of ghee price.
b. Figures in parentheses represent percentage of aggregate income.
c. Figures in parentheses represent percentage of total employment in all activities.

The landless households in the cooperative villages were found to be better off than their counterparts in the control villages in terms of most of these criteria. The most vulnerable section of the rural populace, that is, children below age 6 and expectant and nursing mothers, had on average better nutritional status in the cooperative villages than in the control villages.

Parthasarathy (1991) cites a number of reasons why the 'white revolution' was thought to be more equitable than the green revolution. He notes that (a) the distribution of milch cattle is more equitable than the distribution of land; (b) higher income elasticity of demand for milk in comparison to cereals provides more opportunities for the employment of landless people in dairying; (c) it is easier to provide poor households with cattle, which multiply biologically, than to provide them with land through redistribution; and (d) there is greater scope for the employment of women in the dairy industry, with favourable consequences for family health and nutrition.

Arora and Bhogal (1996: 747–48) found the performance of the Meerut Milk Union to be highly satisfactory, with about 50 per cent of the milk markets in rural areas captured by dairy cooperatives. The prices paid by milk cooperatives were higher than those paid by private vendors. However, the authors emphasize the need for dairy cooperatives to play a more proactive role in order to meet the stiff competition from private milk vendors. Singh and Chattaraj (1996: 822–23) found that the average number of cross-bred cows per household and the average family labour income per milch animal per year were both higher in the villages with milk cooperatives than in those without milk cooperatives. The authors conclude that the dairy cooperatives had a positive impact on incomes of the members. Koli (1996: 818–19), in a similar study of the Gokul Cooperative Dairy in Kohlapur district of Maharashtra, found that the cooperative had played an important role in securing fair prices for milk producers, in providing various inputs and services to them, and in increasing employment opportunities.

EMPOWERMENT ELEMENTS

The question of how the cooperatives have affected village households and livelihoods raises the issue of their potential impact as a means of empowerment for the rural poor. At the outset, one must admit that Operation Flood was not conceived as an all-purpose poverty eradication programme. It cannot be, because it focuses on a single productive activity, dairying, while the ranks of the rural poor include many different categories of the disenfranchised: the old, the infirm, tribal people, the landless, small farmers, artisans, and so forth. Nonetheless, it is notable that the increased income from milk under OF encouraged a process of change in other activities of the milk-producing households and contributed to their overall socioeconomic development (Verhagen 1990).

We have used the framework suggested by the World Bank for assessing the Operation Flood programme on three dimensions: social empowerment, economic empowerment, and political empowerment.

Social Empowerment

Social empowerment deals with issues of exclusion and inclusion. These become important in a religiously diverse, multicultural, and highly stratified society like India where the rural poor face many forms of exclusion. While Operation Flood is not an all-purpose development programme and cannot hope to sweep away economic and social inequalities that have existed in rural India for centuries, it has nonetheless had a profound impact on the social landscape of the countryside.

In its 1976 report on rural employment, the National Commission on Agriculture observed:

Next to crops, animal husbandry programmes have the largest employment potential. The most important features of these programmes are that they provide subsidiary occupation, offer gainful employment at the location itself, and make better utilization of female and child labour ... Most of these programmes are particularly suitable for weaker sections of the rural community and have redistributive effect on rural income in favour of them. (quoted in Mascarenhas 1988: 47).

Baviskar (1988: 346) explains that Operation Flood was considered a means of overcoming the barriers of caste, class, and power, something earlier rural development programs had been unable to do.

Since milk production does not require much land, but family labour which the poor have amply, the landless poor can easily and profitably participate in the white revolution, deriving employment and additional income from it. Since milk is not a polluting substance in the Hindu religious ideology, people belonging to any caste, even the lowest, can and do participate in producing milk. ... Also cooperatives which organize only milk producers can successfully bypass the constraint of village power structure.

Although OF was not designed to eradicate the problems of poverty and unemployment, it is true that millions of landless, marginal, and small farmers who were engaged in milk production benefited greatly from the increased income and employment opportunities generated by the programme. Of the farm families covered under OF, 21 per cent had no land and another 66 per cent were marginal and small farmers owning less than 2 hectares of land. Over 70 per cent of the participating households had just one or two milch animals (NDDB 1987: 7). Thus, OF turned out in practice to be a pro-poor programme that made the distribution of incremental income from milk among rural milk-producing households more equitable.

As far as empowerment of women is concerned, this took place mainly through the women's dairy cooperative societies that were promoted seriously during the third phase and in the post-OF period. In these women's cooperatives, members find themselves empowered, as they are authorized to make their own decisions in meetings held outside the home. Income from dairying enables the women to make most household expenditures without being dependent on their husbands. OF has also played an important role in generating employment for women. With 3.5 million milk suppliers, 'it is reasonable to assume that 5 per cent represented women who were able to stay at home rather than go out for work. This withdrawal of women from the labour force will have created an additional 175,000 labouring jobs, predominantly for the very poor' (Candler and Kumar 1998: 50–51).

Cooperative dairying also empowers people at another level. The village dairy cooperative is a clean, well-lit, and orderly place. The villages have gone through a similar transformation ever since the cooperatives began to operate. When the people of a village see cleanliness, sanitation, hard work, and discipline in the cooperative, and when they know that the cooperative serves them well, it probably inspires them to bring more of these qualities into their own lives.

The women members of dairy cooperatives visit dairy cooperative unions and are shown the mysteries of artificial insemination under a microscope. Does not their knowledge of conception in animals help them to better understand their own lives and to begin to control what was simply accepted as a matter of fate?

When our village people see a veterinarian cure an animal that would otherwise have died, they learn about the efficacy of modern medicine. They see that with feed and care, animals produce better milk; as their income from milk increases, they become hopeful of a better future for themselves. And they learn that fate does not determine their future—that they can take control of their own destinies.

Economic Empowerment

The economic empowerment aspects of OF deal with connecting people and their institutions with markets. Efficiency and effectiveness of operations is an essential prerequisite for economic empowerment.

In the words of Peter Drucker (1977: 33), 'Efficiency is concerned with doing things right. Effectiveness is doing the right things.' In the pre-OF era, milk pricing was not used as an instrument of dairy development. No effort was made by any government to ensure a remunerative price to the producer, but the consumer price of milk supplied through government-run city milk schemes was invariably subsidized. This had two adverse effects on dairy development. First, in the absence of a year-round remunerative price for milk, the producer did not have any incentive to increase milk production through better breeding, feeding, and management of animals. Therefore, milk production increased at a miserably low rate of 1 per cent per year in the pre-OF era. Second, by selling milk for less than its cost and less than the open market price, city milk schemes incurred huge losses year after year, and as a result were not able to save and plough back any money into modernizing and expanding their activities. Thus, the milk pricing policy followed before 1970 was both anti-producer and anti-dairy development.

For the first time, OF accorded the highest priority to ensuring a year-round and dependable market at remunerative prices for rurally produced milk. Indeed, OF was originally conceived as a marketing project. The producer price of milk in most OF areas is determined by the state government concerned and is set at a level that is considered remunerative to milk producers. Although the cost of milk production is not explicitly considered in setting the producer price, there is some evidence to show that the terms of trade over the last decade or so have been favourable to milk producers. The time-series data on the producer price of milk and the wholesale price of oilcakes used for feed, which account for nearly three-fourths of the total cost of milk production, confirm this. Over the period 1987 to 1996, the compound annual rate of growth in the producer price of milk was 10.9 per cent as compared to 5.8 per cent growth in the wholesale price of oilcakes (Singh and Singh 1998: 21–22).

The strategy evolved by early dairy cooperatives in Gujarat proved decidedly superior to alternative ones being tested in the 1960s, such as the Key Village Scheme or the system under which government-owned milk plants collected and processed milk produced by contractors. The Anand Pattern emphasized keeping cattle in the hinterland and transporting milk to cities by farmer cooperatives, rather than transporting cattle and their fodder to cities. Thus the system had strong comparative advantage (Shah 1996). As a result, the early dairy unions in Gujarat—such as Kaira, Mehsana, Sabarkantha, Banaskantha, and others—rapidly emerged as large and successful farmer organizations, with hundreds of thousands of members dominating the economies of their locales.

Political Empowerment

The political empowerment aspect of the milk revolution deals with connecting poor people with the government. The OF programme was able to connect the grassroots-level dairy cooperatives not only with the state and central governments, but also with international agencies. In a public message on the first International Day of cooperatives, on July 1, 1995, United Nations Secretary-General Boutros Boutros-Ghali observed:

Cooperative enterprises provide the organizational means whereby a significant proportion of humanity is able to take into its own hands the tasks of creating productive employment, overcoming poverty and achieving social integration. They constitute a model for a people-centred and sustainable form of societal organization, based on equity, justice and solidarity.

As 'schools of democracy', cooperative enterprises also contribute to the promotion of social stability. It is clear that governments, although they may create an enabling environment, cannot achieve or maintain sustainable development without an interactive social partnership, actively involving all of civil society in an empowered, democratic manner. Thus, with its globe-spanning dimensions and diversity and its insistence on social partnership, participatory democracy, empowerment, and 'people-centred sustainable development', the cooperative movement reflects a strong, deep current of humanism that forms the bedrock of social development.

In a country like India, democracy rests on a fragile foundation. One must underpin democracy with a plurality of rural institutions through which people can take direct control over matters that have an immediate effect on their lives. The Anand Pattern dairy cooperatives of India are such institutions.

ISSUES AND LESSONS

By following the experience of the pioneering Amul, the dairy cooperatives in Mehsana, Sabarkantha, and elsewhere succeeded with the leadership and managerial inputs that were available locally. Six key principles, briefly outlined below, together embody the core of the design concept underlying the Anand Pattern and help to explain its success. Failure to adhere to these principles can also explain numerous failures, not only in attempts to replicate the Anand Pattern but also throughout the arena of development experimentation (Shah 1996).

Market Access as a Precondition

In order to raise the production and productivity of subsistence farmers so that they can move to post-subsistence production, we must first stimulate and expand the market to which they have easy, low-cost access. This access will help the producers use up the slack available in their production system and reap benefits. Only when they have such a market will production enhancement programmes make sense to them. Thus, in order to create a milk production system such as Anand, one must first develop a milk demand system linked to an urban market such as Mumbai.

Marketing: First Step to Cooperative Organization

In efforts to organize cooperatives, it is best to begin by studying the demand system rather than the production system. Steps to mount a successful marketing strategy should be taken before organizing the producers. Where marketing is underemphasized or mishandled, dairy and other cooperatives tend to fail. This means that production enhancement programmes must follow and not precede the commissioning of the procurement, processing, and marketing system. Many income generation activities promoted by cooperatives and non-governmental organizations have failed for want of access to a remunerative market, rather than because of limitations in the production of goods and services.

The Anand Pattern: A Superior Design Concept

The key advantage of the Anand Pattern structure is that it combines procurement, processing, and marketing within one unified federal structure (Doornbos and Nair 1990: 15). In many other cooperative models, the critical marketing function is not under the control of the cooperatives. Often brands are owned and distribution is handled by multinational companies. The cooperatives must take the prices they are offered, and as a result, they earn very little for their member producers.

The design of the cooperative enterprise must avoid mismatch between demand and supply and must also free the cooperative from cut-throat competition with small-time players. A dairy cooperative can capture and retain an urban market and provide its farmer members a stable remunerative market for milk only if it has an effective procurement system—to collect small marketable surpluses from many members—and efficient processing facilities.

Priming the Pump

The best way to organize a producers' cooperative is to start with marketing. However, unless producers' cooperatives are organized, they have nothing to market, and unless cooperatives know how to dispose of the produce, they cannot start the procurement process. NDDB found 'pump priming' the best answer to this problem that all new cooperatives face, and this principle became central to the design of the OF programme. OF used donated dairy commodities to prime the pump by marketing them in the domestic market. If used instead as external resource flows, the donated powder and butter oil could have destroyed the domestic milk production base by further depressing the prices of perishable milk and milk products and increasing the country's dependence on imports.

The SNF Surplus: A Competitive Advantage

The technological capacity to convert buffalo milk to skim milk powder has given the Anand Pattern dairies a distinctive competitive advantage. For dairy cooperatives, especially those without direct access to a large liquid milk market, conversion of milk into ghee and powder has in most years been as profitable or more profitable than marketing liquid milk. Seizing this competitive advantage has been one of the keys to their success.

The advantage of the SNF surplus exists only as long as the household sector dominates in ghee manufacture. Over the past two decades, there has been a shift in this position as cooperative dairies have increased their share of ghee making. As a result, the SNF surplus has been progressively diluted. This process will most likely continue in the future and weaken the competitive advantage of the Anand Pattern cooperatives over traditional as well as modern sector operators in dairying (Shah 1996).

Professional Management, Farmer Control

Finally, an important reason for the cooperatives' success is the work of committed professional managers under the control of an honest and enlightened elected leadership of farmers. Without access to professional expertise, it would be difficult for farmers to quickly gain a market foothold on the scale needed and exploit the full advantage offered by technology. However, accountability must be honoured in principle and in practice. If the development of producers is the goal of building the business and the business is to serve their interests, then the venture must be managed by professionals and technocrats who are, and feel, accountable to producers through the producers' elected board.

Explaining the secret of Amul's early success to the prime minister of India in 1964, I said: 'Sir, this is a dairy owned by farmers. It is managed by an elected board of farmers. They, in their wisdom, have appointed me as a professional manager, to manage it for them even as I remain subordinate to them. I am not sent by the government; I am an employee of this cooperative. They can hire me, they can fire me. So when you have this combination, that is, the power of its people with professional managers like me, many good things can happen.'

References

Arora, V.P.S. and T.S. Bhogal, 1996, 'Integrated Milk Co-operatives in North-West Uttar Pradesh: Organisation, Functioning and Performance,' *Indian Journal of Agricultural Economics* 51 (4): 747–48.

Baviskar, B.S., 1988, 'Dairy Co-operatives and Rural Development in Gujarat,' D.W. Attwood and B.S. Baviskar (eds), *Who Shares? Co-operatives and Rural Development*, New Delhi: Oxford University Press.

Candler, W. and N. Kumar, 1998, *India: The Dairy Revolution*, Washington, DC: World Bank.

Doornbos, M. and K.N. Nair, 1990, 'The State of Indian Dairying: An Overview,' M. Doornbos and K.N. Nair (eds), *Resources, Institutions and Strategies: Operation Flood and Indian Dairying*, New Delhi: Sage.

Drucker, P., 1977, *People and Performance*, New Delhi: Allied Publishers.

Government of India, 2002, 'Basic Animal Husbandry Statistics, 2002,' Department of Animal Husbandry and Dairying, Ministry of Agriculture, New Delhi.

Gupta, P.R. (ed.), 1997. *Dairy India*, 5th ed. New Delhi: P.R. Gupta.

Khurody, D.N., 1974, *Dairying in India*, Mumbai: Asia Publishing House.

Koli, P.A., 1996, 'Dairy Co-operatives and Rural Upliftment: An Empirical Analysis,' *Indian Journal of Agricultural Economics* 51 (4): 818–19.

Korten, D.C., 1980, 'Community Organisation and Rural Development: A Learning Process Approach,' *Public Administration Review* 40 (5): 480–511.

Kumar, N., 1997, 'Operation Flood: Literature Review and Reconciliation,' Occasional Publication 13, Institute of Rural Management, Anand, India.

Mascarenhas, R.C., 1988, *A Strategy for Rural Development: Dairy Cooperatives in India*, New Delhi: Sage.

Mergos, G., 1997, 'Production Increase: Is It Real?' Paper presented at the OED-IRMA Workshop on the Impact of Operation Flood, Institute of Rural Management, Anand, India, March 17–18.

Mergos, G. and H. Alderman, 1987, 'Production Effects of Co-operative Dairy Development in Madhya Pradesh and Karnataka.' Paper presented at the IFPRI Workshop on the Economics of Dairy Development in Selected Countries and Policy Implications, Copenhagen, January 6–8.

NDDB (National Dairy Development Board), 1987, 'From a Drop to a Flood.' Anand, India.

——, 2001–2, *Annual Report 2001–2002*, Anand, India.

——, 2005, 'Achievements of Dairy Cooperatives: Facts at a Glance,' Anand, India. www.nddb.org.

Parthasarathy, G., 1991, 'White Revolution, Dairy Cooperatives and Weaker Sections,' *Economic and Political Weekly* (Mumbai), December 28, A177.

Shah, T., 1996, *Catalysing Co-operation: Design of Self-Governing Organisations*, New Delhi: Sage.

Singh, K., 1999, *Rural Development: Principles, Policies and Management,* New Delhi: Sage.

Singh, K. and V.M. Das, 1984, 'Impact of Operation Flood I at the Village Level,' Research Report 1, Institute of Rural Management, Anand, India.

Singh, K. and V.P. Singh, 1998, 'Dairy Development in India: Retrospect and Prospect,' Research Paper 15, Institute of Rural Management, Anand, India.

Singh, L. and J. Chattaraj, 1996, 'Enhancement of Family Labour Income through Service of Dairy Co-operatives,' *Indian Journal of Agricultural Economics* 51 (4): 822–23.

Verhagen, M., 1990, 'Operation Flood and the Rural Poor,' M. Doornbos and K.N. Nair, *Resources* (eds), *Institutions and Strategies: Operation Flood and Indian Dairying*, New Delhi: Sage.

3

Collective Action by Women Workers
The Self-Employed Women's Association, India

John Blaxall

The vast majority of women workers in India earn their living in the informal sector. Acting alone, they are powerless to improve their working conditions, the security of their precarious livelihoods, or their access to basic services. When they organize and act together, however, their strength is formidable. The thirty-year history of a grassroots movement shows how collective strength can be harnessed and translated into better lives for hundreds of thousands of poor women.

The Self-Employed Women's Association (SEWA) is a membership organization—a movement rather than a programme. Members are poor women working in the informal sector who have organized themselves into a labour union to struggle for their rights and into nearly 100 cooperatives to improve their economic security. From small beginnings in 1972, SEWA's membership has grown to over half a million in its home state of Gujarat and to about 700,000 if six other states in India are included. More than 100,000 new members have joined each year recently. In 2003, some 300,000 people used SEWA-provided primary health services and more than 110,000 members were covered by the organization's insurance.

SEWA members see themselves first and foremost as workers, and identify their primary need as gainful and secure employment. Many members have increased their incomes as a result of their involvement with SEWA, both through the collective pressure that the organization's members can exert and through the creation of alternative employment opportunities. Members have gained access to markets through information campaigns, assistance with product improvement, and SEWA-run marketing services. They have gained access to services (such as health care, childcare, insurance, and housing) that are essential to a secure livelihood. And they have gained access to banking facilities that allow them both to save and to borrow in small amounts and on reasonable terms, and so gradually to build up their assets.

In the process, large numbers of members have achieved a measure of self-reliance. By providing training and capacity building of various kinds, SEWA has developed its members' leadership abilities, self-confidence, and life skills. The stories of three women presented below illustrate some of the ways in which SEWA has helped poor women change their lives.

This chapter focuses on SEWA's efforts to empower large numbers of poor self-employed women. It is not an evaluation of SEWA as an organization or of particular activities that SEWA has promoted. However, it does include some evidence on SEWA's impact on members and on the wider environment, drawn from a recently published study.

ORIGIN AND EVOLUTION OF SEWA

The Self-Employed Women's Association was formed in 1972 in Ahmedabad, Gujarat, the textile capital of India. Some poor, illiterate women, seasonal migrants from rural areas, approached the Textile Labour Association, one of the oldest unions in India. They were making a meagre income as casual labourers, pulling carts and carrying head loads of cloth between the 100 or so wholesale textile markets in the city. The women's most urgent need was for shelter, but they also knew they were being cheated by the cloth merchants. Seeing the benefits the union had brought for its (mostly male) members in the textile mills, they sought its help. They were directed to the union's Women's Wing, and Ela Bhatt. A lawyer, Bhatt had represented the textile union in court disputes and in policy discussions with government for some years, and later worked for the state Ministry of Labour before returning to the union to head its Women's Wing. She was much influenced by the example and teachings of Mohandas Gandhi, who lived for many years in Ahmedabad and had helped to found the Textile Labour Association in 1917.

To counter the unfair and corrupt practices that kept these women's earnings low and their lives precarious, Bhatt conceived the idea of organizing them into a union, along with other women working in the informal sector as vegetable and used-garment vendors, construction workers, carpenters, and the like. The poor and uneducated women who became members of SEWA organized campaigns and peaceful demonstrations to draw attention to their plight. They slowly gained ground on issues such as differential rates for cart-pulling depending on distance and the right of vendors to sell on the street without harassment by the police, seeking bribes. These achievements added to their self-confidence and led to new initiatives, which in turn resulted in a growing membership and an expanding field of activities.

SEWA has kept its focus on one overriding reality: that poor women are above all *workers*, whose empowerment depends on achieving the twin objectives of secure employment and self-reliance. SEWA sees its core role as organizing women and building their capacity to accomplish these ends. As a membership organization with firmly democratic procedures, based explicitly on Gandhian principles, SEWA develops all its activities in direct response to members' needs. There is no a priori view on what these needs may be or how they should be served—though SEWA is convinced, on the basis of its experience, that all the needs of poor women are interrelated and all deserve attention. It is, as Ela Bhatt has often emphasized, a movement rather than a programme or a non-governmental organization in the usual sense. The movement flows slowly at times and faster at other times, and it may occasionally be deflected around an obstacle, but it always moves in the same direction.

A structure has evolved that gives SEWA great flexibility to grow and respond to its members' needs. Apart from their participation in the union's formal election and governance arrangements, members are engaged in three main ways:

- Through a *union* with both urban and rural branches, that helps members in their collective struggle for fair treatment and access to justice, markets, and services
- Through *cooperatives* that help members produce and market the fruits of their labour and build their assets
- Through *member services*, which are financed partly by user charges but also partly by donors and by government departments that have been unable to provide the services for which they are responsible by law.

SEWA members evoke the image of a banyan tree in describing these activities and their interactions. SEWA is the central trunk that draws its strength from the roots. The trunk puts out branches, each of which helps poor women advance in a trade or provides a service that they need. Each branch then lets down new roots that connect it to the soil, nurturing and sustaining the branch and at the same time strengthening the whole tree.

A list of some organizations in the SEWA family and their founding dates illustrates the wide range of activities:

- SEWA Cooperative Bank (1974)
- First milk cooperative (1979)
- Anasuya (newsletter, 1982)
- SEWA National Association (1982)
- First artisans' cooperative (1982)
- Video SEWA (1984)
- First childcare cooperative (1986)
- First tree growers' cooperative (1986)
- First rural programme, in a drought-prone area (1987)
- First vegetable and fruit vendors' cooperative (1989)
- SEWA Academy (1990)
- First health care cooperative (1990)
- First salt farmers' cooperative (1991)
- Vimo SEWA (insurance, 1992)
- SEWA Cooperative Federation (1993)
- Gujarat Mahila Housing Trust (1994)
- First midwives' cooperative (1994)
- Kutch Craft Association (1995)
- SEWA Gram Mahila Haat (local marketing, 1999)
- SEWA Trade Facilitation Centre (2000)

Ela Bhatt retired from the post of general secretary in 1996, and since then the general secretaries and the two secretaries have each served three-year non-renewable terms. SEWA is proud of its rotating 'collective leadership' approach. Its corporate management is in the hands of a small but remarkably stable cadre of women who remain fully involved in running SEWA's affairs whether or not they happen to be office holders. A large majority of the management cadre have professional backgrounds, but SEWA has provided intensive training for some uneducated women to equip them to take on roles for which professional training is normal. By custom, 80 per cent of SEWA's own employees are poor women, and only 20 per cent have professional backgrounds.

SEWA continues to emphasize Gandhian values, in particular simplicity and tolerance. For example, the highest-paid employee receives no more than three times the salary of the lowest-paid. All meetings begin with both

Hindu and Muslim prayers. While SEWA as an organization was careful to make no public statements on the communal violence in Gujarat in 2002 and 2003, because of the danger that would have created for members in affected areas, there were many cases in which SEWA members (of both religions) took heroic steps to protect people of the other faith. SEWA organizations also played a large role in assisting victims and their families in the affected communities.

SEWA's Growth and Expansion in India

At the end of 2003, SEWA had a membership of over 700,000 women and was still growing.[1] The average annual rate of growth in membership was 25 per cent in 1988–92, 35 per cent in 1993–97, and 27 per cent in 1998–2003, with more than 250,000 new members joining in 2002 alone. About two-thirds of the members live in SEWA's home state of Gujarat. SEWA organizations have been started in six other Indian states in recent years, with a combined membership of approximately 230,000. There are also SEWA associates in South Africa, Turkey, and Yemen.

The urban branch of the union, with a membership of 153,000 in Gujarat, has organized workers in over 70 occupations or trades. They are clustered into four groups: home-based workers, vendors, producers, and manual labourers/service providers. SEWA recognizes that mechanization and new production technologies are eroding traditional employment opportunities, and it strives to counter the effects of this inevitable process by upgrading members' skills. In 2002, for example, ready-made garment workers were trained in new techniques that allowed 100 women to gain employment and 30 to restart work (another 3,000 obtained a modest bonus from the merchants). In the same year, major campaigns were mounted in support of better wages and provident funds for *bidi* (cigarette) rollers and incense stick rollers. In the latter case, 10,000 incense workers (half the total number) received an increase in pay, and another 2,000 were able to restart work. However, conditions for the bidi rollers did not improve, and SEWA members will continue the struggle.

The rural branch of the union had about 316,000 members in more than 2,000 villages across 14 rural districts of Gujarat at the end of 2003. In urban areas, access to secure (or less insecure) employment can sometimes be achieved by traditional union activities, relying on solidarity among members and appeals to public sentiment to force employers to offer better conditions. In rural areas, however, SEWA discovered that large labour surpluses make such an approach ineffective.

It has therefore concentrated on creation of alternative employment for rural women. This does not mean inventing completely new full-time jobs, but rather finding various forms of part-time employment so that members have more options. The possibility that some income can be earned by selling embroidery, for example, has changed the bargaining dynamics between poor women and local farm owners for whom they provide casual labour. Opportunities for year-round employment producing handicrafts and some high-value crops have reversed the trend towards declining agricultural wages. Another result has been a decline in the seasonal migration of women agricultural workers to the cities and to other states, which used to be as high as 80 per cent from some districts in Gujarat.

Formation of Cooperatives

Developing alternative forms of employment through production of saleable items raises the daunting issue of market access. SEWA members may be poor and uneducated, but virtually all of them have had extensive (and unhappy) experience of how markets work. In their experience, the only function of middlemen is to exploit and cheat poor people like themselves. They have a lively appreciation of how important *fair* access to markets can be.

For this reason, SEWA has promoted the formation of cooperatives among its members. In general, their purpose is to help ensure that members' products are of high quality and are sold at fair prices. At the end of 2003 there were 86 SEWA cooperatives ranging in size from a tree-growing venture in a single village to the SEWA Bank, which has 35,000 member shareholders. There is also an umbrella federation that provides training and marketing support to individual cooperatives. During 2003 it trained over 1,300 women in various skills, as well as arranging sales of items produced by the cooperatives.

SEWA cooperatives in rural areas have helped women improve the quality and design of the handicraft and woven items they produce for sale. In most cases the women are already highly skilled at embroidery or weaving or other crafts. The task is mainly to ensure consistent quality—the items must be of a size and style that can be sold easily—and timely delivery. Cooperatives have also promoted new agricultural products and techniques that add value to traditional products. For example, tree nurseries are a new activity in areas where traditional tobacco workers are being displaced. Milk cooperatives improve cattle breeding as well as milking and milk handling techniques, raising the value of sales. Salt farmers are being shown how to produce higher-value industrial salt rather than lower-value edible salt. Cooperatives also provide their members with information on market prices for traditional and new products.

SEWA has also become involved directly in marketing what members produce. A rural marketing organization called SEWA Gram Mahila Haat ('village women's market') was set up in 1999. Four years later, in 2003, it arranged sales of nearly $700,000 for 15,000 members organized into almost 4,000 different producer groups. By far the largest shares of total sales were for salt (56 per cent) and agricultural produce (36 per cent), with gum and weaving accounting for the remaining 8 per cent. In 2003 SEWA made an arrangement with a national agricultural firm under which members sold sesame seed directly to the firm through Gram Mahila Haat (members also had the option of selling in the open market). SEWA's intervention increased dramatically the sale price obtained by members.

A separate SEWA organization, the Trade Facilitation Centre, was set up in 2000 to concentrate on designs for and sales of clothing, fabrics, and handicraft items outside local marketing channels. The centre's sales in 2002 totalled $145,000 in the national market, and SEWA's participation in the Smithsonian Folklife Festival in Washington, DC resulted in additional sales of $275,000 that year. During 2003, the centre's sales exceeded $200,000.

By far the largest cooperative is SEWA Bank. The accumulation and preservation of assets is central to the goal of self-reliance for poor women, who are almost always in debt and are easy prey for unscrupulous moneylenders and traders. The need was so obvious to SEWA members that they launched SEWA Bank in 1974, only two years after SEWA itself was founded. In the years since then, the bank has been a major source of SEWA's strength and an innovator in the field of microcredit. At the end of fiscal 2003/04, deposits totalled $14.4 million in 257,000 accounts, and there were 53,000 outstanding loans totalling $3.9 million (for an average loan size of about $73). Historically, SEWA Bank's loan recovery rate has been about 96 per cent. In 2003 and 2004, the bank started innovative mobile 'doorstep banking' arrangements to provide service to members without interrupting their livelihood activities. It also offers training courses in financial planning.

SEWA Bank has introduced the habit of regular saving to tens of thousands of poor women. They still have debts, but they are able to see progress in paying them down. They pay significant interest rates to SEWA Bank (currently over 20 per cent a year, while the rate of inflation is around 5 per cent), but no longer feel powerless and exploited by moneylenders.

And they can seize opportunities when they arise to improve their lives through microenterprise—by setting up a shop-in-a-cart, by embarking on a sharecropping scheme with a local landowner, by buying a mill to grind grain for the neighbourhood, or by investing in machinery that will improve the quality and raise the price of what they sell. They can also borrow for purposes that economists have traditionally regarded as 'unproductive', such as weddings. SEWA Bank's attitude towards such loan requests has become more permissive over time, in recognition that if members are to be self-reliant, they must be allowed to make their own choices.[2] The bank is also aware that if it denies a loan for such a culturally important purpose, the member will probably borrow the money elsewhere on less favourable terms.

SEWA's Impact: Improving Welfare and Empowering Women

SEWA gives priority to initiatives by its members rather than setting long-term programme targets against which progress could easily be measured. There is no doubt, however, that the movement has had an impact on empowerment of poor self-employed women by improving their access to employment opportunities, markets, services, and assets. Indeed, most activities are specifically designed to address problems of 'secure access' (to use SEWA's preferred term). SEWA regards all access problems as closely related. Opportunities for work are essential, since very little can be done without a secure source of employment. But women cannot take advantage of employment opportunities without minimal social security, including access to health care, childcare, insurance, and shelter. They cannot accumulate assets or make effective use of borrowed funds unless they have a degree of autonomy and a secure source of income to repay loans.

Delivering Basic Services to Members

SEWA concentrates its member services in four areas: health care, childcare, insurance, and housing. In SEWA's experience, a poor woman's livelihood security is not complete without access to these four basic goods. In this, as in many other areas, SEWA's approach is above all pragmatic. If a service functions well, provide members the information they need to use it; if a service needs improvement or reorientation, try to influence decision makers accordingly, and offer to assist; if all else fails, provide the service on a sustainable basis. The last option not only provides a service otherwise unavailable but also gives SEWA a louder voice at the policy table as it can speak with the authority of experience. In reality, there are very few cases where the simple provision of information has enabled members to use existing, fully functioning services. Much more commonly, SEWA has linked members to poorly functioning public services while trying at the same time to improve those services.

SEWA members often say 'my health is my only wealth' or 'our body is our capital'. Consistent with this, studies have repeatedly shown that the most important stress factor in poor women's lives is ill health. SEWA's health care activities are carried out in a variety of ways. Health teams are organized as midwives' and health workers' cooperatives in four districts; elsewhere they are adjuncts to other ongoing activities, such as a handicrafts association or childcare centre. SEWA encourages members to use government-run primary health care clinics and to take advantage of the government's immunization campaigns and 'camps' set up periodically to address particular ailments. In 2003 more than 300,000 people obtained primary health services of various kinds through SEWA teams of local 'barefoot doctors'. In addition, external funds were tapped to run a mobile clinic in rural areas affected by the 2001 earthquake, which allows doctors in government hospitals to extend the reach of their services. One of SEWA's most popular health initiatives is the sale of medicines at low cost in medical shops at major hospitals in Ahmedabad. Sales totalled over $250,000 in 2002 (SEWA 2003).[3]

Childcare is important not only to allow poor women time to earn a living, but also to protect children from the hazardous and sometimes toxic environments in which their mothers work. It also frees older siblings from child-minding duties, allowing them to attend school. Centres have been established cautiously, and only when the combination of women's contributions and funds from a variety of philanthropic, employer, and government sources will cover all the costs on a continuing basis. In 2003 there were 73 childcare centres catering to 4,700 children.

SEWA has pioneered the provision of insurance to poor women, drawing on both the SEWA Bank and government insurance companies. Typically, a woman saves Rs 1,000 (about $22) and puts it in a fixed deposit. The annual interest pays the premium and ensures uninterrupted coverage, which includes maternity benefits as well as payments in the event of various calamities such as illness, death, and loss of property. In 2003, more than 110,000 members were covered: over 6,000 claims were paid, for a total close to $180,000 (meaning the average payment was about $30).[4] SEWA is now planning an insurance cooperative, drawing on the example of SEWA Bank.

Finally, housing is enormously important for SEWA members, not just as a safe place to shelter the family but frequently also as their principal place of production and their most significant asset. The SEWA Housing Trust has offered training both to women wanting to build part or all of their own houses and to women working regularly on construction sites who seek to upgrade their skills and earning potential. It organized a scheme that legalized electricity connections to 900 households in three areas of Ahmedabad in 2003, with SEWA members undertaking to read the metres regularly. The women now pay less for better electrical service. In the rural areas affected by the 2001 earthquake, the SEWA Housing Trust built 2,600 houses in 2002 and 4,000 more in 2003, with ownership registered in the women's names; another 1,000 were under construction during 2004.

Increasing Incomes, Assets, and Welfare

Much of the foregoing discussion has focused on the numbers of participants in various activities and aggregate volumes. In an effort to address the question of SEWA's impact more systematically, Martha Chen and associates at SEWA recently published a synthesis of earlier studies of SEWA's impact in a variety of fields (Chen, Khurana, and Mirani 2005).[5] The more robust findings include the following:

- *Increased employment.* In a survey of 798 women, SEWA Bank borrower households reported 50 person-hours worked in household microenterprises during the previous month compared to 41 for control households. They also reported the highest increase over a two-year period in days worked per month (Chen and Snodgrass 2001).
- *Higher incomes.* In a survey of 50 urban women (32 SEWA members and 18 controls), two-thirds of SEWA members reported that their incomes had risen since joining SEWA (Schuler, Hashemi, and Pandit 1995).

  Borrowing from SEWA Bank was associated with monthly earnings from microenterprise substantially higher than the earnings of a control group: for the respondent herself, $16 versus $11; for the household, $42 versus $25, and for total household earnings from all informal sources, $205 versus $150 (Chen and Snodgrass 2001).

  Over a two-year period, SEWA Bank households raised their average incomes by 17 per cent in real terms, compared with

7 per cent for a control group. Repeat borrowers experienced greater increases (Chen and Snodgrass 2001).

- *Higher savings and ownership of assets.* Members of SEWA Bank had considerably more savings ($50) than controls ($20) (Chen and Snodgrass 2001).

  A survey of 470 SEWA members, half of them participating and half of them not participating in a total of 33 different savings groups, found that more of the participants had ownership of assets in their own names. Assets were reported by 26 per cent of savings group leaders, 21 per cent of participants, and 14 per cent of non-participants. In addition, the participants felt much more confident than non-participants in their ability to borrow in the future (Murthy 2000).

There is a completely different side to SEWA's impact that is important, notwithstanding the difficulty of measuring it in any rigorous way. Most observers would agree that over the years SEWA has played an important role in shifting attitudes and changing policies in India and even internationally. The 2005 study by Chen's team includes a 10-page list of 'influences' in a wide variety of fields, of which just two will be mentioned here. First, India's National Policy on Street Vendors, promulgated in 2004, undoubtedly owes a great deal to SEWA's experience and input. Second, SEWA has played a central role in initiating and establishing several 'global grassroots institutions' such as Women's World Banking, HomeNet, StreetNet, and WIEGO.[6]

Empowering Women

No account of SEWA's impact is complete without reference to the gains in self-confidence and dignity that members repeatedly mention and demonstrate in their everyday behaviour. While these gains are extremely hard to measure, they are at the heart of SEWA's work. Their significance is enormous in enabling members not only to assert their rights, but also to make effective use of the access they achieve.

During the five-day visit with SEWA workers on which this chapter is based, the foreign guests were impressed and deeply moved to hear their hosts speak proudly, in individual conversations and in group meetings, of becoming leaders in their communities and developing dignity and self-respect. The women were starting to participate in the wider society and economy and were acquiring new knowledge and skills, including management and literacy skills. They had strengthened their capacity to deal with the kinds of disasters that so often wreak havoc in the lives of the poor, ranging from natural disasters affecting whole communities to personal and family crises such as illness. And they spoke of having gained a feeling of security and comfort with their culture and heritage, despite an increasingly competitive environment.

These empowerment outcomes are in part the by-products of SEWA's other activities. When an illiterate woman borrows and saves money in her own name, for example, she gains in self-esteem. But empowerment is also the result of a conscious strategy of capacity building in which SEWA has invested since its early days.

Towards this end, the SEWA Academy was formally established in 1990. Its goals are to develop self-confidence and leadership skills among members while also uniting the large and diverse membership by imparting a common ideology and set of values. There were over 1,500 training events in 2003, attended by more than 75,000 members. In response to member demands, literacy and life skills training courses have been added and engaged about 1,400 members in 70 villages during 2003. Women are thrilled by their newly acquired literacy—and not just for practical reasons, such as being able to read the bus schedule rather than relying on someone else who might put them on the wrong bus. They also talk about the dignity they feel when signing their names on documents instead of making a thumbprint.

From the outset, SEWA has recognized the importance of doing research into the conditions affecting poor self-employed women. The SEWA Academy has carried out such studies and circulated them widely to policy makers and the public.[7] The academy has shown that with training, grassroots-level workers can contribute to serious research activities, so that research is not the exclusive concern of intellectuals and professionals.

The SEWA Experience through the Voices of its Members

The impact of SEWA can be seen most clearly in the life experiences of its members. The following accounts present the stories of three SEWA members who participated as hosts in the Exposure and Dialogue Programme organized in 2003 by SEWA and the World Bank. The accounts, based on conversations with the host women, were written up by three of the guests and reflect the SEWA members' situations at the time of the visit.[8]

Bhavnaben's Story

Bhavnaben is a 32-year-old salt farmer and a member of SEWA since 1997. Salt farming involves pumping underground brine into salt pans laid out on the desert floor, rimmed by low mounded walls. The brine evaporates until a certain level of salt concentration is reached and is then transferred via ditches to larger 'finishing' salt pans nearby. The low dikes and connecting ditches require constant repairs; this is done mainly by women, while men attend to the pumping engine and brine flow. Women usually also take care of compacting the floor of the finishing pans by trampling it with their bare feet. Then a heavy roller is pulled by hand over the entire floor. More semi-concentrated brine is gradually added to the pan, and the trampling and rolling process is repeated, until evaporation brings the brine concentration to a critical level for efficient crystal formation and the entire floor of the pan turns into a giant carpet of salt. The final steps involve raking to separate the salt from underlying sand and stones and piling the salt for transportation.

Conditions in the desert are harsh. There is no vegetation or water; intense heat during the day and cold at night are complicated by regular dust storms and occasional cyclones. The glare from the sun reflecting off the sand, brine ponds, and salt causes eye problems including night blindness, while constant exposure to chemicals and salt causes severe discomfort to the skin and more general health problems. The story repeated often by people in the area is that the feet of a salt worker never burn completely (or burn last) in the funeral pyre, because of the high salt content.

Bhavnaben and her family live at the salt farm during the seven-month salt season. They have built their desert home next to the brine well by digging a rectangular hole about 3 by 5 metres and half a metre deep, and erecting over it a simple tent-like structure made of wood poles, sticks, desert clay, and matting. The next hut and well can be seen on the horizon, amid shimmering mirages. Between November and February the nights are cold and the whole family of seven sleeps inside the hut; at other times the husband and a son sleep outside. Cooking and eating also take place inside the hut: the cooking area is in one corner, and a few receptacles with basic ingredients are stored on a shelf carved in the clay wall of the pit. The family sits on the floor in a circle at meal times and shares food from a common plate. There are few utensils, and the food is more or less the same for all three meals: flat breads made from millet flour, called *rotlas*. At breakfast they are accompanied by sweet tea served in a saucer, and sometimes at lunch or dinner by some potatoes and spinach and jaggery (raw sugar). But most of the meals consist simply of rotlas.

Once or twice a week Bhavnaben walks 10 kilometres to the village to bathe and fetch basic supplies, including fuelwood and water. She sometimes gets a ride from a relative with a bicycle or from a tractor or tanker, but most of the time she walks, often carrying her four-month-old baby. Her small one-room house in the village was recently finished with the help of SEWA and a programme financed by the government and international agencies after the original house was destroyed by the 2001 earthquake. However, the family's lack of funds means that there is no underground water storage tank or latrine in the compound.

Water is a precious commodity, in the village almost as much as in the desert. Its scarcity is evident from the way Bhavnaben uses only two or three glassfuls to wash dishes after each family meal. Bathing is done only once or possibly twice a week. Sanitation is primitive. Garbage is thrown into the common areas outside dwellings, where cattle and pigs devour almost everything. Most dwellings in the village have no latrine of any kind, and people relieve themselves in the fields.

Two months after her baby's birth, Bhavnaben fell ill and could not work for a month. She did not go to the clinic immediately and the fever got worse. When she eventually went to the clinic her fever was lowered, but before recovering fully she developed a severe cough and symptoms similar to pneumonia. Other members of the family also became ill, and as a result, they lost about a month at the start of the salt production season. Bhavnaben has four older children: daughters aged 12 and 2, and sons aged 8 and 6. None go to school; the two boys tend the diesel engine that pumps water from the ground, while the 12-year-old girl helps her mother with everything, including taking care of the baby and cooking.[9]

Bhavnaben's mother-in-law has been a dominant and domineering influence in her life. She is very conservative, insisting that Bhavnaben follow every local tradition. That includes such outdated customs as covering her face in the presence of elder males from her husband's side of the family. It also means not leaving the house on her own for any reason, so that for all her SEWA activities Bhavnaben has to be accompanied by another relative, usually an aunt who is also a SEWA member. The mother-in-law also objects whenever Bhavnaben is asked to leave the village for a SEWA meeting. She insists that a female relative accompany Bhavnaben, and demands, 'What does she know? How can she take part in such meetings?' Bhavnaben tells the story of going to a SEWA meeting in Baroda. Later, when her mother-in-law asked if she said anything, Bhavnaben replied that not only did she speak, she even sat in a big chair that went around in a full circle!

Since joining SEWA, Bhavnaben says she has found the courage and encouragement to take an active part in matters affecting her. She opened a SEWA Bank savings account, putting aside the equivalent of 40 cents per month plus other occasional deposits. The balance has grown to $23; this is important, as she can borrow from SEWA Bank three times her savings balance whenever needed. Other benefits from SEWA include a credit line that advances about $110 per month for operating and living expenses during the seven-month season of salt production. If the family has stayed within the limit of the advances they received plus interest, the entire season will yield a net income of about $450. SEWA has helped the salt workers negotiate better prices for their salt, bypassing the middlemen who used to exploit them both by paying too little for salt ($2.00 per ton against the renegotiated price of $2.65) and by charging ruinous interest rates on advances.

Although quite shy and relatively junior within the community, Bhavnaben has been very active in SEWA and is becoming a leader. At a village meeting, she was one of only two villagers who stood up in response to an invitation to talk about the benefits of joining SEWA. Her intervention was impressive and eloquent. In response to a heckler trying to be funny, Bhavnaben shot back, 'You did not have the courage to stand up and speak; if you wish to speak now, I will sit down.' That silenced him (and the audience), and she went on to make her points.

Kamlaben's Story

Kamlaben is a 37-year-old agricultural worker who lives in a single-room house with her husband and two of her three sons. The room is about 3.5 by 2.5 metres, with a roofed verandah. She rises every day at 5:30 a.m., starts a fire in a corner of the room, and cooks breakfast for the family— chapatis and rice plus tea with milk and sugar, all of which takes an hour or so to make from scratch. After washing the dishes and cleaning the house, Kamlaben usually goes to the tobacco field with other women for the morning or all day.

As a fieldworker, she performs tasks that vary with the season, but most involve back-wrenching work and constant bending. All the fields, as well as the tobacco factory and related infrastructure, are owned by one extended family. The owners contract with various 'village managers' to tend different fields, and the managers in turn recruit fellow villagers, typically four or five women, to do the work. The manager is paid an agreed amount per kilogram of tobacco harvested for managing the recruitment and payment of labour, and shares some of the risks if weather or other conditions reduce the crop. Kamlaben earns the equivalent of about 25 cents for a half day's work and 43 cents for a full day.

In addition to her work as a casual labourer in the tobacco fields, Kamlaben earns income in two other ways: as a member of a tree nursery cooperative and as owner of a 'shop' near her home. The nursery cooperative was recently formed with other village women, with financial and technical assistance from SEWA. Kamlaben took a SEWA loan of $110 to be repaid in 10 instalments at a 21 per cent interest rate. All loans are made solely to the women members, not to their husbands, with a guarantee provided by a respected and literate person in the village. With the help of family members, including Kamlaben's husband, the women have cleared and levelled two small areas in the village, bought tree seeds and other inputs, and mixed and bagged enriched soil for the seeds. The business appears promising and they have already sold a number of saplings for planting around the perimeter of fields. Kamlaben is the 'spearhead leader' for the cooperative, providing guidance to the other women and managing and collecting on their loans; for this she receives a small stipend from SEWA.

Her third source of livelihood is a simple wooden box on stilts, about one metre square, stocked with small food and household items. This was purchased with another $110 loan from SEWA. The shop is open from 9 a.m. to 9 p.m. and is run by her 14-year-old son, with some assistance from her husband and her husband's brother. They have started buying fresh vegetables to sell, and are making sales of about $5 to $6 a day. Here again, Kamlaben is the sole borrower and proprietor of the shop. She plans to start paying her son a salary once she has repaid the loan.

Kamlaben suffered great hardship as a child because of her father's heavy drinking and abuse of her mother and subsequently of her, coupled with the family's poverty. Her mother ran away and was never found. Kamlaben went to school through grade 5, and was then obliged to work in the tobacco fields.

She was married at age 16 and moved to her in-laws' home. Her inability to conceive for the first four years brought on the wrath of her husband and mother-in-law, and both beat her. Her mother-in-law said that the family would have been better off with a buffalo, which would at least have provided milk. Eventually her mother-in-law threw the couple out of the house, and they were forced to rent accommodation. They lived in vacant houses or sheds belonging to other villagers, and had to move often.

Kamlaben finally went to a health clinic and was given medicine that corrected her infertility, and she gave birth to three sons at two-year intervals. The eldest (now 16) completed grade 9, but dropped out after injuring his ankle and missing school for a couple of months. He is living with an uncle in another town in hopes of finding a job. The second (14) dropped out of school after grade 8 and is currently looking after the family's little shop. The youngest (12) is in grade 5, but is not keen about school and sometimes skips classes. The family does not put much stock in education, not seeing any connection between schooling and their livelihoods.

Kamlaben's primary asset, as she says herself, is her body. She has worked since she was a child and expects to work until she dies. Health and its fragility are key concerns for her. She sometimes has back problems that prevent her working as long as she needs to. The doctor is not the first resort when illness strikes; Kamlaben may visit the temple or just hope the problem goes away.

Kamlaben has been a member of SEWA for many years and is one of its local village leaders. She has received training through its member and leadership education programmes, and loans from SEWA Bank have helped build her economic assets in the form of working capital for the plant nursery and her shop and its stock. The biggest asset is her house. It was built with a grant of $130 provided by the government after she was sterilized, plus a series of three loans from SEWA Bank ($45 followed by two loans of $110 each, all now repaid). Having a roof over the family's head—no longer relying on rental housing or living with her husband's mother—is a great source of mental security for Kamlaben.

With SEWA's help, Kamlaben and other women in the village have found solutions to some of their families' basic problems, obtaining day care for children and modest health care centres. Advanced leadership training for the forestry cooperative has brought Kamlaben skills in accounting, report preparation, and business planning.

But most of all, in Kamlaben's opinion, SEWA has been instrumental in helping her overcome an abusive family situation and develop a sense of self-confidence that is evident in her manner of speaking and even in the way she walks—proudly, with assurance and conviction. Membership has also brought a very real solidarity with other women, who have come together not only as workers but also as women. If a member's husband beats her, a group of women will descend on the house to confront him, as happened in Kamlaben's own case. In an environment where women have traditionally had little choice, these are impressive signs of empowerment.

Shantaben's Story

Shantaben is a 47-year-old street vendor in the city of Ahmedabad, one of around 100,000 people who earn a living by selling fruit, vegetables, flowers, fish, clothing, and other items for daily use. They carry their wares in baskets on their heads or on handcarts. Some wander from street to street, while others sit on the ground in one place.

Shantaben buys small quantities of vegetables at the wholesale market early each day and tries to sell them by the end of the day. Her negotiating power is minimal and she is regularly shortchanged by the wholesalers and forced to pay inflated prices for produce; as a result, her profit margin is very small. Her vulnerability is not only economic. She sits and waits for customers for up to 14 hours a day on the street, where she is defenceless. She is exposed to floods and rains in the monsoon and to the burning sun in the hot months. At the major intersection where she has sold vegetables for many years now, the air she breathes every day is heavy with toxic engine emissions.

But rain, sun, and pollution are the least of her problems. Far more serious is the fact that she has no rights whatsoever. Street vendors are a thorn in the side of the city administration because they block pavements with the goods they lay out and impede traffic with their countless handcarts. By law, street peddlers must obtain a license from the city. However, to obtain a license one needs to know the right people, and one must be willing and able to pay a large sum of money. Since Shantaben has neither the money nor the right contacts, she is at the mercy of the police, who stop at her stand every day and charge her Rs 40 (about $1, one-fifth of her daily sales) as a 'penalty' for not having a license.

For Shantaben, it is a struggle each day to earn enough money to feed her family and still have enough left over to buy vegetables at the wholesale market the next morning. She cannot borrow from commercial banks, because the loans she would take (the equivalent of $10 to $20) would be considered too small. The wholesale merchants and the moneylenders who have set up shop around the wholesale market charge exorbitant interest rates.

Shantaben's father died when she was a year old, and her mother worked as a headload carrier to provide for the family. When Shantaben was 17 she married, and she and her husband moved to the country to grow vegetables with his family. Droughts forced them to return to Ahmedabad after only a few years. Shantaben's husband found work in a textile factory and Shantaben took care of their two young children, living in a small room about 10 metres square in a simple house on the city outskirts. The owner and his family lived in the other two rooms, and they all shared the toilet. Then her husband had an accident at work and lost a hand, leaving him unable to work for several weeks. Shantaben began selling vegetables in front of their home to provide for the family. Her best friend fell seriously ill and Shantaben promised to take care of her two small children as well. When the friend died a short time later, Shantaben took in the two orphans. More bad luck followed: a few years after his accident on the job, her husband died. Shantaben was left alone, raising four small children on her own.

A few years later, Shantaben joined SEWA when a friend told her about the way members fight for their interests and about the possibility of loans through SEWA Bank. Her first loan from SEWA was very small, the equivalent of about $10, which she used to buy more vegetables at the wholesale market. This increased her income marginally. When she repaid the first loan on time, she was able to borrow progressively higher amounts, and in this way gradually expanded her selling area from the original 2 square metres to 6 square metres.

Later she took out a larger loan to buy the room in which she and her family had been living, plus an additional room from the owner of the house, and a few years later she took another SEWA loan to purchase the remaining room. She is now the proud owner of the entire house with three small rooms and a small terrace, not more than 40 square metres in all, where she lives with her four grown children and two grandchildren. Shantaben will be repaying the loan for quite some time. Each day the SEWA member in charge of her district stops by her vending site and collects the instalment, which corresponds to roughly one-third to one-half of her daily intake, depending on sales. She has no difficulty repaying the loan.

In many ways, this is a success story. But Shantaben remains vulnerable. She cannot afford to fall ill or to have an accident because she would lose the means of existence for herself and her family. Earthquakes, floods, and violent conflicts between Hindus and Muslims are recurring catastrophes that keep the lives of poor people in Ahmedabad in constant jeopardy. If her modest possessions were to be damaged or destroyed, the fruit of decades of hard work would disappear. And old age looms: for the poor, there is no retirement, and people work until their dying day. In most cases their children have either moved away long ago to seek work or are themselves so poor that they cannot support their parents.

The SEWA women have resolved to break out of this vicious cycle. But progress is slow, and even the best-laid plans sometimes go awry. For example, after a long effort, in 2002 SEWA opened its own shop at the wholesale vegetable market. The idea is to pay fair prices to rural members who grow vegetables and to charge fair prices to urban members who buy and resell them, by cutting out the middlemen merchants and the high commisions they charge. But when Shantaben arrives at the wholesale market at 4:30 a.m. to purchase her vegetables, she buys only small quantities at the SEWA shop and the rest from the established wholesalers. She explains that at that time in the morning, the SEWA shop has only a few different kinds of vegetables, forcing her to continue to rely on purchases from the merchants.

The social cohesion among SEWA members is very strong, and not just because they are all poor women. There is also a new spirit emerging among women who no longer regard poverty and marginalization as their destiny, but are increasingly willing and able to take action. SEWA meetings invariably begin and end with everyone singing not just prayers but also 'battle songs' that describe their independence (from brothers, husbands, mothers-in-law, etc.) and their struggle for their rights. Change is in the air.

DRIVERS OF SUCCESS

Each of the life stories recounted above is unique, but they have two obvious features in common. All three women are struggling against grinding poverty, and in all three cases membership in SEWA played a central role in helping the women to empower themselves so that they could improve their situations. How does SEWA have an impact in such disparate circumstances, and what does this tell us about why SEWA has grown so rapidly?

Four common threads run through these stories and the larger story of SEWA as an organization: organizing, values, flexibility, and leadership. Woven together, these threads form a strong fabric that supports the growth and impact of SEWA's empowerment strategy.

Organizing Members Increases their Collective Strength

SEWA is first and foremost an association of self-employed women whom the rest of society excludes and exploits. They have almost no resources except the potential of their large numbers. To mobilize their collective strength, SEWA organizes the women into a trade union that helps members obtain a variety of benefits. Sometimes these benefits are new, but very often they are rights and services to which the women are already legally entitled but have not been receiving, either because they are unaware of them or because more powerful and organized forces in society deny them access. SEWA's highly successful approach to organizing relies heavily on tapping the latent capacities of poor and uneducated women (Box 3.1).

The organizing process increases the number of members and therefore their collective strength. But it has other purposes and consequences as well. When poor women become better informed about their rights, this increases the accountability of various public service providers, including the police, to the clients whom they are supposed to serve. By helping new members articulate their needs, SEWA focuses their attention on the future and reinforces the notion that their views are valuable and that SEWA belongs to its members; at the same time, this ensures that SEWA activities are 'demand-driven'. And in identifying potential activists and leaders among new recruits, organizing lays the groundwork for SEWA's future growth.

At different times in its history, SEWA has embarked on major organizing campaigns in order to increase the size and influence of its membership. For example, during the late 1990s it became clear that more attention would be paid to SEWA's voice in the national policy dialogue if it had the status of a national union. SEWA met the registration requirement of having activities in at least five states, but not the minimum requirement of 500,000 members. So a campaign to recruit new members began in 1999, with the rallying cry *Five lakhs!* (a lakh is 100,000). A surge in membership of almost 50 per cent in 2000 was followed by another 32 per cent gain in 2001. The 500,000 figure was passed easily in 2002, and SEWA was able to register as a national union.

Extraneous factors also play a role in recruitment. In January 2001, a devastating earthquake killed 14,000 people in Gujarat and injured more than 150,000, while destroying or damaging 230,000 homes in rural areas of the state. And in 2002 and 2003, communal violence caused wide suffering and disrupted the livelihoods of tens of thousands of poor families, especially in Ahmedabad and other urban areas. SEWA was able to respond quickly and provide effective assistance to the victims of both crises, whether or not they were members. In addition, it became well known that SEWA members with insurance were receiving payments in partial compensation for their losses. Both the favourable publicity and the vivid demonstration of the benefits of SEWA insurance encouraged new members to join. Of course, once they are members, women often became involved in a variety of SEWA activities extending well beyond their original motive for joining.

Box 3.1 Organizing at the Grassroots

SEWA has three levels of staff outside corporate management at its headquarters, and also relies heavily on members for volunteer activities (with expenses reimbursed). A coordinator is assigned to each rural district where SEWA is active; in urban areas, each coordinator is responsible for several neighbourhoods. Each coordinator is supported by several team leaders, and each team leader in turn by several organizers.

The first steps towards organizing the women in a village are carried out by a SEWA team leader and one of her organizers. They visit the village and talk with the village council about SEWA and the benefits it could bring to the whole community. If the village council agrees— and it does not always do so—the team leader and organizer hold discussions with village women and recruit one or more volunteer village leaders. These volunteer leaders are not employed by SEWA, but receive a small stipend to cover their expenses associated with SEWA activities. The team leader, the organizer, and the volunteer village leader then explain the benefits of SEWA membership, help the women identify their urgent needs, and begin the process of capacity building. The approach is made easier as SEWA becomes known in an area, and women from nearby villages or neighbourhoods can come to meetings to talk about their own experiences with SEWA.

Women who join SEWA become members of a particular trade group and are encouraged to participate in cooperatives or other collective activities related to that trade. In addition, a deliberate effort is made to develop the women as 'barefoot managers' of activities ranging from integrated production campaigns (as in water, forestry, or agriculture) to health care, childcare, training and education, insurance, savings, housing, research, and video production.

For each activity in a district, a spearhead team usually consists of 10 people—two SEWA staff organizers and eight volunteer village leaders from different villages. Thus the savings spearhead team for a rural district would include eight volunteer village leaders from eight different savings groups. Members of the spearhead teams receive on-the-job training from SEWA and attend classroom sessions periodically to help them become proficient in record keeping, managing money, writing, and presentation. They learn about the government's administrative structure and programmes and receive

(Contd)

Box 3.1 (Contd)

technical training in the activity for which they are responsible. As they gain proficiency and confidence, volunteer village leaders play a growing role in the recruitment and training of new groups. They train individual members in the skills that they have learned and help new groups to overcome problems, drawing on their own experience and what they have learned from each other.

Over time, spearhead team members acquire considerable experience and expertise in the activity in which they specialize. Many go on to become promoters of savings groups, or distributors of raw materials and collectors of finished products for craft groups. They may take on responsibilities for accounting and record keeping, or win election to committees of cooperatives, or undertake training as barefoot veterinarians or builders. In this way they increase their options for earning income and contribute more generally to the welfare of their families and the larger community. Some are recognized as especially promising by SEWA staff and are recruited to positions as SEWA organizers, eventually becoming team leaders or coordinators.

Adhering to Core Values

From its inception, SEWA has been steeped in the Gandhian beliefs and practices of Ela Bhatt and her associates. Their clarity of vision provides the foundation for SEWA's consistency of purpose and its perseverance, for example in the long-term struggle to shift the policy environment in which SEWA works. Gandhi's 11 principles are often sung in chant form at the beginning of meetings, and they are an integral part of what the SEWA Academy teaches.[10] There are constant reminders of a consciously practiced egalitarianism that stands in marked contrast to the norms of Indian society. SEWA staff insist that members address each other and even 'distinguished' foreign visitors using the suffixes *ben* (sister) and *bhai* (brother). These traditional Gujarati forms of address are becoming less common today, but are used within SEWA as a way of emphasizing the members' sense of equality and self-worth.

All meetings are conducted in a highly participatory manner and thus consume far more time and energy than would be considered efficient in the West. It is said that no SEWA staff member has ever been fired—though some have moved to a different kind of work, better suited to their talents.

There is, accordingly, a willingness to take risks, to learn from mistakes, and to try new approaches until something works. Because the value structure is so well understood, staff and organizers have great freedom in deciding how to carry out their responsibilities. At the same time, because of frequent meetings any successful new approaches are quickly made known to and adopted by others, while unsuccessful approaches are labelled as such.

Ela Bhatt notes that the Gandhian principles that underlie SEWA are age-old and embedded in Indian culture and traditions, as Gandhi himself freely acknowledged. She adds modestly that her only contribution is the notion that, in contemporary India at least, women are the conservers and source of strength in society and the natural leaders of any movement to improve the general welfare. They have the future orientation that leads them to save and to invest, they have the courage to face adversity and despair and just work harder, and they have the nurturing instinct that keeps children fed and families functioning. If only they were allowed to get on with it! In her view, the key to SEWA's consistency of purpose and success over three decades is very simple: they have always focused on the women.[11]

Employing a Flexible and Decentralized Approach

SEWA's flexible style and decentralized organization can be confusing to a first-time visitor, but it is a huge source of strength. The image of the banyan tree is helpful once again here: it is easy to get lost among the multiple root-trunks that grow down to support the branches, but the whole tree provides marvellous and extensive shelter, and an injury to (or even the loss of) a particular branch or root-trunk does no great harm to the rest of the tree. So each branch of SEWA, and each individual organizer, has a great deal of autonomy. What binds them is not a set of rules telling them in specific terms *what* to do, but a set of principles governing *how* they should set about working towards whatever ends they choose. Characteristically, SEWA's statement of what it does is phrased in rather abstract terms ('organizing women for full employment and self-reliance'). Most of the details are left to members on the ground.

This leads to wide variation in approaches intended to achieve the same broad objective, and thus to the emergence of natural experiments in which the outcomes of different approaches can be compared. Since no approach is considered the 'right' one, staff and members tend not to become strongly wedded to any particular approach, and they are happy to share the results in frequent meetings in which they also learn about the achievements and problems of their colleagues. These habits are reinforced by SEWA's long-term commitment to enquiry and fact finding, reflected in the establishment and work programme of SEWA Academy. SEWA seems in this way to have become a natural 'learning organization' well before the term became popular.

Four additional consequences of SEWA's organizational style are worth noting. First, staff become used to risk-taking rather than averse to it, and think of innovation and adaptation as normal. Crises such as earthquakes, droughts, or communal violence are seen as opportunities rather than as setbacks. When asked to describe a failure, SEWA staff say they do not think in terms of success versus failure or victory versus defeat, but in terms of a long struggle in which there are ups and downs and periodic realignments of strategy to achieve the larger goals. To cite one example, SEWA's attempt to gain higher pay for agricultural workers by withholding labour in rural areas did not work out. But this was not a 'failure', as SEWA eventually found a way to achieve the same end by promoting alternative income-earning opportunities, which both benefit those who participate and raise agricultural wages in the area.

Similarly, SEWA Bank's feasibility depended initially on the innovative use of passport-size photos as a substitute for signatures for identification purposes, a concept that was completely new to the financial establishment at the time. More recently, SEWA Bank has also pioneered various ways of bringing bank services to members for whom a visit to the bank's office means lost time and therefore lost income. There are now extension counters in several parts of Ahmedabad; in addition, in some areas members act as agents, collecting deposits, and performing other transactions.

The second important consequence of SEWA's flexible and decentralized style is that staff are highly motivated, energetic, and committed. They feel trusted to control their own work. Nobody is looking over their shoulder, telling them how to do their jobs, criticizing them for not following rules, or evaluating their performance. This contributes to a strong sense of loyalty and to low turnover and allows SEWA to attract highly competent professionals despite long hours and low pay. Job satisfaction has to come from the substance of the work rather than from financial reward.

The third consequence of SEWA's flexibility is the capacity to grow. Since the whole structure is built around members and their concerns, it adapts and grows in whatever direction those concerns may lead. Some of the normal constraints on growth in a large organization do not seem to apply—there is no rigid central bureaucracy to overcome, and any new procedures needed can be introduced fairly easily. There are, of course, problems associated with growth, discussed in more detail below, but SEWA's flexible organization and style are forgiving.

The final aspect of SEWA's flexibility that deserves attention is its focus on pragmatism rather than rhetoric. There is a firm commitment to core values, but a readiness to work with any organization that might be helpful to poor self-employed women. SEWA has accepted funding from a variety of Indian foundations and foreign donors; among the latter are the Consultative Group to Assist the Poorest (CGAP), the Ford Foundation, the German technical cooperation agency GTZ, the International Fund for Agricultural Development, the International Labour Organization, and KfW, a German bilateral development bank. SEWA is cautious about entering into substantive partnerships but has no qualms about engaging in dialogue with parties sometimes considered controversial, such as industrial conglomerates or government departments with poor reputations. Some activists criticize SEWA for this attitude, accusing the organization of 'selling out'. SEWA's response is very simple. It seeks to bring its members into the mainstream, and it cannot do that without being willing to talk and work with mainstream actors. Indeed, SEWA has (in the words of Ela Bhatt) the audacity to think that it can slowly change the minds of mainstream actors, including the Government of India and the World Bank.

Fostering Leadership at All Levels

Ela Bhatt founded SEWA and led the organization as its general secretary for 24 years, until 1996. She nurtured leadership at the grassroots as well as at the centre, and her vision inspired a cadre of professional women to join and stay with SEWA's corporate management. Collectively they have developed a remarkable set of participatory management and behavioural practices that help to close the social distance between members and managers, and that have resulted in great consistency of purpose over more than 30 years—including the years since Ela Bhatt's departure.

Because SEWA is registered as a national labour union, it is subject to all the requirements imposed by India's state and national labour legislation. The formal electoral and governance arrangements are described in Box 3.2. Transparency in union elections is treated very seriously, and SEWA staff make a point of absenting themselves from meetings where they might appear to influence election outcomes. SEWA's constitution stipulates that the president and vice presidents, one of the secretaries, and all the generally elected members of the executive committee must be working-class women. The only elective offices available in practice to professional members are two corporate management posts—the general secretary and one of the secretaries.

By custom, the corporate management offices are treated as one-term posts, so that there is a regular rotation of office holders. This practice (SEWA uses the term 'collective leadership') helps ensure that no individual becomes or appears to become unduly powerful. Its apparent disadvantage, loss of continuity, is avoided because the core management cadre remains remarkably stable. There has been very low turnover among the professional women who have committed themselves to SEWA, and they stay fully involved in running SEWA's affairs regardless of their current title or office. Some of them occupy the 'invitee' chairs on the Executive Committee mentioned in Box 3.2.

In addition to these arrangements for the structure of corporate management, there are other mechanisms through which SEWA's management reduces social distance between the membership at large and the centre. First, the Gandhian value of equality is constantly emphasized. Meetings favour participation over the speedy conduct of business, while seating arrangements, songs of solidarity, opening and closing prayers, and even the use of the ben and bhai suffixes all serve as reinforcing behaviour. SEWA delegations to national and international meetings invariably include working-class members (usually travelling outside their home area for the first time) as well as headquarters staff. Second, pay scales are highly compressed: the rule is that the highest-paid staff member may earn no more than three times as much as the lowest-paid staff member.[12] This means that managerial staff are unlikely to be resented for their high salaries—just as it means that their commitment and motivation have nothing to do with financial rewards.

SEWA has a conscious policy of finding and developing new leaders among the poor women who become members. Much of this takes place informally. An organizer or coordinator notices a new recruit with energy and drive, and encourages her through personal interactions and by assigning her special tasks that gradually increase in significance. Because poor women have usually had no outlet for any latent leadership talents (indeed, any signs they showed early in life were probably suppressed harshly), it quite often happens that modest encouragement from SEWA releases remarkable abilities that were previously untapped. Many women have come into their own in this way and attained leadership roles in SEWA, despite illiteracy and limited exposure to the wider world.

A more formal role in leadership development is played by SEWA Academy as part of its capacity-building mission. Courses at the academy include very basic 'self-presentation' skills (such as talking into a microphone and introducing oneself), more advanced courses to build self-confidence, and quite sophisticated courses that include, for example, material on how to deal with politicians. The one organizational form that SEWA regards as completely off-limits is the political party, because the leaders know from experience that politicians will use them, to the disadvantage of the members. Now that SEWA has grown so large, members with leadership roles are constantly being wooed by politicians seeking votes at election time or the endorsement of party positions at other times. SEWA Academy teaches members why and how to avoid such entanglements.[13]

Box 3.2 SEWA's Governance

Each SEWA member belongs to a trade group (such as bidi rollers, construction workers, dairy workers, gum processors, hawkers, salt farmers, weavers, and so on). The trade groups, more than 125 in all, provide the foundation for SEWA's governance arrangements.

Every three years, the members of each trade group elect their own trade committee. At the same time they elect a certain number of trade committee members to be their trade representatives (one for every 400 members of the trade group). The trade representatives become members of the Council of Representatives, SEWA's main source of authority and governance, which meets monthly. The Council of Representatives had 1,422 elected members in 2004.

Once the council is elected for a three-year term, one of its first duties is to elect 25 of its members to an Executive Committee, the composition of which once again broadly reflects the relative size of the trade groups. The Executive Committee numbers 30 in all, since it also includes five appointed members from the senior management staff of SEWA. In addition, it has a limited number of chairs for 'invitees', members who have made a particularly significant contribution to SEWA over the years.

The Executive Committee, following the same three-year cycle, elects seven of its members to serve as officers: a president and three vice presidents, and a general secretary and two secretaries. The president and vice presidents are from the largest trade groups in SEWA's membership. The general secretary and the two secretaries assume responsibility for the management and administration of SEWA; at least one of the secretaries must be a working-class member.

(Contd)

Box 3.2 (Contd)

By custom, the corporate management officers hold office for only one three-year term, though unlike most of the provisions mentioned earlier, this is not a requirement of SEWA's constitution.

Since SEWA is by constitution and registration a trade union, it is required to file audited annual accounts and the proceedings of its annual general meeting with the government registrar. It also has to submit membership records annually to the government's Department of Labour for scrutiny and control.

Lessons Learned and Remaining Challenges

This concluding section looks at the lessons that can be drawn from SEWA's experience and their possible applicability elsewhere. It briefly addresses two questions: What challenges did SEWA face and how were they overcome? What key factors led to SEWA's successful outcomes and steady scaling up of activity?

Challenges

SEWA's initial challenge was to overcome the assumption, even the strong conviction, that organizing workers in the informal sector 'just can't be done'. This was accomplished by the determination and inner strength of the few women who were then involved. This same determination, combined with a shrewd eye for what the general public would support, carried SEWA over many hurdles as it organized self-employed women in Ahmedabad in its first few years. This quality of determination is probably essential during the start-up phase of any major undertaking. What is interesting about the SEWA experience is that the same quality has been required throughout its life, simply because SEWA is constantly embarking on new ventures and modifying old ones in response to its members' needs. Every reversal or setback is seen as a challenge and an opportunity. It seems likely that this repeated interplay of 'challenge and response' contributes significantly to the solidarity and continued enthusiasm of SEWA members, even as their numbers continue to grow.

The challenges SEWA faced in its initial start-up were in part problems with the policy environment. India is not a country that is hostile in principle to civil society organizations or unions or to the empowerment of women—on the contrary, public rhetoric and a considerable body of legislation strongly favour such endeavours. The problem for SEWA (and India's myriad other civil society organizations) is not the rhetoric but the practical realities of operating in a huge country with strongly entrenched interests, an unwieldy bureaucracy, and a painfully slow and congested legal system. SEWA had to struggle for two years, for example, before it could register as a union, because the registrar was not convinced that self-employed women were legally entitled to form a labour union. Who were their employers? Similarly, the banking authorities were at the outset very reluctant to allow the establishment of SEWA Bank. How could a bank be financially viable if it lent only to self-employed women without collateral?

Over the years, almost every step in SEWA's growth has meant engaging with the policy environment in a very practical sense and patiently pushing the boundaries so that SEWA members are actually covered by the programmes and agencies and rules that are ostensibly in place to help India's poor. It was not until 2002, for example, that the informal sector and self-employed workers were recognized as major contributors to the economy; this was an outcome of the National Labour Commission chaired by Ela Bhatt. SEWA's successful and continuing efforts in this direction have benefited self-employed workers, as well as civil society organizations assisting them, throughout India—a broad impact that goes far beyond SEWA's own membership.

Other challenges have taken three main forms. The first is resistance to SEWA's organizing activities, the foundation on which all subsequent activities are based. The resistance invariably originates in the suspicions of a community's menfolk, with their wives sometimes echoing their objections. There are many, many stories about how SEWA organizers eventually overcame such resistance through patience and sometimes guile. In the vast majority of such cases, even the men who originally objected are pleased by the eventual outcome. But there are communities where opposition remains firm, and organizers have simply not been allowed to enter the area. SEWA's tactic in these cases is to wait. Sooner or later, the time will be ripe—and there is plenty to do in other communities in the meantime.

The second challenge is the financial viability of various enterprises. In preparing this chapter, no attempt was made to investigate to what extent the cooperatives and member services promoted by SEWA are financially viable in the long run. SEWA's policy in this area is clear: all such activities should be sustainable. But actually making them so, and deciding when initial subsidies have gone on long enough, is always difficult. Up to now, SEWA has been able to rely on funds from donors to make good any deficits. In the future, financial issues are bound to loom larger, for several reasons.

Although donor funds are likely to keep flowing as long as SEWA maintains its reputation, and may even increase, they are unlikely to grow as rapidly as SEWA's membership—and new members bring new demands for activities and services. In effect, whatever subsidy funds are available will have to be divided among more activities, and the pressures of tight financial discipline will become steadily greater. Moreover, some of the new activities in which SEWA is engaging, such as insurance, require a much longer planning horizon and more refined risk management than SEWA's traditional activities. SEWA is already engaging private sector partners and expertise to address these issues, and additional donor support would be helpful.

The third challenge is that of growth. As noted earlier, SEWA's membership has grown very rapidly for an extended period, with an average annual growth rate of over 25 per cent in each of the last three five-year periods. This has proved possible because of the decentralized, flexible structure and management arrangements described earlier. One can hope that the same principles, if not precisely the same arrangements, will work well for an organization with 1 million members ... or 2 million. But there are bound to be challenges. With such large numbers, will it be possible to maintain the 'flat' structure that today ensures participation at the grassroots as well as responsive governance arrangements? Will SEWA find the necessary numbers of organizers and team leaders and village volunteers? Will it be possible to recruit professionally qualified women to enlarge the dedicated management cadre and to absorb the new recruits quickly? As outside support grows, will the different and sometimes conflicting oversight and reporting requirements imposed by different donors become a major burden? Will it be possible to avoid political entanglements as SEWA becomes an ever more attractive potential 'vote bank' for politicians seeking election?

One other aspect of growth deserves attention. The expansion of SEWA's membership in other states has been uneven, and certainly less dramatic than in Gujarat. At the end of 2003 membership exceeded 175,000 in Madhya Pradesh and was more than 50,000 in Uttar Pradesh, but in most other states it numbered in the hundreds rather than thousands. What light does this cast on scaling up?

There are several reasons why SEWA's success in Gujarat was not simply replicated, after some years, in other states. Probably the most important has to do with timing. SEWA's activities in Gujarat in the 1970s and 1980s were truly path-breaking, and provided a firm foundation for subsequent growth in the state. But SEWA's expansion into other states came later, when the ideas pioneered by SEWA had gained wider currency and could already be found in the programmes of many organizations. While SEWA still has a unique approach, in other states it does not have the innovative edge that worked to its advantage in Gujarat. A second reason flows from the first: because it is by now so well known and respected in Gujarat, SEWA can attract funds from the state government and other sources that are tied to expenditure in Gujarat.[14] In other states, SEWA faces more competition for local funds from other local organizations, and this hampers its rapid growth. A third, more speculative, reason is that Gandhi's principles have a special intensity and following in his home state of Gujarat. While these principles are embraced widely throughout India, it may be that this core feature of the SEWA movement has somewhat less resonance in other states.

This discussion points to a paradox. Perhaps SEWA's very success in introducing innovations in Gujarat in the 1970s, innovations that were later adopted widely by civil society activists elsewhere, had the effect of slowing down SEWA's subsequent expansion in other states. This highlights a classic problem in measuring the scaling up of almost any development activity: How does one take into account the spread of ideas, as opposed to growth in the number of participants? There are no obvious answers to be drawn at this stage from the uneven pattern of growth of SEWA activities outside Gujarat.

Key Factors for Success and Growth

While no single model of organizing can fit all populations and contexts, SEWA's impressive record in scaling up its membership and activities over the past three decades may offer useful lessons to other initiatives with similar aims. In sum, four significant features can be seen to account for SEWA's success in mobilizing large numbers of poor women and encouraging them to empower themselves.

First, member-based organizations promote *ownership* and help ensure that activities are based on members' demands and needs. Such organizations can harness energy hitherto untapped and generate it anew as members attain self-confidence and learn new skills. Membership organizations can grow rapidly if attention is paid to organizing and recruiting new members, and to selecting and training new organizers among them.

Second, an organization based on *values* must emphasize them constantly. If it does so, it can maintain consistency of purpose and function very flexibly. Values generate strong loyalty from staff and members, as well as support from the wider public, and underpin the patience and perseverance required to change a difficult policy environment.

Third, a *flexible style* encourages learning and innovation and therefore facilitates adaptation to changing circumstance, including the ability to see crises as opportunities. At the same time, flexibility motivates high performance and low turnover among staff and makes it possible to take advantage of partnerships with external actors.

Finally, *leadership skills* are crucial, not only to define and uphold the vision of an organization, but also in establishing management and behavioural practices that minimize social distance between the management cadre and the organization's members (or clients). Moreover, with proper attention to training and practical research, an organization can find and develop new leaders among its members or clients despite their poverty and lack of formal education, and in this way ensure its continuity and growth.

NOTES

This chapter combines contributions of the participants in a five-day Exposure and Dialogue Programme conducted by SEWA in November 2003 at the request of the World Bank. The six SEWA hosts were Bhavna Kali, salt worker; Gauri Koli, water line woman; Kamla Parmar, tobacco worker; Shanta Parmar, vegetable seller; Hira Vaghela, construction worker; and Hansa Vankar, weaver. The group of 13 visitors included guests from the World Bank (Judy Edstrom, Basil Kavalsky, Ad Melkert, Deepa Narayan, Fred Nunes, and Praful Patel), BMZ (Dorothee Fiedler), KfW (Nassir Djafari), India America Foundation (David Fuente and Purvi Tank), and the Institute of Development Studies at Sussex University (Robert Chambers); the two remaining guests were John Blaxall, a consultant, and Amanda Melkert, a student. The 12 SEWA staff and coordinators, who also acted as translators, were Chhaya Bhavsar, Mirai Chatterjee, Mona Dave, Renana Jhabwala, Jyoti Mecwan, Reema Nanavaty, Manali Shah, Nisha Shah, Uma Swaminathan, Labhu Thakkar, Beena Trivedi, and Jayshree Vyas.

The author wishes to acknowledge, in addition to contributions from those named above, the thoughtful comments of Ela Bhatt in a personal interview. Thanks also to Poonam Shroff of SEWA's staff for pulling background material together and reviewing successive drafts. Figures cited here without specific attribution are from internal SEWA sources or from presentations by SEWA staff. Two books that proved useful as background are K. Rose, *Where Women Are Leaders: The SEWA Movement in India* (London: Zed, 1992), and D.W. Crowell, *The SEWA Movement and Rural Development: The Banaskantha and Kutch Experience* (New Delhi: Sage, 2003). Much information about SEWA can be found on the organization's three Websites: http://www.sewa.org, http://www.sewaacademy.org, and http://www.sewaresearch.org.

References

Chen, M.A., R. Khurana and N. Mirani, 2005, *Towards Economic Freedom: The Impact of SEWA*, Ahmedabad, India: SEWA Academy.

Chen, M.A. and D. Snodgrass, 2001, 'Managing Resources, Activities, and Risks in Urban India: An Impact Assessment of the SEWA Bank,' AIMS Project, US Agency for International Development, Washington, DC.

GRIP (Grass Roots Immersion Programme), 2005, 'GRIP Program @ SEWA in India, November 9–14, 2003: Notes and Photographic Record of the Salt Workers Team.' Updated with notes from follow-up visit in January 2005. Collaborative Program of SEWA and the World Bank, Washington, DC.

Murthy, S., 2000, 'Assessing the Impact of SEWA's Rural Microfinance Program,' SEWA Academy, Bhadra, Ahmedabad, India.

Schuler, S., S. Hashemi and H. Pandit, 1995, 'Beyond Credit: SEWA's Approach to Women's Empowerment and Influence on Women's Reproductive Lives in Urban India,' Washington, DC: John Snow International.

SEWA (Self-Employed Women's Association), 2003, *Annual Report 2002*, Ahmedabad, India.

——, 2004, *Annual Report 2003*, Ahmedabad, India. http://www.sewa.org.

Notes

1 Except as otherwise noted, data are from the SEWA annual report for 2003, available at http://www.sewa.org.

2 Borrowing for such a purpose would have to be approved by the local branch of SEWA Bank. Some branches are holding out against the trend towards more permissive lending, fearing that family pressures will oblige women to take on burdensome and unwanted loans. This theme—the need to keep expenditures (and therefore debts) associated with family rituals within reasonable bounds—was the special topic at SEWA's annual membership meeting in January 2004.

3 Patients at Indian hospitals (or their relatives) are expected to go and buy whatever medicines or supplies are prescribed by attending doctors, and the medicines or supplies are then administered by hospital staff. SEWA does not subsidize the medicines, but keeps costs low through bulk purchases and low profit margins. Purchasers do not have to be SEWA members.

4 Payouts for earthquake damage in 2001 and for violence-related damage in 2002 raised questions about the insurance scheme's long-term solvency. This led to

a complete revision of financial plans and targets, including requests for additional financial support from international donors.

5 The Chen study team reviewed a wide variety of materials and selected 21 reports that address the impact of SEWA's work. Eight of the reports were prepared by SEWA for its own use and 13 were done by outsiders, usually to measure the impact of specific services provided by SEWA. The authors note that 'none [of the 21 reports] were explicitly designed to measure the impact of SEWA's key strategies: namely, organizing its members into either trade groups or cooperatives and collective bargaining to improve their living and working conditions' (Chen, Khurana, and Mirani 2005: 9). They also acknowledge a variety of methodological problems in the studies. In addition to the general problems of selection bias and attribution, for example, they note that of the 10 reports based on surveys, only five used random samples with matched control groups, and only three tested statistical correlations (51).

6 HomeNet and StreetNet are global alliances of home-based workers and street vendors respectively. WIEGO (Women in Informal Employment: Globalizing and Organizing) undertakes research and policy work on the informal economy in a global context.

7 Some of the studies are available on the SEWA websites at http://www. sewaacademy.org and http://www.sewaresearch.org.

8 The life stories of Bhavnaben, Kamlaben, and Shantaben are excerpted with minor editing from reports by Praful Patel, Judith Edstrom, and Nassir Djafari, respectively. A longer report by Praful Patel documents the visit and is illustrated with photographs of Bhavnaben's family and their salt farm, taken during the November 2003 visit and a return visit in January 2005 (see GRIP 2005).

9 By the time of the return visit in 2005, the four older children had started some literacy instruction at home with a visiting teacher.

10 The 11 principles are being truthful, being non-violent, being honest, retaining minimum possessions, controlling one's desires, relying on one's own labour, rejecting caste divisions, being free from fear, supporting local livelihoods, adopting a simple lifestyle, and practicing equality of all faiths. Sometimes the principles are simplified into a list of four: truth, non-violence, integrating all faiths and peoples, and promoting local employment and self-reliance.

11 Interview by author with Ela Bhatt, Ahmedabad, December 5, 2003.

12 This rule applies to SEWA's headquarters and district staff, not necessarily to all cooperatives in the SEWA family or all projects for which SEWA draws on external funding.

13 SEWA members may of course join political parties and vote for them, but they may not stand for election as members of a party. Some SEWA members have been elected to village assemblies as independents.

14 Notwithstanding SEWA's cultivation of its independent reputation, politics still intrude. In the fall of 2005, a dispute arose between SEWA and the Gujarat state government, as a result of which all state funding of SEWA programmes was suddenly cut off.

4

Empowerment through Self-Help Groups
Andhra Pradesh Shows the Way in India

Swaminathan S. Anklesaria Aiyar,
Deepa Narayan, and *K. Raju*

In the south Indian state of Andhra Pradesh, a programme to empower poor women, historically at the bottom of class and gender ladders, has begun to break down social and income barriers. Originally called Velugu and recently renamed Indira Kranti Patham, the programme had organized 7.8 million poor women into 617,472 self-help groups by the end of 2005. These groups mobilize up to $250 million in savings every year, obtain additional credit of up to $475 million from banks, and use the credit and government grants to improve livelihoods and community infrastructure. The programme also provides food security through rice credit lines and household security through community insurance schemes. It works for the abolition of social evils like child labour and temple prostitution, creates community-based health systems, and establishes residential schools to promote education of the girl child.

In the Indian context, a self-help group, or SHG, is a group of 10 to 20 people, almost always women, who come together to find a collective solution to their common problems. Mobilized with government facilitation, such groups typically start by pooling their savings and lending to members in need, but then go on to tackle broader livelihood and social problems. They get matching grants and training from the state government.

This strategy has been adopted widely by Andhra Pradesh, a state that accounts for over 40 per cent of India's self-help groups (Indian NGOs 2005). SHGs in Andhra Pradesh have federated into 27,350 village organizations, which in turn have federated into 864 organizations at the level of the *mandal*, or subdistrict.[1] This federated structure gives the groups unprecedented social and political influence. Velugu thus represents one of the most sweeping organizational attempts in the world to empower poor and marginalized women.

Conventional anti-poverty programmes have found it difficult to reach those at the bottom of the social ladder. The SHG approach helps overcome these difficulties, as the groups consist of self-selecting poor women. The groups are empowered with access to facilities previously available mainly to those at the top of the ladder: credit, organizing capacity, training, opportunities to become entrepreneurs, and safety nets. This approach has given many women the courage and confidence to rise above their historical disadvantages. Illiterate women who had seldom ventured out of their houses have, thanks to Velugu, become entrepreneurs and heads of village organizations and subdistrict federations (Box 4.1).

Box 4.1 From Landless Labourers to Community Leaders

Lakshmi and Pedaramana were once an illiterate, landless couple. They worked as agricultural labourers and had no assets, only debts. They managed to clear their debts with some assistance from Lakshmi's family, yet the future seemed to hold little for them. But today, thanks to Velugu, they own a sheep business and a shop, and are about to buy 10 acres of land. They have been transformed from objects of pity to objects of envy.

Lakshmi and Pedaramana first heard about the self-help group movement on a visit to a neighbouring village where a non-governmental organization had operated for some time. Lakshmi approached the programme's coordinator and invited him to start self-help groups in her village too. This was the start of a transformation: today, every household in Lakshmi's village is covered by SHGs.

Lakshmi soon became the president of her SHG. As her stature grew, she also became chairperson of the watershed committee in her village. Using the Velugu community investment fund, the SHGs in the village built *anganwadis* (childcare centres) and a community hall. They are now building a school. Villagers today have confidence in their collective strength to meet any challenge.

Lakshmi and Pedaramana used loans from the SHG to pay off moneylenders and acquire productive assets. Their good loan repayment record enabled them to get bigger and bigger loans, so they have received cumulatively almost Rs 200,000 ($4,400). Their

(Contd)

Box 4.1 (Contd)

> shop and sheep business are yielding good returns, so they feel
> confident of repaying the loan they have just taken to buy 10 acres
> of land.
>
> 'Despite being illiterate and uneducated we have travelled far with
> our minds,' says Lakshmi. 'We know what it means to be proud.'
>
> *Source*: *Velugu: Voices of Women* (SERP n.d., 56–58).

The progress of self-help groups in most Indian states has been slow, as established elites have resisted giving up power to those who traditionally have been powerless. Andhra Pradesh is an exception. Enlightened local champions among bureaucrats and politicians have, for more than two decades, been innovating and improving institutions for empowering women through SHGs, and the women of the state have responded enthusiastically. The state is the fifth-largest in India in terms of population, with 76 million people, of whom three-quarters live in rural areas. It is not among the poorest states, but many of its social and economic indicators are below the national average (World Bank 2003). It ranks low on the gender-related development index of the United Nations Development Programme (UNDP), reflecting persistent gender inequalities in access to education and health (Murthy, Raju, and Kamath 2005). However, the state has a strong reform agenda in terms of information technology, economic liberalization, and participatory rural development (World Bank 2003).

Non-governmental organizations (NGOs) first introduced self-help groups in Andhra Pradesh in the 1970s. The state government then experimented with variations and adaptations of the approach in the 1980s and 1990s, and eventually decided to scale up SHGs with World Bank support. It designed a new initiative called Velugu, which in the local language means 'light'. Launched in 2000, Velugu initially covered six districts with high levels of poverty. It fared so well that the state government and the World Bank decided to launch a second phase of Velugu in 2003, extending the project to the remaining 16 districts of the state (SERP 2005a).

Various studies suggest that the impact of SHGs has been wide-ranging, though uneven. This is a significant achievement given that the programme is trying to reach the most marginalized women, with limited resources, and that resistance to change from traditional power centres is substantial. The high potential of such an empowerment approach has been demonstrated vividly. To convert the potential fully into performance, however, various risks and challenges will have to be tackled effectively.

The main impacts of SHGs can be summed up as follows, adapted from a framework developed by Deshmukh-Ranadive (2004):

- *Increased economic space* for the poor, in the form of increased incomes, assets, marketing linkages, and partnerships with banks and corporations.
- *Increased security*, which reduces the grave risks poor people face from natural disasters, illness, or the death of breadwinners.
- *Increased socio-cultural space.* SHGs combat discrimination against women, widows, low castes, and landless labourers. Women are able to fight for better access to education and gender rights.
- *Increased political space.* SHGs give collective power to the unorganized poor through a federated structure. Individual groups are federating into village organizations and *mahila mandal samakhyas* (women's federations at the mandal level). These will later federate at the district and state levels, providing them with political clout.
- *Increased physical space.* Once confined to the home, women are increasingly able to move out of the house and village and play a role in public life at the mandal and district levels.

This chapter first describes the historical evolution of the self-help groups in Andhra Pradesh and the scaling up of SHGs under the Velugu programme. It then elaborates the main achievements and risks of the initiative and draws lessons for other states and countries.

EVOLUTION OF SELF-HELP GROUPS
IN ANDHRA PRADESH

Ancient India had self-help groups in the form of grain banks: villagers pooled grain, which was lent out to those in need. Another SHG forerunner was the chit fund, in which a group of villagers pooled savings that were then loaned to the highest bidder or distributed by lottery (Noe 2003a).

In more recent times, the SHG movement evolved through five phases prior to the launch of Velugu in 2000: (a) the creation of women's thrift cooperatives by the Cooperative Development Foundation, an NGO, in the early 1970s; (b) the Development of Women and Children in Rural Areas (DWCRA) programme in the 1980s; (c) the South Asia Poverty Alleviation Programme supported by UNDP in the 1990s; and (d) partnerships of

SHGs with banks in the 1990s, catalysed by the National Bank for Agricultural and Rural Development.

The Cooperative Development Foundation

During the 1970s, several NGOs began working with poor, marginalized groups in rural villages of Andhra Pradesh. The most important of these was the Cooperative Development Foundation. Believing that lack of access to credit kept people in chronic poverty, the foundation began creating thrift and credit groups. Men opposed the inclusion of women in their groups. But the NGO believed that women would make better use of microcredit, and launched women's thrift cooperatives to ensure that women would be included.

The groups were large, averaging 228 members. Each member contributed Rs 20 (about 50 cents) per month to her group's pool of savings, and the money was lent at nominal interest rates to needy members. The maximum loan available was three times a member's savings. According to Galab and Chandrasekhara Rao (2003), 50 per cent of such loans were used for immediate needs. But, more encouragingly, the remaining 50 per cent were used for productive activities such as agriculture, animal husbandry, and small businesses. The very act of meeting regularly for saving and credit created social capital among group members through bonding and common aims. Although small in scale, the initiative showed the potential of SHGs.

Saving a Rupee a Day: The DWCRA Programme

In 1979, the government of India launched a national poverty alleviation effort called the Integrated Rural Development Programme. Its main component was the provision of subsidized loans from government banks to purchase assets, and it was targeted at the poorest of the poor: Scheduled castes and tribes, women, and the disabled. Women's participation increased sharply from 10 per cent in 1985 to 33 per cent in 1996. This was partly because of a subcomponent created with assistance from UNICEF: the Development of Women and Children in Rural Areas (DWCRA) programme.

DWCRA aimed to provide credit for self-employment to rural poor women and empower them in the development process. Women of similar socio-economic backgrounds in the same neighbourhood were organized into self-help groups of 25 members each. Each SHG chose to undertake one economic activity, such as animal husbandry. Members had to save Rs 30 (70 cents) per month for a year, and could then get matching grants of Rs 15,000 (later raised to Rs 25,000, or $550) as a revolving fund for their group. They also received some training and marketing assistance.

DWCRA at first made little headway in the state, partly because of inappropriate guidelines. SHGs were supposed to have 25 members, but many villages did not have that many families engaged in a single activity. The groups were to consist of people of the same occupation/caste, but this added to the problem of getting 25 members. Poor women often said the saving target was too high. The guidelines also set a low ceiling of 50 groups per development block or 800 per district, making rapid expansion impossible. DWCRA withered in many states, but took on a life of its own in Andhra Pradesh thanks to innovations by enlightened bureaucrats in Anantpur and Nellore districts.

In Anantpur, the district collector and the project director of the District Rural Development Agency stepped in to change the inappropriate DWCRA guidelines. SHGs of less than 25 members were permitted, as were groups with members of different castes and occupations. These groups soon proved that the common goal of thrift and credit was strong enough to create social capital and cohesiveness among women of different castes and occupations. The savings target for poor women was reduced to one rupee per day, and NGOs were harnessed to mobilize and train SHGs. These adaptations were successful. An independent evaluation by SK University, in Anantpur district, showed improved indicators for income, nutrition, and health access for SHG members compared to non-members (Noe 2003a).

In the 1980s the Government of India launched a National Literacy Mission supervised by district collectors. The district collector of Nellore saw literacy as a means to poverty alleviation and empowerment, not as an end in itself. He deployed volunteers to teach illiterates, and 400,000 villagers achieved literacy this way. But the campaign taught more than reading and writing: it also focused on social problems facing the poor and on social mobilization to enable poor people to assert their rights through group power. This message resonated with poor women and encouraged them to tackle a stubborn social problem: the sale and consumption of 'country liquor' known as *arak*.

Male consumption of arak drained family resources and led to domestic violence. Women who were organized around literacy decided to fight the sale of arak in Nellore, and the anti-arak movement soon spread to other districts. Previously disempowered women smashed liquor shops and stopped country liquor sales all over the state. They then persuaded the state government to ban arak.

The anti-arak campaign gave poor women a sense of empowerment they had never before experienced. So they responded with enthusiasm when the next district collector urged them to organize themselves into self-help groups. The women pledged to create their own microfinance fund by saving one rupee a day each. Bolstered by their success in the anti-arak campaign, they also tried to address broader issues of social justice. As SHGs arose in almost every village in Nellore, the district became known for them, and other district collectors began to emulate the Nellore model. The chief minister of the state saw development potential in SHGs and encouraged their proliferation.

The South Asia Poverty Alleviation Programme

Another chapter in the evolution of SHGs started with the 1993 summit of the South Asian Association for Regional Cooperation, which focused on poverty alleviation. One outcome of the summit was that UNDP decided to support a pilot project called the South Asia Poverty Alleviation Programme (SAPAP). UNDP chose three districts in Andhra Pradesh because of the state's poverty and severe gender inequality (Murthy, Raju, and Kamath 2005). SAPAP built on earlier SHG efforts, with adaptations. It started with thrift and credit groups, but designed these to also stimulate social change and improve the status and power of women and poor groups. It focused on mobilizing the poorest women into SHGs, stressing rights and empowerment as much as savings and credit.

The project adopted a three-pronged strategy:

- *Social organization.* The poor were organized with the help of NGOs at three levels: self-help groups, village organizations comprising all SHGs in a village, and mahila mandal samakhyas comprising all village organizations in a mandal (subdistrict). Creating federations entailed substantial costs, but paid off in the end as the federated structure gave influence to once-disempowered people through the sheer force of numbers (Noe 2003a).
- *Skill development.* Earlier schemes had neglected skill creation among members of SHGs. This reduced their capacity to organize, manage finances, and keep books. Accordingly, SAPAP included a bigger training component for group formation and bookkeeping.
- *Capital formation.* SHGs were required to engage in savings and internal lending. The programme also provided credit at three different levels, through the SHGs, village organizations, and mahila mandal samakhyas.

By 2000, 5,201 SAPAP groups had been formed in the three project districts. These groups had 56,256 members, 90 per cent of whom were women (SERP 2002). The SAPAP groups were generally stronger than the SHGs that had preceded them: Galab and Chandrasekhara Rao (2003) gave 48 per cent of the SAPAP groups an A grade, against only 16 per cent for groups formed under earlier programmes. A recent study compares outcomes for SHG members and nonmembers, finding that SHG members have better access to food, nutrition, health, shelter, and education (Murthy, Raju, and Kamath 2005). The study also found that members have a lower percentage of assets mortgaged to moneylenders and lower seasonal migration.

Bank–SHG Linkages

Meanwhile, national credit institutions in India were becoming interested in using the SHG model to extend microcredit to the rural poor. Government banks had already set up a substantial rural network, but these catered mainly to better-off farmers with collateral. Default rates were high and many rural banks suffered serious losses. High transaction costs made it impossible for banks to give small loans to the poor.

The success of microfinance in Bangladesh suggested a new approach. In that country, Grameen Bank and other microfinance organizations had proved that lending to groups of poor women could succeed, with very low default rates and commercial rates of interest. In India, the National Bank for Agricultural and Rural Development (NABARD), a subsidiary of the country's central bank, the Reserve Bank of India (RBI), saw the group approach as a viable way to get credit to the poor. NABARD ran a pilot project in 1991–92 to provide finance from government banks to 500 SHGs. It succeeded in reaching the poor at relatively low interest rates, and with little default.

Encouraged by this, in 1996 the RBI decided to mainstream the bank–SHG linkage. It issued guidelines asking all commercial, rural, and cooperative banks to lend to SHGs without asking for collateral; NABARD then refinanced these loans. RBI rules on priority lending had long obliged banks to allocate 18 per cent of all loans to agriculture and rural development, and the RBI decided to classify loans to SHGs as part of this 18 per cent quota. These developments integrated SHGs with the formal banking system. Bank-SHG linkage made innovative use of the large existing network of commercial, rural, and cooperative banks in India. This network of 160,000 retail outlets provided more than 90 per cent of the population with a bank branch within 5 kilometres. Linking these branches to SHGs facilitated a major scaling up of credit to poor women (Reddy 2005).

Today, Andhra Pradesh accounts for close to 40 per cent of the cumulative SHG–bank linkages nationwide. By March 2003, a total of 281,338 groups in Andhra Pradesh had been linked with banks, with total loans coming to Rs 9,753 million (approximately $212 million). In 2002–03 around 62 per cent of these loans in the state were provided by commercial banks, 36 per cent by regional rural banks, and 2 per cent by cooperative banks (NABARD 2003). The cumulative loans extended had risen to $850 million by October 2005.[2]

SCALING UP SELF-HELP GROUPS: VELUGU

By the late 1990s, the various SHG experiments in the state had produced several pockets of success. But progress was uneven and uncoordinated. The poorest had not been well-targeted, and loans given by SHGs mainly went to non-poor members (Noe 2003a). District rural development agencies were often not equipped to mobilize and build capacity in SHGs. The institutional emphasis of the South Asia Poverty Alleviation Programme in three districts, linking SHGs to social awareness, had not been extended to other districts.

The chief minister of the state was a champion of women's empowerment, and he had been impressed by the ability of women to organize themselves in the anti-arak agitation. He decided that the time was ripe to blend the best features of earlier SHG experiments into a new programme that would make women's power a force for reducing poverty and social ills. He also probably saw this as a means of gaining popularity with the electorate (Noe 2003a). In consultation with the World Bank, the state government devised a programme that would harness the existing SHG base and scale it up to cover the six poorest districts of the state. This programme was called Velugu. Launched in 2000, it was supported by a World Bank loan of $134 million, with $16 million coming from the government and $7.2 million from the communities.

Key Design Features of Velugu

The state government established an independent organization called Society for Elimination of Rural Poverty (SERP) to help implement Velugu. SERP was to be a bridge between the state and the self-help groups, and would oversee social mobilization and the diverse components of the programme.

The chief minister himself headed SERP, staffed it with high-calibre bureaucrats, and ensured continuity in staffing. This strong 'ownership' of Velugu at the highest level sent a powerful signal to the bureaucracy and lent encouragement to the self-help groups.

Velugu incorporated several adaptations and innovations. At its core were microfinance and bank–SHG linkages to enhance livelihoods, but it went well beyond that, to embrace holistic empowerment and social justice (SERP 2005b). Its innovations and adaptations included, among others, the creation of capable, socially aware grassroots institutions using community coordinators; the use of female village leaders of earlier successful SHGs as trainers for new groups; the provision of community investment funds with untied grants, which empowered SHGs to use funds according to their own preferences; the training of SHGs to fight against gender and caste injustice; the mobilization of SHGs to abolish child labour and ensure that all children were in school; and the creation of community-based health systems.

Building strong grassroots institutions

Mobilizing poor communities and raising their social awareness is a complex, difficult task. A key innovation of Velugu was the hiring of well-educated, highly motivated youths as community coordinators who would live and work in the villages and build strong SHGs. The youths were typically university graduates, some with MBAs or PhDs. They had to pass a written test and undergo a village immersion programme. The process aimed to select those most sensitive and empathetic to the needs and aspirations of the poor. This cadre of community coordinators mobilized poor people, helped them to express their aspirations and problems, and helped generate village-level 'livelihood enhancement action plans' that the programme could then implement.

Creating community specialists

Capacity-building has often been a problem in community projects. Velugu sought to overcome this by training women from within communities as community resource persons, in some cases using persons from mature SHGs who had already acquired skills from experience and could be role models for new group members. These community resource persons were given training to function as para-professionals in the village, delivering community services such as basic health care, veterinary services, and childcare. As Velugu expanded, so did this cadre of home-grown community specialists, and they greatly improved the sustainability of the programme. As of 2005, over 5,000 community resource persons were in place, and their number is projected to rise to 100,000 by the end of the programme.

Self-identification of the poor

Velugu introduced participatory techniques for social inclusion. One criticism of earlier programmes was that the poorest were often left out of SHGs, which tended to give most of their loans to the non-poor. Lists of poor people drawn up by village heads excluded many people known to be poor. Therefore, Velugu mandated that communities should themselves prepare a list of the poor through open meetings and have the findings ratified by the village-level elected bodies. This innovation improved targeting and encouraged the poorest villagers to participate.

Emphasizing information and communication

The social mobilization approach of Velugu placed heavy emphasis on disseminating information, and on sensitization and training programmes. Awareness of the programme and its aims was raised through the print media, radio, and TV, and through folk theatre. Face-to-face meetings involving the community coordinators also played vital role.

Community investment funds

A major innovation of Velugu was the provision of grants to communities through community investment funds that could be spent as decided by local people. Villagers typically chose to spend funds on small infrastructure, microenterprises, improved marketing arrangements, and the hiring of specialists. This availability of untied funds substantially empowered communities: they could now spend in line with their own preferences, not those of the authorities. They achieved major success in the creation of marketing organizations at the village and subdistrict levels to obtain higher prices for their agricultural produce and lower prices for agricultural inputs (Box 4.2).

Box 4.2 A Bountiful Groundnut Harvest

Groundnut growers used to be poor and powerless in Kothapalem, a village in Chittoor district that had low average rainfall and no

(Contd)

Box 4.2 (Contd)

irrigation. Moneylenders charged 60 per cent interest, making it difficult for farmers to repay loans for seeds or fertilizers. Many small landowners who could not repay loans end up losing their land to moneylenders.

Then Velugu arrived. A community coordinator of Velugu persuaded nine villagers to come together and form a self-help group. The new SHG made a joint cultivation proposal to the community investment fund, seeking a loan of Rs 41,040 ($900) to buy seeds and fertilizers. It obtained the loan, which carried only 12 per cent interest. The group was able to get benefits of bulk buying of inputs and bulk selling of output. The groundnut harvest yielded a net profit of Rs 99,000 (about $2,000), more than twice the loan they had taken.

Villagers are now confident of their ability to improve their livelihoods and reduce their dependence on moneylenders. They are no longer powerless individuals, now that they have banded into strong groups.

Source: *Velugu: Inspirational Series* (SERP n.d., 5–7).

Strengthening federations

Velugu envisaged the federation of SHGs not only at the village and mandal levels but also at the district level, with a view to ultimately creating a statewide federation. Self-managed federations provided organizational strength and identity to SHGs, providing them the benefits of a large organization without losing the advantages of small size (Nair 2005).

A different role for NGOs

Earlier experiments had channelled funds through NGOs for mobilization and capacity building. But Velugu decided to cut out NGOs as intermediaries between the state and communities, and directly hired community coordinators and community resource persons. Community investment funds gave SHGs freedom to hire NGOs or specialists for perceived needs. In some cases NGOs had to compete with private sector suppliers of services.

Accountability to the poor

Right from the beginning, the line of accountability of community coordinators and community resource persons was to communities, rather than to administrative superiors. This provided downward accountability of staff to SHGs, as distinct from traditional upward accountability to bureaucrats. Accountability to SHGs was further strengthened by the groups' ability to hire service providers and professionals using the community investment funds. Improved accountability to villagers constituted real empowerment, something that earlier top-down programmes had not provided. Group rules on transparency, bookkeeping, and loan payments at weekly meetings provided accountability on the part of members, too. The group approach itself used social pressure to ensure the accountability of borrowers to the group.

Clear vision

Velugu drew up a road map, with benchmarks at different points of the programme to transfer power to communities. Groups were graded based on their level of maturity, and the programme withdrew support as they became self-sufficient in skills. Support focused on new groups that needed it most. For mature groups, the emphasis shifted to livelihood skills and the development of new income opportunities. Mature groups were better prepared and trained for entrepreneurship.

Working for social justice

The programme aimed to reduce discrimination against women and lower castes by improving their voice and organizational strength. The very fact that Velugu created groups of women and empowered them with training and loans was a step towards gender justice. Folk theatre and other communication strategies were used to increase awareness of social injustices and ways to combat them. In some districts, women's rights protection committees arose and investigated cases of gender and caste injustice. The programme mandated that every subproject of the community investment fund should address the concerns of women as well as men. In consequence, subprojects included community bathrooms, smokeless stoves, and crèches for working mothers.

All children to be in school

A basic rule of Velugu was that SHG members had to keep their children in school. This aimed to tackle the twin evils of child labour and school-leaving.

Community coordinators motivated groups to campaign for abolishing child labour. 'Bridge schools' were created to prepare child labourers and dropouts to re-enter regular school. A series of 24 residential schools were set up for young girls who had been child labourers or, in some cases, were children of working women.

Improving health

Velugu aimed to empower communities to take care of their own health in a holistic manner. It sought to integrate curative and preventive medicine with other factors relevant to health, such as education, safe drinking water, and agriculture. Communities selected health activists from among the members of mature SHGs to be trained as community health development workers. These trained workers became paramedics, delivering basic health services that did not require doctors. They were linked to base hospitals that could provide specialized services when needed.

Linking up with other government programmes

As the programme evolved, attempts were made to link Velugu with other rural government programmes in areas such as education, health, and infrastructure. This aimed to reap synergies and improve the access of poor households to the other programmes.

Rice credit lines

A pilot project in the first phase of Velugu provided 50,000 tonnes of rice as a three-month loan to needy SHGs. This scheme was received with enthusiasm, and led to demands for expansion.

The Next Stage: Velugu II

Velugu soon proved a success, as described in the next section. Building on this, the state government and the World Bank decided to launch Phase II of Velugu in 2003, at a cost of $275 million (with Bank support of $150 million). The expanded project aimed to cover the remaining 16 districts of the state, organizing 2 million families into 187,500 self-help groups, 15,000 village organizations, and 500 mahila mandal samakhyas.[3]

Velugu II introduced a number of design innovations. First, the community investment fund was greatly increased to $157 million, accounting for over 60 per cent of the project outlay. This enabled communities to take up more ambitious schemes, especially marketing schemes, which expanded greatly after 2003. Velugu II for the first time permitted the community investment fund to be used for the purchase of land by poor women. Poverty and inequity in India are closely linked to land ownership—roughly 10 per cent of households in Andhra Pradesh are landless, and another 36 per cent own less than half an acre. Only 6 per cent own more than 5 acres. Land ownership is also an important status symbol in rural India. Velugu II, by enabling poor women to become landowners, changed both class and gender relations.

Second, while communities had started formulating village development plans in the first phase of Velugu, this was strengthened and expanded in the second phase through livelihood enhancement action plans. These provided value chain analysis, starting with resource and social maps of villages that identified items traded in and out of villages as well as the income and spending patterns of villagers. This made it possible to identify critical gaps in the livelihoods of the poor and to examine the credit system, risks, uncertainties, and best practices for each livelihood sector. One outcome was the creation of successful marketing federations at the village and subdistrict levels. By late 2004 these federations were marketing 15 agricultural and horticultural commodities including soybean, red gram, castor, groundnut, cashew, and lac (Table 4.1).[4]

Third, Velugu II mitigated risk and improved security through a comprehensive insurance package covering health, life, crops, and livestock. Experience in the first phase had shown that families needed safety nets to protect them from risks such as bad weather, pests, falling water tables, illness, and death of breadwinners. The new insurance package provided life insurance and hospital health insurance to SHGs. In addition, a comprehensive basic health package aimed to provide basic care through community-managed paramedics. And, for the first time, Velugu II introduced a programme for people with disabilities.

Fourth, Velugu II greatly expanded a food security measure piloted in the first phase, the rice credit lines. Access to food in times of distress was recognized as a key safety net. Rice credit lines enabled communities to borrow rice at controlled rates from the government and repay the loan later.

Fifth, a state election brought a new party to power in 2004, and the new government started subsidizing bank credit to SHGs. The interest subsidy popularly known as 'Pavala Vaddi' brought down interest rates to just 3 per cent, reducing interest costs to SHGs. However the subsidy is structured in such a way that the SHG's continue to pay the banks the usual rate of 8 to 11 per cent per annum. Those who repay bank loans promptly become entitled to a subsidy which is equal to interest paid in excess of 3 per cent per annum. The difference goes directly into a corpus fund for the use of group activities. This process is still risk prone, as women might be tempted not to pay back loans.[5]

Sixth, Velugu II linked SHGs to the private sector, yielding partnerships with considerable potential to raise incomes and reduce poverty. And finally, the second phase expanded the target of eliminating child labour to 300,000, from 100,000 in the first phase. The target for residential girls' schools rose from 24 to 64.

VELUGU'S ACHIEVEMENTS AND CHALLENGES

It is too early to judge the long-term impact of Velugu, but Phase I was assessed in a 2005 midterm appraisal by the Centre for Economic and Social Studies in Hyderabad (CESS 2005). Other studies have also thrown light on what SHGs have achieved, and on the risks and challenges that remain.

As mentioned, the major achievements of SHGs in Velugu can be categorized as increased economic space, increased security, increased socio-cultural space, increased political space, and increased physical space. We consider each of these in turn.

Increased Economic Space

Improving poor people's access to credit, income, assets, and marketing facilities is central to poverty alleviation. The impact assessment of the midterm appraisal is not yet complete, but preliminary indications are that poverty has fallen faster in Velugu areas than in others. Among poor people, the share of superior foods (such as milk, eggs, and meat) in food consumption has increased faster in Velugu households than in others. At the same time, the share of food in total consumption has fallen faster in Velugu households than in others, a classic sign of growing prosperity (CESS 2005).

The midterm appraisal and other studies show that, compared with non-Velugu households, the households covered by Velugu have, on average:

- higher incomes;
- less dependence on wages from migration;
- increased dependence on self-employment rather than wage labour, and lower sale of assets;
- increased income from livestock, and increased use of common property resources (such as grazing livestock on village pastures);

- increased ownership of and leasing-in of land, and less leasing out;
- fewer assets mortgaged to moneylenders;
- more access to credit for both women and their husbands, and higher savings for women.

SHG-bank linkage is much stronger in Velugu areas than others. Borrowing from external sources (mainly banks) has benefited 57 per cent of SHGs in Velugu areas as against 23 per cent in others. Old DWCRA groups folded into Velugu have fared best: they typically borrow Rs 50,000 ($1,200) externally, while new groups average Rs 36,000 ($880) each.

Velugu has provided members with control over marketing, a common demand of small and marginal farmers who are victims of the unfair practices of traders. Federations of SHGs have made a major breakthrough by marketing agricultural produce. They have the bulk-buying power required to ensure higher prices for local produce and lower prices for purchased inputs. Even while improving prices for members, marketing federations are making profits that are partly shared with members. By 2004, the village organizations and mandal mahila samakhyas were marketing 15 major commodities. Between October 2003 and July 2004, 207 of the mandal-level groupings were able to procure nearly 7,300 metric tonnes of various commodities, valued at Rs 63.4 million ($1.45 million), yielding a profit of Rs 6.38 million ($145,000) and benefiting almost 71,350 producers and collectors (Table 4.1).

These data do not capture the full benefits, however. Earlier, traders often cheated farmers through rigged weighing or by levying excessive deductions for impurities and moisture content. They also paid below-market prices, taking advantage of poor farmers' lack of information, and deferred payment for delivered produce, obliging farmers to get into debt. Marketing federations enable producers to avoid these losses. Taking into account these additional gains, the real benefit from marketing federations in the above example was not Rs 6.38 million ($145,000), but Rs 15.1 million ($340,000).[6]

The subsequent scaling up of such marketing activities has been phenomenal. Against just $222,000 worth of maize procured in 2004–05, the figure for 2005–06 is expected to be $26 million (it touched $17 million by December 6, 2005). In the following year, 2006–07, procurement is expected to be $44 million. To date, 260 village procurement centres have been set up, and the number is projected to rise to 1,500. Procurement by SHGs has forced traders to increase payments to all farmers, cutting down the share of the middlemen.[7]

TABLE 4.1 Velugu's Marketing Interventions, October 2003–July 2004

Item	No. of MMSs	No. of VOs	Quantity procured (quintals)	Value (Rs millions)	Quantity sold (quintals)	Value (Rs millions)	Gross profit (Rs millions)	No. of beneficiaries
Red gram	51	145	11,086	18.3	10,028	18.0	1.14	12,520
Soybean	14	28	16,300	18.6	16,191	21.5	3.10	16,400
Neem	30	218	29,773	4.5	25,307	5.7	1.23	25,000
Lac	17	26	433	2.9	361	3.1	0.46	660
Groundnut	15	34	3,630	6.2	3,447	6.5	0.30	620
Maize	2	6	1,556	0.7	1,556	0.7	0.04	750
Other non-timber forest products	77	124	9,676	10.5	5,604	7.1		14,200
Coffee	1	6	243	0.6	243	0.8	0.11	1,200
Total	207	587	72,698	62.3	62,737	63.4	6.38	71,350

Source: SERP.
Notes: $1 = Rs 44. MMS = mandal mahila samakhya; VO = village organization.

A more recent development has been the interest shown by private sector companies in building partnerships with SHGs. Companies have long faced difficulties in dealing with hundreds of individual small farmers, and believe they can more easily do business with federations. It is too early to measure the impact of these partnerships, but they show promise (Box 4.3).

Box 4.3 Partnerships with the Private Sector

Velugu II envisages partnerships between private sector companies and self-help groups for mutual benefit. This echoes the philosophy of management expert C.K. Prahalad, author of *The Fortune at the Bottom of the Pyramid* (2005), which shows how big companies can find a huge market potential in poor, rural, badly served communities. Rural folk can serve as suppliers of raw materials to large companies, and also as consumers of (and in some cases marketers of) their finished products. Some examples of partnerships being developed:

Maize. Godrej, the largest cattle feed company in India, has contracted with SHGs in Andhra Pradesh to grow maize on 7,000 acres. The company has implemented a similar project in two other states, Chhattisgarh and Maharashtra. Godrej will provide technical expertise to the farmers and buy the produce.

Farm forestry. Two major paper companies, ITC and BILT, have agreed to create a partnership with SHGs for growing trees on community wastelands. The companies will provide the best clonal saplings and oversee planting. The SHGs will safeguard growing trees from grazing and unauthorized felling, and sell them to the companies on maturity. The clones reduce the gestation period of trees from seven years to just four years.

Shrimp. ITC is setting up an e-choupal (electronic kiosk) at Nellore for aquaculture, in collaboration with the village organizations and the Marine Products Export Development Authority. ITC will help train and finance villagers to set up shrimp ponds and will provide shrimp seed and feed. ITC guarantees it will buy the output, but shrimp farmers can also sell to rival traders. The electronic kiosk will enable villagers to check prices at all markets and sell at the highest possible rate.

Gherkins. The Thapar group exports gherkins to 22 countries. It has made a beginning with contract cultivation of 100 acres in the state. The company provides the inputs and buys the output.

(Contd)

Box 4.3 (Contd)

> *Kiosks and sales jobs.* Hindustan Lever, a multinational producer of soaps and household needs, has started training rural women to be door-to-door sales agents. It is working simultaneously with the state government to set up rural computer kiosks to allow the public to access information locally and affordably. The company aimed to have 1,000 kiosks by the end of 2004, growing to 5,000 in 2005.
>
> *Source*: SERP.

Increased Security

Natural disasters, illness, and deaths of breadwinners constitute major risks for poor people. Such tragedies frequently oblige people to sell their few assets at distress prices, get into debt at interest rates exceeding 100 per cent, or become bonded labourers. Seasonal migration is a widespread risk-mitigation strategy, but involves considerable costs. The midterm appraisal of Velugu finds that the proportion of households able to withstand drought effects has increased from 4 per cent to 11 per cent, and the proportion able to withstand health shocks has risen from 5 per cent to 13 per cent. Food security schemes and insurance have benefited 36 per cent of SHGs in Velugu districts, but none in other districts (CESS 2005).

Velugu has addressed risk mitigation in several ways. The very fact that credit is available at reasonable interest rates constitutes a major improvement in security: poor people can get funds in an emergency and do not have to sell assets at throwaway prices, become bonded labourers, indenture their children, or migrate (Box 4.4). Moreover, microcredit enables poor people to buy assets—animals and equipment in Velugu I, and land as well in Velugu II. A greater asset base, land ownership above all, is an important form of security.

Velugu II has expanded rice credit lines, which provide SHGs with three alternatives. In the first, groups can borrow up to 50 kilograms of rice, with repayment due in one month. In the second, they can borrow 100 kilograms, repayable in two months. In the third, they can borrow 100 kilograms, repayable in six months or on a schedule linked to local harvests. This has become a major form of food security.

Some federations have opened fair-price shops. Such shops were traditionally run by private operators, who were supposed to sell grain at a government-controlled fair price using subsidized supplies from the government. But private operators sold much of the subsidized grain they received on the open market, not at controlled rates. Their shops were often shut when poor people came. Fair-price shops run by SHGs have overcome these problems, providing enhanced food security to villagers even while creating new businesses.

Velugu II has introduced a comprehensive insurance package for SHGs covering life, health, crops, and livestock. This is still in its early stages and no impact analysis has been done. But the midterm appraisal mentions that the poorest have pointed out that while loans are typically taken by better-off members, rice credit lines and insurance benefit all members. Since the poorest are the most vulnerable, they gain the most.

Through improved information and voice, SHGs encourage and empower poor members to make better use of existing government amenities such as primary health centres. The midterm appraisal says that Scheduled Castes accessed and benefited from less than one government scheme per year in the pre-project days, as against more than one benefit during the post-project period. For instance, in one district Scheduled Caste households got on average 0.67 benefits per household in 2000, before Velugu, but this went up to 1.69 per household in 2003.

Box 4.4 Bonded No More

Bojju Upendra used to be an agricultural labourer whose family often lacked money for two square meals a day. She belonged to the dalit caste, the very lowest, which traditionally had no hope of social advancement. Her family found it difficult to get loans even at high interest rates from moneylenders. In order to raise money for her daughter's marriage, she had to give her son as a bonded labourer to a landowner.

Then she joined a self-help group that had formed in her village, enabling her to obtain loans in times of distress. She obtained small loans on three occasions, for medical expenses, rice, and miscellaneous expenses. She also obtained larger loans to start a fruit-selling business.

Her success in taking and repaying loans has gained her recognition and social status within the SHG. Best of all, she has been able to buy her son's release from bonded labour.

Source: 'Warangal District Profile' (Warangal DPMU 2005: 14).

Increased Socio-cultural Space

SHGs are helping to reduce discrimination against women, widows, low castes, illiterates, and landless labourers. Women used to regard themselves as powerless, passive victims, but group mobilization has helped them take charge of their own destinies. SHGs have given women and lower castes access to credit and assets, improving not just their income but their social status; some have even become presidents of federations (Box 4.5). Many poor members of mature SHGs have been hired by Velugu as community resource persons. Lower-caste members have been able to organize and strengthen their voice, and so improve their access to justice (Box 4.6).

BOX 4.5 The Tied Rabbit Now Runs Free

Maloom Bi, daughter of a Muslim construction worker, was married at the age of 12. She struggled for years rolling bidis (leaf-wrapped cigarettes), tailoring, and working as an agricultural labourer. Then in 1993 a government officer persuaded women of her village to form a self-help group. The women met their savings target and got a matching grant of Rs 1,000 ($22) from the government. Maloom Bi took a loan to start a tent-supply business. She also bought a machine for grinding spices, which she then packed into sachets for sale to local hotels and restaurants. This made a big change to her family's income and lifestyle.

Initially there was much criticism among the village elders, who objected to Muslim women going out of the house for meetings and as far afield as Delhi for training. But the women persevered, and SHGs came to be seen as a major force for progress. The groups began to run residential schools for girls, facilitating education for the daughters of working women. The SHGs federated at the village level, and then at the mandal level.

In 1996 Maloom Bi was elected president of her local mahila mandal samakhya. She says: 'As a Muslim woman, it was unthinkable for me to even come out of the house, let alone become a community leader. I think that the little rabbit tied to the kitchen table is now running free in the open forest.'

Source: *Velugu: Voices of Women* (SERP n.d., 5–8).

Box 4.6 Self-Help Group Members Fight for their Rights

In Ketavaram village, like many other villages, people of the lowest caste, known as Dalits, were traditionally regarded as untouchable and were barred from collecting water from public wells and ponds. They were supposed to wait until an upper-caste person collected water and poured some into their pots. One day Sushila, a Dalit member of a self-help group, tired of waiting for an upper-caste benefactor directly scooped water from the village pond. This outraged upper-caste villagers. Sushila was attacked and beaten for her impudence.

In the old days, Sushila would have had no redress. But she was on the executive committee of a mahila mandal samakhya, which included four Dalit SHGs. She turned to them for support. The local village head advised them against any further action, and gave Sushila Rs 50 ($1.20) for medical costs. Undeterred, Dalit members approached the local UNDP programme officer. He encouraged them to go to the district collector's office, something no Dalit would have dared do in the old days. The outcome was also unprecedented: the police arrested and filed cases against the upper-caste assaulters. Dalits are now seen as a force to be reckoned with in this village. Discrimination against them has not ended, but they can no longer be beaten with impunity.

Source: *Velugu: Voices of Women* (SERP n.d., 12–14).

The midterm appraisal found that targeting of the poor was better in Velugu than in earlier schemes, and the percentage of borrowers belonging to the poorest of the poor had gone up. Awareness of and participation in local government bodies was much higher in Velugu districts. Better awareness had positive side effects: the proportion of households indicating that they used other government programmes was 34 per cent in Velugu areas against 24 per cent in other areas. The proportion of households in which men alone made decisions on debt, income-generating activities, and education was sharply lower in Velugu areas. The consumption of alcohol by men fell significantly, and women had greater voice and control over household spending (CESS 2005).

An internal review carried out for SERP (CESS 2002) found that the greatest achievements for women were increased mobility, access to savings and credit, access to friendships outside the family, access to leadership positions, and a reduction in the gender division of income earning. Achievements were moderate in relation to reproductive and bodily rights, including freedom from physical abuse. State government statistics showed that population growth in Andhra Pradesh slowed from 2.42 per cent annually in 1981–91 to 1.39 per cent annually in 1991–2001, a trend that could be partly due to women's empowerment through SHGs (GoAP 2002). The proportion of children in school was much higher in Velugu areas than others, and the dropout rate much lower (CESS 2005). At the community level, the programme improved the status and power of women and lower castes. They were able to fight for the rights of children, and for ending social evils like temple prostitution (Box 4.7)

However, despite some progress, gender and caste discrimination have by no means ended. Male preference in distribution of food and clothing, for instance, has not declined significantly (Murthy, Raju, and Kamath 2005).

Box 4.7 Ending Temple Prostitution

A multivillage joint action committee comprising men as well as women was formed to end the *jogani* system, which involves the virtual enslavement of Dalit women as temple prostitutes (locally called *jogans*). These women, who often are also the daughters of jogans, are inducted into the system at a young age. They typically are first used by the local landlord until he tires of them, after which they are left in the temple to service any man who is willing to pay (the priests, not the jogan). The system has existed for more than 300 years and is couched in religious ideology: the jogan is supposedly very privileged because she has been chosen by the goddess.

'But why does the goddess only want Dalit women?' was the question that the joint action committee addressed to the district temple committee during their campaign to end the jogani system. The campaign used several approaches including street theatre, visits to local authorities, and even visits to leaders of the state government. Although the gender adviser to the joint action committee advised its members to accept a symbolic compromise offered by the temple, the committee was determined to end the system once and for all. It accomplished this in one temple and is now focusing its efforts on other temples, and on getting the children of jogans into school.

Source: Mason 2004.

Increased Political Space

Self-help groups in Andhra Pradesh have created new political space for poor women. The anti-arak agitation was the first manifestation, and Velugu went on to widen this political space. The political strength of SHGs has improved with the formation of federations, which now interact with local government bodies, government line departments, formal financial institutions, and the corporate sector. One outcome has been increased access of poor women to other government programmes and to the redress of social injustices (Boxes 4.6 and 4.7). Velugu II federations are currently being formed at the district level, and these will ultimately federate at the state level. It remains to be seen whether social capital inherent in each SHG can be transmitted to the higher-level federations. If so, their political clout will become substantial, and they should able to influence legislation and executive directives.

Problems and Risks

Despite many positive outcomes, self-help groups also face several challenges. First, better-off members with education are able to make much better use of credit than the poorest of the poor. The poorest are often not well-equipped to become entrepreneurs, and many SHG members remain below the poverty line (CESS 2005). The poor may benefit more from other aspects of Velugu, such as food security and improved social status. Public investment in village infrastructure and a good investment climate may alleviate poverty faster by increasing jobs and wages (GoAP 1999; Raju and Ali 1996a, 1996b; Noe 2003b).

Second, the impact of SHGs on improving education and family planning has been uneven. Households in remote villages and Scheduled Tribes have benefited less than others (Youth for Action 1996; Kanchanya 1998).

Third, a village has a limited need for businesses such as vegetable and fruit vendors. Credit from SHGs can lead to 'overcrowding' in a particular activity, which then forces some businesses to close (BASIX, CARE-AP, and Vikasa Darshini 1999; Raju and Ali 1996a; Kanchanya 1998; ICM 1996; Jayalakshmi 1997; Narayanaswamy and Jagannathan 1999).

Fourth, the rapid expansion of SHGs through Velugu has meant a loss of quality in internal controls and discipline. On average, the midterm appraisal found, Velugu groups held only 65 per cent of meetings as scheduled and only 62 per cent of members attended, against 83 per cent and 79 per cent respectively for earlier SHGs (CESS 2005).

Fifth, conflicts within groups worsened with rapid expansion. Other experiences with similar programmes show that decision-making is generally delegated to poor people. Often there is more conflict, but people gain experience and the ability to resolve conflicts (Woolcock, Smith, and Barron 2004). Serious conflicts affected performance in 11 per cent of Velugu groups against 16 per cent of other SHGs. Temporary conflicts affected 40 per cent of SHGs in Velugu against 13 per cent in others (CESS 2005).

Sixth, while Velugu created new political space, this mainly benefited a limited number of SHG leaders who tended to monopolize leadership positions. One survey of DWCRA groups showed that while the election of leaders was usually democratic (87 per cent of cases), leadership did not rotate in 94 per cent of cases. Often one leader remained in charge and managed all activities including accounts, loans, and attendance. A similar pattern was observed in Velugu (APMAS 2002; OMRL 2000).

Seventh, husbands in many cases controlled the credit and assets that were nominally in their wives' names. That reduced to some extent the gender empowerment effect of the programme.

Eighth, the midterm appraisal (based on a survey ending December 2005) says that almost half the external loans from bank–SHG linkages were overdue in 2005 (CESS 2005). This contrasted with default rates below 10 per cent for internal lending to members. Peer pressure seemed to ensure repayment in internal borrowing, but not necessarily in external borrowing. This sounds alarming. However, SERP claims that repayment rates of SHGs to banks exceed 96 per cent overall, and exceed 98 per cent on loans after April 2003. It is difficult to reconcile these two dramatically different claims, and more research is needed to establish the actual situation. One possible clue is that SHGs that have failed to repay principal to banks are nevertheless paying interest. Possibly banks are willing to live with this practice (which amounts to rolling over the principal), and do not view overdues of principal as default, as long as interest is being paid. Bank lending to SHGs has been rising fast, and this suggests confidence in the debt-servicing capacity of SHGs.

LESSONS LEARNED

Velugu is still a programme in progress. But it already has substantial achievements to its credit, and holds lessons for other Indian states and for other countries. Some of the main lessons learned from the Velugu experience to date are as follows.

Empowering poor women through self-help groups has the potential to bring about an economic and social transformation. If properly designed and implemented, these groups can help to begin a shift of power from existing elites to the powerless, from national capitals to the grassroots, from the well-off to the poorest, from high castes to the lowest, and from males to females. There are several risks and challenges in designing successful programmes, but their potential for social transformation is not in doubt. This is the key lesson for other states and countries.

Poor women should be treated as clients who are potentially valuable assets, not as objects of pity or largesse. Velugu has shown that illiterate women can emerge as leaders and managers at the village and subdistrict levels. They can be role models for others. Over 5,000 women have become community resource persons, and their number is expected ultimately to reach 100,000. These women provide the human resources required for scaling up programmes at low cost. The programme's beneficiaries, therefore, are not simply passive recipients; they are assets.

Accountability in empowerment programmes should be downward to poor women, not only upward to state capitals. Unlike traditional top-down programmes, Velugu mandates that staff such as community resource persons be accountable to villagers. Untied community investment funds have empowered groups to hire service providers who are now accountable to them. As the saying goes, he who pays the piper calls the tune.

Empowerment programmes require strong local champions. Andhra Pradesh has been fortunate in having local champions for women's empowerment in both the bureaucracy and the political parties. Champions in the bureaucracy pioneered the Anantpur and Nellore experiments. The anti-arak movement opened the eyes of all political parties to the potential of women's groups. The Telugu Desam Party, which launched Velugu and remained an active supporter of the programme, envisioned the political power of millions of women organized into SHGs. However, the party lost the 2004 state election. The new chief minister, belonging to the Congress party, has continued supporting Velugu, changing only its name. The new chief minister has also provided a large interest subsidy to bank–SHG loans. This shows that women's groups in Andhra Pradesh have become a political constituency to be wooed by both sides. Most other states lack such strong support from highly placed local champions.

Learning and experimentation are vital. Velugu built on decades of earlier experiments with SHGs. The experiences with the Cooperative

I _____ on in the 1970s, with DWCRA in the 1980s, and with SAPAP and bank SHG linkage in the 1990s meant that new ideas and practices were constantly tried. Velugu built on what had already worked well, devised new solutions to old problems, and scaled up. The programme evolved considerably between its first and second phases. The lesson: SHG programmes in other states and countries should also make bold use of experimentation and learning to evolve over time.

Institutional innovation is important. Andhra Pradesh's experience shows that institutional innovation is critical to make good ideas work. The Integrated Rural Development Programme looked like a good poverty alleviation scheme, giving microcredit at subsidized rates to the poor, yet it failed because of corruption and political encouragement to default. The SHG approach turned out to be a better form of microcredit, ensuring high repayment rates by using peer pressure within communities. SAPAP innovated further by stressing social mobilization and empowerment of the poor and forming federations of SHGs. NABARD devised the bank–SHG linkage.

Velugu I introduced innovations such as self-identification of the poor, channelling funds and training directly to communities instead of going through NGOs, creating community investment funds, scaling up federations, and enabling federations to run businesses like fair price shops and bulk marketing. Velugu II has introduced additional innovations such as an expanded community investment fund that can also be used by the poor to buy land, security innovations such as rice credit lines and the comprehensive insurance package, and aid to disabled people. Important innovations in the human resources area include the creation of community resource persons and community coordinators. These have given Velugu institutional strength and sustainability.

External catalysts can play a valuable role. The evolution of SHGs in the state was influenced in fair measure by external catalysts. UNICEF helped create DWCRA in the 1980s, and UNDP played a similar role with SAPAP in the 1990s. The experience of Grameen Bank in Bangladesh provided an example of bank–SHG linkage that helped catalyse parallel efforts by NABARD. The World Bank provided support for Velugu. In none of these cases did the external organization force anything on the borrower through conditionalities. On the contrary, external organizations supported local efforts, bringing knowledge of practices that worked well in other places and might work in Andhra Pradesh too. These were partnerships in which the external organizations always played a supporting catalytic role, with local champions in the lead role.

As empowerment programmes evolve, they should link up with other government programmes, local governments, banks, and the private sector. This enables small microfinance groups to be integrated into holistic rural development and helps to extend the participatory approach to other rural programmes. This in turn can leverage the role of SHGs as agents of social change. Bank–SHG linkages can greatly increase the financial and commercial strength of groups. Linkages with the private sector have considerable potential for improving incomes and skills.

Such programmes also face several challenges and risks. Experience suggests that self-help groups by themselves will not solve poverty problems. They will be most effective in a context of dynamic rural growth. Linkages with banks are desirable, but groups need to be more carefully differentiated based on maturity or quality to qualify for successively larger loans to ensure that repayment rates remain high. Interest subsidies from the government carry the risk that the programme will be perceived as a government handout and so encourage large-scale default, as happened in the earlier rural development programme. Rapid scaling up of diverse activities can lead to a dilution of quality and increased tensions within SHGs.

But these risks pale in comparison with the potential gains. The risks can be reduced through innovation, adaptation, and a constant search for design improvement. This continuous questioning and adaptation will also strengthen the eventual gains. Empowerment is an idea whose time has come.

References

APMAS (Andhra Pradesh Mahila Abhivruddhi Samithi), 2002, 'Evaluation of Self Help Groups in Adilabad, Cuddapah, and Visakhapatnam Districts.' Report prepared for the Government of Andhra Pradesh, Hyderabad, India.

BASIX, CARE-AP and Vikasa Darshini, 1999, 'Women's Savings and Credit Movement in Andhra Pradesh and a Proposal for a New Institution, APMAT.' Report prepared for the UK Department for International Development India Office and Commissionerate of Rural Development, Government of Andhra Pradesh.

CESS (Centre for Economic and Social Studies), 2002, 'Andhra Pradesh District Poverty Initiatives Project: Baseline Survey Report in Sustainable Livelihood Framework.' Prepared for the Society for Elimination of Rural Poverty. Centre for Economic and Social Studies, Hyderabad, India.

_____, 2005, 'Mid Term Appraisal of District Poverty Initiatives Project.' Prepared for the Society for Elimination of Rural Poverty. Centre for Economic and Social Studies, Hyderabad, India.

Deshmukh-Ranadive, J., 2004, 'Women's Self Help Groups in Andhra Pradesh: Participatory Poverty Alleviation in Action.' http://info.worldbank.org/etools/docs/reducingpoverty/case/82/fullcase/India%20SHGs%20Full%20Case.pdf.

Galab, S. and N. Chandrasekhara Rao, 2003, 'Women's Self-Help Groups, Poverty Alleviation and Empowerment,' *Economic and Political Weekly* (Mumbai), March 22–29.

GoAP (Government of Andhra Pradesh), 1999, 'DWCRA and Women's Empowerment: A Success Story of Self Help Movement in Andhra Pradesh,' Panchayati Raj and Rural Development Department, Hyderabad, India.

———, 2002, *Economic Survey 2001–2002*, Department of Planning, Hyderabad, India.

ICM (Institute of Cooperative Management), 1996, 'Evaluation of Rural Development Programs in Nizamabad District of A.P.' Hyderabad, India.

Indian NGOs, 2005, 'Governments and Microcredit,' Citigroup Micro Finance Forum, IndianNGOs.com. http://www.indianngos.com/issue/microcredit/govt/.

Jayalakshmi, R., 1997, 'Evaluation of Rural Development Programmes in Adilabad District.' Report submitted to the Government of Andhra Pradesh, Institute of Cooperative Management, Hyderabad, India.

Kanchanya, K., 1998, 'Women and Development: A Case Study of DWCRA Programme in West Godavari District of A.P.,' Master's thesis, Dr B.R. Ambedkar Open University, Hyderabad, India.

Mason, K., 2004, 'Women's Empowerment in Karnataka and Andhra Pradesh: Swa Shakti and the DPIP,' http://www.velugu.org/Go_Reports/karen.html.

Murthy, R.K., K. Raju and A. Kamath, 2005, "Towards Women's Empowerment and Poverty Reduction: Lessons from the Participatory Impact Assessment of South Asian Poverty Alleviation Programme in Andhra Pradesh, India,' N. Burra, J. Deshmukh-Ranadive, and R. Murthy (eds), *Can the Triad Work? Micro-credit, Poverty Reduction and Women's Empowerment*, New Delhi: Sage.

NABARD (National Bank for Agriculture and Rural Development), 2003, 'Progress of SHG-Bank Linkage in India 2002–2003,' NABARD, Mumbai.

Nair, A., 2005, 'Sustainability of Microfinance Self Help Groups in India: Would Federating Help?' Policy Research Working Paper 3516, World Bank, Washington, DC.

Narayanaswamy, R. and P. Jagannathan, 1999, 'Evaluation Study of IRDP, TRYSEM, Tool Kits and DWCRA Schemes in Adilabad District.' Report prepared for the Government of Andhra Pradesh. Institute of Cooperative Management, Hyderabad, India.

Noe, D., 2003a, 'History and Evolution of SHGs in Andhra Pradesh,' World Bank, New Delhi.

____, 2003b, 'NABARD Support to Self Help Groups,' World Bank, New Delhi.

OMRL (ORG-MARG Research Limited), 2000, 'Consultancy on Strengthening Self Help Groups in Andhra Pradesh: SWOT Analysis of the Groups Surveyed in Andhra Pradesh.' Report of study sponsored by Department of Rural Development, Government of Andhra Pradesh, Hyderabad, India.

Prahalad, C.K., 2005, *The Fortune at the Bottom of the Pyramid: Eradicating Poverty through Profits*, Upper Saddle River, NJ: Wharton School Publishing.

Raju, B.Y. and A.F. Ali, 1996a, 'Evaluation of DWCRA in Cuddapah District.' Report prepared for Government of Andhra Pradesh. Administrative Staff College of India, Hyderabad.

____, 1996b, 'Evaluation of DWCRA in Adilabad District.' Report prepared for Government of Andhra Pradesh. Administrative Staff College of India, Hyderabad.

Reddy, Y.V., 2005, *RBI Bulletin*, September.

SERP (Society for Elimination of Rural Poverty), 2002, 'Andhra Pradesh Rural Poverty Reduction Project: Project Implementation Plan,' Hyderabad, India.

____, 2005a, 'Program Plan,' http://www.velugu.org/.

____, 2005b, 'What Is Velugu?' http://www.velugu.org/.

____, n.d., *Velugu: Voices of Women*, http://www.velugu.org/downloads/Voice_women.pdf.

____, n.d., *Velugu: Inspirational Series*, http://www.velugu.org/Features/ins_series.pdf.

Sharma, S., 2002, 'Is Micro-credit a Macro Trap?' Financial Daily, the *Hindu*, September 25.

Warangal DPMU, 2005, 'Warangal District Profile,' District Rural Development Agency, Indira Kranti Patham, District Project Management Unit–Warangal, Andhra Pradesh Rural Poverty Reduction Project.

Woolcock, M., C. Smith and P. Barron, 2004, 'Understanding Local Level Conflict in Developing Countries: Theory, Evidence and Implications from Indonesia.' Working Paper 19, Conflict Prevention and Reconstruction Unit, World Bank, Washington, DC.

World Bank, 2003, 'Project Appraisal Document for the Andhra Pradesh Rural Poverty Reduction Project.' Report 24771-IN, World Bank, Washington, DC.

Youth for Action, 1996, 'Evaluation Report on DWCRA in Mahaboobnagar,' Hyderabad, India.

Notes

1 Personal communication from Vijay Kumar, CEO of SERP, December 9, 2005.

2 Personal communication from Vijay Kumar.

3 Personal communication from Vijay Kumar.

4 Lac is an insect resin that is a popular source of red dye used for making bangles.

5 There is a discrepancy between different estimates on repayment rates. According to SERP managers, repayment stands at 90 per cent and has not been affected by the change in interest rate. But a midterm appraisal of Velugu by CESS in 2005, estimates overdues at almost 50 per cent. The discrepancy between the two estimates is large, and needs to be resolved by further research.

6 Personal communication from Vijay Kumar.

7 Personal communication from Vijay Kumar.

5

Scaling Up Rural Support Programmes in Pakistan

Stephen F. Rasmussen, M. Mujtaba Piracha,
Rashid Bajwa, Abdul Malik, and *Aadil Mansoor*

For decades, a service delivery gap has co-existed alongside high levels of poverty in rural Pakistan. The inability of successive governments to deliver basic social services to millions of poor people has left the country near the bottom of many human development rankings. In the early 1980s, however, the vision of one of South Asia's foremost development practitioners helped transform Pakistan's approach to rural development. Dr Akhter Hameed Khan inspired the launch of an experimental scheme in an impoverished region in northern Pakistan, planting the seeds of what would later become a nationwide movement.

The first Rural Support Programme (RSP) began on a small scale, organizing poor people in several remote and sparsely populated districts in the mountainous north. From these modest beginnings the scheme scaled up rapidly countrywide, led and promoted energetically by Shoaib Sultan Khan, the head of the first RSP. By 2005 there were 10 Rural Support Programmes working in more than 70 of the country's 106 districts. The work reaches almost 1.2 million members and their households, perhaps 8 million people overall, and is helping to transform the face of rural Pakistan.

The RSPs rely on a community-driven model of development that seeks to simultaneously empower poor people and improve service delivery. Communities are mobilized around their needs and organized to stimulate more effective demand for services. RSPs frequently partner with government, civil society, and the private sector to improve the quality and delivery of social services—sometimes by linking people to existing service providers, and sometimes by providing services themselves. Importantly, however, the RSPs are autonomous structures that retain independence from government.

From a poverty reduction perspective, the assumption behind the model is that poor people are willing to do many things themselves and invest their own resources in order to improve their own welfare and that of their communities. The model draws its strength from being participatory rather than representative. In economic terms, it is geared towards achieving economies of scale for poor communities.

In the districts covered by the oldest RSP, the Aga Khan Rural Support Programme, per capita incomes have increased substantially. There have also been significant improvements in health and education outcomes. These advances appear to reflect, at least in part, the success of the RSP in organizing poor people and including them in mainstream development opportunities. This is something the RSPs have been able to do better than any other large-scale development effort in Pakistan.

The RSP movement has also influenced development policies and practices in the country, both drawing on and encouraging government support for rural development at the grassroots level. By demonstrating success in the pilot stage and fostering a cooperative relationship with government, the movement has been able to expand to new areas. The institutional model based on mobilization in communities proved resilient, allowing new autonomous entities responsive to local conditions to emerge. But it is important to note that the process has required consistent work over time to build a solid base at the community level.

Pakistan's experience with Rural Support Programmes demonstrates that social mobilization can work on a large scale even in an unfavourable climate of low growth, high poverty, weak democracy, and frequent changes in regime. This chapter details the evolution of the RSP model, from its beginnings in northern Pakistan to its emergence as a national programme. It reviews some evidence on the programme's impact, explains its main features, and suggests lessons that have emerged from the RSP experience.

PAKISTAN'S DEVELOPMENT CHALLENGE

The RSP initiative evolved against a backdrop of persistent poverty in Pakistan, marked by two principal problems—the service delivery gap, on the one hand, and the exclusion of the poor from mainstream economic activities, on the other.

Efforts to reduce poverty in Pakistan have historically shown mixed results. Poverty declined in the 1970s and 1980s, but increased again in the 1990s. Even in the best years of economic growth, however, the overall incidence of poverty has remained high. Underlying factors include weak governance, slow economic growth, lack of social services, and degradation of environmental resources (ADB 2002). In 2002, more than 38 per cent of families in Pakistan remained below the poverty line (CRPRID 2003).

There are two important lessons from the experience of the last three decades. First, for many reasons, including political volatility, weak governance, and corruption, successive governments have failed to deliver on their basic responsibilities to reach the poor and to provide them with adequate social services. Second, even in the best years of economic activity, the so-called trickle-down effect has remained elusive. Most of the benefits of development have gone to the better-off, while the poor have mostly been excluded.

These circumstances have led stakeholders in government and civil society to seek development solutions that go beyond the public domain, supplementing and complementing the government's efforts to combat poverty. This has included efforts to fill the gaps in service delivery where government services are weak or even non-existent, by seeking more active partnership with communities. In other cases, where government has been active and economic opportunities are available, non-government initiatives have focused on helping poor people build their resources and skills so they can participate more actively in mainstream development opportunities.

From Regional Experiment to National Effort

The RSP model of grassroots organizing among the poor is based on ideas and practices learned from more than a century of experience, beginning with the cooperative movement in nineteenth-century Germany. It was tested with work in Comilla (in then East Pakistan, now Bangladesh) in the 1950s and 1960s. In Pakistan, it was first put into practice in an organized fashion in 1982 by the Aga Khan Rural Support Programme (AKRSP), inspired by Dr Akhter Hameed Khan (Box 5.1).

The AKRSP was formed with support from the Aga Khan Foundation, an international development agency established by His Highness Prince Karim Aga Khan.[1] The task of setting up the programme was entrusted to Shoaib Sultan Khan, a former civil service officer who had worked in the Comilla project in the 1960s and in the Daudzai project in the 1970s. The AKRSP focused its work in the impoverished Northern Areas of Pakistan.[2] It acted as a catalyst for rural development by organizing communities, working with them to identify development opportunities, and promoting the provision of services needed to tackle the specific problems of high mountain regions.

Box 5.1   Dr Akhter Hameed Khan: Originator of the RSP Approach
in South Asia

Over five decades, Dr Akhter Hameed Khan inspired and motivated
thousands of development professionals in South Asia, winning a
reputation as a visionary practitioner and teacher. Beginning with the
Comilla Thana Pilot Project, he moved on to a project in Daudzai, in
North-West Frontier Province, and then to the Aga Khan Rural Support
Programme, culminating his efforts with the Orangi Pilot Project.
Akhter Hameed Khan always saw the brighter side. He relied on the
resilience and success of poor people and the informal sector and
was also a firm believer in making the public sector more efficient.
He used to advise that development in Pakistan would come not
from the top but from the bottom, and would happen in pockets:
one island will be formed here, one island there, and 'one will be
formed by you.'

   Pakistan's rural development model is based on this approach.
The experimental phase, embodied in the AKRSP and the Orangi
Pilot Project, was later expanded countrywide. After his death, the
government of Pakistan awarded Akhter Hameed Khan the Nishan-
I-Imtiaz, its highest civil award.

   With support from a number of donor agencies, AKRSP expanded
rapidly to cover almost all the territory of the five districts in the Northern
Areas as well as Chitral district in North-West Frontier Province (NWFP). It
worked with a population of about 1 million people widely dispersed over an
area of about 72,000 square kilometres astride four of the highest mountain
ranges in the world. In its second evaluation of AKRSP, in 1990, the World
Bank noted substantial progress: 'At a time when "rural development" as
a development strategy is out of favour, the AKRSP experience provides a
hopeful prospect that rural development can be made to work, given half-
way favourable circumstances' (World Bank 1990).

   North-West Frontier Province was the first to show a willingness to
try out this model at the provincial level. This led to the establishment of
the Sarhad Rural Support Corporation, renamed the Sarhad Rural Support
Programme (SRSP) in 1989. SRSP began operations with financial support
from the provincial government and a bilateral donor. At about the same
time, the Pak German project in Balochistan, which had begun operations
in 1982, was restructured as the Balochistan Rural Support Programme.

By 1990 the three RSPs were working in about 10 districts of the country. Two years later the Government of Pakistan decided to support replication of the RSP model on a countrywide basis. Towards this end, it created the National Rural Support Programme (NRSP) and pledged initial financing of Rs 1 billion as an endowment fund. The first instalment of Rs 500 million was allocated in October 1992 for start-up operations in an additional eight districts. Due to a change of government soon after that, further funding to NRSP was discontinued and the ambitious expansion plan had to be postponed. Later on, however, NRSP was able to expand beyond the initial eight districts as other resources became available.

In the mid-1990s, NRSP helped the Water and Power Development Authority to establish the Ghazi Barotha Taraqiati Idara, a resettlement-cum-rural-development project. It was designed to complement the construction of a large hydroelectric project by working with communities displaced by the project. This was followed by creation of the Lachi Poverty Reduction Programme and the Tardeep Rural Development Programme, both in 1997. The Punjab Rural Support Programme (PRSP) was launched in 1998, and the Sindh Rural Support Organization (SRSO) in 2003.

By 2005 there were nine Rural Support Programmes active in more than 70 of the country's 106 districts, including larger rural districts and even some poor urban communities (Box 5.2). This work engages more than 72,000 community organizations. It affects almost 1.2 million members and their households, perhaps 8 million people overall (Figure 5.1). Expansion continues: in 2005, work was under way in three districts of Azad Jammu and Kashmir to lay the groundwork for establishing a Rural Support Programme in that area.

In the evolution of RSPs over the years, the common practice has been for older RSPs and their senior managers to play important roles in setting up new programmes. For instance, in the establishment of NRSP as well as the RSPs in Sarhad and Punjab, experienced staff from AKRSP helped introduce the programme to local communities and set up management systems.

In the late 1990s, however, it became evident that a more organized approach was needed to support not only expansion but also the evolving roles of existing RSPs. This led to the creation of a resource group within NRSP that was later transformed into an independent organization called the Rural Support Programme Network. The support network has a small group of professionals with extensive experience in participatory rural development. They provide support to the RSPs in the initial phase of development and also work on matters such as expansion and portfolio diversification. More recently, the support network has also played a significant role in policy dialogue at the national level, linking the work of the RSPs with national initiatives.

Box 5.2 Expansion of the RSP Movement, 1982–2005

1982 Aga Khan Rural Support Programme

The AKRSP was set up on the initiative of His Highness Prince Karim Aga Khan, with Shoaib Sultan Khan as general manager, to work in the Northern Areas.

1989 Sarhad Rural Support Corporation

When the US Agency for International Development (USAID) decided to withdraw from Pakistan, the North-West Frontier Province government and USAID asked AKRSP to expand its work into other districts of the province. AKRSP presented an alternative proposal, to which USAID and the government agreed, that a new organization be established to replicate the AKRSP approach. Initially called the Sarhad Rural Support Programme, it became known as the Sarhad Rural Support Corporation.

1991 Balochistan Rural Support Programme

A project funded by the German technical cooperation agency GTZ that had begun in the early 1980s was converted into the Balochistan Rural Support Programme.

1992 National Rural Support Programme

The opportunity to set up a large-scale replication of AKRSP came in 1991 after the prime minister visited AKRSP. He subsequently requested Shoaib Sultan Khan to begin the same kind of programme for the rest of the country. The central government provided an initial grant to establish the autonomous NRSP. The same approach was later successfully followed to set up provincial RSPs.

1995 Ghazi Barotha Taraqiati Idara

The Ghazi programme was set up by NRSP following a commitment by the government, with support from the World Bank, to mitigate the problems of communities being displaced by a large hydroelectric project.

(Contd)

Box 5.2 (Contd)

1997 Lachi Poverty Reduction Programme

The Lachi programme began in two districts of NWFP under the United Nations-funded South Asia Poverty Alleviation Programme, with technical and organizational support from the RSP in Sarhad.

1997 Tardeep Rural Development Programme

Save the Children UK had supported a relief and development programme in one of the most remote desert districts in Sindh Province in the mid-1990s. In 1997 that project was transformed into the Tardeep Rural Development Programme.

1998 Punjab Rural Support Programme

By the mid-1990s the relevance of the RSP approach in reducing poverty began to be more widely recognized. The government of Punjab committed $10 million for a provincial RSP to concentrate on districts not already covered by NRSP.

2001 Sindh Graduates Association

The Sindh Graduates Association was begun in 1972 by several university graduates who wanted to do something for the poor rural areas of Sindh. Over time it adjusted its approach to work more like the RSPs, and in 2001 it officially joined the RSP movement.

2003 Sindh Rural Support Organization

The programme in Sindh was established on the same pattern as the PRSP in Punjab, with initial funding from the government of Sindh and management support from NRSP.

2005 Azad Jammu and Kashmir Rural Support Programme

Plans were approved in 2004 for setting up an RSP in Azad Jammu and Kashmir, following the pattern of the provincial RSPs in Punjab and Sindh. Preparatory work was under way in 2005.

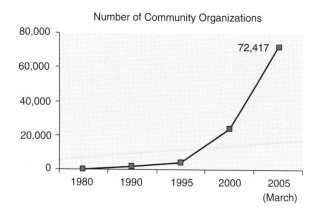

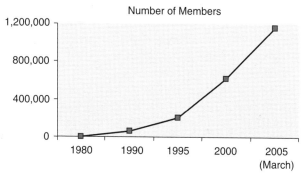

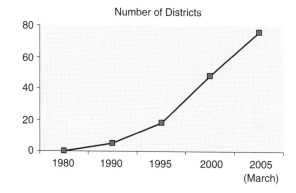

Source: Rural Support Programmes Network.

FIGURE 5.1 Growth of RSP Coverage, 1980–2005

IMPACT OF THE RURAL SUPPORT PROGRAMMES

The contribution of the RSPs can be seen most clearly in the area where these programmes have been in place for more than a decade, namely the areas in northern Pakistan where the movement started. There are sufficient economic data over this period to show significant trends. Elsewhere in the country, although systematic data over such a long period are lacking, there are also encouraging indicators of positive effects.

Economic Impact of AKRSP

Economic impact can best be assessed by examining changes in incomes and poverty in the communities and by calculating rates of return on investments made by the RSPs. Both of these approaches require data collected over long periods of time. So far, such are only available from the AKRSP experience. This evidence on incomes and poverty in northern Pakistan (Northern Areas and Chitral, or NAC), available from 1991 onwards, indicates significant positive economic change.

The average income per capita in northern Pakistan was less than one-third of the national average in 1991. By 2001 it had risen to more than half the national average. Even though national economic growth slowed considerably in the 1990s, the NAC region experienced impressive growth in per capita income, showing an 84 per cent increase from 1991 to 2001 (Table 5.1).

TABLE 5.1 Trends in Income Per Capita, 1991–2001

(US dollars)

Year	Pakistan	Northern Areas and Chitral (NAC)	NAC as percentage of Pakistan
1991	424	131	31
1994	440	176	40
1997	487	232	48
2001	415	241	58

Sources: Government of Pakistan, Federal Bureau of Statistics; AKRSP 2000.

This economic growth had a direct impact on poverty as well. While poverty at the national level rose between 1991 and 2001, in NAC it dropped dramatically from about two-thirds to one-third of the population. More detailed measures show that even those still living below the poverty line benefited from this growth. The indicators for depth of poverty (poverty gap), intensity of poverty (poverty gap index), and severity of poverty in NAC all show that the consumption levels of even poor households have improved.[3] Not only did the percentage of the population below the poverty line decline faster in NAC than in the country as a whole, but the benefits of growth were increasingly well distributed to the poorest households—that is, there was growth with equity (Table 5.2).

TABLE 5.2 Trends in Poverty, 1991–2001

	Pakistan	Northern Areas and Chitral			
Year	Percentage of population below poverty line	Percentage of population below poverty line	Poverty gap	Poverty gap index	Severity of poverty
1991	26.1	67	0.53	0.36	0.75
1994	28.7	54	0.49	0.27	0.55
1997	29.8	45	0.42	0.19	0.41
2001	32.1	34	0.38	0.19	0.27

Sources: Government of Pakistan, Planning Commission; Wood and Malik 2005.

Although there is no conclusive proof that these advances in the NAC region can be attributed to the AKRSP programme, the available evidence suggests that the contribution has been substantial. For instance, one study showed that the incomes of member households in village organizations were 15 to 20 per cent higher than those of non-members. This difference increased with the number of persons per household holding membership and with the length of their membership. The economic rate of return on AKRSP investments provides another confirmation that the programme has generated substantial benefits. Using conservative assumptions, the estimated rate of return calculated for AKRSP's investment falls in the range of 16–24 per cent, well above the usual experience in similar programmes (World Bank 2002).

The work of AKRSP also influenced efforts to improve the education and health status of communities in the Northern Areas, albeit in a less direct manner. AKRSP often played an active role in forging partnerships between community organizations and service providers, both governmental and non-governmental, to improve social service delivery. The existence of organized communities created numerous opportunities to improve the delivery and quality of services, sometimes through partnerships and at other times through efforts directly managed and financed by communities themselves. Partly as a result of these efforts, infant mortality rates in the Northern Areas declined dramatically, from 161 per 1,000 live births in 1986 to 33 per 1,000 in 1997. And between 1994 and 1998, the literacy rate rose from 14 to 33 per cent.[4]

Economic Impacts in Other Areas

The impacts of the RSP programmes also appear to have been significant in other parts of Pakistan, although other regions do not have the same level of quantitative data as the Northern Areas. In the case of the NRSP, which was launched throughout Pakistan in 1992, it has been estimated that membership in a community organization raises a household's income by about 7.5 per cent per year. Similarly, NRSP's own estimates show that poverty levels are lower in member households (Khan 2002). According to a report on Pakistan issued by the United Nations Development Programme (UNDP) in 2003, 68 per cent of NRSP members surveyed said they ate their fill daily, and the same percentage said they ate better than before they become involved in the programme. Fifty per cent reported improvements in health, and 82 per cent said they had experienced a sustainable increase in income after accessing credit. In Punjab, a study of 35 rural water supply schemes concluded that NRSP schemes had a higher success rate in sustainable service delivery than schemes undertaken directly by government, and were more cost effective as well (Khan 2002).

Impact on Policy

More generally, the RSP movement has had a visible impact on development policies and practices in the country. When the movement began in 1982 there was little talk of community-based development in national policies, much less of what later came to be called 'community-driven development'. The RSP experience was a major factor in changing thinking about development to give greater attention to the community.

Terms such as community participation, community-based development, and community-driven development now appear in all significant development policies and projects at the national and provincial levels, including the Pakistan Poverty Reduction Strategy Paper (Government of Pakistan 2003). RSPs have also had significant influence on poverty reduction strategies, on approaches to local governance, and on the adoption of microfinance and community-owned infrastructure as mainstream development strategies. This influence has come from demonstrating in practice what can be accomplished by working directly with communities and households.

Impact Issues

The long-term impact of AKRSP thus came through the combination of direct service delivery and indirect influence on the policies and working of public and private sector players, both in its geographic area of concentration and nationally. Within the Northern Areas, AKRSP focused on building up the asset base (physical, human, social, and financial) of rural households on an equitable basis. It worked both directly through its own interventions and indirectly by improving the efforts of government and the private sector. As a result, economic growth in NAC directly translated into reductions in poverty levels and improved the share of the lowest income groups (Wood and Malik 2005).

The choice of interventions made by AKRSP had important implications. By mobilizing communities and improving infrastructure, the programme was able to enhance access to markets and to education and health services. This improved health and education outcomes and also reduced vulnerability to health shocks and food shortages. Efforts to improve the condition and position of women were also key elements in the AKRSP portfolio of interventions.

It is important to note that the effects of RSP interventions are best felt when there is greater macroeconomic growth and when communities are more closely linked to mainstream markets. Thus the growth of incomes in northern Pakistan was higher in the first half of the 1990s and much lower in the second half, following broad national trends (Parvez and Rasmussen 2004). Similarly, better integration with national markets and improved public policies, such as greater investment by government, clearly added to the effects of AKRSP's interventions. A comparison between Chitral and Gilgit, two districts in NAC, showed differential gains owing to differential access and public investment (Malik and Piracha 2003).

Overall, the most recent World Bank evaluation of AKRSP found that the programme's high level of inputs (consistent delivery of considerable resources) was effective in ensuring delivery of a high level of outputs, had a high economic rate of return, and achieved a positive, measurable impact on reducing poverty (World Bank 2002). Such a high-input model was particularly appropriate for an underserved area such as northern Pakistan and helped to make a dent in the region's widely prevalent and persistent poverty.

Elsewhere, in areas where service providers exist and can be mobilized, and where there is already some degree of integration into mainstream markets, the tendency has been to rely on a less intensive approach focused on forging partnerships with organized communities to increase the effectiveness of service providers. Such an approach has been adopted by most of the RSPs that followed AKRSP, and it is possible that it may also prove effective. So far, however, measurable reductions in poverty for large numbers of people have remained elusive in these areas. It may prove necessary to move in the direction of a high-input, high-output approach. This, however, would require more resources than the other RSPs have so far been able to mobilize.

The RSPs now form the largest group of non-governmental organizations (NGOs) working for poverty reduction in Pakistan. As of 2005, they were working in over 70 per cent of the districts in Pakistan and their coverage was still expanding. Key drivers in the movement's success to date include political commitment at the national level, institutional innovation and learning, and the role of external catalysts.

POLITICAL COMMITMENT AND RELATIONS WITH GOVERNMENT

The relationship between the RSP movement and the Government of Pakistan has been an important factor in enabling the movement to scale up. Several aspects are of particular note. First, a model was developed in the field that clearly demonstrated effectiveness at a grassroots level. On this basis it was possible to 'sell' the model to government, to donors, and, importantly, to other poor communities. Second, the RSPs consciously maintained a non-confrontational and politically neutral approach in dealing with government and other stakeholders. Advocacy for change was important, but it was done by demonstrating practical, useful results at the community level. This allowed the RSPs to take advantage of opportunities to expand the RSP movement with direct government funding.

Third, although government was instrumental in supporting the growth of the movement, government did not try to control the RSPs it established. Instead, it set them up as independent, self-governing organizations with control over their own decisions and financial resources. Fourth, while government initially expected the RSPs only to complement and help improve the delivery of social services, officials did not interfere when RSPs took on roles that went well beyond those initial expectations. And, finally, the RSP model gained further credibility as it influenced thinking on development issues within government circles.

Developing and Marketing the Model

Fundamental to other components of success at the national level was the successful experience of the AKRSP. For the first six years, from 1982 to 1988, it was the only RSP, operating in a handful of remote districts in northern Pakistan. Taking ideas from earlier projects such as Comilla and Daudzai, the programme began with a few villages and ultimately expanded to six districts. In this phase, AKRSP had no direct government financing. However, the Aga Khan had sought and received the support of the president of Pakistan to begin the project, and the first general manager of AKRSP was a well-respected person from the bureaucracy who had excellent links within the government. There was still a distance from government, in that AKRSP worked in a remote region outside of the development limelight. This allowed it to focus on demonstrating what could be done in villages, first proving itself to people living in those communities.

With a working model on the ground, the Aga Khan Foundation, as the founder of the AKRSP, was able to market this model of rural development to a wider audience—one of the original objectives of the programme. Many political leaders, senior government officials, and donor representatives in Pakistan, as well as people from outside the country, visited the villages where AKRSP worked. Participants in training courses for top government officials at the Civil Service Academy and the National Defence College came to AKRSP to get field experience as part of their training. Gradually a cadre of influential decision makers who had some exposure to the RSP model was built up. Some of them later played important roles in expanding the RSP movement.

AKRSP also benefited greatly from the strong support of the international Aga Khan Foundation. This allowed it to gain credibility more quickly and to establish patterns of governance and management that set the standards for the RSP movement as it expanded. AKRSP was thus able to serve as the successful pilot project that created the basis for scaling up.

AKRSP gained additional recognition and credibility from World Bank evaluations affirming the efficacy and impact of the approach. Later, UNDP evaluations of the NRSP reached similar conclusions. A 1998 evaluation of NRSP observed: 'In sum, the NRSP model is unique. It is highly responsive to community motives and aspirations within the context of community participation. NRSP has shown that institutional sustainability is an achievable goal through the creation of the endowment and access to a virtually unlimited line of credit [from a commercial bank]. Clearly, NRSP's experiences suggest that it is feasible to unlock the productive and entrepreneurial potential of Pakistan's rural people' (UNDP 1998). These reports, which were widely circulated, put development in Pakistan in a positive light. This helped build credibility with donors as well as national pride in a locally developed approach that appeared to be working.

Particularly crucial in building momentum for scaling up was the enthusiasm of the partner communities themselves. The confidence and exuberance of community members in northern Pakistan was evident to visitors. The inclusive nature of the RSP approach was also instrumental in encouraging the poor to organize themselves. Once the process of forming organizations took off in an area, it quickly created a demonstration effect and gained a momentum of its own. This process of social mobilization gradually changed a long-entrenched cultural attitude that had seen the poor merely as passive recipients of services planned, financed, and delivered by others. Through the social mobilization process, people were organized not simply to receive services but to act as catalysts of change and improvement.

This experience in the northern region set the precedent. Beginning in the late 1980s, when the second RSP was created in Sarhad, a pattern was established that was crucial in promoting replication. Influential decision makers who supported the replication of the RSP model did so because they had themselves visited villages where the model had worked.

Within the basic context of a good example being effectively communicated to political decision makers, there were other specific elements that were conducive to success in scaling up. These included political neutrality, government funding combined with support for RSP autonomy, and realistic expectations accompanied by willingness to learn on the part of government.

Maintaining Political Neutrality

In volatile and unpredictable political environments such as Pakistan's, political neutrality may increase the chance that non-government programmes will be able to work effectively over long periods of time on a relatively large scale, or even continue to exist. The RSPs maintained their autonomy and integrity by taking a non-confrontational approach. Advocacy for changes in development policies and practices took place mainly through demonstrations that practical, useful results could be achieved on the ground. It was also important that the RSP movement was scaled up through replication—by creating multiple organizations rather than by building a single large entity that might have been perceived as a rival to established government structures and thus a potential political threat. The focus was on fostering community organizations primarily engaged in practical development work. Despite its growing scale and influence, therefore, the RSP movement was largely, although not entirely, successful in staying clear of political controversies.

While the internal dynamics of the RSP movement that allowed it to grow were consistent over time, the external political and economic environment fluctuated wildly. The RSPs managed to take advantage of opportunities to scale up when they came along, while maintaining existing programmes during times when the political environment was less supportive. In general, the RSPs pursued a partnership with government, at least in terms of seeking support from high-level officials and identifying ways of complementing government efforts to improve service delivery for the poor. This posture allowed the RSP movement to grow when the political environment was supportive. This was the case in the emergence of three of the largest RSPs (SRSP, NRSP, and PRSP) as well as two of the smaller ones (GBTI and SRSO). In all these cases, the main officials involved in creating these opportunities had been persuaded by visits to AKRSP that the RSP model did work.

Government Support for RSP Autonomy

A critical factor was that government funds, or funds sought from donors with government support, were used to create new institutions that operated outside of government control. This feature helped make the RSPs credible to external donors and served to generate additional resources (Boxes 5.3 and 5.4). When autonomy from government and donors was not successfully institutionalized, however, institutions found it more difficult to sustain their operations (Box 5.5).

A few key government people were convinced that the RSPs must remain free of government control and political or bureaucratic interference. Decisions by these officials had a long-term impact in making the programmes sustainable in line with the approach taken by

AKRSP. Two specific mechanisms allowed this to happen. First, the RSPs were established as private, not-for-profit companies regulated by the independent Securities and Exchange Commission that also regulates for-profit companies. Thus the RSPs had a legally defined autonomous governance structure that was self-perpetuating. Second, each RSP received an initial lump-sum endowment that did not require ongoing government oversight. These endowments provided core financial stability that was especially important to sustaining momentum through difficult political and financial circumstances.

Since the expansion of RSPs to the national level, NRSP has enjoyed a special relationship with the central government that is mutually supportive and remarkably congenial. While this has been a great advantage in linking NRSP to line agencies and drawing on resources from government departments, the programme has had to maintain a careful balance to ensure its independence (UNDP 1998). The fact that it has been possible to maintain such a balance is one of the factors responsible for success.

Box 5.3 Scaling Up: The National Rural Support Programme

When the 1990 elections brought the Pakistan Muslim League to power at the national level, Nawaz Sharif became prime minister and Sartaj Aziz became finance minister. Both officials had experience that led them to be receptive to expanding the Rural Support Programme then operating in the north. Prime Minister Sharif, previously chief minister of Punjab, had observed that the common government approach of investing heavily in buildings and infrastructure was not sufficient to produce positive development outcomes. He noted, for example, that there were many empty school buildings in rural villages and that teachers were often absent. For his part, Finance Minister Aziz had been following AKRSP from its beginning, having first visited the Northern Areas in 1983. He also had extensive international experience in rural development, having served as assistant president of the Rome-based International Fund for Agricultural Development. He was convinced that the AKRSP model could be widely replicated in Pakistan.

The first UNDP human development report, published in 1991, showed that while Pakistan was doing relatively well economically, its performance on social indicators was woeful. This increased pressure on the government to act. At the donor roundtable in Paris that year,

(Contd)

Box 5.3 (Contd)

the government proposed a programme to improve management of social sector efforts. It launched the Social Action Programme with its own funds in 1992.

The finance minister argued that government efforts could not be successful without a complementary programme to organize and empower communities to be effective partners. This could best be done, he believed, through support organizations such as AKRSP that were autonomous of the government. After a presentation to top officials from the general manager of AKRSP, Shoaib Sultan Khan, the prime minister approved Rs 10 billion for a 10-year plan to set up RSPs in all districts of the country. Of this, Rs 500 million was allocated for a National Rural Support Programme to begin immediate work in eight districts.

The Pakistan Muslim League government lost power to the People's Party of Pakistan in April 1993, and no further funds were released to NRSP. But the NRSP, holding autonomous legal status, was able to continue its work despite efforts by the new government to take back some of the funds already allocated. Thus the NRSP survived to serve as a precedent. Provincial governments established similar programmes in the Punjab in 1998 and in Sindh in 2002. In 1998 the federal government followed the same model when it established the Pakistan Poverty Alleviation Fund as an autonomous institution.

Box 5.4 A Different Approach to Scaling Up: Ghazi Barotha Taraqiati Idara

The Ghazi Barotha Taraqiati Idara (GBTI), based on the need to assist thousands of people being displaced by a large hydroelectric project, represents a unique approach to establishing a sustainable RSP.

In 1994 the central government's Water and Power Development Authority (WAPDA) began construction of the 1,450-megawatt Ghazi Barotha power generation project on the Indus River, backed by loans from the World Bank and other donors. About 60,000 households in three districts faced resettlement as a result of the project. In order to try to work in a more participatory way with these people, an NGO was established to 'promote the participatory development of [those

(Contd)

Box 5.4 (Contd)

affected] ... including advocacy of the rights of affectees in matters of (re)settlement and compensation.'

The power authority sought help from NRSP, and GBTI was set up as an autonomous, self-governing organization. Its board of directors included representatives elected from the communities as well as people with experience in development and resettlement matters. WAPDA provided an initial grant of $1.5 million as an 'endowment fund,' with income used to pay GBTI's operating costs. NRSP organized the new programme and recruited and trained its staff. Participatory baseline surveys were used to develop an integrated rural development plan, with an additional $5 million commitment from WAPDA.

GBTI fostered community organizations that had an unprecedented voice in the overall project. Acting as an intermediary, GBTI was able to help negotiate fair and generally acceptable market prices for land acquired from local people. Previous WAPDA projects had used an average 'registration price' to acquire land forcibly, usually at prices that were only 20 per cent of market value. This approach had resulted in considerable conflict between WAPDA and affected communities. In contrast, GBTI worked with poor people to prepare land records and assess a fair value for each parcel of land. In addition, many people from the communities were hired by the contractors, and GBTI was able to mobilize funds for community development projects. Although WAPDA was not always supportive of GBTI, GBTI had sufficient autonomy to be effective. Its endowment allowed it to continue operations after the power project came onstream in 2003.

Box 5.5   Failure to Establish Autonomy: Balochistan Rural Support Programme

The Balochistan Rural Support Programme (BRSP) did not begin life as an RSP. Instead, it joined the movement later, after gradually adopting the RSP approach. It was started in 1982 as a rural development project funded by the German government and managed by GTZ, the German technical cooperation agency. This successful initial project was transformed into the Balochistan Rural Support Programme in 1989 and registered as a local organization in Pakistan.

(Contd)

Box 5.5 (Contd)

BRSP was a well-managed organization that was setting down roots in Balochistan. In the mid-1990s, however, GTZ began to interfere directly in management of the organization. This resulted in problems that eventually forced the closure of most operations, and by 1997 BRSP was in serious decline. Although recent efforts to revive it have met with some success, it is clear that two of the driving factors underlying the successful experiences of the other RSPs were not present in Balochistan.

First, the organization lacked autonomy in relation to the donor. The donor retained strong influence over BRSP, even after setting it up as an autonomous local organization; it appointed a senior management person and kept a seat on the board of directors. BRSP also remained dependent on external donor funding. Thus, when differences arose between BRSP and the donor, the donor stopped providing funding and BRSP had no core funds of its own to sustain its operations. Second, BRSP lacked autonomy from the Pakistani government, as government officers sat on the board of directors and also had some influence over decisions about the use of funds. So long as people in key positions were supportive of BRSP, things functioned well, but ultimately the organization proved vulnerable to bureaucratic interference—with negative results.

RSPs and Government: New Partnerships, New Expectations

The decision makers who created expansion opportunities for RSPs were convinced that governments in the past had not been able to provide adequate or effective economic and social development opportunities for the poor. They saw empowering communities as a way to increase demand for better service delivery mechanisms as well as a way to gain political credit for reaching out to the poor. It was not always clearly articulated, however, what specific roles the RSPs would play, and government expectations were different in the cases of different RSPs.

For instance, in 1992 the NRSP was essentially seen as complementary to the government's Social Action Programme for improving primary education, primary health care, and rural water supply and sanitation services. Service delivery would be supplied by government, while the NRSP's role would be to organize the poor so they could access those services.

With the PRSP, there was a similar expectation that the programme would complement the development work of government, largely by creating community demand for better services and by establishing community-based mechanisms to make better use of the services government did provide. Such a complementary role is often still cited as the main reason for government support to the RSP movement.

Nevertheless, RSPs have also taken on the role of service providers themselves, sometimes parallel to government and sometimes as subcontractors to government. The AKRSP, supported by outside donor funding, began to fill gaps in service provision almost from its inception. This role was especially important in the relatively impoverished and underserved communities of mountainous northern Pakistan. In the 1980s, for example, AKRSP was the largest provider of agricultural inputs, credit, and advice to farmers in the Northern Areas. Slowly it handed over to community-organized initiatives responsibilities for supplying these inputs and services, and it has since sought to support private providers of agricultural services as well. Similarly, in the late 1990s, RSPs collectively became the largest providers of microfinance services in the country, serving about 80 per cent of all clients of microfinance institutions. Although RSPs were not primarily established as service provider organizations, they assumed such a role with government consent because they were able to provide more efficient and effective services, drawing on direct community involvement and providing services in villages that government services often did not reach.

In the establishment of RSPs in Pakistan, the government provided seed capital for private, independent organizations designed to work in partnership with government programmes. This public–private partnership approach was also followed in setting up other development organizations such as the Pakistan Poverty Alleviation Fund, the National Commission for Human Development, and the Devolution Trust for Community Empowerment. Such partnerships have included not only community mobilization and capacity building, but also direct involvement of RSPs in delivery of social services.

Cases where grassroots projects complement delivery of services by government departments include the Khushhal Pakistan Programme as well as area development and agriculture development projects in Punjab and NWFP. More direct involvement in service delivery is illustrated by one of the few successes in the Social Action Programme that began in 1992. This was the partnership between the government and AKRSP to establish 500 community-managed schools to provide access to primary education, especially for girls, in remote communities. This model was later adapted by the Punjab government in partnership with the Punjab Rural Support Programme, with more than 400 community schools established by the end of 2004 and further expansion planned.

The NRSP also has an agreement with the Punjab government to improve the quality of education in schools in one district by improving the curriculum and introducing new teaching methodologies. In NWFP, the Sarhad Rural Support Programme is working with one district government to improve the quality of education in an extremely remote area with very low female literacy. In 2005 the NRSP and the PRSP entered into an agreement with the Punjab government to set up 2,000 school councils to improve management of schools and increase accountability of the public sector to communities under the World Bank-funded Punjab Education Sector Reforms Programme. These partnerships employ a 'learning by doing' approach in which RSPs and government are learning how to use their respective strengths to work towards a common goal.

In the health sector, NRSP entered into a partnership with the government in 2001 to manage three basic health units in southern Punjab. This experiment formed the basis for what became in 2003 the Chief Minister's Initiative for Primary Health Care, starting from Rahim Yar Khan District and extended to 10 other districts. By early 2005 the PRSP was managing 1,100 frontline health care facilities, more than 20 per cent of the total number of such facilities in the country, serving a population of more than 20 million. The key to this partnership was the handing over of the management of public financial and human resources to the PRSP. While it is too early to judge the full impact of this experiment, there have been clear improvements in the management and delivery of the primary health care services. For example, patient visits more than tripled in the first year as public confidence in the services increased.

The opportunity for such district-level partnerships increased substantially with passage of the Local Government Ordinance of 2001, which transferred the management of departments involved in providing basic services from the provincial to the district level. The ordinance also envisages the creation of community-based organizations, called community citizen boards (CCBs), that will implement projects and have access to 25 per cent of each district's annual development budget. Through a memorandum of understanding signed with the Devolution Trust for Community Empowerment, the RSPs are training elected local government representatives and other actors to mobilize CCBs and train them in formulation of projects to be funded by the district governments. Over

9,000 community organizations mobilized by RSPs have registered as CCBs in order to access funding for infrastructure projects. To an extent, the RSPs' work with the Devolution Trust for Community Empowerment has mainstreamed their social mobilization efforts into the local government system. Government is increasingly realizing that the creation of effective community-based organizations is a task best undertaken by supporting structures like the RSPs and not by government departments that have no such experience.

As the RSP model gained visibility, it also began to influence overall development practices. Social mobilization, previously not given much attention, became a part of many other development projects, including large projects initiated by provincial governments and funded by multilateral agencies. The first example was in 1990, when North-West Frontier Province received funding from the Asian Development Bank and the International Fund for Agricultural Development to establish the Chitral Area Development Programme. Other even bigger projects followed in NWFP as well as in other provinces. Donor funding was available partly because of the promise of the successful RSP model.

The record of these efforts, however, is mixed. Although they instituted structures, staffing patterns, and programmes paralleling those of RSPs, in fact such projects were not autonomous from normal government procedures and accountability mechanisms. As a result, these projects did not have the autonomy required to work independently of political interference or bureaucratic procedures. The public viewed such projects as extensions of the government system and were reluctant to take on an effective partnership role, often preferring to treat them as sources of funding to be demanded through the normal representative governance system. Moreover, these projects were not able to internalize within government the community partnership approach used by the RSPs as government typically executed them through separate project management units with project staff on short-term contracts. More sustainable than this approach are the linkages that the RSPs forge between 'regular' government departments and the communities they work with.

It is clear that RSP partnerships with government take on many forms that change over time. The driving force behind these partnerships, though, is the trend to outsource public services and to involve communities in their management in order to create greater efficiency, service impact, and accountability.

Institutional Innovation, Learning, and Experimentation

In addition to the twin principles of cooperation with and autonomy from government, institutional innovation and learning has been key to the expansion of the RSPs. The first important innovation was adoption of the social mobilization approach, which contrasted to the widely practiced top-down approach to development. Second, expansion was achieved not by scaling up the work of a single organization but by setting up autonomous RSPs in different geographic areas. While replicating the RSP approach, these programmes had the advantage of being more adaptable to local needs and conditions than a single large organization would be. A holistic approach to development, beginning with organizing communities, gave people the flexibility to decide their own development priorities.

Third, most RSPs were able to establish core capital funds that provided a basis for sustainability. These helped them avoid overdependence on any single external funding source while giving them leverage to obtain additional funding from government, commercial banks, donors and others. Finally, a long-term outlook was essential. The experience of the RSPs showed that at least 10 years of concerted effort was needed to create a critical mass at the community level sufficient to enable a programme to influence policy and to allow its impact to be measured.

Social Mobilization

Social mobilization lies at the heart of the RSP approach. It is based on the premise that people's potential can best be harnessed through mobilizing their own initiative, and that this is especially true for poor people. Development is also recognized as an ongoing process rather than a one-time transition. When the RSP movement began in the early 1980s, it was conceived as a clear departure from the approach to rural development then widely practiced, in which a carefully planned and uniform set of interventions, or 'blueprint', was applied to all communities. Instead, the RSP approach called for starting from what organized communities identified as their priority needs. It also required that communities invest some of their own resources in order to become eligible for benefits from an RSP, such as improved access to services. The focus was on learning by doing and adapting what had been learned, rather than attempting to plan everything in advance. The RSPs share a commitment to maintaining this 'purity of concept', a phrase that is still often invoked by those in the movement.

Social mobilization focused on the household, bringing households with common interests together into an organization where each one could potentially have a voice. It encouraged participation on a modest local level in contrast to representation through elected government systems. The point was not only to increase the assets of poor people and improve their access to services, but also to promote strategic empowerment, getting people effectively involved in making decisions that affected their lives. Practical benefits became the means to more important strategic gains. One example of the results can be seen in the influence that organized communities had in choosing local government representatives in the elections held during 2001. Many community activists were elected to local government positions.

The RSPs did not set out to do things for poor people. Rather, it was expected that people would do things for themselves, making optimum use of whatever assets they had. Particular emphasis was placed on promoting collective action, building human capital by training people in leadership, management, and vocational skills, and increasing financial capital by encouraging people to save money. The basic goal was to make the development process locally sustainable. This also included identifying and developing activists from the communities who could lead the process in their respective communities. As time went on, these activists played increasingly important roles.

Expansion through Replication

Scaling up is often understood as expansion of a single organization and its work, but the RSP movement deliberately chose a different path. The RSP approach was replicated by creating new, independent organizations for each new environment. When an opportunity arose to scale up in North-West Frontier Province in the late 1980s, the initial request of the provincial government and the donor was for AKRSP to expand its operations to new districts. Instead, SRSP was created as a separate, autonomous organization. The same philosophy guided the creation of the other RSPs. The fourth evaluation of AKRSP noted: 'Expansion is a slow process even with skilled facilitators, as there are few economies of scale. However, expansion by grafting new programmes into locations with similar circumstances offers substantial leverage' (World Bank 2002).

Eventually the process of encouraging regional autonomy within the larger RSPs took localization further. There was further subdivision by regions within each of the larger RSPs, which allowed local ownership to develop and programmes to be customized to suit the particular conditions in each locality. Thus each provincial government could feel that it was supporting its own RSP. As noted, the approach of scaling up through replication also was conducive to central government support. Eventually a network was created to help support the movement as a whole, sustain necessary links within the movement, and use the collective experience and strengths of the RSPs to influence national policies and practices. Today there appears to be a shared core philosophy and approach within the RSP movement, but programmes are increasingly differentiated.

Outside Pakistan, this approach expanded to the South Asia Poverty Alleviation Programme in 1994, creating autonomous implementing organizations in each country. In addition, the Aga Khan Foundation has replicated the RSP approach in several other countries where it is engaged in rural development work.

Another important aspect of institutionalization is that RSPs do not mobilize communities for a specific intervention or sectoral programme. Instead, they foster community organizations that can deal with a wide range of issues that affect people's lives. To the extent that necessary funding can be obtained, an RSP's activities in a region are a function of the needs of the communities it works with. When the needs of the communities change, the priorities of the RSP change as well. In AKRSP, for example, the development of village infrastructure was followed by demands for skill-building programmes. This in turn led to the expansion of microfinance and enterprise development activities. Experience shows that such a holistic approach using multiple interventions is necessary for effective poverty reduction.

Core Capital and Leveraging Funds

Just as with private companies or financial institutions, the fact that RSPs have core capital that they control gives them a basis for sustainability. For some RSPs this came through initial grants provided by government. In other cases, RSPs have been able to build up core capital over the years through grants from donors. Where this has not been possible, RSPs have been in a more precarious position, finding it difficult to continue their work. Government and donors generally provide grants only for current expenditures; if this is the only source of funding, the organization lives hand to mouth and it is difficult to sustain or expand operations. When an organization has its own capital, however, this provides a solid basis for making good use of additional funding. In fact, RSPs have built a track record of leveraging their core funds through the addition of donor- or government-funded projects. Some RSPs have also used their core capital as collateral to obtain lines of credit from commercial banks to expand their microfinance programmes. Core capital allows considerable flexibility to the RSPs and makes it possible to think long-term.

Patience and Perseverance

The experience of the RSPs, beginning 20 years ago when AKRSP was founded, makes clear that having an impact requires long-term vision and sustained effort. It took AKRSP 10 to 12 years to foster community organizations that eventually included 80 per cent of all households in six districts. Such extensive coverage provided a critical mass that allowed the process of social mobilization to become embedded in the communities and to gain momentum of its own. It took a similar period of time for a positive impact on reducing poverty to become evident and measurable.

It is probably not coincidental that it was 11 years after AKRSP began its work that the Northern Areas government officially adopted a development approach based on partnership with the community organizations, by recognizing them as part of a community-based movement rather than simply as an extension of AKRSP. Influence on national policies and practices also became visible at about the same time. Although there were earlier examples of efforts to replicate the RSP approach, the creation of NRSP in 1992, 10 years after AKRSP began its work, was the first time that government directly and significantly contributed to scaling up the RSP movement. The process of scaling up was neither easy nor predictable. Consistency and continuity were required over a long period to achieve results on a significant scale.

The commitment of specific persons was clearly a central factor in scaling up the RSPs. This began with the role of the Aga Khan, who took a personal interest in establishing and promoting AKRSP, and Akhter Hameed Khan, the thinker and activist who inspired the RSP movement. It also included key politicians and senior government administrators and, at the level of administrative leadership, Shoaib Sultan Khan, the first general manager of AKRSP (Box 5.6). But the RSP movement has not been dependent on these figures. It has suffered relatively little from the kinds of succession battles or failures that have characterized many organizations and movements. One reason for this has been the considerable investment made in developing competent people to take on management roles. Another reason has been the creation of strong and accountable governance structures that require periodic reelection of directors. In addition, the replication approach used by the RSPs has helped to make the RSP movement less reliant on a few personalities, since it has been necessary to identify and develop people who could lead independent organizations.

Box 5.6 Shoaib Sultan Khan: Principal Driver of the RSP Movement

Shoaib Sultan Khan accepted Akhter Hameed Khan as his mentor from the time of the Comilla Project in the early 1960s. Akhter Hameed Khan was a former member of the Indian civil service, and Shoaib Sultan Khan would in time become a former member of the civil service of Pakistan. Each had gained from his experience a profound understanding of why and where governments fail. Akhter Hameed Khan showed that development could happen in pockets, Comilla and Orangi being the outstanding examples, when communities were empowered by 'social guidance' to take charge of their own destinies. Shoaib Sultan Khan extended the same principle to AKRSP and from there to what became the RSP movement.

While Akhter Hameed Khan was a social scientist, Shoaib Sultan Khan was a social activist convinced that the art of development could be practiced countrywide, not just in pockets. Despite occasional setbacks over the years, Shoaib Sultan Khan never wavered from his drive to scale up the RSP movement and make it a success at the national and regional levels.

THE ROLE OF EXTERNAL CATALYSTS

While cooperation with government and the social mobilization approach were the vital driving factors in RSP success, consistent funding from external sources has been an essential component as well. Support from a variety of external programmes aided the RSPs over the years, while from 1998 onward the Pakistan Poverty Alleviation Fund (PPAF) provided another regular source of support.

In addition to the Aga Khan Foundation, other donors soon realized the potential of the RSP approach and began to provide backing to AKRSP. From 1983 to 2003, donors provided more than $100 million to the programme. The Canadian International Development Agency and the UK Department for International Development, in particular, provided the continuity of support that was crucial to achieving results. Donors also did much to create credibility for the movement and convince the government of its value. While this was especially important at the beginning, it continued to be true even after the scaling up of RSPs.

In 1998 the government created the Pakistan Poverty Alleviation Fund with Rs 500 million as an endowment from which to pay core administrative costs. It worked with the World Bank to secure a $90 million soft-loan fund for programmes to be carried out with NGO partners, primarily related to microcredit and community infrastructure. In its first phase, from 1998 to 2004, PPAF met its targeted expenditure goals before the end of the planned period. A second phase is planned with double the endowment, and an additional $238 million from the World Bank has also been approved. The relationship between PPAF and the RSPs is mutually beneficial, since the RSPs provide the institutional capacity to absorb the expanded funding being made available. Collectively the RSPs soon became the largest PPAF partner, absorbing more than 60 per cent of PPAF funding given out in the first phase.

Lessons Learned

The lessons emerging from the RSP experience can be summed up as five main points. First, communities engaged in community-driven development require support, and support organizations in turn need autonomy from government and some independent means of sustaining themselves. Second, these organizations should complement and support the work of government and other development organizations in order to connect communities to multiple development opportunities. Third, scaling up can take place through a process of replication, with many separate organizations following the same basic approach. This has the advantage of fostering local ownership and support as well as adaptation to local needs and opportunities. Fourth, impact requires consistent effort over time. Fifth, while individual champions can play pivotal leadership roles in sustaining and spreading the core values of the movement, it is also crucial from the beginning to offer many opportunities for new leadership to emerge, rather than allowing organizations to remain dependent on a few people.

Support Organizations Should Be Autonomous and Sustainable

The history of the RSPs shows that government can support poverty reduction efforts in other ways than by doing things exclusively through its own mechanisms. In the RSP experience, government achieved an impact by supporting organizations that were effective precisely because they were autonomous, with independent governance structures and sustainable core funding. They also had relatively free access to donor funding, the use of which was controlled by the RSP, not the government. This was not an abdication of government responsibility, but rather a recognition that development could be more effective if it engaged autonomous support organizations. While government agencies often did not have the credibility with poor people to form effective partnerships on their own, the RSPs were able to establish credibility and trust on the ground. Autonomy not only allowed them to replicate structures and systems that had proven to be effective, but also fostered a process of internalizing values that were essential to partnership with communities.

Support Organizations Should Complement and Support Government Efforts

The RSPs did not attempt to function in opposition to or in isolation from government, but rather sought to complement the efforts of government, the private sector, and civil society. This commitment to partnerships was an inherent component of the movement and enabled it to leverage limited resources for greater effect. Partnership has taken on different forms over the years. In an environment that was highly charged and politically volatile, it was essential that the RSPs remain 'apolitical'. This helped them survive during periods when the political environment was hostile, but also position themselves to benefit from government support when it was offered. The RSP movement managed on the whole to transcend political divides, retaining its base of support within communities and gaining support from other stakeholders on the basis of performance.

Scale Up by Replication Instead of Expansion

The RSP movement scaled up by replicating the model through different local organizations rather than by expanding a single large organization. This required a clear conceptual model and core values that could be expressed with considerable flexibility by several different organizations at the same time. A balance had to be found between standardizing principal aspects of the model and diversifying programmatic interventions to adjust to local conditions and opportunities. All RSPs adopted the social mobilization approach that characterized the movement, but each RSP was left to find the best fit to its environment and the needs of poor people in its area. Each also could explore opportunities for partnership and for mobilizing resources. This increased diversity within the RSP movement and eventually made necessary a formal network to help enhance and sustain core approaches and values.

The replication of the RSP model through many organizations of varying size and scope also helped to reinforce the apolitical nature of the movement and win government cooperation and support. Small, localized organizations were perceived as less threatening than a single large organization would have been. They were also better able to promote local ownership and access to local resources. Finally, this approach also supported the emergence of a wider set of leaders.

Impact Requires Consistent Effort over Time

The RSP approach of providing social guidance and capacity building to poor and marginalized communities created the opportunity for poor people to benefit from macroeconomic growth and development. But this was not accomplished overnight. It required an organic and often slow process of growth that clearly demonstrated the potential and effectiveness of what was being done. The pace of growth depended on the pace at which communities could organize themselves and bring their own resources to bear.

The experience of the first RSP, the Aga Khan Rural Support Programme, was that it took 10 or more years to create a critical mass of organized communities able to influence public policy and become an effective force for development. It also took a decade to begin to see a measurable impact on reducing poverty. Advocacy for change and for expansion of the work of the RSPs depended on showing success in the field. Most government and donor approaches to development demand quicker results with higher initial visibility via short-term projects. The RSPs had to find ways to sustain their work to suit much longer time horizons, resisting top-down control focused on achieving immediate outputs.

Champions and New Leaders are Both Important

Every movement needs leadership by people who are committed to its values and practices. Replication requires champions at all levels of the movement. For the RSPs these champions were certain influential political figures and people in government who created important opportunities for the movement to grow and scale up. There were also several highly visible and influential personalities who provided overall continuity of leadership. But the movement also mobilized thousands of community activists who saw the potential to change long-established and entrenched patterns in which poor people were excluded from the mainstream. The RSPs were able to attract many competent managers and technical experts and to ensure that some of them developed into second-generation leaders who could take the movement forward in the coming years.

NOTES

In an effort to ensure objectivity and wider insight into the process of scaling up RSPs, a working group representing the RSPs, the Government of Pakistan, and others was constituted at the beginning of the process of developing this case study. The members of the group made considerable contributions to the content of the study as well as commenting upon and improving working drafts. The working group comprised Pervez Tahir, Abdul Wajid Rana, Qazi Azmat Isa, Farooq Haroon, Masood ul Mulk, and the authors. We are also grateful for the time taken by Shoaib Sultan Khan, Sartaj Aziz, Jehangir Khan Tareen, Tariq Sultan, Azam Khan, and Kamal Hyat to provide useful insights that helped the authors understand important lessons. We thank Ghias M. Khan and his staff, especially Ghulam Hafeez, for providing the figure and tables as well as technical support.

This case study was produced with financial support from the World Bank and the UK Department for International Development.

References

ADB (Asian Development Bank), 2002, *Poverty in Pakistan: Issues, Causes and Institutional Responses*, Islamabad: ADB.

AKRSP (Aga Khan Rural Support Programme), 2000, 'An Assessment of Socio-Economic Trends and Impact in Northern Pakistan (1991–1997). Findings from AKRSP's Farm Household Income and Expenditure Surveys,' Policy and Research Section, AKRSP Core Office, Gilgit, Northern Areas, Pakistan.

CRPRID (Centre for Research on Poverty Reduction and Income Distribution), 2003, *Pakistan Human Condition Report 2003*, Islamabad: CRPRID.

Government of Pakistan, 2003, 'Pakistan Poverty Reduction Strategy Paper. Accelerating Economic Growth and Reducing Poverty: The Road Ahead,' Islamabad.

Khan, M.H., 2002, 'Rural Support Programmes in Pakistan: Methods for Assessment of Cost and Impact,' Rural Support Programmes Network, Islamabad.

Malik, A. and M. Piracha, 2003, 'Poverty Trends and Issues in Northern Pakistan,' Paper presented at Chronic Poverty Conference, University of Manchester, UK.

Parvez, S. and S.F. Rasmussen, 2004, 'Sustaining Mountain Economies: Poverty Reduction and Livelihood Opportunities,' M.F. Price, L. Jansky, and A. Iatsenia (eds), *Key Issues for Mountain Areas*, Tokyo: United Nations University Press.

UNDP (United Nations Development Programme), 1991, *Human Development Report 1991*, New York: Oxford University Press.

_____, 1998, 'Interim Evaluation of the National Rural Support Program,' Islamabad.

_____, 2003, *Pakistan National Human Development Report 2003*, Islamabad: UNDP.

Wood, G. and A. Malik, 2005, 'Sustaining Livelihoods and Overcoming Insecurity,' G. Wood (ed), *Valleys in Transition: Twenty Years of AKRSP's Experience in Northern Pakistan*, Karachi, Pakistan: Oxford University Press.

World Bank, 1990, 'The Aga Khan Rural Support Program in Pakistan: A Second Interim Evaluation,' Operations Evaluation Department, World Bank, Washington, DC.

_____, 2002, 'The Aga Khan Rural Support Program. The Next Ascent: A Fourth Evaluation,' Operations Evaluation Department, World Bank, Washington, DC.

Notes

1 Created as a private, non-profit foundation under Swiss law, the Aga Khan Foundation has branches and independent affiliates in 15 countries, primarily in Asia and East Africa.

2 The Government of Pakistan refers to this territory as the Federally Administered Northern Areas. These five districts are part of the territory that is disputed by Pakistan and India, though they are separate from the Pakistani-overseen Azad Jammu and Kashmir. The Northern Areas has a special status and is not governed by the constitution of Pakistan.

3 The poverty gap is the proportion by which the average income of the poor falls below the poverty line. The poverty gap index is calculated by multiplying the poverty gap figure by the overall incidence of poverty in the population to show the relation of income shortfall of the poor with the overall incidence of poverty. The severity of poverty builds on the poverty gap index by factoring in the unequal distribution of incomes within the poor population.

4 Figures on infant mortality are from unpublished reports of the Aga Khan Health Service, which did a baseline survey in 1996 and then established an information system to report progress on an annual basis. The literacy figures are from AKRSP (2000).

6

Afghanistan

Integrating Community-Driven Development with Governance Reform

Abi Masefield

A quarter century of war and natural disasters has left Afghanistan one of the poorest countries in the world, with disastrous economic and social indicators. For the first time in more than two decades, however, the people of Afghanistan have a chance to build a peaceful, prosperous society. One of the central pillars of this rebuilding strategy is the National Development Framework, adopted in early 2002 by the transitional government that came to power after the Taliban's fall. Two key components of this framework are the National Emergency Employment Programme and the National Solidarity Programme. While both programmes are designed to provide immediate assistance in a post-conflict environment, their participatory structures are helping to lay the foundation for local-level democracy.

The National Solidarity Programme (NSP) supports small-scale reconstruction and development projects in communities across Afghanistan. Its uniqueness lies in the fact that the communities themselves make decisions and control resources throughout the project cycle, beginning with identification of projects to be funded. Towards this end, NSP works through community development councils (CDCs) elected at the village level. By August 2005, only two years into operation, 10,000 CDCs had been established in all 34 provinces of the country, and were being managed by 278,000 elected representatives. Working with the CDCs, NSP had supplied safe drinking water to 2,000 communities and has connected another 2,000 to district centres with rural access roads.

The National Emergency Employment Programme (NEEP) provides a safety net to unemployed Afghans.[1] It does so by focusing on labour-based infrastructure projects, especially roads and irrigation systems, with the twin purpose of building new infrastructure in the ravaged country and providing cash-for-work opportunities to local people on these projects. By the end of 2005, NEEP had generated an estimated 11.2 million labour-days, benefiting some 375,000 households. Through the programme, Afghan workers have built or rehabilitated about 6,000 kilometres of access roads, 11,000 metres of bridges and culverts, and 187 irrigation schemes.[2]

The national budget provides $1.3 billion to these programmes over the next seven years, affirming the political commitment of the transitional government to these programmes. How are these two flagship programmes contributing to Afghanistan's reconstruction? And what factors will underpin their scaling up and increased impact? This chapter attempts to answer these questions while suggesting how community-managed projects and cash-for-work programmes can be used for reconstruction and development in post-conflict environments.

THE NATIONAL DEVELOPMENT FRAMEWORK

War, autocratic rule, and natural disasters spanning the last 25 years have left Afghanistan one of the poorest countries in the world. By 2001 over 25 per cent of the population was displaced within the region, and more than 3 million refugees returned to the country between 2002 and 2004 (UNHCR 2005). During this period Afghanistan had social indicators ranking at or near the bottom among developing countries. According to the United Nations Development Programme, Afghanistan in 2003 had one of the lowest adult literacy rates in the world, at just under 29 per cent. Seven in 10 girls were not attending school. Life expectancy was a mere 44.5 years, at least 20 years lower than in any neighbouring country (UNDP 2004).

The three years following September 11, 2001 saw seismic shifts in the political landscape of Afghanistan. The quick fall of the Taliban government was followed by the Bonn Agreement establishing an interim government in December 2001.[3] In January 2002 the international community pledged $4.5 billion in assistance for Afghanistan at the Tokyo Conference. At the conference, Hamid Karzai, then chairman of the Afghanistan Interim Authority, outlined an ambitious initiative to enhance democracy, generate employment, and rebuild productive infrastructure.

Given the context of political transition and continued insecurity, there was little clarity or agreement regarding development priorities. The de facto economy in post-Taliban Afghanistan was, and remains, highly dependent on cultivation of the opium poppy. Opium contributes an estimated 60 per cent of the country's gross domestic product, and Afghanistan accounts for some 87 per cent of world opium production. Nevertheless, in the National Development Framework adopted by the transitional government in early 2002, the state is seen as the enabler of development to be driven primarily by the private sector. Community development was presented as the centrepiece of the development strategy for Afghanistan.

It was clear that Afghans' acceptance of the transitional administration would depend in no small measure on its ability to deliver long-awaited assistance throughout the country. Programmes were needed that could guarantee immediate and tangible benefits to the Afghan people. At the same time, cross-country experience, particularly in post-conflict contexts, suggested that while it may appear attractive to bypass dysfunctional institutions in the short term so as to meet urgent needs, this may simply postpone the development of well-functioning and accountable institutions. Moreover, it was known that projects planned and managed by communities typically show higher rates of return than those planned and managed by government agencies.

In dialogue with international development partners, the transitional government recognized the need to strike a balance, ensuring the prompt provision of essential services to the population while at the same time building sustainable institutions of public administration and finance and supporting the emergence of a vibrant private sector. At the heart of Afghanistan's National Development Framework was the government's commitment to ensure that Afghans themselves are in the driver's seat for development. Given the transitional situation, the government was kept at the centre of the framework, with the budget as the central vehicle for public expenditure management (AIA 2002). A series of National Priority Programmes (NPPs) were launched with the intention of strengthening the budget process and building ownership and capacity. NPPs were to be managed as programmes, as opposed to fragmented projects (TISA 2004a). They were to incorporate oversight from the central government through specific ministries and involve different stakeholders including United Nations agencies, the private sector, and non-governmental organizations (NGOs).

By the end of Islamic year 1382 (March 2004), the government had launched eight NPPs (Table 6.1). These accounted for a major share of the increase in development expenditures from 1382 to 1383 (March 2003 to March 2005).[4]

TABLE 6.1 Initial Round of National Priority Programmes Launched by the Government of Afghanistan

(millions of US dollars)

	Core			External		
	1382 (2003–04)	1383 (2004–05)	1384 (2005–06)	1382 (2003–04)	1383 (2004–05)	1384 (2005–06)
National Transport Programme	28.3	173.3	250.1	423.9	627.5	263.4
Education and Vocational Programme	5.8	23.8	31.5	104.1	253.2	304.0
Health and Nutrition Programme	10.2	22.3	29.7	143.2	267.1	199.9
Afghanistan Stabilization Programme	0.2	75.4	16.8	0	5.6	0
National Emergency Employment Programme	52.6	42.2	15.0	15.6	29.9	8.4
National Solidarity Programme	18.6	140.4	115.0	14.0	28.4	211.7
National Irrigation and Power Programme	7.0	25.5	51.6	15.4	70.3	128.4
Feasibility Studies Facility	0	30.0	24.3	0	0	0

Source: Based on author's analysis of data drawn from the National Development Budget and World Bank 2005.

Note: 'Core' refers to domestic revenue plus international assistance managed directly by the government (through the Treasury). 'External' refers to the majority of international assistance, which is programmed outside the Treasury. Figures for 1382 are for expenditure, while those for 1383 reflect resources anticipated in the budget.

The National Solidarity Programme and the National Emergency Employment Programme were born as twin initiatives in late 2002 and early 2003, with start-up funding from the World Bank. They were designed to put two commitments at the core of Afghanistan's agenda for reconstruction: (a) accelerated support for community mobilization and local governance through transparent collective action, and (b) the immediate generation of employment through infrastructure projects directly contracted by the government. Such a strategy, Karzai told the Tokyo Conference, 'would allow communities to manage their own resources [and] would allow legitimate leaders to emerge and deal with issues facing their communities ... forming a basis for consultative democracy in the future' (Karzai 2002).

The National Solidarity Programme

NSP was launched in April 2003 to support small-scale reconstruction and development activities identified by communities across the country. While building on lessons learned through international experience with similar models, it introduced a new development paradigm hitherto unknown in war-torn Afghanistan. For the first time, rural communities would be empowered to make decisions and control resources during all stages of the project cycle. Nationwide coverage and the promotion of awareness through local media were recognized as crucial from the outset. In addition to the initial $22 million start-up grant, the World Bank's International Development Association (IDA) provided $95 million, and additional commitments from international partners raised another $65 million by 2004.

NSP sought to build grassroots confidence in the new central administration by establishing a national mechanism for recurrent transfer of block grants to all villages in the country. The government's target was to have NSP cover the country's estimated 20,000 rural villages over a four-year period. NSP has four key elements:

- *System of direct block grant transfers.* Block grants support rehabilitation or development activities planned and implemented by community development councils, which are elected at the village level. NSP-supported projects include access roads, school and clinic construction, micro-irrigation schemes, and so on. They are implemented by communities and/or by local private contractors.

- *Facilitation.* NGOs serving as 'facilitating partners' help villages elect CDCs, reach consensus on priorities and corresponding project activities, develop eligible proposals that comply with NSP appraisal criteria, and implement approved projects. In most cases separate CDCs have been established for women in order to promote the identification and articulation of gender interests.
- *Capacity building.* Steps are taken to enhance the competence of CDC members (both women and men) in financial management, procurement, technical skills, and transparency.
- *Institutional linkage.* Activities are undertaken to strengthen links between community-based institutions and public administration and aid agencies to enhance access to increasingly responsive services and resources in the long term.

The National Emergency Employment Programme

Launched in 2003, NEEP provided a strategic framework for labour-based infrastructure projects. The programme built on earlier grants of $16.5 million and $25 million for emergency employment creation, and eventually included a total of $126 million.

Unemployment and underemployment were obviously major issues for Afghanistan, with rates reported as high as 50 per cent in Kabul and even higher outside the capital, particularly in the agricultural off-season. NEEP's first objective, therefore, was to provide a timely, efficient, significantly self-targeting social safety net based on cash for work (World Bank 2003b). NEEP activities are intended to reach a range of rural populations including the poor, vulnerable women, the disabled, destitute pastoralists, and agricultural labourers affected by the ban on opium poppy production.

The second objective was to establish effective mechanisms for building infrastructure assets, based on a private sector-led approach. NEEP created infrastructure in a wide range of sectors including roads, irrigation, urban development, natural resource management, soil conservation, and reforestation. Rural access infrastructure lends itself particularly well to large workfare programmes and is therefore one of the key areas for investment under NEEP. In addition to the short-term employment benefits, investment in rural access infrastructure can create assets that will have a lasting impact on poverty reduction and improve access of the rural poor to economic opportunities and basic services.

Translating Commitment into Action: Implementation Structures

Implementation of the two programmes has depended upon a significant commitment of resources, both by the national government and by donors. It has also entailed development of a management structure that coordinates the crucial connection of stakeholders, including ministries and provincial governments, with local communities.

Resource Commitment

The national development budget provides the clearest expression of the level of national commitment to NSP and NEEP. The overarching national Livelihood and Social Protection (LSP) programme of 1383, within which NSP and NEEP are housed, came to $352 million, with investments for NSP alone accounting for 62 per cent of the total. NSP and NEEP also constitute 58 per cent of the $2.272 billion projected for the LSP over the next seven years.

This represents a significant demonstration of commitment to NSP and NEEP, given the fiscal constraints faced by government, its narrow revenue base, and competing claims for finite resources. The government's stated preference is for joint co-financing, with funds from different donors channelled through the Treasury. However, in practice the Afghanistan Reconstruction Trust Fund (ARTF), administered by the World Bank's IDA, has been a key mechanism for co-financing of both NSP and NEEP.[5]

Oversight Bodies

Both NSP and NEEP cut across sectors and the mandates of specific line ministries. Accordingly, national policy bodies have been established for coordination, with technical oversight being provided by consultants contracted on a competitive basis.

NSP is coordinated by a single ministry, the Ministry for Rural Rehabilitation and Development (MRRD), through an oversight consultant. The MRRD underwent a fundamental restructuring to prepare it for taking responsibility for management of NSP. With community empowerment as a core vision, MRRD has moved away from its former role as a direct implementer of projects and now carries out the following functions: (a) policy and strategy formulation; (b) programme coordination; (c) programme and project execution, with implementation through contracting partners such as NGOs, UN agencies, and private sector entities; (d) monitoring and supervision; and (e) information dissemination.

In delivery of NSP to communities, the ministry is assisted by what it calls its 'facilitating partners'. These include agencies such as UN-Habitat as well as 22 NGOs, both Afghan and international. In each province, one or more facilitating partners maintain community facilitators and technical specialists. They pay special attention to recruitment and deployment of female field staff in order to include more women in decision-making and implementation of projects. The output of the facilitating partners is measured by agreed quantifiable indicators, including the number of eligible project proposals developed and the number of projects satisfactorily completed.

During implementation of NEEP, it was recognized that the development of high-quality and affordable engineering capacity within the public sector would not be realistically possible in the short term, nor would it be desirable in the longer term. The emphasis therefore was on strengthening the government's policy and regulatory role to support private firms that could be hired through competitive contracting. NEEP was thus carried out by the government in partnership with the private sector. A number of line ministries were involved from the government side, including the Ministry of Public Works, the Ministry of Rural Rehabilitation and Development, and the Ministry of Energy and Water.

For NEEP, a joint programme management unit (JPMU) was established to perform core oversight functions and provide a mechanism for coordination of technical assistance. It reports to an inter-ministerial board. Technical assistance to the JPMU is provided by international agencies (the United Nations Office for Project Services and the International Labour Organization). However, the JPMU has not had the same level of responsibility or institutional authority as has the oversight consultant for NSP. The direct involvement of several ministries, the proliferation of multiple funding mechanisms under the NEEP umbrella (including food-for-work interventions), and the absence of a consolidated oversight mechanism have posed challenges to effective coordination.

Local Governance

The basic structure for local governance within NSP consists of village-level community development councils. To be eligible for support through NSP, communities are required to elect a CDC as a representative decision-making body. To begin the process, the facilitating NGO carries out sensitization in the community, attempting to reach consensus on such as questions as the village boundaries and whether women will have a separate CDC. Elections are then held by secret ballot on the basis of household clusters (groups of families), with each cluster electing one representative to the council.

The elected CDC, working with the NGO partner, oversees the preparation of a community development plan (CDP) for the preparation and implementation of individual projects. The CDC obtains endorsement through community meetings for decisions on development priorities, the final selection of project proposals, the size and composition of community contributions, the use of project funds, transparency arrangements, and the operation and maintenance of completed projects.

Within NEEP, the emphasis has been on strengthening a broader range of national and local institutions for management and delegation of development activities such as subprovincial planning, contracting, targeting for social protection, and supervisory and evaluation activities.

Coordination and Convergence

NSP faces competing demands. On the one hand, its long-term aim is to strengthen local governance, transparency, accountability, and people's participation in development processes. On the other hand, the pressure to establish credibility has resulted in the need to accelerate financial transfers for approved CDC plans. Therefore, the strategy for linking CDCs and local government is based on a phased approach, to ensure that linkages do not act as bottlenecks that impede efficient approval and financing of CDC plans.

Three strategic components link the CDCs with subnational administration and broader rural infrastructure investments (Table 6.2). In addition to NSP, other programmes such as the National Area-Based Development Programme, the Afghanistan Stabilisation Programme, and, increasingly, decentralized counternarcotics initiatives have been developed to strengthen subnational administration and improve service delivery.

TABLE 6.2 Strategy for Linking CDCs with Subnational Administration

CDCs strengthened to …	Short term	Long term
Demand improved services	CDPs provided by MRRD to line ministry district representatives to inform annual planning for budget CDPs provided to district administration for information purposes only	CDCs encouraged to collectively organize within a district so as to be more proactive in presenting specific demands to district administration and line ministry representatives
Leverage additional resources	District officials may harness CDPs to coordinate assistance and highlight priority needs for additional external resources	CDCs can determine whether to use their block grant allocations individually or as coordinating entities to leverage additional resources from district or provincial government Coordinating CDCs could leverage resources for possible large investments such as roads linking villages or towns
Monitor service delivery	No direct and formal monitoring arrangements in place, although facilitating partners may raise issues with district representatives	CDCs will be asked (by facilitating partners) to provide quarterly monitoring reports to district officials of the ministries of education and health

Preliminary Results and
Programme Adjustments

Stakeholder expectations for scaling up NSP and NEEP in the first year of the pilot initiatives were high. But there were unavoidable delays. These related to setting up procedures for rapid disbursement of funds, defining the decision-making roles of various players (government, World Bank, oversight consultant), and issuing contracts. Particularly important were the market constraints related to the high level of demand for technically qualified engineers.

Nevertheless, there is broad consensus among those involved that initial progress with both NSP and NEEP has been encouraging (Tables 6.3 and 6.4). For NSP, the recruitment of the oversight consultant in September 2003 was a significant step forward. By early 2004 oversight consultant offices had been established not only in Kabul but also in each of the 34 provinces nationwide, supported by subregional centres. Elections of Afghanistan's first CDCs began in August 2003; by the end of 2005, almost half the villages in the country had voted in CDC elections. Block grant disbursements started in December 2003. By March 2005, almost 8,000 village project proposals had been approved and had received their first payments.

TABLE 6.3   NSP Targets and Achievements

Performance indicator	Original target for year one (September 2003– August 2004)	Actual achievement (through March 2005)
Facilitating partners	23	23
Field staff deployed	3,000	2,995
Communities mobilized	5,000	8,268
CDCs elected	3,280	7,348
CDPs completed	3,280	7,127
Projects submitted	3,280	9,247
Projects approved	3,280	7,935
Projects completed	2,050 (50% of communities)	535
Block grant disbursements	$80.0 million	$82.2 million
Block grant commitments	$98.4 million	$128.0 million

Source: Ministry of Rural Rehabilitation and Development.

TABLE 6.4   NEEP Achievements

Performance indicator	Achievement (through March 2005)
Labour-days generated	Estimated 8–10 million
Direct beneficiaries (workers)	Estimated 250,000
Total number of (direct and indirect) beneficiaries	Estimated minimum 1.5 million household members
Total donor allocation	Approximately $140 million
Total disbursement	Approximately $80 million
Cost per labour-day	Approximately $10
Infrastructure completed	Approximately:
	6,000 km access roads
	3,000 road structures
	180 irrigation canal systems
	110 shelters
	230 water supply systems

Source: Ministry of Rural Rehabilitation and Development.

Note: First-year targets for NEEP are not clearly specified because multiple projects operate under the programme's umbrella framework.

NEEP, for its part, had directly benefited a quarter million workers by March 2005, with a broad impact on an estimated 1.5 million household members. Local people employed by the programme had built or rehabilitated approximately 6,000 kilometres of access roads, 180 irrigation canal systems, and 230 water supply systems, as well as smaller numbers of schools, clinics, shelters, and government buildings. NEEP activities have taken place in 308 districts in all 34 provinces.

Although the original vision for both NSP and NEEP has not changed fundamentally, the early experiences of scaling up have resulted in several programme modifications. They include, among others:

- *Change in eligibility of microfinance proposals under NSP.* It was originally thought that community grants could be used for self-help savings and credit schemes, but this was challenged on the basis of a critical assessment indicating that it would be preferable to avoid the creation of unsustainable new institutions within the framework of NSP.[6] Instead, individuals are expected to engage directly with existing microfinance providers where available (World Bank 2003a).

- *Change in block grant allocations for NSP.* Given the financial uncertainty facing the government, it was agreed at the end of 2003 to allocate grants based on an open entitlement *per family*, subject to different caps for villages depending on their size. One block grant therefore was allocated to each community at a rate of $200 per family, with an upper limit of $60,000 per community, to be used for one or more projects. It was supplemented by the community's own contribution of 10 per cent. It was decided that annual follow-up block grants would be allocated at a lower per-capita rate to be determined. In the first year of operation of NSP, the average block grant value was $30,000, based on an average community size of 150 families.

- *Shift in strategic orientation of NEEP.* A central purpose of NEEP was to serve as an emergency safety-net intervention by providing immediate targeted wage transfers for vulnerable groups. However, as the programme evolved, it was recognized in policy circles as an instrument for effective integration of certain social policy objectives. Government policies related to NEEP, for instance, are now focused increasingly on partnership with the private sector, on enhanced maintenance of pro-poor productive assets, on improved national systems for area targeting, and on effective labour legislation.

- *Rationalization of the use of cash and food resources.* The simultaneous use of both cash and food as labour payments in rural infrastructure projects has been a particular challenge to NEEP.[7] However, an evaluation of food aid programmes and food policy was carried out in 2004, and it is anticipated that the strategic utilization of food assistance will improve with the emergence of a more coherent framework.

IMPACT: SHORT-TERM GAINS, LONG-TERM ISSUES

It is too early for a full evaluation of the impact of NSP and NEEP, which are among the first priority public investment initiatives presented to the international community for financing in post-Taliban Afghanistan. The immediate and most tangible outcomes have been the transfer of cash to villages and households and the delivery of small- and medium-scale rural infrastructure. But these are best understood as instrumental to broader and longer-term governance outcomes. Therefore, the challenge for impact assessment is to go beyond immediate quantitative results such as the number of projects financed and the number of labour-days generated.

National Solidarity Programme

In mid-2004 the performance of 20 of the 23 facilitating partners (FPs) was assessed by an outside contractor, Altai Consulting.[8] The assessment revealed considerable variation in the approaches of the FPs, as well as some variation in the quality of implementation. While some FPs could be identified as leaders with strong outputs, others were found to be hampered by external constraints or internal weaknesses. Still others were identified as innovators, showing average performance but a strong and innovative social approach. Notwithstanding these differences, the evaluation concluded that all the facilitating partners had performed satisfactorily in terms of efficient use of resources.

In general, the assessment found that the programme was progressing well across the country. It drew attention to the ways in which, for the most part, communities in Afghanistan are embracing the CDC model as a means to launch a grassroots democratic process at the village level, with very few cases of rejection observed.

Resource efficiency

Given the high profile of NSP and the pressure to justify the use of scarce resources on contracts with oversight consultants and facilitating partners, MRRD has been acutely sensitive to cost efficiency issues.[9]

One possible model for evaluating efficiency crudely juxtaposes aggregate delivery costs (that is, the total value of contracts with oversight consultants and facilitating partners) against the value of block grants delivered. During the first year of programme implementation, the ratio between these two components was roughly 1:1—that is, it cost $1 to deliver every $1 of community block grants. For the second year of implementation the comparable ratio was around 26 per cent.

However, a more realistic model of efficiency recognizes that capacity building is one of the core objectives of NSP. It therefore disaggregates delivery costs into administrative and management costs, on the one hand, and the costs of facilitation, capacity building, and strengthening local governance structures, on the other. The latter can be considered as valuable as the block grants themselves in contributing to programme objectives.

Together, the costs of block grants and the portion of delivery costs dedicated to facilitation and capacity building accounted for some 72 per cent of expenditures during the first year of field implementation and 88 per cent during the second year.[10]

Effectiveness and outcomes

One of the programme's strengths has been the government's attention to defining clearly measurable core indicators for effectiveness as the contractual basis for FP involvement. These indicators include: (a) identification and selection of communities completed, (b) community mobilization process completed, (c) CDC elections undertaken and concluded, (d) community development planning resulting in finalization of a plan, (e) submission of CDC proposal to centre through FPs, (f) approval of projects by centre and release of funding, and (g) implementation of projects finalized.

The process of implementation has progressed somewhat more slowly than originally envisaged (Table 6.3). The most obvious bottlenecks have been, first, the shortage of technically qualified engineers and experts at the field level for most FPs, and second, the cumbersome financial management and procurement systems at various levels. The sense of a trade-off between ensuring the quality of social mobilization and the technical implementation of infrastructure has also emerged as central to the experience of the FPs, given time constraints, finite resource availability, and limited human resources.

Nonetheless, there have been gains. The Altai evaluation carried out in 2004 found that a majority of communities under NSP had voted to use their block grants to implement a succession of smaller projects. The consultants note, 'The whole notion that the Afghan Government is actually helping rural communities is new and surprising for villagers' (Altai Consulting 2004). This substantially reinforces the governance objective of the programme, despite its delayed disbursement.

Another detailed qualitative study of the CDC election process by the Afghanistan Research and Evaluation Unit (AREU) confirms that there has already been an impact in terms of a participatory approach to local development (Boesen 2004). The AREU study reports that at one level, 'the NSP appears to go against many customs, traditions and power relations in Afghan society and history.' In this sense, the programme can be seen as an attempt to introduce democracy 'from above'. But the rationale for the CDCs is also resonating with the social identity and traditional resilience of village communities across Afghanistan. The AREU study provides several important insights into local perspectives on the project to introduce grassroots democracy.

First, regarding elections for CDCs, the high levels of voter participation among both men and women and the positive descriptions of the voting experience by community members suggest that the system of secret ballot election has been well received by Afghans. Interviews indicated that there is a generally high level of trust in the honesty and fairness of the election arrangements and in the agencies responsible for managing the process, although men tended to have more information regarding the election process than women. There were some reports of attempted interference by landlords, commanders, or mullahs.

Second, all stakeholders recognize that female participation in CDC elections represents a significant challenge to existing values and norms regarding gender relations. In many communities there was evidence that gradual shifts in women's roles are under way in response both to facilitation and to the impact of war and displacement. However, many communities displayed signs of anxiety regarding externally imposed requirements for female participation in the elections, and offered only symbolic compliance. Women voted, but they were often obliged to obtain permission from male relatives and to follow male lead in casting their votes. The approach taken by the facilitating partner was found to be crucial in determining how effectively such fears of threats to conservative norms were addressed.

In general, social inclusion, and women's participation in particular, have exceeded the expectations of government, donors, and FPs. NSP has functioned effectively to promote opportunities for gender inclusion even in areas considered to be culturally conservative. Nevertheless, in many cases the elected CDC representatives are also the traditional male village leaders. The substantive involvement of women in local decision-making remains limited (Box 6.1). For example, the creation of women-only CDCs alongside male CDCs, while a crucial innovation and necessary first step to facilitate the involvement of women, has often resulted in the de facto exclusion of women's priorities in the final submission of project proposals.

Box 6.1 NSP and the Gender Challenge

Gender issues have been central to the development agenda in Afghanistan, shared by national and international stakeholders alike in the post-Taliban era. Increasingly, Afghan women appear to be emerging as a force in their own right. The National Solidarity Programme, with the creation of community development councils,

(Contd)

Box 6.1 (Contd)

has proved instrumental in facilitating the increased presence and visibility of women.

At the same time, it is important to be realistic about the scale of the gender challenge that lies ahead for Afghan women. Emerging evidence suggests that in some ways the new CDC bodies continue to face problems similar to those of traditional institutions, even though they explicitly seek to promote greater inclusion of women in both their elections and their membership. In a recent study of 30 sample communities, only three women were found to be participating as full members of a joint male–female CDC (Wakefield and Bauer 2005). The study notes that 'in other communities, even if women were officially elected to the CDC, they were not permitted to attend mixed gender meetings and discussions ... in these instances a separate "women's shura" was sometimes formed, though communication between the women's shura and the male-led CDC was often uncoordinated or nonexistent.'

Continuing facilitation of gender awareness and services for enhanced empowerment is clearly required. At the same time, policy makers will need to recognize that a participatory approach cannot provide a fast track to progress in tackling deep-rooted gender inequities. In particular, although the physical presence of women in local-level institutions is an important first step, indicators based on this do not present a full or true picture with regard to the achievement of gender objectives.

Third, a particularly positive indicator is the finding that in many districts CDCs were regarded as legitimate 'national' institutions of local governance. Their credibility thus appears to go beyond the immediate requirements of NSP. Preliminary analysis suggests a degree of generational shift, as the CDC representatives appeared to be generally younger and better educated than the membership of the existing *shuras* (unelected village authorities). It was also true, however, that the CDC election process often reproduced existing authority structures and thus served to reinforce established power relations.

Fourth, the process of generating community development plans highlighted the priority that both women and men placed on employment and income generation. However, such activities for women in particular were narrowly restricted, often confined to home-based crafts such as sewing and carpet weaving. Education and training were also identified as key development priorities for girls, boys, and adults.

Finally, security was a central issue affecting implementation of NSP. In the run-up to the presidential election of 2004, a general downturn in security across much of Afghanistan proved a major challenge. In some areas local commanders sought to influence villagers' decision making, and fears of intimidation led to reluctance to participate in NSP. At times security concerns also negatively influenced the performance of the FPs.

Central to NSP are concerns about the long-term strategic direction of the programme and its outcomes. Enhanced social inclusion and empowerment of communities through village-based institutions cannot take place in a vacuum. It will depend in large part on improved linkages with other development projects and local tiers of public administration, as was done in a pilot project for rehabilitation of schools. It is also recognized that there is a continuing need to strengthen CDC capacities for planning and implementation and that facilitating partners will have to continue their support and capacity building over a much longer period than originally envisaged. This will have significant implications for programme management costs.

National Emergency Employment Programme

A well-designed and well-executed workfare programme can have multiple benefits.[11] The most obvious one is the direct transfer of benefits in cash or in kind to participating households. Accordingly, the direct transfer impact has predominated in reporting on NEEP.

Also significant, though, are the wider impacts on local labour markets. These may come through the programme's effects on overall wage and employment levels, through the economic benefits of assets created, and through the 'consumption smoothing' or insurance function of short-term employment. The relative significance of these kinds of impacts has not always been clear for NEEP. There have been few systematic attempts to monitor employment rates in Afghanistan; employment is strongly seasonal, and the high incidence of internal and cross-border migration complicates the picture. And given the extent to which employment generated by poppy cultivation dwarfs that created by NEEP, labour market dynamics are difficult to attribute to the programme's impact. Nonetheless, based on international experience with cash-for-work schemes, it can be assumed that a narrow focus on transfers underestimates the aggregate impact of the programme.

Resource efficiency

Monitoring resource efficiency has proved more challenging for NEEP than for NSP. This is in part because of the dual objectives of NEEP, which was initially designed both as a social safety net for the poorest people and as a way to provide productive rural infrastructure. It also reflects the absence of centralized management. Since 2002, various labour-intensive cash-for-work and food-for-work infrastructure projects have been funded and implemented by various international development agencies and facilitating partners under the NEEP umbrella. Original measures of results focused primarily on the number of labour-days generated with available resources and the cost per person-day of employment generated. Initial indications based on a multi-stakeholder review led by government in early 2005 suggested that the average cost per labour-day was relatively high, and that the average labour cost as a share of total cost was relatively low when compared to international experience.

Given the objectives of NEEP, greater attention should be paid to the costs and efficiency associated with the infrastructure created. These nontransfer benefits of workfare programmes may exceed direct transfer benefits. A significant share of the road works executed in the pilot stage consist of spot improvements such as pothole filling, drain repairs, surface levelling, and so on. These are highly labour-intensive, low-cost, and effective, but such repairs may last only 6–12 months and are likely to require recurrent expenditures. Improved documentation of costs and efficiency is important to sustain the case for these investments.

Effectiveness and outcomes

The core indicators for NEEP reflect its dual objectives of providing a social safety net and rural infrastructure. Available data suggest that since the programme was launched, employment opportunities and wage rates have risen significantly in many parts of the country. But it is highly unlikely that this is primarily due to the impact of NEEP, as opium poppy cultivation through the informal economy is believed to generate much more employment than any development programme.

It is estimated that NEEP has generated large direct transfer benefits for approximately 10 per cent of all rural households in Afghanistan. While the majority of the programme's beneficiaries are poor or highly vulnerable to poverty, NEEP does not seem to have been effective in targeting the extreme poor and some of the most disadvantaged groups. In this sense it may be viewed as somewhat disappointing as a safety-net mechanism, although expectations of its effectiveness in this regard were perhaps unrealistic (World Bank 2005). Low institutional capacity, nascent local governance structures, and poor availability of data severely constrain the effectiveness of targeting systems at present. Little is known about the indirect impact of NEEP transfers on the most vulnerable households through indirect access to benefits. However, it has become increasingly apparent that workfare programmes, by their structure, tend to exclude certain groups that are disproportionately poor, including female-headed households, disabled people, the elderly, communities in remote areas, and nomadic communities.

NEEP was launched shortly before the return of millions of refugees and internally displaced people, when the conflict-ravaged nation was suffering the devastating effects of an extended drought. In this context, short-term transfers, accompanied by the generation of millions of labour-days, were an appropriate palliative mechanism to meet immediate needs.

However, while NEEP's original focus and rationale remain historically valid, the programme also requires adjustment to take into account long-term goals of addressing rural poverty and vulnerability and strengthening livelihood risk management strategies. As an employment-based safety net, NEEP is not in itself adequate to address the root causes of widespread chronic poverty and entrenched vulnerability. While the programme will continue to be useful if appropriately targeted to address seasonal and geographically specific shocks, better planning is needed to balance its two objectives of social protection and rural infrastructure investment. Such planning needs to take account of the proper balance in duration, seasonality, wage rate, sectoral prioritization, structural exclusion, sustainability, and cost.

Driving Factors

In the complex environment of post-war Afghanistan, scaling up both NSP and NEEP to the level of nationwide programmes has presented a stiff challenge. That it has been possible at all reflects the convergence of four key factors: a high level of political commitment, continuing institutional innovation, learning and experimentation, and support from external catalysts.

Political Commitment

Both NSP and NEEP have enjoyed an exceptionally high level of political commitment from the government and its key international partners. The government recently issued a seven-year investment plan that includes the $1.3 billion required for the two programmes. This reflects, in part, the strategic role of these programmes that goes beyond stand-alone interventions for service delivery.

So far, the political commitment to NSP and NEEP has resulted in adequate financial support for these programmes, despite the narrow revenue base of the government.[12] Sustaining existing levels of support from both the government and international partners through multiyear budget commitments will be critical in order to avoid undermining government credibility through resource shortfalls in the future.

One indicator of continuing government commitment has been the involvement of senior government officials in weekly meetings with representatives of the oversight consultant and the World Bank. Government officials also participate actively in monthly meetings of the facilitating partners. At the subnational level, securing the political commitment of resource-poor provincial administrations has been crucial. However, governance of NSP could be further strengthened by activation of the steering committee that was originally envisaged, with representation from multiple ministries and donors.

Institutional Innovation

In 2002 the public administration of Afghanistan was extremely weak, the result of more than two decades of conflict, an exodus of trained personnel, low pay, and lack of exposure to new approaches.

Striking an appropriate balance between the delivery and capacity-building imperatives of NSP and NEEP has not been easy, although the requirement to strengthen capabilities within government agencies has been of paramount importance. Nevertheless, careful investment in the institutional architecture of the two programmes in the first year appears to have paid off. In particular, contracts with the oversight consultant and facilitating partners have resulted in the establishment of effective management incentives among key stakeholders. Considerable progress has been made with the establishment of core capacities for contract management and for maintaining fiduciary standards through externally recruited advisers. A key task of the oversight consultant is managing the disbursement of block grant funds, which are the largest component of costs under NSP.

The National Development Framework stressed the need for the state to shift its primary role from that of provider and employer to that of enabler of the private sector. NSP and NEEP were conceived as pioneers in this shift. Nevertheless, their development has also had to respond to the requirement to strengthen central institutions of the state after an almost total collapse of public institutions. NSP and NEEP have been harnessed as vehicles for driving long-term institutional reconstruction within the state, providing capacity-building support to provincial and district governments. This support focuses on planning, monitoring, and coordination roles rather than on implementation.

The two programmes have also had to confront the weaknesses and capacity limitations of the commercial private sector and civil society, building in various checks against risks to effective management. These risks include elite capture of benefits, which has been minimized by external facilitation of CDC elections through secret ballot. They also include corruption and delays in disbursement; these have been addressed through the development of financial disbursement procedures, although delays are still occasionally encountered. Notably, formal banking arrangements were established within the first two years in almost all provinces. Communities open bank accounts, and block grant funds are transferred to these accounts. Only in a few places such as Badakshan, where it takes several days on foot to reach the provincial capital, are informal financial networks called *hawalas* still being used.

Learning and Experimentation

Opportunities for learning and experimentation have been built into the design of both NSP and NEEP, with particular emphasis on eliciting feedback from the communities themselves and on the difficult but essential area of empowering women.

Given the diversity of reconstruction and development needs across regions and among socioeconomic groups, flexibility is the key for both NSP and NEEP. The intent has been to harness people's own knowledge and ability to identify and address their priorities for reconstruction and development through a participatory planning process. Through the process of scaling up, it has also become clear that communities need enough time for planning to ensure full understanding and ownership of the process, although this can be speeded up with good facilitation. It is also evident that community contributions towards capital costs in the form of labour or reduced daily wage rates can be supplemented with other forms of contributions (such as cash) from more affluent families.

Monthly meetings of the 22 facilitating partners, both independently and with the participation of senior government representatives, ensure that constraints and challenges are systematically identified and explored. The future role of the oversight consultant will be to ensure that potential solutions are tested in an experimental manner and evaluation is incorporated in the decision-making process.

Equally important is the continued development of learning opportunities at the community level, and between communities and local government institutions. Such interaction can promote poverty reduction by increasing the responsiveness of public investments to the priorities of rural people and enabling the village-level information base to increase awareness of opportunities and entitlements.

It is still true, however, that the challenge of addressing issues of gender in particular is great. To date, despite the recent establishment of a gender advisory group, these issues have not been dealt with systematically at the national level. For the majority of government officials in Afghanistan, a gender approach is regarded as an illusive theoretical import with little contextual relevance.

International experience shows that where programmes can apply a gender-sensitive approach, the sustainability of investments will be enhanced in the long run. Feedback from NSP facilitating partners and recent monitoring missions have drawn attention to the need to invest more in strengthening female trainers and facilitators as a means of reaching poor women.

External Catalysts

Finally, the model for addressing the enormous challenge of Afghanistan's reconstruction agenda has benefited both from aid received from the international community and from the experience in other post-conflict situations in recent years. World Bank experience in implementing a community-driven approach in post-conflict contexts has been particularly influential. Based on these experiences, planning for NSP and NEEP emphasized the importance of:

- rapid scaling up and adaptability of modular design;
- initial investments in transparent and participatory mechanisms and regulatory frameworks;
- open menus enhancing responsiveness to local priorities;
- opportunities for high-quality technical support and training for communities by private sector and NGO providers; and

- opportunities for strategic linkages between community projects and district/provincial administration.

LESSONS LEARNED

NSP and NEEP were launched as pilot initiatives to provide immediate and tangible benefits to poor and vulnerable Afghans across the country in the fragile post-war period. As nationwide initiatives, both programmes have provided complementary mechanisms through which tiers of smaller projects can be implemented according to the principles of equitable resource allocation, equality, and efficiency. The programmes have successfully brought into being a multilateral coalition of international partners who finance and monitor jointly to avoid the creation of parallel implementation systems.

Guiding the reconstruction process in this way, NSP and NEEP have confirmed the new government's role as the driver of reform. Community-driven development has emerged as a centrepiece of the national development strategy that is taking shape. Together the programmes have provided an essential focus for key stakeholders at all levels, building consensus and generating, through extensive consultation, a clear vision for policy development and institutional reform. Experience with scaling up these programmes therefore suggests three key lessons.

Lesson one: Pilot programmes can play a key role in building experience, confidence, and consensus (both technical and political) regarding appropriate policy directions.

The Government of Afghanistan has recognized that tension exists between the desire to promote national ownership of public administration and the political imperative to accelerate delivery and meet ambitious targets for disbursement. In this context, it has been important to keep programme designs as simple as possible. Both NSP and NEEP, as pilots, have provided important lessons in how to balance these requirements. Government policy makers feel increasingly confident that they are in touch with the priorities of ordinary Afghans.

In both programmes, the communities themselves have emphasized their need for private sector-driven employment of sufficient duration to have meaningful impact on their lives. They have challenged early assumptions within NEEP that the poor would be most interested in short-term gains, and they are increasingly pushing NSP to provide direct support to rural enterprises through vocational training, financial services, and so on. The rural poor prioritize development objectives because they know that only through improved infrastructure and broad rural development will their livelihood opportunities improve on a sustainable basis so that they can lift themselves out of poverty. As a result, there is increasing consensus among government and its key partners that the dual objectives of NEEP have at times proved incompatible.

There is no doubt that the cash injections through direct wage transfer have helped many poor households to smooth essential consumption, retain assets, and pursue broader livelihood strategies. However, with such a blunt targeting instrument, the extent to which the safety-net objective of NEEP can be prioritized in the future is questionable. The emerging consensus is that given the acute capacity constraints of key stakeholders, a focus on effective investments in high-quality and sustainable rural infrastructure, in the broader context of initiatives to strengthen local development, may be justified.

Experience with NSP has also made clear that reliance on organized community groups can exclude the most vulnerable and marginalized, such as female-headed households, the elderly, and disabled people. As a result, the government is exploring the feasibility of a national programme to directly target the chronic and extreme poor. Another possibility is that communities may decide to commit a proportion of the block grant allocation for direct targeting of vulnerable groups.

Lesson two: Transformative poverty reduction programmes can be harnessed as catalysts for broader national policy reform.

The experience with NSP and NEEP offers a model for creation of a framework for multilateral cooperation around a national strategy, with the budget as the central vehicle for public expenditure management. Through their status as priority national programmes, both NSP and NEEP have become catalysts for policy and institutional reform. They are addressing the challenge of public and private sector roles and demonstrating how scarce resources can be channelled for social transformation. For the first time, national policy dialogue is addressing head-on concepts of community ownership and governance, decentralization, and consultative dialogue. Despite the achievements of NSP and NEEP, however, the proliferation of parallel investments and implementation mechanisms outside the core government budget and priority programmes continues to slow the transition from a state-controlled to a private sector-led economy.

A critical question is whether these programmes have been able to create the conditions for sustainable and normative resource transfer systems. Such an achievement would ensure that poverty reduction activities were not forever dependent on government borrowing, unpredictable international assistance, and fragmented NGO interventions. In this context, scaling up should be taken to refer not only to the increased coverage of districts and villages, but to incorporation of the principles of community-driven development into national and subnational institutions and programmes for poverty reduction and the establishment of lasting pro-poor resource transfer mechanisms.[13]

Probably the most significant institutional innovation to have emerged to date in the Afghan context is the establishment of community development councils and the corresponding formation of social capital. The CDCs have provided a catalyst for learning among multiple stakeholders regarding how best to nurture the organic growth of democracy from below. It is too soon to predict the longevity of these institutions and the extent to which their emergence in every village of Afghanistan may affect the political economy of rural communities.

For NSP, the establishment of CDCs has been a central step towards strengthening the framework for local development. The challenge now is to ensure NEEP's evolution into an effective district investment fund capable of building the capacity of local governments to support NSP activities. Through NSP and NEEP, opportunities have been created to reform and strengthen local government structures in Afghanistan with respect to technical design, procurement, financial management, participatory processes, monitoring and evaluation, and communications. Both programmes help to instill principles of accountability and transparency in the flow of information down to the community level, as well as community-based accountability for project performance.

Both NSP and NEEP ultimately depend on the reconstruction of the private sector as a precondition for their effective and sustainable implementation. But this reconstruction is hampered by various problems, including the acute shortage of skilled construction workers; problems with the availability, quality, and cost of construction materials; and lack of engineering capacity, with a limited domestic pool of skilled engineers. Therefore, while NSP and NEEP are instrumental in promoting the private sector through their use of private contractors for key services, at the same time the current mismatch between demand and supply threatens to significantly constrain the drive to scale unless complementary initiatives are also scaled up.

Steps to catalyse the emergence of a capable private sector include appropriate public policy actions, business development services, and an effective legal framework to allow businesses to start up easily and function efficiently. These efforts will take time. The government is reviewing a number of laws, but the problems caused by a weak legal framework are compounded by administrative barriers that affect entry and raise transaction costs, thereby reducing the competitive strength of the private sector and increasing the scope for discretion and corruption.

Lesson three: The long-term agenda for successful scaling up and sustainability must be pursued at the same time as other reforms.

Strengthening capacities for domestic revenue mobilization remains a long-term priority. The vision underlying both NSP and NEEP suggests that Afghanistan's consolidated national budget will eventually need to provide provinces and communities with a predictable and transparent share of revenue. However, in the short term, efforts to empower both communities and local governments require an assured flow of funds from the international community through the central government.

NSP has helped to operationalize the concept of 'community.' But the empowerment associated with the start-up of the CDCs will only take root in an enabling and stabilizing political context. The establishment of effective and trusted local administration across the country is a precondition for peace and pro-poor growth. While CDCs can provide the basis for village-level governance, options for their integration into the broader structure of local administration will need to be carefully considered. With the parliamentary and provincial elections scheduled for September 2005, the agenda for devolution and decentralization is increasingly central to discussions about scaling up both NSP and NEEP.

Indeed, without a coherent and realistic national strategy for coordinated decentralization, the capacity of both programmes to achieve effective impact may be seriously undermined. International experience confirms that democratic decentralization and the development of local government capacity are pillars of community-driven development. In their absence, the performance of CDD projects is inhibited in a number of areas, including commitments, disbursements, and number of projects approved (Davis 2005). If local governments lack the legal and financial means to support CDD projects, these projects will be poorly integrated into government planning and will continue to depend on NGO support. Under such conditions, communities will be unable to develop voice or to influence local government decisions that affect them. Therefore, a guiding framework for fiscal decentralization that establishes the mechanisms, local capacities, and principles of accountability and transparency will be vital to the sustainability of both NSP and NEEP.

It is clear that local government needs to be further empowered before CDCs can realize their full potential. But the challenges facing local governance structures in Afghanistan today are immense. With few resources and uncertain mandates, they are expected to respond to new kinds of demands from communities that have suddenly found their voice. They must also address the extent of their own empowerment, including relations with line agencies, revenue control, legislative authority, and the ability to effectively tackle corruption. An appropriate legal framework is urgently required to facilitate the formation of accountable and responsive institutions of local governance.

Afghanistan stands at a political crossroads. Together, NSP and NEEP have signalled the government's new policy orientation, and with design features proven through international experience, are taking steps towards its realization. With successful and sustained scaling up, these programmes can contribute to Afghanistan's future by empowering Afghans to decide for themselves where their national interests and priorities lie.

References

AIA (Afghanistan Interim Authority), 2002, 'National Development Framework,' Kabul.

Altai Consulting, 2004, 'Ministry of Rural Rehabilitation and Development/National Solidarity Programme (NSP): Evaluation of the Facilitating Partners,' Kabul.

Boesen, I., 2004, 'From Subjects to Citizens: Local Participation in the NSP,' AREU Working Paper, Afghanistan Research and Evaluation Unit, Kabul.

Davis, D., 2005, 'Scaling-Up Action Research Projects: Lessons from Six Case Studies.' World Bank Institute Learning Programs. 'Community Empowerment and Social Inclusion', paper presented for the workshop on 'Community Driven Development: Training of Trainers', Tanzania, March 2004.

Karzai, H., 2002, 'A Vision for Afghanistan,' Statement of H.E. Hamid Karzai, Chairman of the Interim Administration of Afghanistan, to the Tokyo Conference, January 21.

Ravallion, M., 1991, 'Reaching the Rural Poor through Public Employment: Arguments, Evidence, and Lessons from South Asia,' *World Bank Research Observer* 6 (2): 153–75.

Subbarao, K., 2003, 'Systemic Shocks and Social Protection: Role and Effectiveness of Public Works Programs,' Social Protection Discussion Paper 302, World Bank, Washington, DC.

TISA (Transitional Islamic State of Afghanistan), 2004a, 'National Priority Programs (NPPs): An Overview,' http://www.af/npp/.

———, 2004b, 'Securing Afghanistan's Future: Accomplishments and the Strategic Path Forward,' Report prepared by a government/international agency steering committee and presented at donor conference in Berlin, March 31–April 1.

Wakefield, S. and B. Bauer, 2005, 'A Place at the Table: Afghan Women, Men and Decision-making Authority,' AREU Briefing Paper, Afghanistan Research and Evaluation Unit, Kabul.

World Bank, 2003a, 'Assessment of Microfinance, Livelihood Projects and Income Generating Schemes as an Option for Community Sub-Projects,' World Bank, Washington, DC.

———, 2003b, 'Technical Report on Social Protection Issues: The National Emergency Employment Program (NEEP) in Afghanistan,' World Bank, Washington, DC.

———, 2005, 'Afghanistan: Poverty, Vulnerability, and Social Protection: An Initial Assessment,' Sector Report 29694, World Bank, Washington, DC.

UNDP (United Nations Development Programme), 2004, *Afghanistan National Human Development Report 2004: Security with a Human Face: Challenges and Responsibilities*, Kabul: UNDP.

UNHCR (United Nations High Commissioner for Refugees), 2005, 'Kabul Operational Information Summary Report, January 2005,' UNHCR Office of the Chief of Mission, Kabul.

Notes

1 In 2005, NEEP was renamed the National Rural Access Programme.

2 For updated figures, see the website of the Ministry of Rural Rehabilitation and Development (http://www.mrrd.gov.af/prog/neep.htm).

3 The political transition resulted in adoption of a new constitution and then presidential elections in 2004. The nationwide election of local councils and parliamentary members is scheduled for September 2005.

4 The Government of Afghanistan uses the Islamic solar Hejra calendar. The fiscal year corresponds to the solar year and begins on March 21.

5 The ARTF is one of the main instruments available to the government of Afghanistan to finance key recurrent expenditures (salaries, capital expenditures, operations and maintenance of key government institutions), as well as urgent investments and reconstruction activities planned under the country's economic recovery programme. The ARTF can either finance free-standing projects or co-finance projects funded by IDA or other donors. IDA, as ARTF administrator, allows donors to express preferences for a priority programme or project that is included in the government's multiyear development budget and for which the government has requested ARTF funding.

6 A separate but complementary national programme, the Micro-Finance Support Facility of Afghanistan, was launched in 2003 as an autonomous apex institution.

7 At present, no grain market-based targeting mechanism has been introduced to rationalize the selection of areas for payment in food (most often imported wheat) rather than payment in cash. One proposal being considered involves the use of food-for-work payments or free distribution for social targeting objectives.

8 The evaluation (Altai Consulting 2004) involved assessment of the following parameters: (a) fulfilment of contractual guidelines, (b) awareness of NSP goals and processes, (c) management effectiveness and controls, (d) cost effectiveness, and (e) financial management and facilitation methodology/approach. The evaluation exercise was conducted in 25 provinces and involved 2,500 interviews and discussions with over 200 field staff of the facilitating partners, as well as representatives of the oversight consultant and the MRRD.

9 Total costs for NSP include block grants to communities, community support services delivered by facilitating partners, and overhead costs, including costs towards capacity building by the oversight consultant.

10 Figures from World Bank internal sources.

11 See Subbarao (2003) and Ravallion (1991) for useful international overviews.

12 The 'Securing Afghanistan's Future' report prepared in 2004 estimates that even by 2015 Afghanistan will only be generating sufficient revenue to cover the government's recurrent budget (TISA 2004b).

13 The core principles that make up the CDD framework include community empowerment, local government empowerment, decentralization, accountability/transparency, and learning by doing.

7

Microfinance in Bangladesh

Growth, Achievements, Lessons

Hassan Zaman

As of 2005, the microfinance industry in Bangladesh has been able to provide access to credit to over 16 million poor people, reaching more than 40 per cent of all households in the country.[1] The industry has reached this scale in just three decades, since its pioneering inception in the mid-1970s. There are approximately 1,200 microfinance institutions (MFIs) in Bangladesh, most of which are non-governmental organizations (CDF 2004).[2] The industry is dominated by four large MFIs that serve 80 per cent of all microfinance clients in the country. These four institutions combined have approximately $950 million in outstanding loans and $470 million in savings.

Access to microfinance has had a considerable impact on poverty reduction among clients. In addition to gains in income, participation in microcredit programmes is associated with better health outcomes, social gains for women, and greater school enrolment for the children of borrowers. Also, in a country marked by natural disasters and exogenous shocks that affect the poor, microfinance has almost halved consumption variability for borrowing households (Khandker 2003).

The successful scaling up of the microfinance industry in Bangladesh is the result of three key factors:

- *An enabling environment.* Favourable social conditions, macroeconomic stability, and light government regulation allowed the MFIs to expand.
- *Organizational innovations within MFIs.* These included decentralized structures, performance targets, and close supervision of staff.

- *Strategic use of subsidies.* Subsidies for capitalization of loans and capacity building were channelled directly to non-governmental organizations, and also through a highly professional, autonomous government organization.

The sheer scale of microfinance access in Bangladesh has generated considerable interest in how this growth took place. Two factors have recently enhanced this interest. First, microcredit's appeal in development circles stems from the 'win-win' idea that it can be an effective anti-poverty tool as well as one of the few interventions for which subsidies can be progressively reduced. This notion is somewhat simplistic, however, and debate continues as to whether there are trade-offs between these twin objectives or whether both can be achieved (Morduch 2000).

Second, numerous countries have attempted to replicate the success of Bangladesh's Grameen Bank, but for a variety of reasons (lack of funds, weak management capacity, and regulatory hassles, among others) several of these Grameen replications are struggling to achieve scale or are underperforming financially (Grameen Trust 2002).[3] These practical experiences have led development practitioners to ask which of the factors that contributed to scaling up microfinance in Bangladesh are unique to that country and which ones can be replicated.

This chapter draws primarily from the experiences of the four large MFIs: Grameen, BRAC, ASA, and Proshika. The chapter first describes the evolution of the microfinance industry over the past three decades in Bangladesh, and then examines the factors that contributed to its scaling up. The literature on impact assessment is reviewed to determine the extent to which microcredit reaches the poor in Bangladesh, the benefits the poor may have derived from this intervention, and the likely cost-effectiveness. The chapter concludes with a discussion of lessons from the Bangladesh experience.

Evolution of the Industry

The growth in access to credit by the poor in Bangladesh took place in several distinct phases over the last three decades. The origins of the current microcredit model can be traced to action research in the late 1970s, carried out by academics as well as by practitioners in organizations that were created to deal with the relief and rehabilitation needs of post-independence Bangladesh. During the 1980s a growing number of non-governmental organizations (NGOs) experimented with different modalities of delivering credit to the poor. The various models converged in the beginning of the 1990s to establish a fairly uniform 'Grameen model' of providing microcredit, which in turn sparked a sharp growth in access to microcredit during the decade. In recent years the standard Grameen model has undergone further refinements in order to cater to different niche markets.

The 1970s

Experimentation in providing credit to households considered 'unbankable' by the formal financial system began a few years after Bangladesh's independence war in 1971. The independence movement gave rise to a new generation of young activists who were keen on contributing to the reconstruction of their war-ravaged country. The new government and a myriad of aid agencies that arrived on the scene were unable to cope with the scale of destitution, so NGOs emerged to meet the challenges.

The early years of the NGO movement in Bangladesh focused on relief and rehabilitation, with an emphasis on community development. However, by the mid-1970s two of the NGOs that would subsequently expand, BRAC and Proshika, found that elite capture was a serious impediment to their development objectives.[4] As a result, they introduced the use of target groups in order to focus on the needs of the poor. Meanwhile, an ideological debate within both these organizations erupted between those who favoured 'economic tools' (credit, savings, etc.) to support poverty reduction and those who believed that social mobilization against existing injustices would suffice and that financial services were unnecessary.

Around the same time, a team of researchers at Chittagong University, led by Professor Muhammad Yunus, began an action research programme that provided loans to poor households in a few villages. Borrowers were mobilized in 'peer monitoring groups' composed of four or five individuals who were jointly responsible for one another's repayments. Several of these small peer groups were organized into a larger unit that would meet weekly with the primary purpose of repaying loan instalments. The process of trial and error included combining males and females in credit groups and then changing this to separate groups divided by gender. It also included forming occupational groups that were later dropped in favour of village-based groups.

The demand for loans grew rapidly, and Professor Yunus enlisted the support of the Bangladesh Bank and commercial banks to provide the Grameen Project—as it was then called—with resources. The success of this experimentation paved the way for the establishment of the Grameen Bank under a special ordinance in 1983.

The 1980s

In the early 1980s, several NGOs experimented with different ways of delivering credit. One important test was a comparison between lending to group projects and lending to individuals with peer monitoring. The broad lesson was that individual lending was more effective because problems with incentives and with 'free-riding' often affected lending to groups. Hence, by the late 1980s the predominant model became one of providing individual loans to a target group of poor households, with peer monitoring and strong follow-up by MFI staff.

The Association for Social Advancement (ASA) underwent such evolution. Its initial emphasis was on forming 'people's organizations' mobilized for social action against oppression, but it shifted to the target-group approach and then towards the provision of financial services in the late 1980s. Now ASA is the third-largest MFI in Bangladesh in terms of number of clients, and its unique low-cost credit delivery mechanism is being replicated in several countries. ASA keeps paperwork requirements to a minimum, has decentralized most decision-making to the field, and overall runs a very lean operation (Choudhury 2003).

The 1980s and early 1990s were also important in the development of management capacity within several of the large MFIs, which allowed them to expand their microcredit programmes. It is interesting that development of the know-how and confidence to implement large programmes arose, in some cases, from the experience of scaling up programmes not related to microcredit. For instance, in the case of BRAC, the first major experience with a nationwide programme came about when it implemented an oral rehydration programme to combat diarrhoeal disease. Thirteen million women were trained to use a simple but effective rehydration solution, and BRAC staff were paid according to how many of their trainees used and retained this knowledge.[5]

The Early to Mid-1990s

The early 1990s saw rapid expansion of an approach to microcredit that came to be known as the Grameen model (Ahmed 2004). This growth was driven largely by a franchising approach in which new branches replicated the procedures and norms that prevailed in existing branches. The product provided at the time was fairly narrow, essentially a standard microcredit package offered to all clients. It was considered easier to recruit new staff and train them quickly to provide a simple product during a phase when branches were opening at a rapid rate. Growth was aided by the high population density and relative ethnic, social, and cultural homogeneity in Bangladesh.

A notable shift during this expansion phase was towards greater emphasis on individual borrower accountability for loan repayment, with less reliance on peer monitoring. Staff follow-up of loans became more rigorous and professional with the use of computerized management information systems. Donor funds also helped to expand the revolving loan funds for MFIs during their expansion. This period also saw the emergence of Palli Karma-Sahayak Foundation (PKSF) as a wholesale financing institution.

A geographical mapping of microfinance in Bangladesh suggests that all districts now have microcredit services, though there are many small pockets with little or no coverage (such as Chittagong Hill Tracts). A closer look shows that there is somewhat greater coverage of poor households in the central and western districts. The southeast and pockets of the northeast are areas with room for expansion (PKSF 2003).

Mid-1990s Onward

Feedback from the field, academic research, and international experience all contributed to an increasing emphasis on providing diversified financial services to different groups of households from the mid-1990s onward. The benefit of a narrow focus on microcredit during the expansion phase was that it kept costs low and operations transparent and required relatively straightforward management oversight. However, it became clear that the standard Grameen model of providing microcredit with fixed repayment schedules, and with standard floors and ceilings on loan sizes, was not sufficient to meet the needs of the extremely poor or of households that wanted to graduate beyond microcredit.

Moreover, existing microcredit borrowers also required complementary financial and non-financial services. The standard practice for MFIs until the late 1990s was to collect compulsory weekly savings from their clients, holding the money as a de facto lump sum 'pension' that was returned when a client left the organization. Access to these deposits was otherwise limited, which curtailed a potentially important mechanism to smooth consumption.

Recognizing these limitations, an increasing number of MFIs in Bangladesh have introduced an open-access current account scheme in addition to the fixed-deposit scheme. Moreover, many MFIs have life insurance products under which outstanding microcredit debts are written off and other benefits are paid following the death of a borrower. Non-credit services can also take the form of input supply, skills training, and marketing support for microentrepreneurs.[6] A complementary package provided with microcredit can include underwriting education for the children of borrowers. Grameen Bank, for instance, has a scholarship programme for female secondary education and a student loan programme for tertiary education. Similarly, many MFIs have community health programmes or provide legal literacy training or information on accessing local resources.

Several NGOs have begun providing larger loans to 'graduate' microcredit borrowers and in some cases to households that are not part of the microcredit system but that want a microenterprise loan. These loans typically range from 20,000 taka (about $320) to 200,000 taka ($3,200). Innovative solutions are also emerging to address the problem of access to finance for the small-enterprise sector. For instance, BRAC established a separate financial institution, BRAC Bank, that focuses on lending to the 'smaller end' of the small-enterprise sector, with loans averaging 400,000 taka ($6,400).

Moreover, evaluation studies pointed out that extremely poor households were struggling to benefit from the standard microcredit model, even if they joined the programmes. There were several reasons for this. Minimum loan floors for a first loan sometimes exceeded the borrowers' perceived needs, and households with sharp seasonal fluctuations in income found it difficult to commit to fixed weekly loan repayments. Other members of peer-monitored groups sometimes were reluctant to guarantee loans for extremely poor households. Finally, many impoverished households were located in remote or depressed areas, with limited opportunities for successful microenterprise.

Approaches that have been developed to address these constraints include introducing more flexible repayment schedules, such as ASA's Flexible Loan Programme, and lowering first-loan floors so that amounts as small as 500 taka ($8) can be borrowed. A special Grameen programme offers zero-interest loans to beggars, and another NGO, the Resource Integration Centre, has a programme that specializes in offering loans to a specific vulnerable group, the elderly poor. Various programmes combine food aid with microcredit and training, such as BRAC's Income Generation for Vulnerable Groups Development programme. Finally, efforts are being made to target remote areas through, for instance, ASA's cost-effective minibranch system and the Integrated Development Foundation's work in the Chittagong Hill Tracts.

FACTORS CONTRIBUTING TO GROWTH

Several factors played significant roles in the expansion of access to microcredit in Bangladesh. They include a conducive social and public policy environment, strong organizational development and incentives for staff performance within MFIs, and the strategic use of subsidies.

An Enabling Environment for Microcredit

Aside from the Chittagong Hill Tracts area, Bangladesh is ethnically a relatively homogeneous country, with high population density and good communication networks. The contrast with Nepal in these respects is striking, and the difference in microcredit coverage between the two countries is partly due to these factors. It is also noteworthy that in Pakistan, Afghanistan, Egypt, and certain other predominantly Muslim countries, MFIs have found religious conservatism to be a factor that has depressed demand for microcredit. In Bangladesh, by contrast, even conservative religious forces have been largely tolerant of microfinance activities and of the greater economic empowerment and mobility of women associated with them.

The early experimentation with microfinance and the later scaling up of the industry in Bangladesh was also helped by an appropriate public policy environment. First, the macroeconomy has been soundly managed, by and large (World Bank 2003). The rate of inflation has been kept to single digits and economic growth over the past decade has averaged about 5 per cent per year, creating economic opportunities for investments financed by microcredit. Interest rates are market-determined, and while state banks have offered loan forgiveness schemes for rural credit, these have not affected discipline on microcredit repayment. With respect to public expenditure, the priority given to the expansion of the road network in the 1980s reduced the transaction costs of lending and contributed to the development of the rural non-farm sector where most microcredit-financed investments belong.

Second, the Government of Bangladesh has thus far maintained a relatively light touch in regulating and supervising the activities of the NGO sector. This has been critical in ensuring the operational flexibility required to scale up and adapt programmes rapidly. While this long relationship has not been free from tensions, the Government of Bangladesh has apparently been able to place the interests of the poor at the forefront in dealing with NGO issues. A less charitable view is that the scaling up of NGOs went largely unnoticed, and that once it took place the combined clout of large

NGOs and donors obliged the government to take a largely laissez-faire approach. Accusations that a handful of NGOs have involved themselves in party politics have lately strained the overall government–NGO relationship and have prompted the government to take a more active interest in strengthening oversight over NGOs.

Organizational Strength and Staff Incentives

The impressive leadership skills of the founders of the large MFIs were a key factor in the growth of the microfinance industry in Bangladesh. These skills included being able to recruit and motivate staff; decentralize authority; build management information systems, back-office functions, and internal controls; and manage relations with the outside world. Belief in the possibility of scaling up became part of staff culture, and mid-level managers had the confidence to expand the programmes within their more limited spheres of control. The 1980s and early 1990s were important in the development of management capacity within several of the large MFIs, at times based on the experience of scaling up programmes not related to microcredit. As noted above, BRAC's first major experience with managing a nationwide programme came about when it implemented an oral rehydration programme to combat diarrhoeal disease in the 1980s.

As the large MFIs now have tens of thousands of employees, they cannot rely solely on staff altruism to deliver microcredit and other services effectively. Managing such sprawling organizations has required the development of internal structures and processes that have inevitably led to greater bureaucracy. However, there are important differences between MFIs and public sector agencies in Bangladesh. One key element is the ability of NGOs to recruit staff quickly and dismiss them just as rapidly if they show poor performance. There is a high attrition rate for new staff within the first year of joining the large NGOs, as many cannot adjust to the work culture and/or do not perform well. In some cases, team incentives and competitive pressures are built in by rating the performance of branch offices.[7] Staff motivation is also enhanced by decentralizing significant amounts of responsibility to the lower tiers of the administrative structure. ASA is the best example of a lean credit-delivery structure, with high levels of decision-making authority given to field offices in areas ranging from loan sanctioning decisions to staff human resource issues.

Effective internal controls are also important in ensuring effective staff performance. First of all, the fact that financial transactions are carried out publicly, in the weekly meetings and in the branch offices, is a major check against any form of discretionary behaviour by fieldworkers (Jain and Moore 2003). The standardization of functions due to the relative simplicity of the 'no-frills' Grameen approach also makes it easier to monitor staff performance. The large MFIs have developed measures that include frequent rotation of staff within and between branches, regular field visits by senior management, a strong internal audit team, and annual external audits.

A fundamental aspect of the scaling up of Bangladesh's NGOs, and more specifically the microfinance movement, has been the ability to learn from experiences and adapt programmes accordingly. This learning process takes place both through informal feedback by field staff during regular interactions with management and through a formal monitoring and evaluation process.[8] The shift to more flexible financial services that took place in recent years was an adaptation made largely in response to client feedback and to analysis of the limitations of a uniform microcredit model.

Strategic Use of Subsidies

External resources played an important part in the experimentation process, in subsequent growth in outreach, and in the institutional strengthening of the microfinance industry. International NGOs were involved in financing the initial stages of the NGO-operated MFI industry in Bangladesh. The subsequent expansion and consolidation stage was funded largely by official bilateral agencies and later by multilateral agencies.[9]

A large part of these donor investments went to the capitalization of MFI loan funds, crucial to the rapid expansion that took place in the 1990s, as well as to strengthening institutional capacity through management information systems and human resource development. The setting up of aid harmonization systems also helped this process. Donor consortiums were established that negotiated and monitored assistance to large NGOs. For MFIs this has meant more predictable resource flows and more streamlined financial reporting arrangements. The late 1990s saw dependence on donor resources decline for the overall industry, from 34 per cent of the funds for onlending in 1997 to 13 per cent in 2003, with the current subsidies being channelled to small emerging MFIs (CDF 2004).

The autonomous government organization that channels funds for microfinance, the Palli Karma-Sahayak Foundation, was created in 1990. PKSF's current structure meets the key criteria for effective state provision of financial services (Yaron, McDonald, and Charitonenko 1998). These include having a fully autonomous management; exemption from civil service pay scales; and insulation, by a strong board, from pressures for politically motivated lending and recruitment. In 2004, PKSF funds constituted about a quarter of the funds for microcredit. While PKSF has lent funds to MFIs at lower than market rates, their rates have moved progressively closer to commercial terms, and also vary by the size of the borrowing institution.

There is growing experience with setting up apex institutions worldwide. Examples include the Pakistan Poverty Alleviation Fund (PPAF), the Rural Microfinance Development Centre (RMDC) in Nepal, the Fondo Fiduciario de Capital Social (FONCAP) in Argentina, the Local Initiatives Department (LID) in Bosnia-Herzegovina, and the Microfinance Investment Support Facility for Afghanistan (MISFA). One of the fundamental factors in determining the success or failure of an apex is the underlying retail capacity in a particular country. The overall strength of the MFIs in Bangladesh has been key to PKSF's success. An overestimation of the MFIs on the ground in terms of their capacity to absorb funds is likely to lead to failure of an apex body. However, if a realistic assessment of the underlying retail capacity is made, then apexes offer many benefits, such as the ability to screen MFIs on standard criteria and create a 'level playing field'.

In principle, instead of receiving subsidies through donor grants or through PKSF's concessional lending, MFIs could have raised interest rates to cover the costs of microcredit expansion. However, since the unit cost of lending declines with scale, it can be argued that donor grants or soft loans that effectively keep interest rates at long-run rates from the beginning of a programme can be a 'smart subsidy' to attract poor clients and generate the client volume necessary to achieve economies of scale (Morduch and Armendáriz de Aghion 2005). Such subsidies in the initial stages can therefore be justified on both equity and efficiency grounds. The key to a 'smart' subsidy is enforcing hard budget constraints within MFIs so that subsidies do not breed inefficiency and excessive costs. Donors and PKSF in particular have paid considerable attention to monitoring MFI costs and other specific financial performance benchmarks.

Financial analysis of a sample of MFIs of varying sizes that have accessed PKSF funds shows that most have either reached financial self-sufficiency or are well on their way to doing so (World Bank 2005). However, these ratios are for the mainstream microcredit programme, while the newer programmes that have been set up to cater to the needs of the poorest will require subsidies for considerably longer. The costs and benefits from these newer programmes will need to be compared with those of alternative programmes that reach the poorest in order to assess whether long-run subsidies can be justified.

The Impact of Microfinance in Bangladesh

The evidence on the impact of microcredit can be assessed from two interrelated angles. First, how successful are microcredit programmes in targeting the poor? And second, how do these programmes affect the welfare of different groups of individuals and households?

Targeting the Poor

A recent detailed exercise in mapping microcredit programmes found that although there is nationwide microfinance coverage, a significant number of very poor districts, particularly in the northwest, have relatively few MFIs operating (PKSF 2003).[10] Consequently, these areas have a lower number of borrowers compared to better-off parts of Bangladesh. In particular, the relatively prosperous central districts have a larger-than-average share of their population accessing microcredit. This discrepancy is not altogether surprising. Unlike a targeted safety net programme such as a public works scheme, microfinance depends for its effectiveness on local economic opportunities, so that the extent to which microcredit can be put to good use depends in part on the physical and economic endowment of the borrower's locality. Hence both the demand for and the supply of microcredit are lower in the poorer areas.

Decisions on where to locate microfinance programmes in Bangladesh were modelled by Gauri and Fruttero (2003), using 1995 and 2000 data on NGO programme presence from comparable community surveys. The authors found that the main factor affecting the setting up of a microfinance branch in a community was the presence or lack of competing microfinance programmes in that community. After controlling for competition, they found that the extent of poverty in the community was not a significant variable affecting this decision. However, the authors also show that microcredit programmes reached more poor communities in 2000 than in 1995.

Once an MFI decides to locate in a community, land ceilings, occupational criteria, and asset valuations are standard targeting tools used to identify the rural poor. In practice, the land criterion is the one most closely adhered to in the field. Various household surveys show that a large number of households with little or no land join these programmes (Zaman 1999; Morduch 1999; Khandker 2003). For instance, in Khandker's nationally representative sample, 60 per cent of the sampled microcredit members had less than 20 decimals of land, and 59 per cent of the landless households in the programme villages joined microcredit programmes. There are, however, specific groups such as beggars and the elderly poor who are systematically excluded (Hashemi 1997).

At the same time, several studies also show that 15–30 per cent of microcredit members are from non-target households measured in terms of land (Montgomery, Bhattacharya, and Hulme 1996; Zaman 1999; Morduch 1999). A socio-economic profile shows that these households are typically marginal farmers and can be considered part of the vulnerable non-poor group, prone to transient bouts of poverty. The bottom line is that the literature on targeting suggests that microfinance programmes are less prevalent in the poorest districts of Bangladesh, but that once they locate in an area they are reasonably successful at reaching the poor.

Impact on Welfare

The extent to which microcredit has contributed to reducing poverty in Bangladesh has been the subject of considerable controversy in the literature. For instance, data collected by the World Bank in 1992 have been used to show widely varying results, depending on the methodology chosen to assess impact. Using these data, Pitt and Khandker (1998) estimate that for every 100 taka lent to a woman, household consumption increases by 18 taka; interestingly, the figure is only 11 taka if the same amount is lent to a man.

Morduch (1999) argues that the selectivity bias corrections used by Pitt and Khandker are based on a number of questionable assumptions. Using a different method of controlling for selectivity bias, Morduch finds that microcredit does not have a significant impact on consumption levels and therefore does little to reduce income poverty.[11] However, he finds that consumption *variability* is 47 per cent lower for eligible Grameen households and 54 per cent lower for eligible BRAC households than for a control group. This consumption smoothing is driven by income smoothing, as evidenced by the significantly lower labour supply variability experienced by microcredit members compared to the control group.[12] The importance of this result cannot be over-emphasized, given the fact that seasonal deficits play a key part in the poverty process in Bangladesh. Essentially Morduch's results indicate that programme participants do not benefit in terms of greater consumption levels, but they participate because they benefit from risk reduction.

A repeat survey of the same households in Bangladesh in 1998–99, carried out by the World Bank, was used to create a panel data set. Using a difference-in-difference method to account for selectivity bias, Khandker

(2003) finds a more muted, though still significant, impact of microcredit. This analysis shows that for every 100 taka lent to a woman, household consumption increases by 8 taka, in contrast to the earlier estimate of 18 taka using the cross-sectional 1992 data. Somewhat surprisingly, the impact appears to be greater for households that started off extremely poor than for those that were only moderately poor. The proportion of extremely poor microcredit borrowing households declined by 18 percentage points over the seven years, while the proportion of moderately poor microcredit borrowing households fell by 8.5 percentage points during the same period. These results differ from earlier evidence that suggested that moderately poor borrowers benefit more than extremely poor borrowers because the poorest have a number of constraints (fewer income sources, worse health and education) that prevent them from investing loans in high-return activities.

There has been limited work on the aggregate poverty reduction impact of microcredit at the local or national levels in Bangladesh. Khandker (2003) uses the panel data discussed above to suggest that there is some positive externality due to microcredit programmes but that overall, the spillover benefits are somewhat limited. For instance, the net contribution of microcredit to reducing poverty for non-participants is a small decline of 1.1 percentage points between 1991/92 and 1998/99, compared to a decline of 8.5 percentage points for borrowers in the same village. The impact on extreme poverty is estimated to be somewhat greater, 4.8 percentage points for non-borrowers and 18.2 percentage points for borrowers over this seven-year period.

The impact of microcredit on non-income indicators in Bangladesh is also broadly positive, though not unambiguously so. Sceptics point to evidence that the impact of Grameen Bank credit on contraceptive use and fertility has been negligible (Pitt et al. 1999). There is also a view that microcredit does little to change gender inequities because of limited female control over loans (Goetz and Sen Gupta 1996; Montgomery, Bhattacharya, and Hulme 1996). On the other hand, Pitt, Khandker, and Cartwright (2003), using the 1998 World Bank data, contend that access to microcredit empowers females to discuss family planning issues with their spouses. The same paper argues that microcredit leads to women taking a greater role in household decision-making, having greater access to financial, economic, and social resources, and enjoying greater mobility. These findings are in line with other work on microcredit and female empowerment in Bangladesh (Amin and Pebley 1994; Hashemi, Schuler, and Riley 1996).

On the whole, the evidence presented by those who argue that microcredit helps to empower women appears more convincing than the arguments of the sceptics, for at least three reasons. First, the underlying thread of the 'positive' argument, that access to an important household resource (credit) enhances a female's status within the household, resonates with the theoretical literature on bargaining models of the household (Lundberg and Pollack 1993). Second, by focusing on female control over loans, the sceptics' argument fails to recognize that credit enters the overall household income pool and that household members jointly participate in the loan investment. Third, the work by Pitt, Khandker, and Cartwright (2003), which is based on a nationally representative sample and controls for selection bias, is a highly credible confirmation of the findings from earlier work that showed a positive association between microcredit and female empowerment.

The discussion of the impact of microcredit would be incomplete without referring to the broader range of interventions that are provided with microcredit. MFIs vary significantly in Bangladesh in terms of the non-credit services they offer, though typically these include training, business development services, and social messages on education, health, and civic rights. McKernan (2002) finds that these non-credit interventions raise self-employment profits in rural Bangladesh by 125 per cent, while the combined impact of credit and non-credit interventions on self-employment profits is 175 per cent.

On balance, then, microcredit has had a positive impact on several individual and household outcomes in Bangladesh, most clearly on consumption smoothing and social indicators. However, it is noteworthy that the impact on reducing household-level poverty as well as broader village-level poverty appears more muted. Moreover, it is unclear whether the poorest groups benefited significantly from the microcredit approach prevalent in the 1990s, as there is evidence in both directions. As noted, new microfinance products catering to different types of clients have evolved in recent years. Hence, impact studies based on more recent data are necessary, along with information on the additional costs of these new products, to assess the effectiveness of the enhanced microfinance package that is now on offer in Bangladesh.

CONCLUDING LESSONS

What have we learnt from the experience of scaling up microcredit in Bangladesh and from the evidence on its impact? Do these findings offer any insights for policy makers and MFIs who are seeking to scale up in other countries? This chapter suggests four broad lessons.

First, the role of the state is critical in creating an enabling public policy environment for microfinance. Macroeconomic stability is crucial, though it is difficult to say exactly what level of macroeconomic instability constitutes a serious obstacle to the development of microcredit. Inflation tolerance could be greater in Turkey, for instance, than in Sub-Saharan Africa. The fact remains that high interest rates and high inflation are among the biggest constraints to private sector development, and more specifically to the demand for microcredit. Public expenditure priorities that affect the rural non-farm sector can also boost the demand for, and supply of, microcredit. In Bangladesh the development of the rural road network in the 1980s played an important part in reducing the transaction costs of microcredit and stimulated the demand for microcredit-financed investments.

Government regulations and policies are also crucial in creating the appropriate environment for the growth of the sector. These policies need to strike a balance between protecting the interests of depositors in microfinance institutions that collect savings and allowing growth of the sector by avoiding excessive regulation and unnecessary red tape. The important lesson here is that, whether by design or default, the Government of Bangladesh did not introduce legislation specific to microfinance until the industry went to scale. The advantage of this approach is the ability to tailor the legislation according to the reality of the sector and the operational flexibility this provides to MFIs. The drawback of this lack of supervision is the risk that MFIs with poor financial management will be allowed to grow to a size where their eventual collapse could affect confidence in the entire microcredit system.

Second, the Bangladesh experience suggests that there is a role for 'smart subsidies' by government and donors to expand the capital base of emerging microfinance institutions as well as to develop their technical capacity. These subsidies can be justified on both equity and efficiency grounds as long as hard budget constraints are adhered to. The duration of these subsidies will vary according to local conditions and the level of poverty of the MFI's clients. In most cases, subsidies can be phased out as MFIs become sustainable. However, where MFIs work in remote areas or with the poorest households, there may well be a case for a long-run subsidy whose effectiveness would need to be compared with that of alternative programmes.

The implementation mechanism through which this subsidy is channelled is equally important. In Bangladesh the creation of an autonomous apex wholesaler of microfinance funds has proved effective in expanding access while ensuring that MFIs adhere to a hard budget constraint. However, apex bodies are not a panacea, and at a minimum a rigorous analysis of the underlying retail capacity and demand for funds needs to be carried out, along with the establishment of an independent governing board that can withstand political pressures.

A third theme that emerges from this analysis is that most of the scaling up took place through four large institutions that currently serve 14.2 million clients, or almost 87 per cent of all non-government microcredit borrowers.[13] After the 'big four', only 10 MFIs have more than 100,000 borrowers each. Thus the majority of MFIs are small (with less than 5,000 borrowers), and the bulk of the access to microcredit is supplied by the four large institutions. Hence, another lesson from the Bangladesh experience could be that it is not necessarily a sound strategy to support many different institutions, and risk spreading resources thinly, in order to reach large numbers of poor people. This is particularly important in light of the fact that the leadership skills and professional capacity required to go to scale are in limited supply in most countries. However, this needs to be weighed against the risks of a concentrated market structure in which poor performance by one institution can have industrywide consequences.

This scaling-up strategy is also linked to the extent of the welfare gains due to microcredit. The current focus on improving the quality of microfinance services followed the expansion in access, similar to what has happened in the education sector in many countries. The impact assessment work reviewed in this chapter is based on the 'no-frills' Grameen model that facilitated rapid gains in access. Now that a more diversified package of financial and non-financial services is offered by MFIs, it is likely that the welfare impact of participating in an MFI programme will be greater. However, the costs of these interventions have increased as well, and future research ought to address the cost-effectiveness of the current enhanced microfinance package more explicitly.

A fourth lesson is that while visionary leadership cannot simply be 'franchised', the systems and formal rules that led to scale can be replicated within a long-term framework. The description of the various stages of evolution of the current microcredit model suggests that the institutional development required for scaling up within these MFIs evolved gradually, typically after about 15 years of experimentation. While the details vary, the MFIs that went to scale delegate significant decision-making authority away from head offices, monitor individual staff performance, link staff incentives with programme targets, and have set up appropriate internal controls.

Finally, it is worth pointing out that the Bangladesh microfinance industry faces significant challenges in the years ahead. For one, the microfinance sector needs to build a stronger domestic constituency that understands the economics of microfinance and in particular the reasons why interest rates in the industry are higher than commercial banking rates. Demands for lowering and capping interest rates have gained ground in recent months, and greater public debate around these issues is needed. The apex microfinance body, PKSF, can help to improve transparency by publishing information on interest rates, operating costs, profit margins, and so on.

A second concern relates to how the transition from the highly effective MFI founder-leaders to their successors will affect organizational effectiveness. Many observers believe that the lack of serious organizational in-fighting to date is largely due to the loyalty that staff have to these founder-leaders.

A third challenge is the need to strengthen corporate governance and modernize the legislative framework in line with the scale of the large MFIs. Recent progress on this has been led by the central bank, PKSF, and industry representatives, and steps should be taken to build on these efforts. Given the large variety of institutions that exist, a tiered regulatory structure, as in the Philippines, is likely to be appropriate for Bangladesh.

Finally, the introduction of new financial products, which are key to improving the welfare impact of microfinance, is putting increasing pressure on branch staff and also augments the demands for managerial supervision. Similarly, the increasing number of initiatives that are being undertaken, including replications in other countries, risks stretching management capacity excessively. These challenges are not insurmountable, but will need to be addressed by both government and NGOs in order to ensure that improved financial services can be provided to the large numbers of microfinance clients in Bangladesh.

NOTES

Comments from Sadiq Ahmed, Salehuddin Ahmed, Syed Hashemi, Naomi Hossain, Kristin Hunter, Wahiduddin Mahmud, Frank Matsaert, Iffath Sharif, and Stephen Rasmussen are gratefully acknowledged.

References

Ahmed, S., 2004, 'Microcredit and Poverty: New Realities and Strategic Issues,' S. Ahmed and M.A. Hakim (eds), *Attacking Poverty with Microcredit*, Dhaka: University Press Limited.

Amin, S. and A. Pebley, 1994, 'Gender Inequality within Households: The Impact of a Women's Development Programme in 36 Bangladeshi Villages,' *Bangladesh Development Studies* 22 (2–3), 'Special Issue on Women, Development and Change,' S. Amin (ed.), 121–55. Bangladesh Institute of Development Studies, Dhaka.

CDF (Credit and Development Forum), 2004, *CDF Microfinance Statistics*, Dhaka: Credit and Development Forum.

Choudhury, S.H., 2003, 'Financing the Poor: ASA Experience,' *Daily Star* (Dhaka), March 13.

Chowdhury, M. and R. Cash, 1996, *A Simple Solution: Teaching Millions to Treat Diarrhoea at Home*, Dhaka: University Press Limited.

Gauri, V. and A. Fruttero, 2003, 'Location Decisions and Nongovernmental Organization Motivation: Evidence from Rural Bangladesh,' Policy Research Working Paper 3176, World Bank, Washington, DC.

Goetz, A.M. and R. Sen Gupta, 1996, 'Who Takes the Credit? Gender, Power, and Control over Loan Use in Rural Credit Programs in Bangladesh,' *World Development* 24 (1): 45–63.

Grameen Trust, 2002, *Grameen Dialogue* 50 (April), Dhaka.

Hashemi, S.M., 1997, 'Those Left Behind: A Note on Targeting the Hardcore Poor,' G. Wood and I. Sharif (eds), *Who Needs Credit? Poverty and Finance in Bangladesh*, 249–56, London: Zed.

Hashemi, S.M., S.R. Schuler and A.P. Riley, 1996, 'Rural Credit Programs and Women's Empowerment in Bangladesh,' *World Development* 24 (4): 635–53.

Jain, P. and M. Moore, 2003, 'What Makes Microcredit Programmes Effective? Fashionable Fallacies and Workable Realities,' Working Paper 177, Institute of Development Studies, University of Sussex, Brighton, UK.

Khandker, S., 2003, 'Microfinance and Poverty: Evidence Using Panel Data from Bangladesh,' Policy Research Working Paper 2945, World Bank, Washington, DC.

Lundberg, S. and R. Pollack, 1993, 'Separate Spheres Bargaining and the Marriage Market,' *Journal of Political Economy* 101 (6): 988–1010.

McKernan, S., 2002, 'The Impact of Micro-Credit Programs on Self-Employment Profits: Do Non-Credit Program Aspects Matter?' *Review of Economics and Statistics* 84 (1): 93–115.

Montgomery, R., D. Bhattacharya and D. Hulme, 1996, 'Credit for the Poor in Bangladesh: The BRAC Rural Development Programme and the Government Thana Resource Development and Employment Programme.' D. Hulme and P. Mosley (eds), *Finance against Poverty*, vol. 2, London: Routledge.

Morduch, J., 1999, 'The Microfinance Promise,' *Journal of Economic Literature* 37 (December): 1569–1614.

_____, 2000, 'The Microfinance Schism,' *World Development* 28 (4): 617–29.

Morduch, J. and B. Armendáriz de Aghion, 2005, *The Economics of Microfinance*, Cambridge, MA: MIT Press.

Pitt, M. and S. Khandker, 1998, 'The Impact of Group-Based Credit Programs on Poor Households in Bangladesh: Does the Gender of Participants Matter?' *Journal of Political Economy* 106 (5): 958–96.

Pitt, M., S. Khandker and J. Cartwright, 2003, 'Does Micro-Credit Empower Women? Evidence from Bangladesh,' Policy Research Working Paper 2998, World Bank, Washington, DC.

Pitt, M., S. Khandker, S. McKernan and M.A. Latif, 1999, 'Credit Programs for the Poor and Reproductive Behaviour in Low Income Countries: Are the Reported Causal Relationships the Result of Heterogeneity Bias?' *Demography* 36 (1): 1–21.

PKSF (Palli Karma-Sahayak Foundation), 2003, 'Maps on Microcredit Coverage in Bangladesh,' PKSF, Dhaka.

World Bank, 2003, 'Bangladesh Development Policy Review: Impressive Achievements but Continuing Challenges,' Report 26154-BD, Poverty Reduction and Economic Management Sector Unit, South Asia Region, World Bank, Washington, DC.

———, 2005, 'The Economics and Governance of NGOs in Bangladesh,' Poverty Reduction and Economic Management Sector Unit, South Asia Region, World Bank, Washington, DC.

Yaron, J., B. McDonald and S. Charitonenko, 1998, 'Promoting Efficient Rural Financial Intermediation,' *World Bank Research Observer* 13 (2): 147–70.

Zaman, H., 1999, 'Assessing the Poverty and Vulnerability Impact of Micro-credit in Bangladesh: A Case Study of BRAC,' Policy Research Working Paper 2145, World Bank, Washington, DC.

Notes

1 When converting the number of clients with access to microcredit (16.4 million) to the number of households with access, we need to take into account the number of individuals who borrow from multiple sources and the number of households with more than one individual who borrow from microfinance institutions. A recent survey suggests that about 33 per cent of households meet one or both of these criteria. Hence, we estimate that about 10.8 million households in Bangladesh have access to microcredit, representing about 43 per cent of all households in the country.

2 A notable exception is the Grameen Bank, which is a specialized bank.

3 The Grameen Trust, which offers technical assistance to Grameen Bank replicators, had supported 131 replications in 35 countries by the end of 2004 (www.grameen-info.org/grameen/gtrust/replication.html).

4 BRAC, now known by its acronym, was called the Bangladesh Rural Advancement Committee when it was founded in 1972.

5 In addition to this innovative staff incentive system, a detailed evaluation of the oral rehydration experience also points to a number of other success factors: (a) systematic recruitment and training of staff, (b) an effective feedback loop and the willingness of senior management to learn from experiences in the field, and (c) support from government, donors, and professional experts (Chowdhury and Cash 1996).

6 For instance, in the sericulture sector, BRAC supplies eggs to the silkworm rearer, plants the mulberry trees, trains the entrepreneur in silkworm rearing at home, arranges for extension services by a BRAC rearing specialist, purchases the cocoons from the rearer, and supplies the cocoons to a BRAC silk reeling centre.

7 For instance, Grameen Bank has introduced a system of rating branch offices according to the achievement of specific targets. These include standard loan recovery but also factor in social indicators, such as the proportion of Grameen children going to school.

8 BRAC's Research and Evaluation Division has about 20 professionals whose main function is to evaluate BRAC's multidimensional programmes and give timely feedback to programme staff and management. This process of feedback occurs through long-term research as well as 'quick-turnaround' assessments.

9 Notable examples of international NGOs involved in assisting the sector are the Ford Foundation, Oxfam, and the Aga Khan Foundation. The UK Department for International Development (DFID) has been one of the largest bilateral donors, having provided around $130 million over a 20-year period to MFIs in Bangladesh. The World Bank disbursed $282 million between 1995 and 2004, through PKSF, for development of the microfinance industry.

10 The Nilphamari, Lalmonirhat, Rangpur, Kurigram, Gaibandha, Sherpur, and Jamalpur districts in the northwest all have greater-than-average levels of poverty. However, these districts also have a lower-than-average share of microcredit coverage measured in terms of the ratio of borrowers to population.

11 Morduch compares credit programme members owning less than half an acre of land ('eligible members') with eligible non-members in the programme village and with eligible households in non-programme villages. Using the difference-in-difference method, he is able to account for selection bias arising from both non-random programme placement and non-random household participation.

12 Morduch's estimate of labour supply variability is 39–46 per cent lower for microcredit members than for a control group.

13 As of October 2005, the 'big four' served 86.6 per cent of non-government microfinance clients; their share drops to 80 per cent if government microfinance programmes are included.

8

Computerizing Land Records
for Farmer Access
The Bhoomi Initiative in Karnataka, India

Subhash Bhatnagar and *Rajeev Chawla*

Computerization of land records in the Indian state of Karnataka, under the project called Bhoomi ('land'), has demonstrated the substantial benefits of making government records more open to the public. Citizens are empowered to challenge arbitrary action and civil servants have less discretion at operating levels, making the system less vulnerable to corruption. With the computerization of 20 million land ownership records of 6.7 million farmers by the Department of Revenue, the Bhoomi initiative became fully operational across the state in 2002. Bhoomi replaced a cumbersome manual system in which land records were maintained in register books by 9,000 village accountants.

Under the old system, farmers were dependent on the village accountants to obtain copies of their Record of Rights, Tenancy and Crops (RTC). This essential document is required to qualify for the bank loans that farmers depend on for working capital every year, and it must be updated whenever there is a change in land ownership. Lack of transparency and the frequent unavailability of the village accountants due to travel led to substantial delays, as well as to opportunities for bribery. Before the records were computerized, for example, the village accountant was required to issue notices of requests for changes in the records (called 'mutations') to interested parties and to display such notices at the village office. Often neither of these actions was carried out, nor was any record of the notices maintained. Although revenue inspectors were authorized to update land records 30 days after an initial mutation request, in practice it could take as long as one to two years for a record to be updated.

Under Bhoomi, printed copies of RTCs can be obtained instantly from computerized kiosks, and mutation requests are recorded online. Farmers can now access the database and monitor the results of their mutation requests. Although user fees for the new system are higher than for the old, an increased number of mutation requests as well as the results of user surveys indicate substantial public approval of the new system. By the end of 2004, revenues had already covered the cost of computerization, with enough surplus for further development of the system.

Despite some limitations in access related to literacy status, gender, and other factors, Bhoomi's positive impact in terms of improved service delivery and reduced corruption is unmistakable. These benefits have been confirmed by independent evaluation and are reflected in growing use of the system. The Government of India regards Bhoomi as a model for replication in other states that have lagged in the computerization of their land records.

THE NEED FOR REFORM OF INDIA'S LAND RECORDS SYSTEM

From the beginning of the state in India, historical evidence suggests, taxes on land have played a pivotal part in the evolution and maintenance of governance systems. In ancient times, land revenue was generally the primary source of income for government. Most of the population was affected by this tax, as the vast majority depended on land for their livelihood. British colonial rule brought changes in the methods of assessment and revenue collection. Lands were measured, albeit crudely, and village records of lands were gradually compiled into an array of systematized land records closely linked to the collection of revenue. Taxes on agricultural land were subsequently reduced in the era of India's welfare state, following the country's independence. Despite the decline in the relative importance of land revenue, however, land records have remained central to governance and of vital significance for the rural population.

Landholding information potentially includes a wide variety of data that are of interest to the government. This includes geographic and geological information such as shape, size, land forms, and soils; economic information related to land use, irrigation, and crops; and information pertaining to legal rights, registration, and taxation. The current land records system focuses principally on information about rights and registration. The key records in this system are the Record of Rights, Tenancy and Crops and the Mutation Register, which records a change to the RTC.

Furthermore, land records are important to government policies. The state needs to ensure the maintenance of accurate and genuine land records to further its policy objectives of land reforms and protection of ownership rights. As noted in the plan document for the Seventh Five-Year Plan (1985–89), 'Land records form the base for all land reform measures and therefore regular periodic updating of land records is essential in all States' (Planning Commission 1985). This requires efficiency and transparency, a requirement that was not met by the system of manual maintenance of land records.

Farmers, too, rely heavily on land records. A copy of the RTC is required to qualify for the bank loans that farmers depend on for working capital every year. Moreover, no improvement in land can be made without acquiring rights to the land, and these rights cannot be acquired until ownership is established. Since land records form the basis for assignment and settlement of land titles, they must stand the test of legal scrutiny and safeguard the rights of legal owners. It is essential that they be updated whenever there is a change in land ownership.

A System Plagued by Distortions

In Karnataka state, the land records system until the 1990s was exceptionally cumbersome. It involved 9,000 village accountants, each serving a cluster of three to four villages. Eight registers were maintained to record information such as the current ownership of each parcel of land, its area and cropping pattern, disputes and changes pertaining to the land, and village maps showing the boundaries of each plot. Farmers wishing to alter land records upon the sale or inheritance of a land parcel had to file a request with the village accountant.

The old system was rife with opportunities for distortion and corruption. Village accountants frequently ignored mutation requests because of a dispute or simply to extract money from farmers for speeding up the process. In theory, the village accountants were obligated to issue notices of the request to interested parties and post the notice at the village office. If no objections were received within a 30-day period, then a revenue inspector was responsible for updating the record. In practice, however, the procedure often was not followed, and no record of the notices was maintained. It could take as long as two years for a record to be updated.

Accessing land records proved difficult for farmers because village accountants travelled frequently. The wait time for an RTC ranged from three to 30 days, depending upon the importance of the record for the farmer and the size of the bribe. Bribes were commonplace and typically ranged from Rs 100 to Rs 2,000 (approximately $2 to $40). They could exceed Rs 10,000 if some details of the record were to be written in an ambiguous fashion out of self-interested motives. Such corruption was encouraged by the fact that land records in the custody of village accountants were not open for public scrutiny.

Inaccuracies crept into the system in part through improper manipulation by the village accountants, particularly with respect to government land. Mutations became an instrument for rural corruption, exploitation, and oppression. Large landowners simply bribed the village accountants to change the titles of poor farmers' lands to their own names. Small farmers, mostly illiterate, could do little to change this, either because they did not know what was happening or because they could not afford the accountants' bribes. Even where accountants were law-abiding, the practice of parcelling land into very small lots over generations made it difficult to keep accurate records. Although the system provided for supervisors of the village accountants to physically verify the records, the capacity to check became weaker as the number of records multiplied and the supervisors were burdened with other regulatory and development tasks.[1]

Early Attempts at Reform

The central and state governments have long been aware of the need to reform the land records system. As early as 1985, state revenue ministers resolved to computerize land records throughout India on a pilot basis. Centrally funded pilot projects were initiated to computerize core data contained in land records so as to assist development planning and make records accessible to planners, administrators, and others. The programme began in eight districts in 1988–89 and was extended three years later to an additional 24 districts in different states. However, a comprehensive evaluation conducted in 1998 in eight districts concluded that the project had accomplished very little. The programme's effectiveness was crippled by a variety of bottlenecks including delayed funding, poor training, a lack of good data entry vendors, and delays in software development and installation of hardware.

By then it was apparent that the district was not the appropriate administrative level for computerizing land records. In 1997–98, a decision was taken to operationalize the scheme at the *taluk*, or subdistrict, level and to target delivery of computerized land records to the public at large. Under this programme, the central government earmarked Rs 0.4 million for the purchase of hardware, software, and other peripherals for each taluk. Nearly

2,500 taluks out of a total of 6,000 were to be covered. During the Ninth Five-Year Plan (1997–2002), the central government released a total of Rs 1,545 million. By the end of 2002, the scheme was being implemented in 569 out of 599 districts in India. From the inception of this programme through the end of 2001, the central government released Rs 21,894 million, of which the states and union territories utilized around 53 per cent.

The efforts to computerize land records systems throughout India were hampered by a range of debilitating factors. The federal government lacked a clear strategy for implementation of the scheme and failed to require a detailed system design and implementation plan from states before providing funding. In this context, the decision to 'allow a thousand flowers to bloom' instead of requiring each state to have a well-coordinated strategy proved a mistake. The involvement of the Revenue Department officers and district administration was lacking, confusion about roles among staff abounded, and projects lacked institutionalization by the state government. Instead of planning for ongoing maintenance, the one-time distribution of a record was itself regarded as computerization of land records. Moreover, data entry was plagued by errors, poor training, and slow progress. In one case, in Dungarpur district, the pilot projects took 14 years to complete the first stage. With such delays, in a period of rapidly changing technology, even relatively successful pilot projects in one district could not emerge as a standard to be replicated in other districts (Gupta 2002).

As a result, despite large government expenditure by 2004, most states had only a few scattered taluks where computerized land records were being issued. One state stands out as an exception: Karnataka, the only state in India where the system has been working successfully statewide.

IMPLEMENTATION OF THE BHOOMI INITIATIVE

The first initiative to computerize land records in Karnataka was a pilot venture in 1991 under the Ministry of Rural Development's Computerization of Land Records project, fully funded by the Government of India. By 1996, projects for computerization of land records had been approved for all districts in Karnataka state. However, there was no provision to install computers at the taluk level where manual records were actually updated (Department of Rural Development 2001, 2002).

A breakthrough came in February 2001 when the Karnataka state government mandated that the Bhoomi project be completed in all taluks by March 2002. The decision implied support for full development of a land records system designed to serve citizens, even though this would require substantial investment by the state government for those components of the project not funded by the federal government. This political mandate was backed by full administration efforts at all levels.

The following major objectives were defined for the Bhoomi project:

- Facilitate easy maintenance and prompt updating of land records
- Make land records tamper-proof
- Allow farmers easy access to their records
- Compile all land revenue, cropping patterns, and land use information into a database
- Enable usage of the database by courts, banks, private organizations and companies, and Internet service providers
- Utilize the data for planning and for formulating development programmes.

The Karnataka government's Department of Revenue laid out a plan to set up computerized land records kiosks (Bhoomi centres) in 177 taluk offices. These kiosks were to provide farmers with RTCs and records of mutation requests, speeding up delivery while minimizing opportunities for harassment and bribery.

Digitization of Legacy Data

The first and most important step was to digitize the approximately 20 million records of legacy data records in the possession of village accountants. For this purpose a comprehensive data entry software system called Bhoomi was designed through a consultative process involving extensive workshop discussions at the division, district, and state levels. The feedback from these workshops was invaluable in making it possible for department technical staff to design appropriate data entry software.

As records were entered into the new computerized system, manual records were withdrawn from the field across the state in a phased manner. After comparisons with the manual registers to authenticate the data, printouts of computerized records were individually signed by village accountants (100 per cent of records), revenue inspectors (30 per cent), *shirasthedars* (5 per cent), *tehsildars* (3 per cent), assistant commissioners (2 per cent), or deputy commissioners (1 per cent).[2] Seals with the names and titles of official verifiers and the date of verification were affixed to the printouts. Both manual and computerized sets of records now serve as original records and are kept in safe custody in the taluk offices. Once the process of comparison and certification was complete in each taluk, the deputy commissioner issued a notification that only the computerized RTCs should be used for all legal and other purposes, and the transfer was thus finalized.

A New Process for Accessing and Updating Information

The transition to digital access has been completed. Only computerized records are valid, and village accountants are no longer permitted to issue copies of manual records. Computerized land records kiosks are now operational in all 177 taluks in the state. Records are generated using the Bhoomi software running on kiosk computers and a back-end server in each taluk kiosk holding the database. The records are signed by the designated village accountant at the kiosk and are provided to the farmers for a user fee of Rs 15. Farmers can then request correction of small errors on the computerized records at the taluk office, using the printed copy of the record. If the error is found to be genuine, a correction is made in the computerized Bhoomi database and a corrected copy of the record is provided to the farmer free of charge. All that is needed to access the record is the name of the owner or the plot number.

Farmers can also file an application for a mutation of the land record at the Bhoomi centre following a change of ownership through sale or inheritance. Data from the application are entered into the terminal at the counter, and a checklist is generated for manual verification of the data and documents by a supervisor. Each request is assigned a number, which in some of the kiosks can be used by the applicant to check the status of the application on a touch screen. An entry is then made in the back-end server and a notice is automatically generated to be sent to affected parties.

Village accountants collect the notices on regularly scheduled visits to the taluk office and are responsible for delivering the notices to interested parties and getting their written acknowledgment. If everything is in order, the revenue inspector passes on an appropriate mutation order after the prescribed period of 30 days from the date the notice was issued to the parties. The order is then brought to the Bhoomi centre, where it is scanned into the system, authorized by the revenue inspector who has approved the orders, and further verified by the deputy tehsildar. The system then updates the computerized land record and the physical records are filed in the records room.

To update crop records, a private data entry agency inputs data in batches three times a year. After the updating, the village accountant is responsible for verifying the data with checklists, after which the updated data are merged with the Bhoomi land record database.

Previously, the Karnataka Land Revenue Act did not provide for a computerized system. The act has been amended to allow for storage of data on computer storage devices and for use of the Bhoomi software. In the next phase of the project, all the taluk databases will be uploaded to a web-enabled central database.

Overcoming Obstacles and Expanding the System

Since its inception, the Bhoomi initiative has taken steps to address the challenges that have arisen in the course of implementation. First, the programme has had to ensure the technical quality and maintenance of the kiosk equipment at 177 centres, many located in rural areas. Improving the uptime of computers at Bhoomi kiosks is one challenge that has been addressed successfully. Systematic efforts to train staff have been undertaken: 1,000 officials were trained at the district level and 108 village accountants attended a two-month training course on hardware and networking in Bangalore. Four accountants with this training were placed in each district to serve as resource persons for primary diagnostics and repair. Facility managers with service-level agreements carrying stiff penalties for underperformance have also been assigned to each kiosk. Furthermore, the processing of payments to the facility managers has been decentralized to make facility managers more responsive to needs in the field. These measures have successfully improved computer uptime to its current level of 98 per cent.

A second challenge has been countering the prospects for fraud. Measures have been taken to make the printing process more secure to deal with the problem of fraudulent certificates, although officers continue to enjoy a large amount of discretion. The appearance of a forged RTC in one of the taluks has prompted experimentation in making the printing process secure so that forging a document will become more difficult. Various options such as use of holograms and bar codes have been evaluated, and more sophisticated solutions that encode and print the key contents of the land title as an image (like bar codes) on the RTC are being tried. Decoders supplied to key users will be able to decode the image to authenticate the RTC.[3]

A further challenge that continues today is the need to make the Bhoomi system more widely available to farmers at the village level. In an effort to expand access and reduce the travel time of many farmers, the programme is planning to upload the data from all 177 kiosks to a central database. RTCs will then be available not only at taluk offices but also at multipurpose Internet kiosks in rural areas, which will be able to connect to the central database.[4] The centralized data centre has been designed by Microsoft and the National Informatics Centre in Bangalore to upload data daily using a VSAT network, and data transport has already begun in a handful of taluks. As of December 2004, data from 15 taluks had already been ported to the central platform. Funding support has been sought from the Government of India to establish the central repository in Bangalore. The plan is that multipurpose rural Internet kiosks will be able to access the data after appropriate verification of password, machine ID, and phone ID. The rural telecentre will be charged a fee for each transaction.

The programme is also planning to open an additional 1,000 kiosks through public–private partnerships. A pilot experiment in Mandya district in partnership with the n-Logue company has established 20 private kiosks. These telecentres not only have the capacity to view, print, and distribute land records over the Internet, but also provide other services such as the download of forms for services and beneficiary-oriented schemes from a variety of departments, including forestry, animal husbandry, sericulture, and cottage industries. The telecentres will charge clients a fee of Rs 25 for retrieving an RTC instead of the standard Bhoomi kiosk fee of Rs 15, enabling the owners to retain Rs 10 per record to cover their operational costs and provide a small return on investment.[5] This fee structure is expected to make 1,000 rural kiosks economically sustainable in Karnataka.[6]

The programme is also exploring mechanisms for collecting crop data. A pilot initiative in 2003 designed to aid in collecting crop data provided about 200 village accountants with Simputers, or locally developed handheld computers, at a cost of about Rs 3.5 million. The Simputers were used during two rounds of updating crop data for 600 villages. Further expansion of this pilot depends on reduction in the cost of such handheld devices.

While the current scope of the Bhoomi programme is limited to maintenance of land records, there is potential for collaborative efforts to expand the system's reach to deal with registration of deeds and collection of land revenue, functions that are related to land records. The Department of Stamps and Registration, responsible for registration of deeds in case of a change in ownership through sale or inheritance, has recently computerized the registration of such deeds in a project called Kaveri (Karnataka Valuation and E-registration). There are plans to link up the Bhoomi centres with the newly computerized Kaveri centres so that information on these registrations can be transmitted over a wide area network.

Land revenue currently collected by village accountants, approximately Rs 100 million a year, will also be collected by Bhoomi centres. However, the issue of RTCs is unlikely to be made contingent on payment of land revenue; such an approach is considered politically unacceptable as it would be deemed coercive by citizens.

Remaining Challenges

Lack of awareness among many farmers and difficulties in reaching illiterate and women farmers are ongoing problems. Furthermore, illiterate farmers may still face difficulties in filling out mutation applications. Both challenges require continuing public education of the rural population to protect farmers from unscrupulous elements. The challenges are reflected in reports such as this one by an independent journalist in 2003:

Ironically, while Bhoomi aims to help the poor, in regions like Bijapur in Karnataka, which has the highest demand for RTCs, it is the poor who appear to be struggling most with the new system. 'We spend Rs 10 ($0.20) as bus fare to reach the town from our villages and pay Rs 15 ($0.30) for an RTC. Sometimes it takes two days because the queue is so long. The VA was better,' complains Mehboob Modi Patel. Another farmer, Amsidda Irrappa Karnal, says, 'I am illiterate. Who will help me fill up the application form [for the RTC] here?' ...

Land ownership has long been a male bastion in India—in Karnataka women own just 12 per cent of the land—and this is reflected in Bhoomi. Women in Dharwad district do not know of the new system. Those from Kalakawatagi village in northern Karnataka say they have not seen their computerised RTC, issued free by the revenue department in 2001 for personal verification. In Kolar district, about 100 km from Bangalore, 42-year-old Pappamma, a feisty leader of some 200 women's groups, says she has visited the local e-kiosk several times to help women obtain RTCs. 'But taluk officials themselves know little of the system and are in no position to even begin helping the women. They need training,' she comments dryly (Acharya 2003).

Some early reports based on small-sample interviews and anecdotal evidence have pointed to other problems with the Bhoomi system. For example, Hanstad and Lokesh (2002), who interviewed 23 users of the Bhoomi system in January 2001 in one centre that had been functioning for six months, reported that 20 of the 23 farmers favoured the old system. Problems such as five- or six-hour power outages at the kiosk seemed to be the main reason for dissatisfaction with the new system. Such initial problems have mostly been overcome, and other changes have been made in response to feedback from various stakeholders. For example, the project decided to redefine the roles of the tehsildar and the deputy tehsildar in processing mutation requests because of indications that this was causing delays.

THE IMPACT OF BHOOMI

The implementation of the Bhoomi system has been widely viewed as a significant improvement over the earlier manual system, particularly in reducing opportunities for corruption and overcoming the bias toward rich farmers. A farmer in Kengeri, a satellite town near Bangalore, was quoted saying of his new RTC: 'This is now pukka [genuine]. The village accountant cannot change names anymore.' Another person reported, 'In one district in north Karnataka where feudalism still prevails, 32 farmers' lands had been recorded in the VA's name prior to computerisation. The man immediately sold the lot before Bhoomi began. I know of hundreds of such cases' (Acharya 2003).

The general public has demonstrated its support of the new system through a marked increase in use of the system, despite an increase in user fees. The simplified process for submitting mutation requests has resulted in an 85 per cent jump in the number of such requests. In the first year after computerization, Bhoomi carried out nearly 1 million mutations, whereas in the previous two years, the average number of mutations carried out under the manual system was about half a million per year. This increase is a clear indication of the population's acceptance of the new system, as reflected in their willingness to update records with changes in land ownership that were previously left undocumented.

Faster, Easier, and Less Corrupt

Bhoomi is one of the few e-government applications that have been evaluated by an independent agency using a systematic methodology. An evaluation conducted by the Public Affairs Centre in Bangalore in July 2002 compared users' experiences with Bhoomi and with the previous manual system (Lobo and Balakrishnan 2002).[7] The study concluded that the computerized system had a significant impact on efficiency of delivery and on corruption in the following areas:

- *Easier use.* The evaluation revealed that users found the new Bhoomi system much easier to use than its predecessor: 78 per cent of Bhoomi users who had also used the manual system found the Bhoomi system simpler. Moreover, 66 per cent of users were able to utilize the Bhoomi kiosks with no help, compared to just 25 per cent under the manual system.

- *Reduced dependence on staff.* More than three-quarters of users at Bhoomi kiosks were able to complete their transaction without having to meet any official other than the counter staff, and just 19 per cent had to meet one official. In contrast, 61 per cent of users under the manual system had to meet two to four officials to complete their business. However, 18 per cent of Bhoomi users reported that their document was not signed by the appointed village accountant operating the kiosk, and 6 per cent reported that they had to fill out an application form for issue of an RTC.

- *Fewer errors in documents received.* The study indicated that 74 per cent of users of Bhoomi kiosks received error-free documents, in contrast to 63 per cent of users of the manual system. Major mistakes in land details were 31 per cent of the errors reported in the manual system, but only 4 per cent the Bhoomi system.

- *Improved rectification of errors.* Given that errors are not unusual at this stage of development of the Bhoomi system, how they are corrected is an important issue. Ninety-three per cent of Bhoomi users had the confidence to complain and seek rectification of errors, as compared to just under half in the manual system. With Bhoomi, 58 per cent of complaints received a timely response, whereas a timely response was reported by only 4 per cent of those using the manual system.

- *Faster service.* Bhoomi has reduced the hidden costs of time and effort to secure land records: 79 per cent of Bhoomi users reported a minimal waiting time in the queue of 10 minutes or less, in contrast with 27 per cent under the manual system. Even more important is the number of times a citizen had to visit these offices to get the certificate. While 72 per cent of Bhoomi users obtained the RTC with one visit to the kiosk, only 5 per cent were successful with one visit under the manual system.

- *Reduced corruption.* The most serious issue is that of corruption and bribery. Only 3 per cent of the users of the Bhoomi system, but two-thirds of the users of the manual system, reported paying bribes.

- *Improved staff behaviour.* While the technical capacity of the system plays an important role in its success, the approach of people who handle the task is of critical significance too. A large majority of

Bhoomi users, 85 per cent, rated staff behaviour at the Bhoomi kiosks as 'good'. None of the users of the manual system rated staff behaviour as good.

Empowering Small Farmers

The Bhoomi initiative has had a striking impact on the empowerment of small, rural farmers. By expanding access, improving transparency and accountability, and reducing corruption, the programme has helped to place small farmers on a more equal footing with the low-ranking civil servants who previously maintained an unequal balance of power through their control over records.[8]

Bhoomi has democratized access to land records. Land record information previously held in registers inaccessible to citizens is now available to be collected by anyone. The Bhoomi process is markedly transparent: a second computer screen facing the clients enables them to view the transactions being performed by the kiosk staff. Furthermore, the system has several built-in elements to enhance accountability. The bio-login procedure and the use of encryption and public–private keys ensures that the entry of data for RTCs and mutation requests can be traced back to the individual operators on duty and the supervisors giving approval.

By processing mutations on a first-come-first-served basis and allowing deputy tehsildars to approve mutation orders if the revenue inspector delays it beyond a predetermined limit, the system strips officials of their arbitrary power to harass farmers and extract bribes. Officials must also justify keeping applications in abeyance and pushing applications down in the priority order. Farmers can now access the database themselves and follow up with complaints about delays or fraud. Reports on overdue mutation orders can point to errant behaviour by officials. Opportunities for corruption still exist, however, and strict field supervision through empowered citizen's committees and non-governmental organization is needed to curb such behaviour.

The Bhoomi system is also more accessible to marginalized individuals. Under the manual system, poor and illiterate people and women found it particularly difficult to obtain land records because of corruption, inefficiency, and cumbersome paperwork. The Bhoomi system removes one key impediment: the requirement of filling out an application. As a result, more people have collected RTCs and more have come forward to have data corrected when errors are found.

The more efficient provision of landholding information has also provided a boost to farmers' collective action. Often, farmers go to bank branches in groups to process crop loans in the hope that corrupt officers will find it harder to demand bribes in the presence of other people. The convenience with which RTCs can be collected facilitates this group approach.

Expected Benefits

The potential for the Bhoomi system to have a significant impact in rural areas reflects the wide-ranging importance of land records for farmers. This impact is particularly promising in the area of credit. Nearly 2,500 bank branches in Karnataka loan approximately Rs 40 billion to farmers as working capital every year. A copy of the RTC is absolutely essential for a farmer seeking to procure a loan. Greater efficiency in the system has the potential not only to assist farmers but also to aid banks in recovery of loans, thus improving the investment climate. Nationwide, India loses 1.3 per cent of potential investments because of defects in the land records system (McKinsey Global Institute 2001).

The adjudication of legal disputes over land, which currently constitutes 70 per cent of all legal disputes in Karnataka courts, is expedited as access to land records is made more efficient. Court challenges to changes in land records are often upheld on technical counts, simply because of failure to produce copies of the notices that were sent to the affected parties. With as many as a million notices a year, the manual storage and retrieval system made it difficult to retrieve old notices for submission to the courts. In the Bhoomi system every notice that is issued is scanned and a copy is easily retrievable from the Bhoomi kiosks, thus reducing the resolution time for disputes and minimizing the opportunity for petty corruption in facilitating or hindering the process of retrieval of manual notices. The number of disputes is also expected to decrease because of the open access to data and the transparent and traceable mutation process.

The Bhoomi initiative has also helped increase the coverage of crop insurance, a compulsory requirement for those who take farm loans in Karnataka. In 2000–01, only 0.38 million farmers insured their crops, paying Rs 112 million as premiums and collecting Rs 40 million in damages. In just two years this figure nearly tripled to almost one million farmers (15 per cent of the farming community) who insured their crops in 2002–03, paying Rs 420 million as premiums and collecting Rs 2,960 million in damages. There has also been a substantial increase in the number of farmers who have not taken loans but who are insuring their crops anyway.

Furthermore, Bhoomi has minimized the opportunity for corruption in crop insurance. Under the manual system, it was relatively easy for farmers to obtain from village accountants a falsified certificate of crops grown. Since droughts usually destroy an entire crop, there was no way of verifying the information on such a certificate, which could then be used to make a fraudulent insurance claim. Often such favours were done for rich farmers who could afford to pay bribes; the poor suffered as premiums rose accordingly. With the implementation of Bhoomi, crop data are specified on the back of the RTC, which is now the only document that can be used to back a claim. Efforts are under way to make the crop data more current and accurate, and the village accountants accountable for the data; as a result, corruption in payout of insurance claims is likely to be reduced. Once Bhoomi is available from a centralized database, insurance companies will have easier access to consolidated data, improving efficiency and equity in insurance pay-outs.

While data are not available to isolate and assess the direct impact of the Bhoomi system on reduction in poverty levels, the benefits to farmers from improved transparency and efficiency are already clear. The new system is expected to facilitate the land sale and rental markets in Karnataka by reducing transaction costs. These savings are particularly important for small and marginal farmers, and if the resulting reallocation of land favours the landless and small farmers, income and overall agricultural productivity may also increase (Hanstad 2001).

The data generated by the Bhoomi system, such as information on land ownership by plot size, soil type, crop, and gender, could be used in planning poverty alleviation programmes, in projecting the need for agricultural inputs, and in other research. Data from Bhoomi could also facilitate better administration of the Land Reforms Act, such as by improving the enforcement of ceilings on landholdings. By assigning a unique number to each landowner, Bhoomi makes it possible to identify and aggregate all land of different types belonging to an individual in a given village, and citizen IDs will also be added to link records across taluks and districts. Analyses of ownership data can be made public, leading in some cases to pressures for reform. Most notably, statistics on ownership by gender indicate a large divide.

Additional benefits will also be possible once the centralized database is online. The application has been enabled to work with a public-key infrastructure, so that computer-generated records can be digitally signed. This means that in the future banks may be persuaded to access the central database directly to obtain land-record data for farmers to whom they are considering making loans, eliminating the need for farmers to collect their RTCs and carry them physically to the bank. Such a system would also help the banks to do advance planning on the amount of lending required. Similarly, the high court as well as district and taluk courts could access the database for resolving legal disputes concerning land.

Cost Effectiveness

The benefits of the Bhoomi computerization programme already substantially surpass the costs of its initial implementation, and user fees supply adequate revenue to support ongoing operations.

The total out-of-pocket expenditure on the project was Rs 185 million, not including the cost of software development (nearly 100 person-months of effort) provided gratis by the National Informatics Centre (NIC).[9] The initial expenditure on data entry operations for about 2 million RTCs in 27 districts was Rs 80 million. The unit cost of providing hardware, construction of computer rooms, and kiosks was in the order of Rs 0.64 million for each taluk.

In comparison, the total revenue generated through issuance of RTCs under the new system was Rs 270 million by the end of April 2004. The monthly revenue had stabilized at approximately Rs 8 million. An amount between Rs 90 and Rs 100 million is expected to be collected each year in charges for RTCs. The current user fee of Rs 15 is projected to cover the cost of processing one RTC, which is roughly estimated at Rs 13, assuming a life of five years for the hardware and an activity level of 2 million RTCs issued from all the kiosks over that period (corresponding to 10 per cent of all landholdings). This cost includes an assumed operational expenditure of Rs 2 for stationery, cartridges, and electricity.

The programme's estimated savings are considerable. The benefit in terms of labour saved is approximately 1.32 million person-days per year, leading to savings of Rs 66 million per year in wages. The weighted average value of bribes paid in the manual system was estimated at Rs 152.46 per person. In Bhoomi this has been reduced to only Rs 3.09. Even if this savings is reduced by the user fee of Rs 15, the net saving is Rs 134.37 per person, translating to a total saving of over Rs 806 million annually.

DRIVING FACTORS IN BHOOMI'S SUCCESS

The shining success of the Bhoomi project is particularly striking in the context of failed programs in neighbouring states. At the core of Karnataka's success are several key factors: political commitment, institutional innovation, learning and experimentation, and external support.

Political Commitment to Change

Unlike neighbouring Andhra Pradesh state, where e-government is considered to have been driven by the chief minister, in Karnataka the implementation of e-government has largely been bottom-up, coming from departmental initiatives driven primarily by civil servants. Yet it is to the credit of the drivers of Bhoomi that they were able to harness a significant level of political support for the project.

The political executive was actively involved in Bhoomi. The state chief minister and revenue minister both highlighted the importance of the project in many public forums (Chawla and Bhatnagar 2001). The chief minister wrote regularly to all district deputy commissioners, imploring them to participate fully in the computerization, and he personally inaugurated a large number of land records kiosks.[10] Meanwhile, the revenue minister regularly reviewed the computerization process and also inaugurated several kiosks. A committee of members of the Legislative Assembly visited the kiosks and deputy commissioners invited assembly members of their districts to witness the functioning of kiosks. It is likely that this level of support from politicians reflected a desire to project a pro-poor image of the government. Whatever the motivation, the high level of involvement illustrated the strong political will for computerization of land records.

Institutional Innovation

Implementation of Bhoomi required its promoters to anticipate reactions from in-service personnel and to build partnerships and institutional arrangements that could sustain the programme. Concerted efforts were made to mitigate the expected resistance from field staff. To allay the fears of field officials about changes in their job descriptions, 12 state-level information seminars were organized for 1,200 senior and mid-level officers. Four division-level workshops also were organized to train 800 officials. The seminars stressed that the maintenance of land records was only one of the officials' many functions and that computerization would remove the drudgery of maintaining the records manually. Revenue officials would continue to be responsible for field enquiry. The primary emphasis at these gatherings was on reassurance, and not on the overarching goal of reducing corruption.

Innovative software design was also an essential component of the programme's success. Selected field-level personnel were invited to participate in the software development process for various Bhoomi modules through a formal state-level Bhoomi committee. Meetings were held with participation from various levels in the Revenue Department to elicit suggestions for improvement, and decisions taken at these meetings were incorporated into the software design. Nearly 125 person-months were spent on software development. By 2004, Bhoomi had already been migrated to version three and all taluks were using the latest version.

The programme also took steps to ensure effective management on the ground. Four independent consultants were hired to tour sites randomly in each division and report on problems and progress. Such field supervision required special effort and additional expenditure as the central government project did not include a line item to cover it. The cost was approximately Rs 1.5 million. Furthermore, the village accountants in charge of the new kiosks were chosen very carefully. The programme recruited and trained young people fresh out of college who had not experienced the power that a traditional village accountant could exercise over farmers. The project leader personally participated in the training given to every batch of accountants to ensure that they felt complete ownership and a sense of importance in being assigned to this new initiative. Accountants were encouraged to talk to the project leader at either his home or his office. Nearly 900 officials, including all deputy tehsildars, were trained in the state headquarters and more than 1,000 officials were trained by the Bhoomi consultants at the district level.

Partnerships were forged across numerous agencies. In particular, the NIC played a pivotal role during various phases of implementation. Since departmental staff were reluctant to enter data, private data entry agencies were used, and an elaborate mechanism was designed for validating the information to ensure that it mirrored the manual records that had legal validity. Every district was provided with a consultant to act as a bridge between the data entry agency and the district administration. After the system was operational, the consultant trained the taluk staff and for an initial period helped district administrators in daily work at the Bhoomi kiosk.

Another measure taken to facilitate the introduction of Bhoomi was to contract private operators for one year to handle data entry at the Bhoomi kiosks to give time for the village accountants to become completely trained. A comprehensive intensive training module for the accountants, lasting seven days with 11 hours each day, was designed jointly by the Revenue

Department and NIC. Village accountants took over the work from the private operators after a year.

Learning and Experimentation

Roll-out of the application to 177 locations was a challenge due to the poor quality of the manual records and the enormity of the data entry task. The approach taken, therefore, was to work in phases, allowing lessons learned from the early experiences in pilot taluks to be rapidly applied elsewhere. In the first phase, the project was implemented on a pilot basis in a controlled environment in four taluks. In the second phase, after experience was gained in data entry and implementation of the software, the scheme was extended to one pilot taluk in each of the 27 districts. In the third phase, the project was rolled out simultaneously in all 146 remaining taluks.

Action was taken to address errors and problems. For example, based on early feedback, indicating unacceptable levels of downtime at certain kiosks, a facility manager with strict service-level agreements was appointed to maintain the computer system. This resulted in satisfactory performance at the centres. At every centre, the minimum configuration—server, kiosk machines, power supply—is expected to be up and functional at all times.

Likewise, the programme took steps to improve the data entry software, which originally was unable to handle all the variations in land titles and had unacceptable error rates due to lack of data validation. A series of workshops was organized at both the division and state levels to help officials understand and correct these software problems. At the division level, workshops lasted four days and involved about 800 people. At the state level, workshops lasted 12 days and involved about 1,200 mid-level and senior officials. These workshops came up with guidelines and requirements for a new Bhoomi system. Following the workshops, the state government worked closely with NIC to adapt the data entry software and to develop the back-end Bhoomi software.[11] NIC set up a team of four people to work full-time on Bhoomi. The technical director also devoted about 10 to 15 per cent of his time to management of the team. The end product was a system that has now become a model for replication in other states.

In general, the system has been responsive to feedback from clients. For example, the initial practice of charging a mutation fee for every survey number in a farmer's total holding was seen to be hurting farmers with very fragmented small holdings. As a result, a new algorithm was introduced to calculate the fee based on the total holding and the number of parcels.

External Catalysts

While the initiative for the Bhoomi project came from the state government, external support was also essential. The state government could not have taken up a project of this magnitude involving an up-front investment of Rs 200 million without central government funding, which was the key catalyst that enabled the project champion to sell the idea within the state. Healthy competition with the neighbouring state of Andhra Pradesh, where progress with reforms and electronic government seemed to move much faster, was another motivator that spurred Karnataka officials into action.

The World Bank, which has provided a structural adjustment loan to Karnataka, has also been quietly supportive of Karnataka's e-government programme. The Bank has provided technical assistance in the form of periodic review of major e-government initiatives. Project leaders have been open to feedback from the Bank's team. In particular, some of the new initiatives such as connectivity for rural kiosks have strong endorsement from the Bank. A Bank-funded evaluation conducted by an independent agency was a very useful exercise for establishing the credibility of the fledgling system. External recognition in the form of awards and positive publicity has also been a major motivator for the Bhoomi team.

Lessons Learned

One of the most important lessons learned from the Bhoomi experience is the need to define achievable goals and resist efforts to expand more rapidly than can be sustained. This strategy is a departure from the traditional wisdom that calls for improving service delivery to the poor by rapidly increasing investments to multiply the number of delivery points. Bhoomi, in contrast, reduced service delivery points from 9,000 under the manual system to 177 in the first phase, and is now in the process of providing 1,000 delivery points in the second phase. Despite this overall contraction, consumer satisfaction has increased. Bhoomi thus reinforces some of the ideas put forth by *World Development Report 2004* for improving services to the poor (World Bank 2003). Programmes with a large number of delivery points often cannot be monitored centrally; unless monitoring can be done by communities, with an equal voice for all groups, such large systems become inefficient.

This approach was tested soon after Bhoomi became operational in all taluks, when elected representatives, district officials, and farmers made demands that Bhoomi be extended to the sub-taluk level. Such expansion, however, would have increased costs without necessarily increasing the number of RTCs issued. The Revenue Department wisely resisted the temptation, as it would not have been able to monitor and support such a widely spread operation. It is worth noting that the Computerized Rural Information Systems Project, developed by the District Rural Development Agency, was replicated in 500 districts in a hurried manner during the 1980s and resulted in failure. In general, systems should be allowed to stabilize and prove their sustainability over a two-year period before attempting any replication.

Instead of undertaking direct expansion, planners explored other opportunities to make RTCs available at the sub-taluk level. Private rural kiosks were allowed to issue copies signed by the village accountants, an alternative that would not have been considered if the focus were only on expansion of the Bhoomi system itself. Even greater efficiency may be possible if such copies can be accepted by banks and verified by accessing the departmental database, without requiring signed copies.

The importance of strong management at the top and proper training at all levels is another legacy of the Bhoomi experience. The scope of the programme required intensive and sustained efforts by the project champion, rising to 80 per cent of his time and 15-hour days during the critical year of implementation. The fact that the project champion had a tenure of more than six years was an important factor in ensuring continuity. Minimizing resistance from staff was essential, aided by extensive training of Bhoomi staff coupled with the participatory style of the project leader.

The experience also shows the need to balance the potential benefits of change against the risk of implementation failure in deciding how much reform (reengineering) to tackle at any one time. In Bhoomi, significant benefits are delivered in issuing RTCs, but much of the old mutation process remains unaltered. For example, there is no change in the role of the revenue inspector in approving mutation orders, but that role is now embedded in a different context that reduces opportunities for corruption.

Despite initial concern about raising the user fee to Rs 15 from the previous rate of Rs 2 in the manual system, this policy proved effective. This shows that concerns about user fees can be allayed if services have genuinely improved. In this case, the response of farmers at the taluk level was overwhelmingly positive.

An important lesson for other rural projects is the high level of effort needed to make the rural population aware of reforms that have been instituted. Despite considerable publicity given to Bhoomi, there is evidence that many farmers still may not understand the implications of all the reforms that have been carried out. The farmers need to be made aware of how the new system works, so that functionaries cannot exploit their ignorance and continue to demand bribes.

EXPANDING BHOOMI AND SCALING UP NATIONWIDE

Both within Karnataka state and elsewhere in India, there is significant potential for building on the Bhoomi experience to further improve the lives of the rural poor. Within the state, the key challenges are to utilize Bhoomi as the main application that can make a large number of privately owned rural Internet kiosks economically viable, and to use it as the basis for a land titling system that will further secure farmers' rights. At the same time, there are plans under way to replicate the first-phase success elsewhere in the country.

The first challenge within Karnataka, making Bhoomi data more widely available, is being addressed by current plans for expansion. The 1,000 rural telecentres, when up and running, will help to further bridge the digital divide in the Indian countryside. The second challenge is to use the Bhoomi data as a platform for a land titling system to enhance the security of land for farmers. Providing full legal land titles requires reforms that extend beyond computerization. The Bhoomi system as such does not provide a title, and the RTC issued by Bhoomi has only a presumptive value. What Bhoomi can do is to ensure the accuracy of records that are essential to pursuing more comprehensive reforms. A land titling system can only be built upon records that are clean and securely maintained so that they cannot be tampered with. Such an assurance, which is rare not only in India but also in other countries, has provided the basis for plans in Karnataka to move to a full land titling system—the first state in India to undertake this.

An even more daunting challenge is to improve the security of land tenancy for farmers who till the land of other owners. During the land reforms of the 1970s and 1980s in India, the tenancy system was overhauled and land was granted to the tiller. The reality on the ground, however, does not necessarily reflect these legal changes, and there are likely still a large number of tenants tilling the land of other farmers without having any legal rights to it. The reforms needed to establish tenancy rights are far-reaching, extending beyond the scope even of a land titling project.

The Bhoomi experience is now serving as the model for computerization of land records across India under a special programme of the Ministry of

Communications and Information Technology called 'Roll Out of Successful E-government Initiatives.' Bhoomi is one of three such initiatives identified for a countrywide roll-out. The ministry is providing funds for pilot implementation of Bhoomi in one district of each of the 13 states that have volunteered to participate. Leading management consulting companies have been chosen to support the roll-out effort, with the communications ministry providing the funding. The project recognizes that replication need not necessarily involve use of the same software that was used in the successful applications. Instead, the consultants are expected to capture knowledge and experience from the three successful projects and transfer such knowledge to the agencies involved in pilot implementations. The key point is to identify the processes that lead to successful implementation, such as digitization of manual data, reengineering of processes, involvement of all stakeholders, and management of change.

One significant challenge in replicating the Bhoomi system is the fact that the procedures governing changes in land ownership differ significantly by state, and documentation of these procedures is poor. In addition to formal legal provisions that can be documented, there are also conventional procedures that have evolved over the years. Successful expansion therefore requires significant effort at the start to understand and document such procedures for designing a computerized mutation process to ensure that the computerized system can handle the different ways in which a mutation can arise. In the case of Bhoomi, it took almost seven years to understand and document these procedures. In replicating the experience it will be essential to find ways to build in such systematic effort, despite the typically short tenure of project managers.

References

Acharya, K., 2003, 'Flaws in Bhoomi, India's Model E-governance Project,' Panos Features, July. http://infochangeindia.org/features120.jsp.

Chawla, R. and S. Bhatnagar, 2001, 'Bhoomi: Online Delivery of Land Titles in Karnataka, India,' Washington, DC: World Bank, http://www1.worldbank.org/publicsector/egov/bhoomi_cs.htm.

Department of Rural Development, 2001, 'Land Reforms,' In *Annual Report 2000–2001*, 92–97. New Delhi: Ministry of Rural Development, Government of India.

_____, 2002, 'Land Reforms.' In *Annual Report 2001–2002*, 126–34, New Delhi: Ministry of Rural Development, Government of India.

Gupta, V., 2002, 'E-governance: Lessons from District Computerization,' *Information Technology in Developing Countries* 12 (1). International Federation for Information Processing and Centre for Electronic Governance, Indian Institute of Management, Ahmedabad, India. http://www.iimahd.ernet.in/egov/ifip/apr2002/article6.htm.

Hanstad, T., 2001, 'How Are Rural Land Sale Markets in Karnataka Impacting the Poor's Access to Land?' Discussion paper, Rural Development Institute, University of Washington School of Law, Seattle.

Hanstad, T. and S.B. Lokesh, 2002, 'Computerization of Land Records in Karnataka: Observations from a Simple Field Study,' Rural Development Institute, Bangalore, India.

Lobo, A. and S. Balakrishnan, 2002, 'Report Card on Service of Bhoomi Kiosks: An Assessment of Benefits by Users of the Computerized Land Records System in Karnataka,' Public Affairs Centre, Bangalore, India. http://www1.worldbank.org/ publicsector/bnpp/Bhoomi.pdf.

McKinsey Global Institute, 2001, *India: The Growth Imperative*. McKinsey & Co. http://www.mckinsey.com/mgi/publications/india.asp.

Planning Commission, 1985, 'Rural Development and Poverty Alleviation Programmes,' Chap. 2 of *7th Five Year Plan*, vol. 2. New Delhi: Government of India. http://planningcommission.nic.in/plans/planrel/fiveyr/7th/vol2/7v2ch2.html.

The *Hindu*, 2002, 'IT for Agriculture: Karnataka Move,' the *Hindu* online edition, April 3, 2002. http://www.hinduonnet.com/thehindu/2002/04/03/stories/2002040303460600.htm.

World Bank, 2003, *World Development Report 2004: Making Services Work for Poor People*, New York: Oxford University Press.

Notes

1 Accountants were supervised by deputy tehsildars, who are the chief revenue officers for taluks, or subdistricts.

2 Shirasthedars and tehsildars are Revenue Department functionaries.

3 This is based on propriety software developed by HP Labs India. The image is printed using the private key of the kiosk operator. The public key is attached to the decoder, enabling it to decode the contents of the image and authenticate the source as the kiosk operator.

4 Internet kiosks are being set up in rural areas by the Department of Agriculture, nongovernmental organizations, and the private sector, but the numbers are very small. See the *Hindu* (2002).

5 Most users spend Rs 25–50 in travelling to a taluk kiosk. When questioned about the additional fee, some users indicated that an additional charge of Rs 10 would be acceptable to the farmer community if the RTCs could be delivered through rural telecentres. To make sure that farmers are not overcharged, the stationery used by the telecentres to print RTCs would be stamped with the maximum price that can be charged for the record (like the maximum retail price stamp on product packages sold in India).

6 User fees being collected by Bhoomi total approximately Rs 100 million per year. If 50 per cent of the RTCs are issued from the 1,000 rural kiosks being proposed, each kiosk will earn an average annual revenue of Rs 50,000. Accounting for variability across kiosks, the floor earning could be in the range of Rs 30,000. At this level of earning a kiosk can be viable.

7 The 'report card' on the Bhoomi initiative sought to assess its impact and benefits in relation to quality of service and user satisfaction. A survey was administered to a sample of citizens who had used Bhoomi kiosks as well as to a control sample of those who had used non-computerized land record providers. Quality of service and user satisfaction were compared across these two groups. Six districts reflecting the geographic regions of Karnataka were selected, and two Bhoomi kiosks were selected through sampling (weighted by intensity of use) from among the kiosks operating in each of these districts. A total of 198 respondents were interviewed across the sample of kiosks. For the sample of non-computerized facility users, four taluks were selected and 59 respondents interviewed. A team from ACNielsen ORG-MARG carried out the field survey and preliminary analysis.

8 When the delegates to a workshop in Bangalore, held in 2004 in preparation for the Shanghai conference, visited a rural kiosk issuing RTCs in Mandya, Karnataka, an old farmer protested that the data should be corrected in Bhoomi records as the printout of his RTC had misspelt his name.

9 NIC is a central government programme with offices in state capitals and districts to provide technical assistance in developing information and communication technology applications.

10 One example of the chief minister's commitment is that he signed letters to revenue collectors regarding Bhoomi while he was ill in a hospital.

11 The data entry software should not be confused with the back-end Bhoomi software, also developed by NIC, which operates on data, creates reports, handles changes, and tracks applications.

9

E-choupals and Rural Transformation
Web-Based Tools for Indian Farmers

Kuttayan Annamalai and *Sachin Rao*

Agriculture is vital to India. It produces 21.5 per cent of gross domestic product, feeds a billion people, and employs 66 per cent of the workforce (EIU 2004). In recent years agricultural productivity has improved, making the country self-sufficient in food and even a net exporter of a variety of food grains. Yet most Indian farmers have remained quite poor. The agricultural system is hobbled by remnants of scarcity-era regulation and by small, inefficient landholdings. The traditional marketing system is inefficient and often unfair to farmers, who generally have to accept the price offered at auction on the day they bring their grain to the *mandi*, or local market yard.

An innovative computer-based project begun in 2000 has addressed these challenges by transforming the agrarian marketing system and re-engineering the supply chain. The scheme was the brainchild of S. Sivakumar, head of the international business division of ITC Limited, one of India's leading diversified private companies. Scaling up rapidly, the company has set up 5,200 computer kiosks with Internet access, called e-choupals, in more than 31,000 farming villages across six states (ITC 2005b).[1] The e-choupals serve both as virtual gathering places where farmers can exchange information about market prices and as hubs for e-commerce. Initially targeting the important soybean crop, the scheme has expanded to serve farmers growing coffee, wheat, rice, pulses, and shrimp. At harvest time, ITC offers to buy the crop directly from any farmer at the previous day's closing price, thus bypassing the inefficient mandi system and delivering a higher price to the farmer.

The network of e-choupals has proven profitable both for ITC and for the 3.1 million farmers who have access to the system. Farmers benefit from more accurate weighing, faster processing time, and prompt payment, and typically receive about 2.5 per cent more for their soy than they would get through the mandi system. At the same time, ITC benefits from net procurement costs that are about 2.5 per cent lower than it would pay through the mandis. The company reports that it recovers its equipment costs from an e-choupal in the first year of operation and that the venture as a whole is profitable. Thus the initiative demonstrates that a large corporation can play a role in increasing the efficiency of an agricultural system in ways that benefit farmers and rural communities as well as shareholders.

Critical factors enabling the success of the venture to date include the key role of information technology, ITC's extensive knowledge of agriculture, and the effort ITC has made to retain many aspects of the existing production system, including maintenance of local partners. Equally important are the company's commitment to transparency and the respect and fairness with which both farmers and local partners are treated. This chapter expands on these lessons and the successes of the e-choupal experience in India. It first examines the inefficiency of the Indian agricultural sector and details the design of the e-choupal initiative, including its business model, trading system, and information technology architecture. The chapter then documents the initiative's impact and explores the challenges facing the programme in the future.

THE CONTEXT: INDIAN AGRICULTURE VITAL BUT INEFFICIENT

Agriculture is economically and socially vital to India, both feeding its population and employing its rural labour force. Agriculture's share of GDP has shrunk steadily, but at 21.5 per cent it remains a critical component of the economy. Few Indian farmers have the education or resources to take advantage of opportunities in non-farm sectors of the economy, such as the burgeoning urban services sector. Efforts to raise farm productivity and farmer incomes are therefore essential to improving the living standards of the rural population.

Despite its economically central role, Indian agriculture has until recently been regulated in an archaic fashion that limits its productivity. Non-optimal farming practices and capricious weather patterns left post-independence India with an underperforming agricultural sector, resulting in acute food shortages and dependence on food imports. Legislation from this period brought heavy government intervention in agriculture, including control of land ownership, pricing of agricultural inputs, and regulation of product marketing. Produce could only be sold to authorized agents in government-recognized locations. Processing capacities, private storage, futures trading, and transport were all restricted. The result was corrupt and inefficient systems in which starvation existed while granaries overflowed with food stocks.

At the same time, the unprofessional business environment made the agricultural sector unattractive to modern companies. Rural India is a difficult business location. Transport, electric power, and information infrastructure are all inadequate. Business practices are underdeveloped or outdated, and lack of access to modern resources has resulted in an undertrained workforce. Rural society is structured around subsistence and is largely unprepared to absorb modern products and services. These constraints, along with many others, have dissuaded most companies from taking on the challenge of rural commerce.

High Production, Impoverished Producers

The goal of achieving self-sufficiency in food brought Indian agriculture into the mainstream of the nation's political and social consciousness. The Green Revolution brought great strides in agricultural productivity in some parts of India and made the country a net exporter of most food grains by the mid-1970s. However, the Indian farmer did not progress correspondingly. After independence the government divided large landholdings into smaller parcels and redistributed them to rectify historical inequities and entrust ownership to cultivators in hopes of encouraging productivity. In subsequent years, ownership ceilings were legislated and inherited land was partitioned into even smaller lots. By 2003 the typical Indian farm was a very small operation, with landholdings often measured in fractions of an acre. Unable to realize economies of scale, most Indian farmers remained very poor (Aziz 2002).

In addition to the problems of small scale, Indian farmers are widely dispersed geographically and heterogeneous in terms of the crops they raise and the soils they cultivate (Sivakumar 2004). This makes it difficult for them to access the different types of information and knowledge they need to improve their practices and take risks profitably. They must also cope with profound weaknesses in rural infrastructure, both physical and institutional. This leads to a multiplication of intermediaries in the value chain; while these intermediaries fill a need in the absence of infrastructure, they also extract profits by blocking the free flow of market information.

As a result, producers get a very small share of the consumer price and can seldom increase their returns despite the risks they assume.

Farmers, then, are locked into a vicious cycle of low risk-taking ability, low investment, low productivity, low value addition, and low margins. Notes Sivakumar (2004), 'All the creativity and innovation of the rural poor is burnt up in fighting for survival, rather than in creation of more wealth which can raise their standard of living.'

The Oilseed Complex

Edible oil from vegetable sources is a fundamental part of the Indian diet. The 'oilseed complex' refers to the class of crops from which edible oils are extracted.[2] The complex is further classified into traditional oils (groundnut, rapeseed/mustardseed, safflower) and non-traditional oils (sunflower, soy, cottonseed). The process of oil extraction varies by oilseed, but generally consists of a two-stage process: mechanical crushing followed by solvent extraction to obtain residual oil. The mealy residue, called de-oiled cake or oilcake, is sold as animal feed.

Oilseed production stagnated in the 1970s, and by 1980 imports accounted for 32 per cent of the domestic supply. Following the Green Revolution in wheat and rice, the government of India turned regulatory attention in the early 1980s to oilseeds, sharply limiting imports. Protectionism brought substantial gains in domestic production, doubling oilseed output by 1994 and increasing the reliability of supply. About 40 per cent of the increased output came from the introduction of new crops, especially soy and sunflower. Soy thus represented an important innovation in the Indian oilseed complex, resulting in better utilization of scarce resources and greater cropping intensity. Soy was exempted from the Small Scale Industries Act to allow for processing in large modern facilities. Nonetheless, the growing of soybeans remains dominated by small farmers. Some 3 million soy farmers produce about 5 million tons of soybeans annually.

Traditional Channels for Marketing Soy

Before the introduction of the e-choupal system, there were three main commercial channels for marketing raw soy: private wholesale traders, government-mandated markets (mandis), and producer cooperatives (Figure 9.1). The bulk of the farmers' crop was sold to the private wholesalers and mandis for resale to private oil mills. A smaller portion went to the producer co-ops for crushing in cooperative mills. The percentage of produce going through each channel varied from district to district and from village to village. On average, however, 90 per cent of soy crops were processed through traders and mandis. These traditional marketing channels still predominate in many parts of the country where e-choupals have not been rolled out or are limited in their reach.

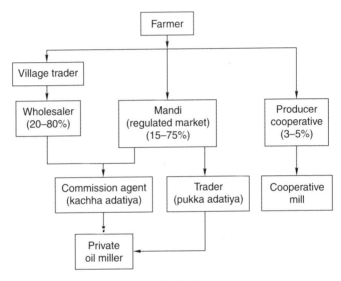

FIGURE 9.1 The Traditional Soy Marketing System

The mandis are the principal marketing channel to have been affected by the growth of e-choupals. The Agricultural Produce Marketing Act mandated the creation of mandis as delivery sites where farmers could bring produce for sale to traders. The area served by a mandi varies by state. In the soy-growing areas of Madhya Pradesh, a mandi typically serves around 700 square kilometres. With traditional grains, large portions are consumed by the farmers' households or bartered for other crops. But as soy is not part of the traditional Indian diet, its major market is the oil mill, and nearly the entire crop must be exported. This makes the mandi a vital part of the soy chain.

Mandi trading is conducted by brokers called *adatiyas*, who buy and sell the produce. They are of two types: *kachha adatiyas* are purchasing agents who buy only on behalf of others, while *pukka adatiyas* finance trade as representatives of distant buyers and sometimes procure crops on their own account. All the adatiyas belong to either the Agarwal or the Jain community, considered an economic class distinct from farmers. These middlemen manage the grain trade across the entire country, a remarkable feat considering the vast cultural and social diversity of the nation. The adatiyas established and grew the soy trading network on the basis of familial and community trust, with buying and selling based upon oral agreements. The lack of professional competition combined with the communal stranglehold on rural trading has made many adatiyas extremely wealthy. Commission agents from medium-size mandis can possess assets and incomes in the millions of dollars.

The operation of the mandi includes a number of different stages, from transporting grain to the market to quality inspection, auction, bagging, weighing, and payment. Based upon local information within the village, farmers choose one of the nearby mandis to sell. They transport their crops to the mandi in carts drawn by animals or tractors. Very often, to avoid peak-time crowds, farmers will arrive at the mandi the night before they intend to sell. When the mandi opens in the morning, farmers bring their carts to display areas within the mandi. Buyers inspect the crops by sight. There is no formal method of grading the produce, and the only instrument used is the moisture meter; the crop is not tested for oil content.

Once potential buyers have inspected the produce, a mandi employee conducts the auction. This is typically an open oral auction in which commission agents place incremental bids. There is a stark contrast between the positions of buyers and sellers. For the farmer, the moment is pivotal: a scant 30 seconds will serve to assess the results of six months of investment and hard work and set the value of his payday, one of only two or three he will have in the year.[3] For the commission agent, on the other hand, the moment is routine: he has many more carts of produce to buy and his margin is ensured irrespective of the price.

Once the price has been established by the auction, the farmer moves the cart to the weighing area run by the buying commission agent. The produce is transferred from the cart into individual sacks. The sacks are then weighed, one at a time, on a manual scale. After weighing, the full value of the grain is calculated. The farmer goes to the agent's office to collect a cash payment. The agent pays a mandi fee (1 per cent of purchase value in Madhya Pradesh) to the mandi. The bagged produce is then loaded onto the buyer's trucks and transported to the processing plant.

Limitations of the Mandi System

The inefficient mandi system does not serve the farmer well. Because farmers are not able to analyse price trends, they cannot time their sales to get better prices. As the price is determined at auction, by the time the farmer knows the price it is too late to go to another mandi. And there are other costs. The overnight stay near the mandi costs the farmer money. Most crops are displayed in open-air courtyards and are therefore vulnerable to the weather. The inspection process is unscientific and often arbitrary, tending to favour the buyer. As a result, there is little incentive for farmers to invest in better seed or farming practices that lead to higher quality, despite the fact that quality, especially oil content, matters to soy processors.

Farmers also point to problems with weighing and payment procedures. Bagging and weighing the crop is done by mandi labourers, part of whose compensation comes from the sale of spilled grain. Not surprisingly, spillage is frequent. Farmers also believe that the weighers consistently underweigh their produce by applying practiced and timely nudges to the scale. Historical intimidation and long queues at weighing stations dissuade the farmers from protesting. Finally, the farmer is not paid the full purchase price immediately, but receives a partial amount and must return to the mandi later for the remainder. Since the crop has already been delivered, the farmers are at the agents' mercy.

Overall, farmers find the auction process demeaning. Agents belong to a close-knit community that is socially and economically distinct from the farmer community. While they may not collude in pricing, they do collude in establishing practices of the trade that uniformly favour agents.

In addition to exploitation of the farmer, there are other inefficiencies in the system. The multiple points of handling in the supply chain require the produce to be bagged. Bagged produce takes four to five times longer than unbagged produce to be unloaded at the processing plant. Traders generally do not have the capacity to separately store and handle different grades of produce, inhibiting efforts to produce better crop grades. Pricing is set locally at the mandis and is not reliably tracked or reported nationally, resulting in a lack of information that reduces the opportunity for arbitrage and improved market efficiency. In addition, regulatory restrictions tend to limit arbitrage to small geographic areas.

The inefficiencies of the mandi system also do not serve the interests of trading companies such as ITC. From the company's point of view, the key problem is the agents' control of the market and the resulting distortions of price and quality. While agents purchase grain on a trading company's behalf, their purchases are of varying quality. The agent often mixes crops of different quality together and charges the trading company a single price near the higher end of the price spectrum. Agents can also stagger their sales to the trading company from day to day, capturing the benefit of price shifts.

When ITC buys from agents, the official commission is 1 per cent of ITC's price. But ITC estimates that the agents' operating margin in fact reaches 2.5 to 3 per cent.

ITC AND THE ORIGINS OF E-CHOUPAL

The ITC group, which originated as Imperial Tobacco Company, is one of India's foremost private sector companies, with a market capitalization of over $8 billion and annual revenues of $2.6 billion (ITC 2005a). ITC has a diversified presence in tobacco, hotels, paperboards, specialty papers, packaging, agribusiness, branded apparel, packaged foods, and other consumer goods.

ITC's International Business Division (IBD) was created in 1990 as an agricultural trading company aiming to 'offer the world the best of India's produce.' Initially, its agricultural commodity business was small compared to that of international players. By 1996, the opening up of the Indian market had brought in international competition. Large international companies had better margin-to-risk ratios because of wider options for risk management and arbitrage. For an Indian company to replicate the operating model of such multinational corporations would have required a massive horizontal and vertical expansion.

In 1998, after competition forced ITC to explore the options of sale, merger, or closure of IBD, the company ultimately decided to retain the business. ITC's chairman, Y.C. Deveshwar, challenged IBD to use information technology (IT) to change the rules of the game and create a competitive business that did not need a large asset base.

S. Sivakumar, IBD's chief executive, recognized a unique opportunity to create value for the company's shareholders while promoting social development in rural India. At the annual planning meeting in 1999, Sivakumar presented an alternative business plan based on using IT to reengineer the supply chain through which ITC sourced its agricultural commodities (Gupta and Rajshekhar 2005). This would benefit the company through lower costs. But ITC also envisioned the scheme as having a social impact, both through the provision of Internet access to rural areas and through the long-term development of rural India as a competitive supplier and consumer of goods and services in the global economy. ITC would serve as a 'network orchestrator', stitching together the supply chain and producing enough value to benefit farmers, other companies, and ITC alike.

ITC approved the plan and decided to test the model in the soy-producing belt in Madhya Pradesh (Gupta and Rajshekhar 2005). When ITC entered the soy industry in the 1990s, it began by buying de-oiled soy cake from the private oil millers and exporting it. But the company soon realized that it needed to establish a presence further up the supply chain. It began renting processing plant time and buying soy directly from local mandis for crushing.

It became clear that with the commission agent structure in the traditional mandi system, ITC was blocked from interacting directly with farmers. This gap created a range of supply-chain issues, limiting ITC's knowledge of its crops, suppliers, and supply risks, and also limiting the company's ability to improve crop quality and quantity by bringing modern agricultural practices to the farmers. The e-choupal strategy was developed as a way to limit the role of the agents and communicate directly with farmers through a 'virtual vertical integration'. While steadily increasing the amount of soy procured directly from farmers through the e-choupals, ITC has also continued to buy a portion of its soy from the mandis.

The E-choupal Vision

The e-choupal alternative was conceived not just as a single innovation but as a transformation of agrarian marketing arrangements that required a broader strategic vision. ITC was able to build on its previous experience in Indian agriculture through its tobacco business, relying on several overarching management principles. These included re-engineering the positive aspects of the established system, conceiving the change in terms of the entire supply chain, and anticipating obstacles and risks.

Re-engineer, not reconstruct

The conventional approach to transforming established business systems begins by examining the failures of the current system and developing the means to change it. ITC took a different approach, first looking at the successes of the current system and then identifying elements to build on. ITC retained the efficient functions within the mandi system. However, some inefficient functions were revamped; as a result, new roles were created for the providers of those functions. This had two benefits. First, it avoided 'reinventing the wheel' in areas where ITC would not have been able to add value through its presence. Second, it found a way to keep the displaced incumbents engaged with ITC, ensuring that ITC maintained a positive relationship with these powerful rural players. Particularly important was ITC's creation of an appropriate new role for the commission agents that were the backbone of the system being replaced.

Address the whole, not just one part

Currently, the village trader services the spectrum of farmers' needs. He is a centralized provider of cash, seed, fertilizer, and pesticides, as well as a marketing channel—in some places the only marketing channel—for crops. As a result, the trader enjoys two competitive benefits. First, his intimate knowledge of farmer and village dynamics allows him to accurately assess and manage risk. Second, he reduces overall transaction costs by aggregating services. The linked transactions reduce the farmers' cost in the short term but create a cycle of exploitative dependency in the long term.

Efforts to reform this system have tended to focus on individual pieces rather than on what the entire community needs. Cooperatives have tried to provide agricultural inputs, rural banks have tried to provide credit, and mandis have tried to create a better marketing channel. These efforts have not been able to compete against the trader's bundled offer of services. Any alternative, therefore, must also address the entire range of farmers' needs, not just provide a marketing channel.

Make good use of appropriate IT

ITC recognized that new information technologies provided opportunities to optimize effectiveness and scalability while reducing cost. While IT represented only about 20 per cent of the effort in the e-choupal business model, it was considered the most crucial 20 per cent. The use of IT offered two critical advantages. First, it facilitated collaboration between the many parties involved in meeting farmers' needs. Second, it ensured delivery of real-time information to farmers independent of the sale transaction. In the mandi system, delivery, pricing, and sales happen simultaneously, thus binding the farmer to an agent. E-choupal technology was seen as a way to deliver critical market information independent of the mandi, thus allowing farmers a choice of where and when to sell their crops.

In deciding to make IT a critical element in the strategy, ITC did not hesitate to install expensive IT infrastructure in remote rural areas. As of 2003, not a single case of theft, misappropriation, or misuse had been reported among the almost 2,000 e-choupals.

Anticipate obstacles and risks

Given the innovative character of the strategy, ITC was careful to plan for modular investment, allowing for incremental advances. Stages of the process included initial roll-out, correcting identified problems, and scaling up operations. This incremental control of investment levels was one of the critical elements in getting approval from management and the company's board for the initiative.

Among risks identified in advance were the possible obsolescence of IT investments because of the emergence of newer, cheaper technology; the possibility that the farmers chosen as local partners would become too influential and would seek greater rents; and the danger that the scope of the venture would pose too great a barrier to efficient management.

One obstacle that was identified and overcome was the effect of existing regulations under the Agricultural Produce Marketing Act. This act, which established the mandi system, prohibits procurement outside the mandis. ITC convinced the government that e-choupals would operate according to the spirit of the act and thus could be considered to fit within the system. Since ITC would not be using the mandi infrastructure to buy from farmers, and would incur its own costs in building the e-choupal infrastructure, the government offered to waive the mandi tax on produce channelled through e-choupals. Nevertheless, ITC recognized that the tax was a major source of revenue for the government and for local mandis. As ITC's competition was also subject to the tax, the tax itself did not place an extra competitive burden on ITC. The company therefore chose to continue paying the tax rather than risk its relationships with the government and the mandis.

The Business Model

The e-choupal initiative is based on a network of information centres located in rural farming villages, each equipped with a computer connected to the Internet. E-choupals serve both as social venues for exchange of information (*choupal* means gathering place in Hindi) and as e-commerce hubs. A local farmer acting as a *sanchalak* runs the village e-choupal, and the computer is usually located in the sanchalak's home. There is also a role in the system for a local commission agent, known as a *samyojak*, who provides logistical support.

The sanchalak

The critical element of the e-choupal system, and the key to managing the geographical and cultural breadth of the network, is the sanchalak. ITC channels virtually all its communication with farmers through the local sanchalak. Recruiting a local farmer from the community for this role serves several purposes:

- It builds trust. For generations, the Indian farmer has been betrayed by individuals and institutions. Trust is the most valuable commodity in rural India. No transaction will happen without trust, irrespective of the strength of the contract. The sanchalak is selected from within the farmer community to provide this vital component in ITC's system.
- It provides physical infrastructure and helps to keep costs low. ITC places each computer in a sanchalak's house and thus need not invest in building and securing a facility to house the computer.
- It overcomes the literacy barrier. The sanchalak is trained in computer operation and offers a familiar and approachable human operator for the often illiterate farmers and other villagers.
- It capitalizes on entrepreneurship. ITC expects to leverage the profit-making power of the small-scale entrepreneur.

Sanchalaks in turn have several motivations for assuming their role. They gain a way to help their community, a profitable business for themselves, and access to a functional computer. The sanchalak receives a commission for every transaction processed through his e-choupal. Farmers also benefit from increased social status that accompanies the position—a significant advantage in rural Indian life. ITC insists that sanchalaks should not give up farming, for this would compromise the trust that they enjoy. To help ensure that sanchalaks serve their communities and not just themselves, ITC projects the role as a public office. The title 'sanchalak' is assumed after a public ceremony in which the sanchalak takes an oath to serve the entire farming community through the e-choupal.

Successful sanchalaks usually have a number of common characteristics, including an ability to take risks, willingness to try something new, ambition, and aspiration to earn additional income. Sanchalaks are usually of median wealth and status in their communities, are able to read and write, and are part of an extended family large enough that they can find time to manage the e-choupal.

Sanchalaks are trained at the nearest ITC plant. They receive instruction in basic computer usage, the functions of the e-choupal website, business skills, and inspection of crop quality. For selling products through the e-choupals, the sanchalaks receive product training directly from the manufacturer. Their role requires considerable entrepreneurial initiative and entails some operational costs, between $60 and $160 per year, for electricity and phone line charges; the latter are gradually declining as ITC replaces phone-based Internet connections with a VSAT (very small aperture terminal) system.

After selecting and training the sanchalaks, ITC continues to encourage sales through a variety of motivation techniques, as most sanchalaks do not have previous retail experience. One technique is to hold a ceremony where sanchalaks are presented with their annual commission cheques and public announcements of earnings are made. Stories of how sanchalaks spent past commissions serve to demonstrate the income potential and spurs non-performers to work. The zeal to perform sometimes leads to territorial disputes, but ITC does not interfere in their resolution because the competition encourages sanchalaks to better serve their customer base.

The samyojak

A secondary but still important role is played by the *samyojak*, or cooperating commission agent. Samyojaks earn income from ITC by providing logistical services that substitute for the lack of rural infrastructure, especially information about products and markets. In effect, ITC uses agents as providers of essential services, not as principals in a trading transaction. The samyojaks play an especially important role in the initial stages of setting up the e-choupals because they know which farmers grow soy, what kinds of families they have, what their financial situations are, and who is seen as 'acceptable' in the villages and thus might make a good sanchalak. ITC is strongly committed to involving samyojaks in the ongoing operation of the e-choupal system. They have opportunities for revenue through providing services such as management of cash, bagging, and labour in remote ITC procurement hubs, and handling of tax paperwork for ITC procurement. They also serve as licensed principals for the retail transactions of the e-choupal.

Since the e-choupal system bypasses the agent-controlled mandis, however, it has reduced the income of the agents. Why, then, do they agree to cooperate with ITC? First, the company has made clear that they will continue also to buy produce through the mandis. Second, the company offers significant commissions for samyojak services. Finally, the agents are fragmented and fear that if they do not agree to work with ITC, another agent will gain the promised e-choupal revenues. One samyojak reported that he saw globalization as an irresistible trend, and although he would lose revenue in the short term, his long-term interest lay in cooperating with an international company.

Coverage

ITC plans to saturate the sector in which it works with e-choupals, so that a farmer will have to travel no more than 5 kilometres to reach one. The company expects each e-choupal to serve about 10 villages within a 5-kilometre radius. Of the e-choupals in Madhya Pradesh, the one in Khasrod serves about 500–700 farmers in 10 villages; another in Dahod serves 5,000 farmers in 10 villages. The average usage is about 600 farmers per e-choupal in the soy cropping area, with fewer in wheat, coffee, and shrimp areas.[4]

HOW E-CHOUPALS WORK: THE TRADING SYSTEM

The e-choupal system works with a re-engineered supply chain that provides gains for both the farmers and for ITC, makes it possible to maintain high volume and scale up operations, and offers scope to add services such as credit and insurance.

The E-choupal Supply Chain

The elements of the supply chain, in sequence, are pricing, inbound logistics, inspection and grading, weighing and payment, and hub logistics.

Pricing is determined by the previous day's mandi closing price, which sets the benchmark 'fair average quality' price at the e-choupal. This is constant for a given day, and is the highest price that a sanchalak can quote. The sanchalak has access to this price and the previous day's price through the e-choupal website. The commission agents at the mandi are responsible for entering daily mandi prices into the e-choupal. If the Internet connection fails, the sanchalak calls an ITC field representative to get the price data.

To initiate a sale, the farmer brings a sample of his produce to the e-choupal for inspection and grading. The sanchalak inspects the produce. Based on his assessment of the quality, he makes appropriate deductions, if any, from the benchmark price and gives the farmer a conditional quote. The sanchalak performs the quality tests in the farmer's presence and must justify any deduction to the farmer. This initial check ensures transparency in a process where quality testing and pricing happen at multiple levels. If the farmer chooses to sell his soy to ITC, the sanchalak gives him a note with his name, his village, particulars about the quality tests (foreign matter and moisture content), approximate quantity, and conditional price.

The farmer takes the note from the sanchalak and proceeds with his crop to the nearest ITC procurement hub. This is ITC's point for collection of produce, as well as for distribution of inputs sold in rural areas. Some procurement hubs are ITC processing plants that also act as collection points; others are purely warehousing operations. ITC's goal is to have a processing centre within a 30–40 kilometre radius of each farmer. As of 2003 there were 16 procurement hubs in Madhya Pradesh, with plans to reach a total of 35 in the state.

At the ITC hub, a sample of the farmer's produce is taken and set aside for laboratory tests. A chemist visually inspects the soybeans and verifies the assessment of the sanchalak. It is important to note that this is the only assessment before the sale. Laboratory testing of the sample for oil content is performed after the sale and does not alter the price. The reason for this is that farmers, having historically been exploited, are not immediately willing to trust a laboratory test. Therefore, pricing is based solely upon tests that can be understood by the farmer. The farmer accepts foreign matter deductions for the presence of stones or hay, based upon the visual comparison of his produce with that of his neighbours. He will accept moisture content deductions based upon the comparative softness of his produce when he bites it.

If later tests show that the quality is actually higher than the norm, this does not alter the price, but the farmer receives 'bonus points'. These can be redeemed through the e-choupal for farm inputs or used to pay insurance premiums. It is hoped that this will contribute to improving quality as well as increasing respect for laboratory testing.

After the inspection, the farmer's cart is weighed on an electronic weighbridge, first with the produce and then without. The difference determines the weight of his produce. Once the weighing is complete, the farmer collects his payment in full at the payment counter. The farmer is also reimbursed for transporting his crop to the procurement hub. Every stage of the process is accompanied by appropriate documentation. The farmer is given a copy of lab reports, agreed rates, and receipts for his records.

Samyojaks, who are adept at handling large amounts of cash, are entrusted with the responsibility of payment, except at procurement centres near large ITC operations where ITC itself handles cash disbursement. Samyojaks also handle much of the procurement hub logistics, including labour management at the hub, bagging (if necessary), storage management, transportation from the hub to processing plants, and handling mandi paperwork for the crops procured at the hub. For his services in the procurement process, the samyojak is paid a 0.5 per cent commission.

Farmer Gains

Before the introduction of e-choupals, farmers' access to agricultural information was incomplete and inconsistent. The only sources of information were the commission agent and word of mouth within the village. The e-choupal system allows farmers daily access to prices at several nearby mandis. Some sanchalaks have taken this a level further by accessing external pricing sources in order to track global trends and determine the optimum timing of sales. With this information, farmers are better able to decide when and where to sell their crops.

Farmers are reimbursed for transport to the procurement hub instead of having to pay their own costs for transportation to the mandi. The transaction at the ITC hub is also much faster than at the mandi, usually taking no more than two or three hours. Moreover, ITC's electronic weighing scales are accurate and not susceptible to sleight of hand like the manual weighing system at the mandi. The system does not require produce to be bagged, which avoids the associated loss of produce by intentional spillage.

In addition to these efficiencies, the ITC procurement hub is a professionally run operation where the farmer is treated with respect and served as a customer. The importance of the dignity accorded farmers by this process should not be understated. ITC recognizes that farmers are not simply agricultural producers, but essential partners in the supply process. Simple provisions such as a shaded seating area where farmers can wait for their paperwork serve as indicators of this respect. Though intangible, the self-confidence created by this professional treatment is affecting the way farmers conduct themselves. Sanchalaks and even commission agents have noted a change in farmer attitudes.

The increased income to the farmer from a more efficient marketing process is about $6 per metric ton, or about 2.5 per cent over the mandi system. Farmers can also make use of the information available to them through e-choupals to improve their yields. Moreover, the seed, fertilizer, and consumer products offered through e-choupals cost substantially less than inputs obtained through other local sources such as village traders. Typically, the sanchalak aggregates village orders for inputs and transmits the combined order to an ITC representative.

ITC Gains

ITC also gains significantly from buying through this process.[5] Although commissions paid to agents under the mandi system were not excessive, other inefficiencies of the system raised the true cost of intermediation to between 2.5 and 3 per cent of procurement costs. Commissions paid for the sanchalaks' services, at a level of 0.5 per cent, are significantly less than the costs associated with the mandi system. Direct reimbursement of transport costs to the farmer is estimated at half of what ITC used to pay the commission agents for transport to the processing plant. The ability to reward farmers for higher quality results in higher oil yields, which in turn leads to higher profits for the company.

In the mandi system, transaction costs add 7 to 8 per cent to the price of soybeans from farm gate to factory gate. The farmer bears transaction costs of 2.5 per cent, while 5 per cent is borne by ITC when it buys through mandis. With e-choupals, ITC's costs are now down to 2.5 per cent. Table 9.1 shows transaction costs incurred by the farmer and ITC per metric ton of soy procured through the mandi and e-choupal systems. In absolute numbers, both the farmers and ITC save about $6 (Rs 270) per metric ton on transactions through an e-choupal.

TABLE 9.1   Transaction Costs for Soy under the Mandi and E-choupal Systems, 2003

(rupees per metric ton)

Cost item	Farmer		ITC	
	Mandi	E-choupal	Mandi	E-choupal
Commission	0	0	100	50
Handling and transit losses	50	0	10	0
Labour	50	0	70	85
Bagging and weighing	70	0	75	0
Transportation	100	0	250	100
Total	270	0	505	235

Source: ITC.

E-choupals also allow ITC to develop long-term supplier relationships with farmers and attain some degree of supply security over time. Risk is managed in the e-choupal system by a far stronger information infrastructure than exists for the mandis. Sanchalaks and samyojaks working on behalf of ITC provide excellent bottom-up information on pricing, product quality, soil conditions, and expected yields. This allows ITC to better plan future operations.

Sustaining Commercial Volume and Scaling Up

ITC has been able to sustain commercial volume in this virtual vertical integration by scheduling procurement year-round and by fostering the flow of information between the e-choupals and ITC. Maintaining procurement and sales operations year-round ensures a continuous flow of commission cheques through e-choupals. Purchases and sales take place during both *kharif* (the rainfed cropping season that coincides with India's southwest monsoon, July through October) and *rabi* (the winter cropping season in irrigated areas). Thus, there is a steady stream of revenue for sanchalaks and of produce for the ITC factories.

This also facilitates communication. Because of the number and physical dispersion of the e-choupals, this communication must be initiated by the sanchalaks. If their motivation to communicate with ITC diminishes, the channel will still function for procurement but will fail to supply enough information for risk management, distribution, and product design. One example of the power of local information was seen early in e-choupal implementation. A competitor attempted to divert produce coming to the ITC factories by stationing representatives on the roads leading up to the plants. These individuals would stop farmers on their way to the ITC hubs and offer them a price higher than the ITC rate. Farmers alerted the sanchalaks and they in turn provided ITC with the information necessary to address the situation.

By 2005, the company was opening six to seven new e-choupals a day (Gupta and Rajshekhar 2005). In addition to expanding the number and coverage of the computer kiosks, ITC also sees opportunities for scaling up the system into a broader distribution channel that reaches out to rural Indian consumers. The company has identified three main options:

- Expanding the e-choupal model to other crops such as spices, horticulture, and cotton (Sivakumar 2004). Agrarian systems vary by crop, with different configurations of inefficiencies in the supply chain and varying opportunities for the e-choupal system. For example, the systems for coffee and shrimp are very different from those for soy. In the case of soy, ITC could realistically target recovering the entire cost of infrastructure from procurement savings. With coffee and shrimp, however, the investment recovery horizon is much longer.

- Channelling other sales through the distribution system. The same system of physical and information exchange that brings produce from the villages can be used to transfer goods to the villages. Given that the infrastructure has already been paid for, it is available at marginal cost for distribution. Products and services such as herbicides, seeds, fertilizers, insurance policies, and soil testing are already being sold through e-choupals. ITC is extending the scope of sales to include consumer goods and services, offering villagers new options not available through traditional traders.

- Providing an avenue for farmers to suggest innovations. For example, farmers have demanded that ITC make available improved varieties of seed. Some farmers have urged ITC to become involved in onion and potato crops, arguing that availability of high-quality seeds and market information would enable them to compete with Chinese onions in the world market.

ITC's strategy is to position itself not as a provider of third-party products and services but rather as a network choreographer for two-way demand and supply of goods through a collaborative business model. The company intends to differentiate itself by handling only those products and services to which it can add value. ITC regards its core asset as its knowledge of the customers, in this case the farmers. Through e-choupals, procurement hubs, and processing centres, ITC is setting up the infrastructure needed to implement an alternative channel for distribution of goods and services to rural India. In the long term, ITC sees vast opportunities from its e-commerce platform and low-cost distribution system; indeed, company officials have expressed an ambition to become 'the Wal-Mart of India'. ITC chairman Y.C. Deveshwar told the media that the e-choupal network will serve an area where nearly 70 per cent of the country's population resides, including 'villages with populations of less than 5,000 people where most businesses never venture' ('ITC Hopes' 2003).

In addition, ITC anticipates that this information infrastructure can be used to enhance its business decision-making, manage risk more effectively, and identify opportunities for cross-selling and up-selling. Data mining and data warehousing will help company executives better understand the behaviour of their customers, identify unfulfilled needs, and devise ways to meet these needs efficiently. Thus, the communication infrastructure can help to compensate for the lack of physical infrastructure needed for marketing products and services in rural India. It can enable rapid, low-cost information dissemination, with a trusted brand for introducing new products, while minimizing the need for a travelling sales force. Online ordering and order management can decrease the need for physical facilities. And the IT infrastructure, working with local sanchalaks, can provide customer intelligence that can be used to maximize customer satisfaction and profitability.

Additional Services: Credit and Insurance

There are significant opportunities for scaling up the e-choupals to address longstanding problems with rural credit. Farmers' low incomes and their difficulty accessing credit severely limit their capacity to pursue opportunities within and outside the agriculture sector. Demand for rural credit is estimated at $31.6 billion (Rs 1.43 trillion) per year. But many financial institutions are hesitant to serve rural India because of borrowers' lack of credit history, high transaction costs, and a perception of high risk, all of which lead to high costs of borrowing for farmers.

Providing credit has long been considered an important poverty alleviation strategy in India. The Indian government has implemented a number of subsidized credit-related programmes. The Integrated Rural Development Programme (IRDP), started in 1978, had a large credit component, but the programme's impact did not match the resources expended. The loans were not tailored to meet individual needs and the programme lacked the support systems necessary to help farmers.

ITC proposes to address these problems through e-choupals and through partnerships with financial institutions. For example, e-choupals can assist in capturing credit history. Farmers in rural India borrow money from local moneylenders, friends, relatives, or traders, as well as through government programmes. Local moneylenders and intermediaries are aware of farmers' creditworthiness and are therefore willing to loan money, albeit at a high interest rate. Through e-choupals, ITC now has the capability to manage credit risk through its sanchalak network, which can be used not only to verify the creditworthiness of individual farmers but also to continuously monitor credit risk. ITC will be able to create a consolidated farmers' database with information pertaining to their holdings and transactions that can be used as a source of credit profiles.

Using e-choupals can also help reduce transaction and administration costs. For major financial institutions, transaction costs involved in servicing the rural market have been high because of the difficulty in reaching this market. E-choupals can help overcome this problem by leveraging the IT infrastructure and the sanchalak network, thereby lowering administrative costs.

ITC plans to establish partnerships with larger banks such as ICICI to design products for rural India. Some of the products being designed include:

- Non-cash loans for farm inputs. Instead of giving cash to the farmer directly, the financial institutions will purchase farm inputs on behalf of the farmer. Farmers are expected to pay back loans for the purchase price to the financial institution.
- Loans to sanchalaks. Instead of making loans directly to farmers, loans will be given to sanchalaks for onlending to farmers. Sanchalaks can manage credit risk better than financial institutions because they have better access to farmers and therefore more accurate information.
- Direct loans to farmers based on sanchalak recommendations. In this case, sanchalaks' commissions are based on the loan recovery, giving them an incentive to monitor the risk on a continuous basis.

Insurance services designed to deal with rural cash cycles are already available through the e-choupals. There is recognition that in bad years, farmers may not be able to pay an insurance premium. Rather than penalize the farmer for non-payment, ITC allows catch-up payments in later years or, as an alternative, reduction of the final payout. ITC uses the e-choupal web infrastructure to set up and issue electronic reminders for premium payments. This addresses a major weakness of the current insurance system, in which agents have little incentive to encourage renewals and the lapse rate among policyholders is high.

How E-choupals Work:
The Information Technology

Introducing appropriate computer technology in rural India has required an understanding of the particular constraints of this environment. These include limitations of power, transportation, and telecommunications infrastructure, as well as customers' general unfamiliarity with computers.

Electric power in rural India is unreliable, usually available sporadically for only a few hours a day. Because timely access to the e-choupal computer is critical to the success of this business model, ITC provided a battery-based UPS (uninterrupted power supply) backup system. With this, the sanchalak can use the system at least twice a day, in the morning to check the prevailing mandi prices and again in the evening to check the rate ITC will be offering the next day. Even so, insufficient line power during the day means there may not be enough power to charge the backup battery. ITC therefore decided to use solar battery chargers, which with one full day of sunlight can charge the battery for 70 to 80 minutes of computer usage.

Power quality is also a problem, with endemic voltage fluctuations that can easily damage the UPS unit. To overcome this problem, ITC plans to install specially designed UPS units that remain effective between 90 and 300 volts. To control voltage spikes, they have introduced spike suppressors and filters. Phase imbalances, which can damage equipment, have been addressed through the use of isolation transformers to correct neutral voltages.

Most e-choupal villages lack proper roads, limiting vehicle access. Public transportation service to many villages is infrequent, with some served only once or twice a day by rural taxis. The population relies primarily on bicycles, motorbikes, and bullock carts. Providing system support and maintenance requires the technician to travel from outside areas to visit the e-choupals. Initially, therefore, ITC placed e-choupals in villages that are within 10 to 15 kilometres of a city.

Telecommunication infrastructure in villages is also poor. Telephone exchanges are subject to the sporadic power supply and have limited battery backup. When power is lost, phones cease to function. In addition, there is no local support staff to maintain or troubleshoot telephone exchanges. The turnaround time for fixing problems is often measured in days, not hours. Overhead telephone lines are exposed to the elements and to interference from parallel power lines. Currently, village telecommunication infrastructure is designed to carry voice traffic only, with slow transmission speeds that make Internet access impractical. ITC has accordingly been forced to turn to more expensive VSAT technology.

The final obstacle is that before the arrival of the e-choupals, most villagers had never seen a computer. Recognizing the importance of appropriate user interface, ITC organized meetings and focus groups of farmers to gather information about potential users. The feedback collected from these focus groups was used in the design of the application. Fortunately, the initial assumption that computer literacy and usability would be a major issue in system deployment was not borne out. It quickly became clear that people could master any of the tools as long as the tools functioned well and added value to their lives. In practice, usability proved to be a non-issue for the sanchalaks.

The system designed to implement the e-choupal included four levels of specification: the technical architecture of the hardware and system software, the software application architecture, the information architecture for the data included, and the organization architecture needed to support system operation. While all four are interconnected, having the same goals and comparable constraints, they are best conceived as distinct layers of the system.

Technical Architecture

The initial hardware configuration was a PC with Intel Celeron processor, a printer, a UPS with isolation transformer and spike suppressor, and a solar battery charger, along with a dial-up modem and a VSAT modem and antenna. The initial operating system was Windows 98 with Ankur (a Hindi word processor). Also included were short video clips on the e-choupal system and on soil testing.

The most problematic issue was Internet connectivity. It soon became clear that the existing telecom infrastructure was not capable of supporting data traffic. Working with the Centre for Development of Telematics (C-DoT), ITC determined that the lack of synchronization between the village exchange and the main exchange was a major issue. C-DoT proposed the installation of RNS kits for network synchronization in the village exchanges. Even after the installation of these kits, however, the data throughput was a mere 12 kilobits per second (kbps). With the help of C-DoT, ITC made modifications to the RNS kit that helped them achieve 40 kbps throughput.

Even so, given sporadic power supply in the village exchanges, dial-up was not reliable. ITC therefore decided to adopt VSAT, a satellite-based technology that enables a throughput rate of up to 256 kbps. This was an expensive solution, costing about $2,650 (Rs 120,000) per installation. Nevertheless, e-choupals with VSAT connections produce significantly higher usage and commercial volumes and thus recover the initial investment faster than the dial-up connections.

Application Architecture

The application layer, based on the central server for e-choupal, represents the logical structure for the system. The website www.soyachoupal.com

serves as the gateway for the farmer. It is protected, requiring a user ID and password to log in. So far, sanchalaks are the only registered users. Immediately after a sanchalak is recruited, an account is created, with a user ID and password to access the system.

The application allows the sanchalak access to features specific to e-choupals as well as to other Internet resources. Features on the soyachoupal website include:

- Weather. Localized weather information is obtained from the Indian Meteorological Department, which provides forecasts for rural areas. Users select their district of interest by clicking on the appropriate region of a map. The e-choupal site provides 24- to 72-hour weather forecasts, along with advisories directly related to farmers' activities. For instance, during the sowing season, a weather forecast for days following heavy rains might advise the farmer to sow seeds while the soil is still wet. One farmer observed that before e-choupals, unreliable weather information would result in prematurely planted seeds that would be washed out by early rains. The availability of accurate rain information has cut losses due to weather by more than half.

- Prices, both the ITC procurement rate and the local mandi rates. ITC's next-day rates are published every evening. The prices are displayed prominently on the top of the web page on a scrolling ticker.

- News from various sources, including agriculture-related news, local news, entertainment, and sports.

- Agricultural best practices, organized by crop type. For instance, this section might discuss what kinds of fertilizers to use and when and how to use them.

- Q & A. Farmers can post any agriculture-related questions they need answered.

In addition to visiting the soyachoupal website, sanchalaks and others who use the system have learned that there is a vast amount of information at their fingertips on the World Wide Web. This includes worldwide price trends for soy and other crops. One sanchalak even followed Chicago Board of Trade prices for a month and arrived at a correlation with the local market prices. He used this information to help other farmers decide when to sell. E-choupal users also visit popular news sites such as Dainik Jagran and WebDunia; entertainment sites for movie trivia, CD rentals, and music downloads; and sports sites for cricket news. Students use the Internet to check their exam results and grades online. The e-choupal computers are also used for communication. The sanchalaks have e-mail accounts on Yahoo, and some use chat rooms to chat with other sanchalaks and ITC managers.

Information Architecture

The e-choupal system is designed to gather customer information over time. The sources, structure, management, and use of these data constitute the information architecture. The technical details are routine, but the information itself and its potential uses are exciting. Data about rural customers such as their location, creditworthiness, consumer preferences, financial position, and spending patterns represent the first link between this vast untapped market and urban commerce. Such information will eliminate the 'unknowns' of rural engagement and enable planning, marketing, and sales of a range of products.

Information gathering is currently semi-automated. Information on each sanchalak is gathered during user registration. The sanchalak also keeps a record of visits, inquiries, and purchases by farmers. The Q & A section of the website allows for two-way entry of data that are also stored in a database. The website does not currently process live transactions, but ITC has plans for this in the future.

The web server tracks Internet usage patterns for e-choupals. From these data, ITC extracts information on such topics as peak usage periods, preferred Internet destinations, information most sought after, and so on. ITC intends to use this information to help better understand the behaviour of its customers, identify unfulfilled needs, and develop ways to meet these needs efficiently.

Organizational Architecture

The hardware and software infrastructure requires the critical resources of people, processes, and services to set up, maintain, and run it. Training and support services are essential, forming an additional layer of the e-choupal IT system.

Training

Training the sanchalaks to use a computer effectively is vital to the success of the e-choupal scheme. As the human interface of the e-choupals, they must be able to operate the computers and access the information requested by farmers.

The computer installed in the sanchalak's home is the first computer in most villages. Immediately after sanchalaks are recruited, they are invited to the nearest ITC plant for a day-long training programme to familiarize them with the equipment. The training includes the following elements:

- Fundamentals: What is a computer? What are its purposes and practical applications?
- Basic equipment training: turning the computer on and off; using the mouse, keyboard, printer, and so forth.
- Software training: word processing, including how to open, close, and save files, how to use the Ankur software, how to type in Hindi,[6] and how to create and edit documents; web browsing; and e-choupal applications, including how to use the soyachoupal website.

When the computer is installed in the village, a coordinator usually accompanies the vendor who installs the system. The sanchalak is given some of the same basic training by the vendor. ITC then allows the sanchalak to experiment with the computer for about a week. During this time, typically the younger members of his family also get to use the computer. ITC has observed that children are quick computer learners and are eager to learn more.

After the first week, the sanchalaks are invited to the procurement hub or the processing plant for the second phase of training. In order to gauge their level of comfort, they are asked to operate the computer. Based on observation, customized training is then provided to raise each user's comfort and competency level. Sanchalaks may also bring their children or other members of the family who are interested in learning about the computer. During this phase, sanchalaks are trained to use the e-choupal website and to access information from the site. They are given the opportunity to voice their concerns and ask questions during training. Sanchalaks are generally enthusiastic about learning the computer skills required to carry out their work.

After a month, trainees are brought in for a third and final phase of initial training. By this time, most sanchalaks are fairly familiar with operating the computer and accessing information. The goal of this session is to learn to troubleshoot common problems. ITC hopes that improving the troubleshooting capacity of sanchalaks will significantly reduce maintenance and system support costs. Sanchalaks are taught about the importance of other devices such as the UPS and the battery backup, and they are given guidelines on what to look for when there is a problem. For instance, they are instructed on the significance of the display lights on the devices. When sanchalaks call for technical help, these details help the support staff identify and resolve problems, perhaps even over the phone, without the necessity of a site visit.

ITC considers training to be a continuous process, and one that requires a concerted effort from all field operatives, not just the support staff. All field operatives are encouraged to provide technology assistance when they visit e-choupals. When the local coordinator visits an e-choupal, he may be required to help with usability issues, even though this is not his primary job.

System support

ITC has about 15 engineers who provide field infrastructure support to the e-choupals. They average one or two calls a day. Each e-choupal is visited about twice a month for infrastructure support. In order to overcome transportation problems, ITC purchased a fleet of 25 motorcycles for its support staff. The support cost is estimated at $6.60 (Rs 300) per visit.

A majority of the issues reported are software-related, and many of these reflect users' lack of familiarity with the operating system. For instance, some users inadvertently delete desktop icons and then have to call for help. On other occasions, failures have occurred when users download and install untested or unapproved software.

Another issue encountered by the support staff has been the malfunctioning of equipment due to voltage fluctuations. About 20–30 per cent of the calls to support staff concern a blown fuse in UPS units. Sanchalaks have now been provided with replacement fuses and have been trained to change fuses on their own. Support for hardware failures is provided by the vendor.

In the future, ITC proposes to improve service and lower the costs of infrastructure support through remote help-desk tools and network automation.

IMPACTS OF THE E-CHOUPAL INITIATIVE

The e-choupal system has already positively affected farmers' economic opportunities, and it has had a significant impact in bridging the information and service gap in the rural areas where it has been rolled out. However, not everyone has gained equally from the scheme.

Positive Impacts

As noted above, ITC estimates that farmers using e-choupals increase their soy revenue by about $6 per metric ton, or about 2.5 per cent over the mandi system. Equally important, it costs them substantially less to buy seed and other inputs through e-choupals than from the village traders.

Although aggregate data on the system's economic impact are not yet available, anecdotal evidence suggests that these benefits to farmers are having a measurable impact on what farmers choose to do. Prior to the launching of the e-choupals, soy cultivation was on the decline. Productivity was stagnant and farmers saw no future in it. In areas covered by e-choupals, the percentage of farmers planting soy has increased dramatically, from 50 to 90 per cent in some regions. For example, in the village of Khasrod, the proportion of farmers planting soy had at one point dropped to 50 per cent, and the decline was expected to continue. But since ITC's involvement, soy is seen as profitable again and by 2003 nearly 90 per cent of farmers in Khasrod were planting the crop. And while there has been an overall increase in the cultivation of soy, the volume of soy marketed through mandis has dropped by as much as 50 per cent in some areas, suggesting farmer preference for the e-choupals.

Indian universities and research centres, notably the Indian Council of Agricultural Research, have made significant advances in practices and technologies to improve productivity and crop quality. But means has been lacking for affordable dissemination of this knowledge on a large scale. The e-choupal system leverages technology to reach a wide audience through the click of a mouse. The fact that the key users are the sanchalaks, who are themselves farmers, makes it easier for best practices to make their way from the website to the field.

In addition to the information provided on the website and through e-mail access to experts, ITC offers services that help farmers improve their techniques. Inputs such as fertilizers and pesticides are not generic in their application: the optimal application depends on the soil and crop. ITC therefore offers soil testing services. The traditional village traders offered inputs, but not the information and services required to make them effective. In addition, after sale of a crop is completed, ITC performs laboratory testing on the sample collected. Based on these results, farmers are given customized feedback on how they can improve crop quality and yield.

More broadly, the e-choupals have helped to open a window on the world for the villages where they are set up. Computers are now bringing the same resources to villages as they bring to urban India, and their impact is no less dramatic. This, coupled with higher incomes and changes in farmers' attitudes, is causing shifts in the social fabric of village life. Accounts from villages in the e-choupal programme note that children are using the computers for schoolwork, as well as to play games. In Khasrod, some 2,000 students used the local e-choupal to print their grade sheets, saving them days of waiting and travel time. Sanchalaks use the Internet to chat among themselves about the status of agriculture in their villages. Villagers are accessing global resources to learn about agriculture in other parts of the world, preparing them to compete in the world outside, not merely in the local mandi.

Losing Sectors

Not everyone has benefited from the introduction of e-choupals. Indeed, some income and jobs have been lost as a direct result of the more efficient e-choupal system. Some of the players in the mandi system who have suffered loss of revenue include:

- Commission agents. Despite ITC's best efforts to maintain mandi volumes and compensate commission agents for lost income, there is little doubt that on the whole they have lower incomes as a result of the introduction of e-choupals.
- Mandi labourers. The workers in the mandis who weighed and bagged produce have been severely impacted by the drop in volume. In the Sonkach mandi, for example, some 28 *tulavatis* (weighers) and 300 other labourers have been affected. ITC's long-term vision is to employ many of these people in the procurement hubs to carry out much the same functions as they currently perform in the mandis.
- Bazaars near the mandis. When farmers sold produce in the mandi, they would also make a variety of purchases at local bazaars. This revenue has now been diverted to shops near the ITC hubs. This, however, can be considered a diversion of revenue rather than elimination.
- Some mandi operations. ITC still pays the mandi tax for all the crops procured through e-choupals, but it now pays the tax to the mandi nearest the procurement hub. As a result, taxes are being diverted from a large number of mandis to the few mandis near the hubs. Regional mandis have therefore lost taxes that contribute to maintaining their infrastructure.

- Competing processors. Even before the advent of the e-choupal, the soy crushing industry suffered from severe overcapacity (half of all capacity was excess). The efficiency pressures imposed by e-choupal have spurred industry consolidation.

CHALLENGES FOR THE FUTURE

The e-choupal system is expanding rapidly. By 2010, the company aims to cover over 100,000 Indian villages in 15 states and serve 25 million farmers. Transactions in 2010 are projected at $2.5 billion (Sivakumar 2004). However, the system faces many challenges.

The first is the possibility that radical shifts in computer access could fundamentally alter community-based business models. That is one of the reasons ITC seeks to build and control its own infrastructure. Second, as the number of sanchalaks increases, it is possible that they may join forces to extract rents, that is, unwarranted additional payments based on their increasing influence within the system. Third, ITC's relationship with the samyojaks seems to be uneasy, and competitors with the financial muscle to invest for scale could conceivably use discontented samyojaks as the base to obtain market share. Fourth, the scope of the e-choupal operation, the diversity of activities required of every operative, and the speed of expansion create real obstacles for effective management.

ITC has awakened the aspirations of farmers. If ITC fails to fulfil these aspirations, the farmers will look elsewhere for satisfaction. As an example, in our conversation with a sanchalak about the potential for Indian onions to succeed in the global market, he made clear that he understood the key to success—better seeds. He half-complained that he had told ITC several times to begin selling better onion seeds, but he had not heard back from them. In a competitive environment, ITC will have to provide faster and more responsive customer service to maintain its distribution system.

The introduction of computers to the villages is no doubt revolutionary, but there is also no doubt that villages are still stratified so that some sectors are excluded from access to the sanchalak and the computer. In rural Madhya Pradesh, at least, this includes the entire adult female population. This is not a reflection on ITC, but rather on the nature of society in rural Madhya Pradesh. The mere presence of the computer cannot transcend these social barriers; nevertheless, there may be openings. Village farmers belong to many social and economic strata, and the sanchalaks are serving all socio-economic categories equally. The potential for commerce has thus broken a barrier that society has built. Similarly, engagement with poorer segments of society and women may be possible through the active marketing of products tailored specifically to them.

ITC also recognizes the limitations of today's e-choupals in regard to procurement efficiency. Not every crop lends itself to such an intervention. And in crops such as soy, competitors may eventually imitate ITC and reduce the company's competitive advantage. Looking ahead, ITC envisages an upgrade path in which e-choupals orchestrate an expanding two-way exchange of goods and services between rural India and the world. Taking the e-choupal's handling of soybean commerce as 'wave 1', the company sees possible additional waves of innovation that might take shape as follows.

In a second wave, the key source of value would be identity preservation through the chain. This can be a significant source of value in crops such as wheat, where the grade of the grain determines its end use. The ability to separate different grades from field to consumer could command a price premium. E-choupals in Uttar Pradesh have already started wheat procurement with this feature.

A third wave could take identity a step further by building the concept of traceability into the supply chain. In the case of perishables, for example, traceability could allow ITC to address food safety concerns and again provide extra value that some customers would be willing to pay for. Shrimp is a good example of a product for which this feature would be important. ITC's intervention in such products would reach down to the level of production, with the company defining standards that producers must adhere to and working with farmers to ensure product quality. Farmers in turn would get the best price from ITC, based on the premium for traceability.

A fourth wave could provide an electronic marketplace for commodities that ITC does not itself buy. For soy, ITC is the sole buyer through the e-choupal channel, but for commodities where the underlying markets have already reached a high degree of efficiency, this would not be possible. Instead, the e-choupals could serve as the marketplace where multiple buyers and sellers come together to execute a range of transactions. A good example of such a commodity is coffee. ITC could gain profits from the transaction fees, making use of IT infrastructure already in place.

In a fifth wave, ITC could add rural marketing and distribution on a larger scale to sourcing of products from rural areas. This would go beyond the rudimentary distribution of agricultural inputs that is already in place. ITC could bring together knowledge of the customer, knowledge of the business, deployed infrastructure, its reputation, and experience gained over the first four waves to bring new value-added products and services to rural India.

Finally, ITC envisages the possibility of sourcing IT-enabled services from rural areas. Telemedicine, eco-tourism, traditional medicine, and traditional crafts are some of the services that could be sourced from the villages. While this possibility is still distant, it shows the scale of the vision and potential impact on development in rural India.

The full potential of the e-choupal model has yet to be fully tested. But the results thus far do show that a large corporation can combine a social mission and an ambitious commercial venture. This can be done by rationalizing markets and increasing the efficiency of an agricultural trading system in ways that benefit farmers and rural communities as well as company shareholders. The example also shows the potential of information technology to increase transparency and access to information while facilitating cost savings that help make new systems profitable and sustainable. Critical factors in the success of the venture to date include ITC's extensive knowledge of agriculture, the willingness of the company to retain many aspects of the existing production system, including both farmers and trading agents, and a stance of respect and fairness that has enabled ITC to be seen as a valued contributor to the development of rural India.

Notes

This chapter is based largely on field visits to India in April 2003. In the state of Madhya Pradesh, the authors visited e-choupals in Khasrod and Dahod as well as mandis in Sonkach and Mandideep. Interviews were held with farmers, sanchalaks, commission agents, ITC employees, and industry bodies. Information in this chapter not otherwise attributed was gathered during these field visits.

The authors wish to thank Wharton School Publishing and C.K. Prahalad for permission to revise and update portions of their paper on e-choupals that appeared in C.K. Prahalad, *The Fortune at the Bottom of the Pyramid: Eradicating Poverty through Profits* (Upper Saddle River, NJ: Wharton School Publishing, 2005).

References

Aziz, J., 2002, 'Poverty Dynamics in Rural India,' IMF Working Paper 02/172, Asia and Pacific Department, International Monetary Fund, Washington, DC.

EIU (Economist Intelligence Unit), 2004, *Country Report India*, London: EIU.

Gupta, I. and M. Rajshekhar, 2005, 'ITC vs. HLL.' *Businessworld*, April 25. http://www.itcportal.com/newsroom/press_25apr_05.htm.

ITC, 2005a, 'About ITC.' http://www.echoupal.com/home/itcfamily1.asp.

_____, 2005b, 'ITC e-Choupal.' http://www.itcportal.com/sets/echoupal_frameset.htm.

'ITC Hopes to Go the Wal-Mart Way,' *The Telegraph* (Calcutta), July 26, 2003.

Sivakumar, S., 2004, 'Reducing Poverty by Leveraging IT: ITC e-Choupal Experience Sharing,' Presentation at Bangalore workshop for Shanghai Global Learning Process, January 4.

World Bank, 1997, 'The Indian Oilseed Complex: Capturing Market Opportunities,' Report 15677-IN, World Bank, Washington, DC.

Notes

1 In 2005, there were e-choupals in Madhya Pradesh, Karnataka, Andhra Pradesh, Uttar Pradesh, Maharashra, and Rajasthan. For updated information on coverage, refer to ITC's three websites: http://www.itcibd.com, http://www.itcportal.com, and http://www.echoupal.com.

2 A major source for this section is World Bank (1997).

3 All of the farmers and sanchalaks interviewed during the authors' 2003 field visits were male, and it is generally assumed that most of the farmers presently served by the e-choupal system, at least in the areas visited, are men.

4 Data collected from field visits in 2003.

5 Data in this section were provided by ITC during the 2003 field visits.

6 ITC has worked hard to create interfaces in the farmers' native language, Hindi. The company has also provided software that makes it possible to type Hindi characters using a standard English keyboard. The preferred language for writing e-mail and other electronic communications, however, is 'Hinglish', that is, Hindi typed with English characters. The reason is that combining vowels and consonants to create Hindi letters is a very cumbersome affair on a keyboard, sometimes requiring three keystrokes to render one letter. Many sanchalaks say that this is the only aspect of computer usage they have not been able to master.

10

A School for Every Village

The Education Guarantee Scheme in Madhya Pradesh, India

Vimala Ramachandran

The goal of universal primary education has eluded India for over 50 years. Traditional approaches to expanding access to education have typically resulted in slow, incremental improvements, falling far short of ambitious targets. One Indian state, however, has succeeded in rapidly expanding school coverage through an innovative and large-scale scheme. In less than a decade, Madhya Pradesh has slashed the number of out-of-school students by more than two-thirds and has virtually eliminated enrolment disparities between social groups.

The Madhya Pradesh government's school expansion programme is anchored in the needs of local communities. Through the implementation of the Education Guarantee Scheme in 1997, the government has extended a legally enforceable guarantee to provide a school within 90 days of any written request from a village-elected council. The scheme harnesses local demand to extract accountability from the state government, while at the same time maximizing the participation of the community in management of the new school. To sustain the local demand for education, a complementary adult literacy campaign was launched in 1999.

In just three years, 1997–2000, 26,571 schools were constructed under the Education Guarantee Scheme. Enrolment rates have risen dramatically. Between 1996 and 2004–05, the number of boys out of school statewide fell from 1.3 million to just 198,000; at the same time, the number of girls out of school dropped from 1.6 million to 230,000. The programme has been particularly successful in reaching out to marginalized communities. Of the more than 1.2 million children enrolled in Education Guarantee

Scheme schools, 91 per cent are from Scheduled Castes, Scheduled Tribes, or other socially disadvantaged groups. By enabling the most deprived children to attend school, the programme has contributed to greater equity in primary education access throughout the state.

The successful expansion of school enrolment in Madhya Pradesh was fuelled by a number of critical factors. The political commitment at the highest level of government, and in particular the public support of the chief minister of the state, was key to the initiative's success. Evidence of this commitment is the increase in the state's education expenditure despite fiscal pressures at the state level and a marked reduction in funds under India's five-year plan. The participation of local communities in the management and supervision of schools through parent–teacher associations and village education committees has built ownership and accountability at the local level.

This chapter reviews the evolution of the Madhya Pradesh Education Guarantee Scheme, looking at the design and implementation of the programme and at factors that have contributed to its success. The chapter concludes with a discussion of the issues for the future, including the programme's equity, sustainability, and replicability.

Unequal Access to Education in Madhya Pradesh

In 1996, a statewide house-to-house survey known as Lok Sampark Abhiyan (LSA) was conducted in Madhya Pradesh to gather information on the educational participation of children in the 6–14 age group. The comprehensive survey of school enrolment was based on participatory problem mapping and was carried out door-to-door in rural areas by panchayat-level teams. The survey listed the number of children attending and not attending school and noted the reasons cited by families for lack of attendance. In so doing it created an alternative data set—a people's information system—to complement government enrolment data. The government also took steps to develop a village education register as the basic record of educational statistics of each village, maintained by the panchayat, or elected village council, and the school. This mechanism would be used for cohort monitoring to track primary schooling completion rates. The LSA house-to-house survey was repeated in 2000–01, both to take stock of progress since the first survey in 1996 and to identify future directions for basic education planning.

The 1996 survey covered 53,460 villages, 6.1 million households, and 10 million children. The results revealed that only 70 per cent of homes had access to a primary school within walking distance. Among boys of school age, 24.4 per cent were out of school at the time of the survey, and 19.7 per cent had never been enrolled. Among girls, 35.2 per cent were out of school and 29.3 per cent had never been enrolled. There was also wide variation by region. For example, Dhar district reported 53.7 per cent of girls not in school, while the corresponding figure for Jhabua district was 64.5 per cent—both well above the statewide average.

The survey presented a realistic picture of school attendance and helped authorities understand the causes of non-enrolment or irregular attendance. Notably, it revealed that the problem of non-enrolment was far more severe than earlier estimates had indicated. It also showed that the inability to access primary schools was especially acute in tribal hamlets with highly dispersed populations, and among children from socially disadvantaged communities in non-tribal areas. Political leaders and administrators in Madhya Pradesh took the survey results both as a warning and as an incentive to rework the system to address the twin problems of non-participation and lack of access. With the realization that radically new strategies were needed to get children into schools, the state decided to undertake an innovative education programme.

KEY ELEMENTS OF THE EGS

In 1997, one year after the first LSA survey, the government of Madhya Pradesh launched the Education Guarantee Scheme (EGS). This creative institutional response to the enrolment problem was premised on a rights-based framework for primary education. Using community demand as the starting point, the programme took a fast-track approach to basic education by linking it with local self-government institutions and creating new space for educational innovation. The EGS was seen as a breakthrough in social sector planning. It aimed to strike a balance between the demand and supply issues framing primary education, instead of regarding household demand and service provision as mutually exclusive emphases.

Provision of Schools

Under the EGS, the state government guarantees that if a panchayat forwards a list of 40 children (25 to 30 in tribal areas) who have no schooling facilities within one kilometre walking distance, the government will provide a school *within 90 days.* The district EGS committee that scrutinizes requests for schools is chaired by the president of the zilla parishad, or the district-level elected body. The state government also guarantees teacher training; a teacher–pupil ratio of 1:40; curriculum on a par with that of the formal government primary schools; equivalence in evaluation and supervision; and adequate funds for maintaining the school building, monitoring, and academic evaluation.

The community plays a central role under the EGS framework. Most important, the community has the responsibility of identifying a teacher candidate to be trained by the education department. The community also provides land for the school building, manages provision of midday meals through the panchayat, and participates in the village education committee and the parent–teacher association (PTA).

Special efforts were made under EGS to reach women and disadvantaged social groups. With gender inequality at centre stage, the state reserved 30 per cent of teaching posts for women. Concurrently, social mobilization and special *chalo* ('let's go to school') programmes sought to reach more girls and children from disadvantaged groups.

By 2001 the institutionalization of the EGS was consolidated. The scheme was clearly not a stopgap or temporary strategy, but rather an integral part of the primary education system of the state. Several developments signalled this integration. All 'alternative schools' (non-formal community schools) were brought under the EGS. The curriculum and textbooks for EGS schools and formal government primary schools were merged, thereby ensuring equivalence in all respects. Finally, grade divisions were introduced into the EGS. In the early stages of the programme children had been grouped together according to ability, but by 2000 it became apparent that children would have to be seated by grades, thus bridging the gap between formal schools and EGS schools.

Institutionalizing Local Ownership: Parent–Teacher Associations

One important determinant of the quality of schooling is the extent of local ownership and accountability. The challenge therefore is to create institutional arrangements that help schools respond to the learning needs of the children and the educational aspirations of the communities they serve. The parent–teacher associations (Palak Shikshak Sangh) have played a key role in fostering such local ownership and constitute a critical component of the EGS. Each PTA comprises all parents of children studying in a school as well as the school's teachers. The president and vice president of the PTA are elected from among its members, while the head teacher of the school serves as the PTA secretary.

Meeting once a month, PTAs undertake a range of activities. One of their core responsibilities is to ensure full enrolment of children aged 5–14 and the regular attendance of both students and teachers. PTAs also assist in the development of schools, participate in school fundraising, and maintain, operate, and strengthen the school education funds. Their role extends to daily school activities as well, such as helping teachers provide quality education, monitoring student achievement in various subjects, and motivating illiterate and newly literate learners to continue their education. Managerial and oversight duties of the PTA include the supervision of developmental, academic, administrative, and financial activities of the school. Furthermore, PTAs are expected to prepare a People's Education Plan (Jan Shikshan Yojana), examine and advise on the public evaluation report (Jan Shiksha Prativedan), and present the needs of learners to the gram sabha, or village assembly, in order to access benefits and grants (GMP 2002).

PTAs were granted legal status through the People's Education Act of 2002. More than 100,000 parent–teacher associations have been formed. It should be noted, however, that good schools with motivated teachers tend to have stronger, more involved PTAs; less functional schools tend to have weaker PTAs, even though these schools arguably would benefit most from a strong parent–teacher body. Training of PTAs is of critical importance to their future effectiveness.

Adult Literacy Campaign

The EGS was not understood as a stand-alone universal primary education programme. Rather, it was complemented by Padna Badna Andolan (Learn and Progress), an adult literacy programme that has helped to create and sustain local demand for education. Begun in 1999, the campaign gave adults, especially women, an opportunity to learn to read and write. Just as important, it contributed to a positive climate for basic education and to the emergence of schooling as a social norm for all children.

The initiative established committees at the village level to promote literacy and continuing education (*padna badna samiti*), as well as village women's groups focused on literacy and continuing education (*padna badna sangh*). These were designed to move towards the goal of universal literacy and to consolidate fragile emerging literacy through organized activities. For example, the literacy and continuing education committees run rural libraries and hold social and cultural events. By more actively engaging adults, they also serve as watchdogs for the universal primary education programme. Moreover, the literacy campaign also fostered the conversion of the village women's literacy groups into broader self-help groups that could deal with such issues as water conservation, community health and sanitation, gender empowerment, and eradication of socially discriminatory practices such as untouchability.

GOVERNMENT REFORMS UNDERPIN EDUCATION EXPANSION

The successful implementation of the Education Guarantee Scheme in Madhya Pradesh was made possible by systematic attention to building appropriate institutional and legal structures. A series of reforms implemented between 1994 and 2003 provided the necessary scaffolding to deliver on the promise implicit in the EGS. At the core of these changes was a move towards greater decentralization and local control over education.

The steering body for the EGS is the Rajiv Gandhi Shiksha Mission (RGSM) for primary and adult education. Created in 1994, the RGSM brings together administrative, financial, and academic arms of educational management in the state. Its chairman is the state chief minister, reflecting the high priority accorded to this education mission.

Decentralization and Local Control

The EGS was initiated in the wake of the 73rd and 74th Constitutional Amendments of 1992, which brought greater decentralization of government functioning. The first version of the Madhya Pradesh District Planning Committee Act devolved important planning functions to the district governments through district planning committees. The act gave significant flexibility to these committees in carrying out their functions, which were further specified in an amendment in 1999. The amended act gave the district planning committee authority to prepare and execute plans. However, the chief minister clarified that 'the powers entrusted with this body are those that have not been entrusted to panchayati raj institutions or urban local bodies, but those that were exercised by the secretariat of the state government.'[1]

A new experiment in direct democracy in Madhya Pradesh further bolstered direct local control of education. An amendment to the state's Panchayati Raj Act of 1993 transferred most of the powers previously exercised by gram panchayats (elected village councils) to gram sabhas (mass assemblies of all village residents). Of particular importance, all user committees, previously chosen by bureaucrats, would now be chosen by the gram sabhas. This meant that the village as a whole was empowered to elect members of the village education committee, who previously had been nominated by the teacher. The amendment also stipulated that one-third of the members of each user committee should be women, and another third should be people from 'deprived categories' (Manor 2001). The community's expanded role in choosing the education committee enhanced the sense of community ownership of the schools.

Legal Framework for Expanding Education Access

In 2002, the state government enacted a new legal framework for educational reform (Madhya Pradesh Jan Shiksha Adhiniyam). The legislation established the fundamental right of every child to basic education and made parents responsible for compulsory education up to the age of 14, an obligation enforceable by the gram sabha. The reforms strengthened the institutional partnership between the state government, local elected bodies, and communities for education and created education funds at the state, district, and school levels to mobilize additional resources. It also required that a public education report (Jan Shiksha Prativedan) be presented every quarter at the PTA and district level and annually to the state Legislative Assembly, reporting progress on all educational programmes in the state.

A second legislative act in 2003 took these reforms a step further. The Madhya Pradesh Jan Shiksha Niyam legislative act formalized the constitutional right to education for every child up to the age of 14, a right safeguarded by the gram sabha in rural areas and by the administrative officer in urban areas. The act reinforced this right by mandating a series of monitoring and oversight activities. Among them were the maintenance of records in every school, including village and ward education registers with the recorded status of every child aged 6–14; an annual audit of school accounts, especially the village education fund; preparation of annual academic reports to track progress in quality; formation of parent–teacher associations in every school; and the formation of an education committee in the panchayat. A cluster resource centre (Jan Shiksha Kendra) was mandated in each block and district for academic support of primary schools under the EGS.

At the administrative level, additional institutional reforms in the system during 2003 were aimed at upgrading quality. Learning outcomes of students, rather than reports written by supervisors, became the basis for evaluating teachers and determining their career advancement. Procedures were also set for presenting monthly progress reports on children to the parent–teacher associations.

THE IMPACT OF EGS: INCREASED ENROLMENT AND REDUCED DISPARITIES

The EGS has had a significant impact on both the quantity and quality of primary education in Madhya Pradesh. In a three-year period, between July 1997 and July 2000, an impressive 26,571 EGS schools were created, 42 per cent of them in tribal areas. This raised the total number of primary schools in the state, including both government and EGS schools, to over 82,000 (Table 10.1). As of June 2003 the programme had a total of 31,815 teachers, called *gurujis*, who had been identified by the communities and trained by the education department of the state government.

TABLE 10.1 Growth in Number of Primary Schools, 1995–2002

Type of school and period	*Number of schools*
Government primary schools existing before 1995	51,813
Total primary schools opened between 1995 and 2002	30,780
Government primary schools opened between 1995 and 2002	4,209
EGS schools opened between 1997 and 2002	26,571
Total primary schools as of June 2003	82,593

Source: Based on data from the District Information System for Education, Government of Madhya Pradesh.

Sharp Reduction in Out-of-School Children

The most significant impact of the EGS has been a marked reduction in the absolute numbers of out-of-school children. The first Lok Sampark Abhiyan survey in 1996 found 1,315,000 boys and 1,604,000 girls not enrolled in school. By 2002–03, these numbers had been reduced to 346,000 boys and 428,000 girls, and by 2004–05, they had fallen to 198,000 and 230,000, respectively (Figure 10.1). The percentage of children out of school also decreased, from 29.3 per cent (24.4 per cent of boys and 35.2 per cent of girls) in 1996 to 6.2 per cent (5.2 per cent of boys and 7.5 per cent of girls) in 2002–03.

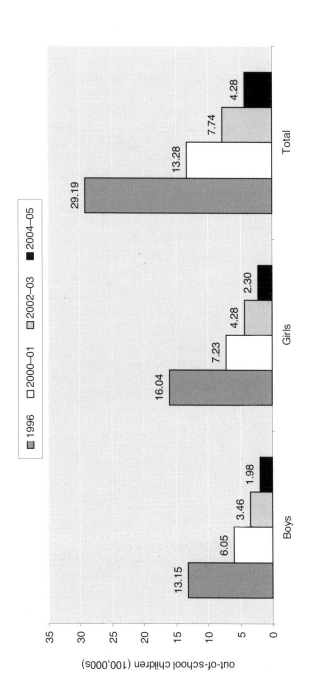

Source: 1996–2003: District Information System for Education, Government of Madhya Pradesh. 2004–05: Sarva Shiksha Abhiyan 2005, Table 9.

FIGURE 10.1 Out-of-School Children 6–14 Years of Age, by Gender

These trends are confirmed by statistics from other sources. The Indian government's National Family Health Survey showed that from 1992 to 1998, the percentage of children ages 6–11 attending school in Madhya Pradesh rose from 61.0 per cent to 80.1 per cent for boys and from 47.3 per cent to 73.9 per cent for girls.[2]

It is still true, however, that the number of children out of school is far too high. The 2002–03 survey revealed that 774,000 children were not enrolled in school. Of these children, the survey reported, 20.7 per cent were busy with sibling care, 20 per cent with agricultural or home-based work, and 17.9 per cent with grazing cattle, while 14.1 per cent said they were not in school because their families could not afford it. Notwithstanding the impressive progress, these survey data confirm that the poorest of the poor are still largely outside the ambit of primary schooling.

Significant Reduction in Inequality

In addition to an absolute increase in children attending school, there has been an easing of inequalities in primary education. The 1996 LSA survey found a significant gender gap at the primary level, with a gross enrolment ratio (GER) of 81.5 per cent for boys but only 70.7 per cent for girls.[3] By 2002–03, the primary GER had risen to 102.9 per cent for boys and 100.3 per cent for girls (Figure 10.2). The gap narrowed even further in 2004–05, with GERs of 104.1 and 103.6 for boys and girls, respectively (Sarva Shiksha Abhiyan 2005). Girls made up 47 per cent of the enrolment in primary schools in June 2003, including both the EGS and government schools.

Over the decade 1991–2001, Madhya Pradesh recorded an impressive increase of 20.9 per cent in female literacy, according to the national census. It ranked third among all Indian states in the percentage of increase. This achievement was an outcome both of the EGS programme for children and of the literacy campaign for adults, primarily women. By 2003 there were 217,000 volunteers working with the literacy committees.

The surveys also showed a trend towards equalization of ratios for disadvantaged social groups. The EGS schools catered to 1,233,052 children in 2003, of whom 45 per cent were from Scheduled Tribes and 15 per cent from Scheduled Castes. Of the children in EGS schools, 91 per cent were from disadvantaged groups living in rural areas. The primary GER for children of Scheduled Tribes rose from 78 per cent in 1992 to 91 per cent in 2000–01 (GMP 2002). By 2004–05, the gap for disadvantaged groups had nearly closed: the primary GER for Scheduled Castes was 103.9 per cent,

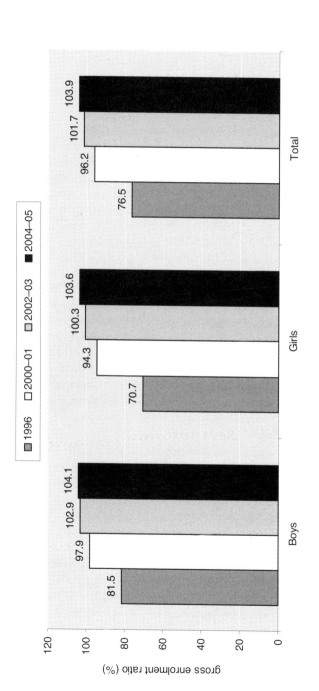

Source: 1996–2003: District Information System for Education, Government of Madhya Pradesh. 2004–05: Sarva Shiksha Abhiyan 2005, Table 8.

FIGURE 10.2 Gross Enrolment Ratios in Primary Schools, by Gender

the same as the overall primary GER, and for Scheduled Tribes it was only slightly lower at 102.2 per cent (Sarva Shiksha Abhiyan 2005).

Positive Learning Outcomes

Field visits by the author in September 2003 and qualitative micro-studies in Betul district (Saihjee 2004) show a pattern of dramatic improvement in access to primary education, especially for children from very poor households and in scattered settlements. All EGS schools were found to be functioning regularly with one or two teachers. Community leaders even reported that some children had moved from government primary schools to EGS schools, partly because of their convenient location and partly because of regular functioning and empathetic teachers.

Regarding community involvement, teachers, classroom processes, and learning outcomes, the following observations were made:

- All EGS schools are housed on land made available by the community.
- Village education committees and parent–teacher associations take full responsibility for regular functioning of the EGS schools. They supervise the conduct and attendance of gurujis, monitor student attendance, and, most importantly, ensure uninterrupted provision of the midday meal. Almost all the teachers are recruited from the villages where the schools are located or from neighbouring villages. While we do not have reliable data on the social composition of EGS gurujis, it is clear that efforts were made to give preference to local candidates.
- Corporal punishment was almost non-existent in the EGS schools visited during the course of fieldwork for this study and the micro-studies done in 2002. This could be attributed to closer interaction between the gurujis and the communities through the parent–teacher associations.
- Given that the community selects the EGS teacher, it was expected that the relationships between parents and teachers would be better than in the formal government schools, and that this would be reflected in the functioning of the PTAs. While we did come across a few proactive PTAs, the sample was too small to make any conclusive statement. There appears to be considerable variation from district to district and even within districts.
- Limited evidence available indicates that there is no significant difference between the learning outcomes of children in EGS

schools and in government primary schools (Kothari, Sherry Chand, and Sharma 2000; Mercer et al. 2002). However, data compiled by the government do not yet include transition from one grade to the next or learning outcomes of children in EGS schools as compared to formal schools.

- There is no difference between the curriculum and textbooks used in the EGS schools and those used in the formal schools. As a result, children can easily migrate from one system to the other.

- The actual teaching time in EGS schools is significantly higher than in formal primary schools. EGS gurujis, unlike teachers in the government schools, are not assigned additional work such as helping with the census or elections and carrying out other data collection and surveillance tasks for the government.

Although comprehensive comparative data are not available, it also seems that the EGS programme has had an indirect positive effect on the government schools as well. An evaluation covering the formal primary schools (Singh, Sridhar, and Bhargava 2002) showed that between 1994 and 2002, enrolment of girls increased 8.2 per cent in Betul, a district with high female literacy, and 13.1 per cent in Sidhi, a low female literacy district. In Betul, the increase in enrolment of girls from Scheduled Tribes was 9.2 per cent. It is clear from this, as well as from our observations during field visits, that more girls than before are entering primary school. However, the data gathered do not capture the shift of children from formal primary schools to EGS schools or the enrolment of children (mostly boys) in private schools. During field visits we observed that there were many more girls than boys in both EGS and formal schools.

One limitation noted during the field visits is that community groups do not yet play a significant role in monitoring the learning outcomes of children. Monitoring of quality and academic support are provided by the block resource centres and cluster resource centres. This situation may change as a result of the introduction of the district annual academic report under the aegis of the People's Education Act of 2002.

DRIVING FACTORS BEHIND THE SUCCESS OF EGS

The success of the EGS scheme in the period through 2003 was driven by a series of interrelated institutional reforms spearheaded by determined political leadership. These reforms, including learning and experimentation as the programme was implemented, received external support from national and international sources. A key question for the future is whether the institutional innovations will be sustained through changes in the political and administrative leadership of the state.

Strong Political Commitment

Political will was clearly a distinctive factor in the EGS from the beginning. The scheme received strong backing from the chief minister of Madhya Pradesh, who made a public commitment to provide adequate state resources. Thus the start-up of the programme was not contingent on availability of foreign funds or grants from the government of India. The government steadily increased actual expenditure on primary education from Rs 2,844 million in 1990/1 to Rs 3,492 million in 1998/99, despite a marked decline in funds allocated under the government of India's five-year plans (Bashir and Ayyar 2001).

Funds were later made available through the District Primary Education Programme (DPEP) between 1994 and 2002, and through the Education for All Campaign, also known as Sarva Shiksha Abhiyan, from 2002 onward. These funds, however, supplemented rather than substituted for state resources in primary education. The Rajiv Gandhi Shiksha Mission also used other innovative mechanisms to garner financial support for the EGS. One example is the Fund-a-School programme, launched in 2000. Anyone can log on to the programme's website, adopt a school, and pay Rs 16,000, which is directly credited to the bank account of the school chosen. By March 2002, close to 1,000 individuals and corporate institutions had adopted EGS schools.[4]

The EGS was positioned as a large programme and not as a small innovation. While the approach was experimental, it was clear from the start that the government was determined to cover the entire state. The state government made the management decision in advance that the programme would have to evolve and be fine-tuned as the scale expanded. Although the basic blueprint was prepared in 1997, the programme adapted and changed as it scaled up.

By 2003, as noted above, key elements of the EGS had been formalized in law and in institutional guidelines. The People's Education Act of 2002, for example, provided institutional mechanisms to foster transparency and strengthen accountability of the educational administration to the panchayat and the community, rather than upward to the bureaucracy. The government also introduced the district annual academic report to publicise information on enrolment, attendance, grade transition, teacher deployment and training, learning achievement of children, distribution of textbooks, and other key educational indicators.

It is still too soon to say how much long-term effect the change of government after December 2003 may have on implementation of the EGS. The Congress party was defeated, and the Bharatiya Janata Party (BJP), previously in opposition, won with a substantial majority. State government employees—especially block- and village-level functionaries—actively campaigned for the BJP. There were reports that many government functionaries were unhappy with the devolution of powers to local elected bodies. Government primary school teachers were also reported to be unhappy with policies such as the requirement that all future appointments be on a contract basis and that the confidential records of teachers include performance outcomes of children. For their part, EGS teachers were demanding parity in tenure and pay with teachers in the government primary schools.

Another issue that remains unresolved and subject to political developments is the extent to which local government institutions such as the panchayats are truly representative. That is, did decentralization of responsibility under the EGS create space for effective participation of the poorest of the poor, including Dalits (formerly known as untouchables) and the more disadvantaged tribal groups? While there is no doubt that devolution of funds to the panchayats has made a difference on the ground, generally increasing representation, there has been considerable variation across districts and even within districts. Given that formal representation of socially disadvantaged groups or women does not guarantee participation, it is still difficult to say whether decentralization has been effective in giving dalits and poor women a voice in local governance.

Institutional Innovation

The Education Guarantee Scheme featured three important institutional innovations. First, it created institutional structures and statutory mechanisms for inclusion of the excluded, that is, poor rural children who previously had no access to primary school within walking distance of their homes. The EGS provided mechanisms for articulating and forwarding the demand for an accessible school through the panchayat. Opening this avenue for public expression showed that, contrary to popular belief, social resistance to education of girls was only a minor reason for non-enrolment. Only 8.2 per cent of respondents gave this explanation for non-enrolment in the 2002 house-to-house survey. Instead, they referred most often to the lack of schooling facilities, to economic pressures on families, and to conditions in the schools as reasons for not educating their children. Open discussions in the panchayat and within the official system not only created a climate for change, but also gave people a specific mechanism through which to demand a school for their children.

Second, the government provided a unilateral, legally enforceable guarantee by pledging to meet its obligation to provide an EGS school within 90 days and to provide training and academic support to the guruji identified by the community. The government provided such a guarantee through formal commitments in the EGS and the People's Education Act. Upon receiving a proper request for a school, the bureaucracy had to respond; if it did not, the panchayat could appeal to a higher authority. Having the necessary statutory institutions and mechanisms in place both enabled state government officials to respond and empowered the panchayats to make decisions and press demands on the administration.

Third, the system forged mutually supportive links between the state government, local self-government institutions, and civil society (Box 10.1). It provided structures for continued participation of the community and the panchayat in educational management and supervision. Lack of coordination between the administrative/financial side and the academic side of education has often been cited as a reason for poor performance in terms of both access and quality. This problem is exacerbated when local self-government institutions are left out of the loop of educational management. The fact that administrative, financial, and academic arms of educational management were all brought under the umbrella of the Rajiv Gandhi Shiksha Mission ensured convergence and synergy.

Making the system responsive and accountable to the gram sabha (an assembly of the entire village, the basic unit of democratic decentralization) effectively flipped the accountability pyramid. The EGS school in a village is owned by and accountable to the parent–teacher association and the village education committee, which is elected by the gram sabha. Funds allocated by the state government for the EGS programme are managed by the panchayat, while the parent–teacher association of each school supervises the use of funds allocated to it. The state government, the panchayat, and the school are each an essential corner of the management pyramid.

Implementing these innovations has depended on the continuity of the two administrators, R. Gopalakrishnan and Amita Sharma, who led educational reform in Madhya Pradesh from 1993 to 2003 and who conceptualized and steered the EGS programme in its formative years.[5] This long tenure was a significant departure from the usual practice of frequent transfers of such personnel. However, after the December 2003 state elections and the change in government, these two officials were transferred. The key test for sustainability will be whether the reforms continue following this leadership change.

Learning and Experimentation

As noted above, the EGS changed over time. Beginning with a concept and a survey, it evolved first into an alternative, cost-effective way of expanding primary education by taking advantage of local initiative. Its success then led to it becoming the primary vehicle for educational expansion in Madhya Pradesh, fully integrated into and on a par with the system of government primary schools.

The crucial first step was the house-to-house survey to gain an accurate assessment of the demand for education, with survey data cross-checked against official government statistics. This was followed by statutory mechanisms for channelling and responding to community demand for schools. Despite the financial pressures facing the government and the deficiencies of the primary school system, this turn to local involvement resulted in a cost-effective strategy for universalization of primary education.

The government acknowledged that local teachers, identified and supported by the communities, would play a critical role in tribal hamlets and in remote areas. Despite having lower qualifications than the teachers in formal schools, these local teachers had the important advantage of being able to communicate with the children and their parents in the families' own languages. In the early stages, the gurujis were seen as paraprofessional teachers. As the programme matured, however, they were recognized as full-fledged teachers on a par with the teachers in the government primary schools.

This was made possible by according priority attention to teacher training and supervision. Credible evidence of the equivalence in quality between the EGS and formal-school teachers was provided by the district annual academic report and the quarterly reports on academic progress to parent–teacher associations. This was an important lesson, demonstrating that when training and supervision are streamlined and made rigorous, it is possible to enhance the skills and capabilities of teachers despite limitations on their formal credentials and their remuneration.

The EGS was initially conceived by the Government of India and the larger education community as an 'alternative stream' to supplement the system of government primary schools. However, in Madhya Pradesh it quickly became an integral part of the primary education strategy, and the government of the state eventually took a decision not to establish any more government primary schools. This dispelled any doubt that EGS had become the central focus in achieving universal primary education in the state.

Institutionalizing community ownership was a key area of learning and experimentation. The parent–teacher associations, which started as local committees specifically for the EGS programme, became an integral part of education management statewide. The EGS marked a significant departure in educational administration by creating an 'organic link between the teacher and the community'. The fact that EGS teachers were selected by the local communities and appointed by the gram panchayats strengthened local accountability, creating a necessary (although not sufficient) condition for quality improvement.

External Catalysts

The principal focus from the beginning of the EGS was to forge a mutually enriching partnership within the state between the panchayat, the larger community, and the administration. These academic and administrative linkages were ensured by the leadership of the Rajiv Gandhi Shiksha Mission, which coordinated all the relevant actors within the state concerned with programme implementation.

The programme also built on supportive external linkages. The Government of India allocated European Commission funds through the District Primary Education Programme to Madhya Pradesh. As a result, the EGS was included in joint review missions of DPEP, as well as in appraisal missions jointly fielded by the World Bank, the European Commission, the India office of the UK Department for International Development, the Royal Netherlands Embassy, and UNICEF. This facilitated national and international exchanges on a range of pedagogy, management, and mobilization issues.

Initially there was some apprehension among external partners about what was viewed as a low-cost alternative programme. But as the programme matured, there was wider recognition of the potential of the EGS model in educationally backward regions. As a result, the programme has received considerable national and international attention.

Box 10.1 The EGS as Described by the Programme's Architects

R. Gopalakrishnan and Amita Sharma, civil servants in the Madhya Pradesh government, conceptualized the EGS programme and steered it from 1996 through 2002. They comment on the programme's implications for decentralized government:

'Historical experience reveals that centralized models of delivery delayed the spread of primary education even where resources were identified. The emergence of working panchayati raj system consequent on the 73rd Constitutional Amendment provides opportunities that need to be seized to share the task of universalization of primary education with the community, mediated through panchayat raj institutions. In Madhya Pradesh a Lok Sampark Abhiyan or door-to-door survey was undertaken jointly by panchayat leadership, teachers, and literacy activists in 1996 for a detailed identification of children not going to school ... This led to the development of decentralized panchayat-level plans for primary education [and] to detailed mapping of gaps in access to schooling facilities ... The survey created leadership roles for panchayats in the management of primary education and provoked policy makers to quickly respond to the gaps in access. The EGS was created in response to this need with an understanding of the potential of collaboration and leadership at the village and panchayat level ... The EGS reinterpreted the definition of responsibility of the state to provide universal primary education by enlarging the understanding of state to mean not only government at the state level but local government or panchayat and the community.'

Source: Adapted from Gopalakrishnan and Sharma 1999.

The state government's *Third Human Development Report* also emphasized the partnership between the state and local self-government bodies:

'Perhaps with the benefit of hindsight, it could be said that institutional change in Madhya Pradesh began with clarity of objectives and instruments in the mid 1990s. The *objective* was to improve the components of human development—health, education, and the like—*in an equitable way in a specified period of time*. And the *instrument* for achieving the goal was the combination of new initiatives and ideas in the capital and implementation through the

(Contd)

Box 10.1 (Contd)

new panchayat and people's collectives at the local level ... The Rajiv Gandhi [Education] Mission brought in new ideas and insights; the panchayat brought in the energies and experience of the people. The panchayats and working with people's collectives brought to the fore people's demands—and the government responded to that demand ... The two developed into a valuable partnership that is institutional in nature. Both, not in themselves, but acting in concert, are crucial to Madhya Pradesh's subsequent experience. This process is perhaps the key institutional change that was made.'

Source: Adapted from GMP 2002.

CHALLENGES FOR THE FUTURE

The development discourse in India invariably leads to comparisons between the more forward states with high literacy, better social services, greater employment opportunities, and informed participation in democratic processes, and the less developed states marked by low literacy, poor social services, a precarious economic situation, and low participation in democratic processes. For several decades Madhya Pradesh was counted among the latter. It was included in the pejorative label BIMARU (Bihar, Madhya Pradesh, Rajasthan, and Uttar Pradesh), a local word also meaning 'sick'.

Thus, it is particularly significant that over the last decade Madhya Pradesh has become a model in the realm of primary education. Education is one of the pillars of social empowerment, as it not only enables people to acquire the knowledge, skills, and confidence to secure a livelihood, but is also the key to accessing information. Education enhances social status and boosts self-esteem and self-confidence, thereby enabling disadvantaged social groups to negotiate an unequal world from a position of strength. Education is also the key to development of human capabilities, thereby creating valuable social capital. Given the tangible gains from education, especially for socially disadvantaged groups and for women, it is recognized in the Millennium Development Goals as an important end in its own right.

In the last decade Madhya Pradesh has made significant progress on several fronts, most notably by linking democratic decentralization to universal primary education and literacy. Political leaders have made public commitments to helping the state escape the downward spiral of poverty, illiteracy, and poor health. Today Madhya Pradesh is cited as exemplary, recording significant improvement in primary education.

A potential problem, however, is that this achievement is often portrayed as the achievement of one political party or, even worse, one dynamic leader. Democratic decentralization, the EGS, and efforts to reduce the state's fiscal burden were all part of a package, with the EGS emerging as a response to both the need for educational access and the precarious fiscal situation of the state. Decentralization was seen as a vehicle for delivery of a people-centred educational programme.

Given that the goal of access to education is widely shared, however, it is not unrealistic to hope that the successful EGS programme will be seen as a non-partisan issue, one that cuts across the specific ideological and political agendas of the state's two main political parties. In the view of the former chief minister, it is essential that such issues be depoliticized. Democratic decentralization, achieving universal primary education, and reducing the fiscal burden of the state need to be seen as issues that are important for the state of Madhya Pradesh. These are common public goods and, ideally, should not be tied up with any individual, social group, or political party.[6]

Whether this perspective prevails and the reforms introduced by the programme are further institutionalized depends on the resolution of a number of issues, as well as on continuing political commitment by the state government. Six critical issues stand out.

Democratic Decentralization

The key message to emerge from the EGS experience is that structural reform in one sector cannot be sustained without continuing reforms in governance that include capacity building. The EGS is a bottom-up innovation in which the panchayats play a pivotal role. It therefore requires that the process of decentralization and devolution of powers to local self-government institutions be carried out fully. That is, greater empowerment of the panchayats through effective decentralization of development planning and resource allocation becomes the logical next step.[7]

The state government has attempted to institutionalize democratic decentralization through the Madhya Pradesh Panchayati Raj Adhiniyan in 2001 and the People's Education Act of 2002. But creation of decentralized structures is not enough; it is also essential that the people elected to various committees and forums have the confidence to participate and know how to access and use information. Building people's capacities is critical for meaningful and sustained participation. So far, ordinances and laws devolving more powers to local bodies and institutions have not been matched by sufficient training and capacity building, especially of disadvantaged social groups. In some senses, decentralization is still a top-down process—participation by dictate.

Sustaining Demand for Education

The effort to universalize education faces the challenge of going beyond simple expansion of the supply of primary schools and sustaining the demand for education beyond the primary level. This not only requires providing access to higher levels of schooling, both formal and vocational, but also raises difficult issues of the quality and relevance of education. It is part of the broader challenge of relating education to people's lives, enabling them to obtain both farm and non-farm work, creating capacities for self-employment, and adapting academic preparation to the rapidly changing economy.

It is clear that primary education by itself is not sufficient. Experience has shown that the presence of a group of demoralized and disillusioned young people, who may have either completed primary school or dropped out, but who have no employment or productive work, discourages other students from staying in school. Younger children and their families see that education does not always improve the situation of the poor, as primary schooling that is not relevant to their life situation may not lead to material gain or even to additional social capital. The growth of a frustrated pool of partially educated youth may even serve to increase adolescent crime, violence, and social unrest.

The EGS model in itself does not yet provide an adequate answer to the problem of educational quality. Conversations with parents and children during recent micro-studies and qualitative studies in Madhya Pradesh indicate that unless the government is willing to invest in schooling quality as well as quantity, most children are not likely to be equipped to go beyond the primary level. The academic rigour, time, and environment necessary for children to move from primary to secondary to professional education are still beyond the reach of poor children. The forward linkages necessary to make primary education a means to livelihood security have not yet been created. This is one of the most formidable challenges for the EGS.

Equity in Teacher Compensation

Closely linked to the quality issue are equity concerns, given that the EGS primarily caters to the most marginalized families. The EGS programme is cost-efficient when compared to government primary schools. EGS gurujis are paid Rs 2,500 per month, equivalent to what contract teachers in the government primary schools earn, but less than the Rs 6,000 per month paid to regular school teachers. Recent debates in the media and among educational planners have raised equity issues with respect to the levels of compensation and training available to gurujis as compared with regular teachers. The state has responded by giving gurujis access to an education diploma correspondence programme on a priority basis. It has also ensured equivalence in academic support, infrastructure development, and most important, minimum learning levels expected from formal and EGS schools.

It is true that available data on performance indicate no appreciable difference in learning outcomes between children in the formal and EGS schools (Kothari, Sherry Chand, and Sharma 2000; Mercer et al. 2002). But learning levels in both systems are still fairly low. Gopalakrishnan and Sharma (1999) argue that given the generally poor quality of education available in the government schools, the 'formal schools are "superior" only as local appendages of a large bureaucratic system' and not in terms of their educational processes. Nonetheless, there remain unresolved issues pertaining to the quality of education in the EGS schools and the ability of poor students to compete with their counterparts from better-endowed schools in both the public and private sectors.[8]

Financial Sustainability

Fourth, the programme's financial sustainability remains a major issue for the government of Madhya Pradesh. The state government has tried to balance the inputs from its own resources with those made available by the Government of India as a part of central sector schemes. Yet it is clear that funding levels are not sufficient to sustain both continued quantitative expansion and badly needed qualitative improvement. Given that it is the poorest of the poor, including those from Scheduled Castes and Scheduled Tribes, who depend on these schools, the government is aware that it cannot mobilize significant funds from the users. Thus, state officials intend to look towards leveraging donor funds and funds from corporate, civil society, and philanthropic institutions. The Fund-a-School initiative was a first step in this direction. But these efforts will need to be expanded in order to take the EGS programme to its ultimate goal of ensuring high-quality education for all.

One issue raised by critics of the EGS is that the financial ceiling for construction of a school may exacerbate existing inequalities. That is, relatively well-off communities may be able to match the contribution of the government with their own inputs, while poor tribal hamlets have to make do with what they receive from the government. State government officials respond that there is additional aid available through the Fund-a-School initiative that can be channelled to remote poor areas.

Ownership and Participation

Yet another pressing question is that of ownership and participation. Travelling around the state, one cannot miss the fact that community forums (the village education committees, PTAs, and panchayats) do indeed believe that the EGS programme is theirs. Community leaders refer to the EGS school as 'our school', an implicit contrast to what they call *sarkari* schools (government schools). They call the gurujis 'our teachers'. The important question here is whether the participation is substantive, by empowered equal partners, or whether it is a mere formality. The hard reality is that, given the prevalent social situation, the economically better-off groups and the higher castes have a bigger say in local government. While the EGS may cater to the very poor and the marginalized, its continuation or strengthening is contingent on the support of panchayat leaders and the local power elite. How these factors evolve will critically influence the sense of ownership of the programme and its long-term sustainability.

Replicability

Finally, the replicability of the programme remains unproven. The larger education community, donors, and the Government of India have all hailed the EGS as an innovation that has changed the face of education in Madhya Pradesh. Suggestions that the model be exported to other states or regions invariably raise the question of whether the programme was only made possible by the coming together of exceptional administrators, political leaders, and practitioners in a unique setting.

Some commentators have concluded that the model is not replicable. The example of Rajasthan is cited as a negative case. There, a variation of the EGS scheme called Rajiv Gandhi Pathashala was introduced. The administration organized a survey, and local legislators and other political leaders selected locations for new schools. But the example is not in fact comparable, as the fundamental feature of the Madhya Pradesh EGS—that is, community demand for schools channelled through the panchayats to an administration that is obligated to respond—was not replicated in the Rajasthan case. This was true even though Rajasthan at the time was governed by the same political party that held power in Madhya Pradesh, and at least in theory shared the commitment to devolve greater powers to local self-government institutions.

Within Madhya Pradesh, the decisive question is the sustainability of key features of the EGS programme through future changes in state government and turnover of administrative personnel. Will a change in leadership result in reversing the bottom-up system of this unique programme? Six or eight years are hardly sufficient to institutionalize new systems and processes, given that the government has operated in top-down fashion for over a hundred years. It is clear that, notwithstanding the encouraging sense of ownership among local stakeholders and the momentum of the programme, more time is needed for the EGS to be institutionalized as an integral part of the state's administrative culture. The scheme will need careful nurturing and support for at least another 10 years before one can speak with confidence about long-term sustainability.

Administrators and community leaders interviewed in 2004 saw some grounds for hope. They firmly believe that democratic decentralization will be difficult to reverse in Madhya Pradesh, and that local self-government institutions are here to stay. Given the scale of the EGS programme, no government can afford to lose the goodwill of so many people who for the first time have real access to schooling facilities for their children.

NOTES

I would like to thank R. Gopalakrishnan, Amita Sharma, Tanuja Srivastava, Kamna Achraya, and the Rajiv Gandhi Education Mission team in Bhopal, Raisen, and Betul for sharing data and studies, facilitating fieldwork, and, most importantly, for giving their valuable time for discussions. Many thanks to Digvijaya Singh, former chief minister of Madhya Pradesh, for readily discussing the EGS programme in an unscheduled meeting at the office of *Seminar* magazine in January 2004. I am grateful for the support of Sumit Bose, then joint secretary in the government of India and now principal secretary for education in the government of Madhya Pradesh. Many thanks to Aarti Saihjee (consultant, UNICEF) and Harsh Sethi (consulting editor, *Seminar* magazine) for valuable substantive and editorial inputs.

References

Bashir, S. and R.V.V. Ayyar, 2001, 'District Primary Education Programme,' New Delhi: European Commission.

GMP (Government of Madhya Pradesh), 2002, 'Universalising Elementary Education in Madhya Pradesh,' in *Third Human Development Report, Madhya Pradesh 2002.* Bhopal, India: Government of Madhya Pradesh.

Gopalakrishnan, R. and A. Sharma, 1999, 'Education Guarantee Scheme in Madhya Pradesh: Innovative Step to Universalise Education,' *Economic and Political Weekly* (Mumbai), 26 September.

Kothari, B., V. Sherry Chand and R. Sharma, 2000, 'A Review of Primary Education Packages in Madhya Pradesh,' Ahmedabad, India: Indian Institute of Management.

Manor, J., 2001, 'Madhya Pradesh Experiments with Direct Democracy,' *Economic and Political Weekly* (Mumbai), 3 March.

Mercer, M., R. Alexander, H. Ramachandran, P. Rao and A. Singh, 2002, 'Final Evaluation (Part I) of EC Support to Primary Education In India,' New Delhi: European Commission.

Saihjee, A., 2004, 'Long Live the Alphabet! Reflections from Betul District, Madhya Pradesh,' in *Gender and Social Equity in Primary Education: Hierarchies of Access,* ed. V. Ramachandran, 130–64. New Delhi: Sage Publications.

Sarva Shiksha Abhiyan Madhya Pradesh, 2005, 'Educational Profile,' http://www.shikshamission.org/educationalprofile.htm.

Singh, S., K.S. Sridhar and S. Bhargava, 2002, 'External Evaluation of DPEP-I States,' Lucknow, India: Indian Institute of Management.

Notes

1 As of 1999, before the bifurcation of Madhya Pradesh, there were 30,992 village panchayats spread over 45 districts and 459 blocks.

2 The National Family Health Survey was carried out in most of larger states and Delhi in 1992–3 (NFHS-I) and repeated in 1998–9 (NFHS-II). The survey focuses on fertility, family planning, child health, and child mortality.

3 The gross enrolment ratio is the ratio of total enrolment, regardless of age, to the population of the age group that officially corresponds to the level of education shown. The GER can be over 100 per cent due to the inclusion of overage and underage students.

4 The Fund-a-School website is at http://www.fundaschool.org.

5 An evaluation by the European Commission found that 'Management of DPEP in Madhya Pradesh has been characterised by sustained, dynamic and

committed leadership by the RGSM Director, who has been in charge of the programme since its inception in 1994. To a large extent this continuity has been crucial to the programme's success' (Mercer et al. 2002).

6 The author interviewed former chief minister Digvijaya Singh in New Delhi, 9 January 2004.

7 Discussions with panchayat leaders revealed that primary schooling (including the issue of the midday meal) provokes heated debates, not only at the village level but also at the district level in the zilla parishad. Women leaders admit that this was not the case even five years ago, when panchayats rarely discussed education. Interestingly, women leaders did not distinguish between the EGS schools and the formal government primary schools, but they made a distinction between those schools that function regularly—where teachers come and teach—and those that are irregular or dysfunctional. Discussions with EGS teachers often led to parity issues, culminating in comments about equal work not being rewarded with equal pay. Since July 2003, however, the monthly salaries for EGS gurujis and grade-3 contract teachers recruited for government primary schools have been equalized, at Rs 2,500 per month.

8 The European Commission evaluation notes: 'There is also an equity question of whether it was intended that marginalized groups [scheduled castes, scheduled tribes, and other backward castes] would receive a cheaper form of primary education than more privileged groups. The issues of the cost effectiveness and the ethics of education provision to different social groups need to be examined in more detail' (Mercer et al. 2002).

11

Expanding Access to Education in Bangladesh

Naomi Hossain

At first blush, Bangladesh appears an unlikely setting for groundbreaking achievements in girls' education. More than 45 per cent of residents in this predominantly Muslim country live in poverty and less than half of adult women are literate (World Bank 2003). As recently as 1985, more school-aged girls were out of school than attending school. Yet despite these unfavourable circumstances, Bangladesh has succeeded in dramatically expanding access to basic education in the last two decades, particularly among girls.

Today Bangladesh boasts some 18 million primary school places, a level that is theoretically sufficient for its entire school-aged population, thanks to a rapid scaling up of education services.[1] Gross enrolment ratios in primary schools have exceeded 100 per cent.[2] Moreover, the once-stark gender disparity has been completely eliminated: today girls constitute 55 per cent of Bangladesh's total primary school enrolment, up from a third in 1990. In just two decades, the number of girls enrolled in secondary school has increased by an astonishing rate of more than 600 per cent, from 600,000 in 1980 to 4 million in 2000.

The explosion in Bangladesh's primary school enrolment is the result of targeted efforts to increase both the *demand* for education services and the corresponding *supply*. A series of programmes were implemented in the 1990s to boost demand for schooling and overcome barriers to enrolment, particularly among historically underenrolled groups such as girls and the poor. Food rations and cash subsidies provided to families who sent their children to school reached nearly 2 million primary school-aged children and 4 million girls in grades 6 to 10. At the same time, a massive investment by the Bangladesh government in school construction, materials, teachers, and administration fuelled a rapid and large-scale expansion of school services to meet this increased demand. Government spending on education during this period increased both in absolute terms and as a percentage of overall social spending. As a result, an average of 1 million new school places were created each year between 1990 and 1995.

The expansion of access to primary education in Bangladesh shines a light on what can be accomplished when political will is strong, partnerships are effective, and funding is sufficient. The steadfast political commitment of the Bangladesh government to universal education has transcended partisan lines and even spanned successive administrations. Non-governmental organizations (NGOs), an important provider of education services, have formed successful partnerships with the government, despite inherent tensions and problems with corruption. And donors, while providing needed financial assistance, have supported the largely national-driven programmes without compromising country ownership.

Despite persistent problems with the quality of education services, the recent experience of education in Bangladesh offers valuable lessons for the scaling up of poverty programmes worldwide. This chapter examines the circumstances and factors that have underpinned Bangladesh's success in expanding access to basic education. The first section traces the emergence of education as a top development priority in Bangladesh. The next sections focus on the scaling up and financing of education services and on the administrative structure and plural provision of services. The fourth section explores the social, cultural, and economic changes that strengthened the demand for education, and describes policies implemented in the 1990s to further increase demand. The chapter concludes with a discussion of challenges ahead and lessons learned.

AN EMERGING NATIONAL CONSENSUS: EDUCATION AS KEY TO DEVELOPMENT

The rapid expansion of primary school coverage in Bangladesh in the 1990s was enabled by the strong political commitment of the Bangladesh government to the goal of universal primary education. After four decades of slow progress, a groundswell of support from elites, civil servants, and political parties in the 1990s paved the way for the ambitious expansion efforts. This support was the result of a propitious convergence of economic, cultural, political, and personal factors that propelled education to the top of the political agenda.

A Slow Start

The sluggish growth of school enrolment in Bangladesh from the 1950s through the 1980s—and the uneven political commitment to primary education during this period—reveals the crucial role of political will in the country's experience of education expansion. During the 1950s and 1960s, when Bangladesh was still East Pakistan, primary education was largely neglected and limited progress was made in expanding access. Gross enrolment ratios hovered between 40 and 50 per cent.

Following independence in 1971, education was accorded heightened symbolic importance when the liberation movement made universal access to education one of its central platforms (Maniruzzaman 1975). Promises to expand access to education, to provide 'a school for every village', were integral to governments' efforts to establish legitimacy, even—and perhaps especially—under unelected regimes. In Bangladesh, as in other postcolonial nations, the economic development goal of education was coupled with political goals such as the promotion of social integration and linguistic harmony.[3] Education was perceived as a means for creating a 'socialistic' society and thus the fledgling nation's new constitution included a mandate to ensure mass-oriented, uniform, and universal education (Gustavsson 1990: 19). At least in theory, the drive for universal primary education was one of the highest government priorities, along with food production and population control.

Despite the rhetoric, however, the government's early commitment was more symbolic than practical, and very little progress was made towards the objective of mass primary education in the 1970s and 1980s. One reason was the priority given to higher education to address the shortage of educated administrative personnel needed to run the new nation. Political resolve to expand basic education was further dampened by the new nationalist government's wariness that an educated rural populace would be susceptible to social mobilization campaigns, as had happened in other parts of Asia (World Bank 1999: 12). Attempts by disaffected groups of war veterans and leftists to mobilize the rural masses in Bangladesh had been hampered by the educational differences that distanced these middle-class activists from those they sought to mobilize, a gap the new government had little desire to close (Maniruzzaman 1980: 200–1; see also Arens and Van Beurden 1980, part 4, and Hartmann and Boyce 1983: 250–4).

In the following years, when support for basic education did grow, the modest efforts to expand the sector under the First Five-Year Plan (1973–80) were crippled by famine, political unrest, severe economic crisis, assassinations, and declining aid flows (ADB 1986). With funding and political attention in short supply, enrolment levels remained largely stagnant through the 1980s.

Education Becomes a Top Priority

By the 1990s a surge of high-level support pushed education to the forefront of the political agenda. At the core of this movement was the emerging consensus that education was essential to the country's development goals. A study of attitudes among Bangladeshi national elites found that they supported mass primary education as a prerequisite for tackling poverty (Hossain 2005). Increasingly, poverty was perceived to be caused by the absence of modern attitudes and behaviour; education of any quality was therefore an antidote to poverty, helping the poor control their fertility and plan for the future.[4] Elites hoped that an emphasis on education would help Bangladesh emulate the economic development success of the country's neighbours in East and Southeast Asia, where education was believed to have been an important factor in the region's impressive growth.

The view of mass education as furthering Bangladesh's national interest was complemented by a deep, personal faith in the transformative power of education. Many political leaders, civil servants, and members of the national elite had experienced rapid social mobility as a result of their own academic attainment, rising from modest rural backgrounds to positions of power within a single generation. One politician recalled that 'in our days, bright boys came out of remote villages' to rise in society (Hossain 2005: 36). The Bangladeshi social structure reinforced this view: in this comparatively undifferentiated society, characterized by a lack of social distinctions based on language or ethnicity, social advancement appeared to be based on merit, based in turn on level of education.

The personal conviction of many leaders that formal schooling could do for the poor masses what it had done for them spurred a generation of education champions within the ranks of the administration. One such proponent was the former secretary in the Ministry of Education (1979–81), Kazi Fazlur Rahman. As secretary and later as adviser to various governments of Bangladesh, Rahman worked to build a constituency for expanding primary education, arguing that this would further elite interests such as population control (personal communication from Rahman; see also Sattar 1982).

Culture and personal experiences likewise played a role in garnering the support of elected officials and focusing their attention on the need to expand access to education in their constituencies. In accordance with the principles of Islamic charity and Bengali elite tradition, private charitable involvement in village schools has been widespread among politicians and other elites. This involvement has resulted in a unique opportunity for direct contact between policy makers and the lowest level of service provision, the village schools. Through their multiple roles—as constituency MPs, local landlords, respected community members, and the charitable rich—education policy makers, providers, and politicians have been exposed firsthand to the vital significance of education for the poor. The elected Parliament members have expressed this support through democratic representation and increased the pressure on the administration to expand services.

Additional political will for educational expansion has come from partisan factions and from teachers' unions. Particularly during the 1990s, rival parties competed politically on the issue of education access, motivated by their desire to control education policy and to enshrine their vision of national identity and history in the national curriculum. Incoming governments have acted swiftly to revise the curriculum, arousing the wrath of opponents and furthering the incentive for each successive government to expand enrolment in order to achieve greater influence than its predecessor.[5]

At the same time, the powerful primary schoolteachers' associations have generated the political coverage for expansion. Bangladesh's teachers, both vast in number and influential as community-level bureaucrats, have wielded considerable political clout, as evidenced by their four successive salary increases between 1992 and 1998 (World Bank 2000, vol. 1). Because the unions benefit from the addition of new members, simple expansion has positive or, at worst, neutral effects for teachers and therefore does not meet with any organized opposition. Quality reforms are more likely to be resisted by teachers to the extent that they stand to lose from closer monitoring and more accountability (Corrales 1999).

Finally, the prospect for corruption is likely to have helped bolster support for school expansion. Expansion efforts were rife with corruption opportunities due to the influx of foreign aid, the rapid and unmonitored increase in the number of teachers, the provision of food and cash subsidies, and the proliferation of school construction and improvement programmes. Indeed, recent evidence from the World Bank suggests that corruption in the education sector causes more concern for the population than all other forms of public sector corruption in Bangladesh. This is not necessarily an indication that leakage or misappropriation of funds is more widespread in education than in other sectors, but it does illustrate the high level of public attention to corruption in education, a service used universally and routinely.

A Rapid Scaling Up of Primary Education

With leaders squarely behind the objective of universal education, the Government of Bangladesh took bold steps during the 1990s to dramatically scale up education services. Between 1990 and 1995, school places were added at the rate of a million seats a year. At its peak in 2000, the primary school system had places for 18 million students, a level that is theoretically sufficient for the entire school-aged population. This rapid expansion was achieved through a massive government investment in school construction and personnel and an increase in external financing from donors.

Thanks to the expansion efforts, enrolment swelled with new entrants to the sector (Figure 11.1). By 1997, more than 18 million students were enrolled in approximately 78,000 primary schools. By the end of the 1990s, gross enrolment ratios in primary education exceeded 100 per cent (Figure 11.2), and net enrolment ratios were about 85 per cent. In addition, secondary enrolments among all students more than doubled during the 1990s, to approximately 8.5 million.

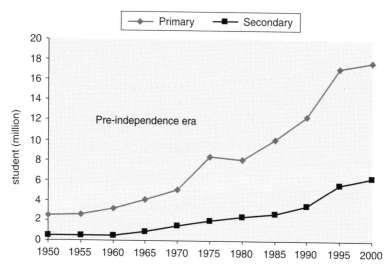

Sources: BBS 1985, 1995, 1999; Government of Bangladesh 2001.

Note: Primary enrolments exclude unregistered non-formal NGO schools.

Figure 11.1   Total Enrolments at Primary and Secondary Levels, 1950–2000

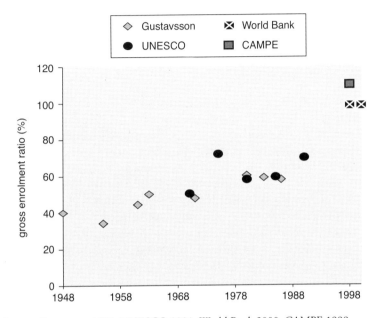

Sources: Gustavsson 1990; UNESCO 2001; World Bank 2000; CAMPE 1999.

Note: Primary enrolments exclude unregistered nonformal NGO schools, except for
             CAMPE figures.

FIGURE 11.2 Gross Enrolment Ratios at Primary Level, 1948–2000
             (Various Estimates)

Massive Investment in Education

The government programmes of the 1980s reflected the shift in priorities
towards education that helped lay the foundation for expansion efforts
over the subsequent decade. A stronger focus on primary education was
incorporated in the Second Five-Year Plan (1980–85), leading to erratic
efforts towards expansion and the establishment of the Directorate of Primary
Education. The Third Five-Year Plan (1985–90) explicitly stated the goals
of universal primary education and mass literacy and placed new emphasis
on reducing gender disparities in enrolments at all levels (Unterhalter, Ross,
and Alam 2003).

Programmes in the 1990s translated these priorities into action.
The Fourth Five-Year Plan (1990–95), which focused firmly on
primary education, introduced legislation making attendance compulsory.

Subsequently, the General Education Project committed the government to a huge effort to scale up the education sector between 1991 and 1997. Under this project, all aspects of the education system were expanded: new schools and classrooms were constructed, teachers and administrators were hired, and additional teaching materials were supplied. As a result, Bangladesh now boasts a universal primary education system that is one of the largest in the world.

The expansion was backed by a large increase in government funding. Beginning in the late 1980s, government spending on education grew both as a proportion of public spending on development and in absolute terms. Education expenditures accounted for only 4 per cent of the government's Annual Development Programme in 1990, but this surged to 14 per cent in 1996 (World Bank 1998). Other social spending rose as well, but more gradually.

As a share of gross domestic product (GDP), public spending on education increased from 0.9 per cent in 1973–80 to 2.2 per cent in 1997–98. Within the budget, education rose from approximately 9 per cent of total spending in 1973–90 to 16 per cent in 1995–96 (World Bank 2000, vol. 1). Households also helped finance the expansion by investing more of their own resources in their children's education.

Donor Funding

The scale and pace of the expansion was made possible by an influx of foreign aid. Between 1990 and 1995, development partners provided half of the total financing for primary education in Bangladesh (Sedere 2000; see also Bennell and Furlong 1998 for a global overview of aid to education after Jomtien). The bulk of their investment was funnelled through NGO education programmes. Government financing for state primary education, therefore, was critical and in fact remained larger and increased more rapidly than foreign aid to that sector (Table 11.1).

The surge of foreign funding marked a positive shift in donor attitudes towards the education sector. Until the 1980s, donors demonstrated little interest in funding education. World Bank staff in Bangladesh in the 1970s were ambivalent about financing what they saw as 'nation-building rather than skill-building', and the first major primary education project was not launched by the Bank until 1980 (World Bank 1999: 12). The World Bank's reservations about channelling donor money to primary education were not unique and reflected the general views of bilateral aid donors during this period (Bennell and Furlong 1998). However, following the World

Conference on Education for All held in Jomtien, Thailand in 1990, donors began investing heavily in the education sector. In Bangladesh, as elsewhere, donors proved increasingly willing to support government efforts in this field, particularly in expanding access (especially for the poor and girls) and improving quality at the primary and secondary levels.

TABLE 11.1   Spending on Primary and Mass Education by the Government and Foreign Donors

(millions of taka)

Year	Government of Bangladesh	Foreign aid[a]	Total
1990–91	5,974	1,397	7,372
1991–92	7,186	3,134	10,320
1992–93	8,249	3,401	11,650
1993–94	11,589	3,375	14,964
1994–95	14,307	3,281	17,588
1995–96	14,562	3,156	17,718
1996–97	15,570	3,073	18,643
1997–98	17,626	1,687	19,313
1998–99	19,008	2,763	21,770

Source: Government of Bangladesh 1999.
Notes: Figures may not sum to total due to rounding.
a. Excludes aid to NGO education projects, for which aggregate data are unavailable.

The comparatively late arrival of donor funding facilitated the scaling up of expansion at a critical moment and also helped Bangladesh avoid the common pitfall of insufficient national ownership in the face of donor involvement. Foreign aid usually bears high transaction costs, a burden that donors in Bangladesh took steps to reduce in the 1990s. In this instance, donor funding and coordination never reached levels that constituted a threat to government control. Instead, the Bangladesh government took the lead, displaying an uncharacteristically high degree of national ownership of policy in this historically aid-dependent country. The fact that the government and other key actors in Bangladesh were already committed to expansion and universal access before donor resources were committed on any scale may explain this success. Donors were thus supporting a preexisting pro-poor government agenda, adding to the incentive to spend aid resources well.

The benefits of donor involvement in the education sector extend beyond just the provision of material resource flows. Donors have long championed domestic and international NGOs within Bangladesh, which they have seen as spearheading the effective provision of services to the poor (Sanyal 1991; Hashemi and Hassan 1999; Hashemi 1996; White 1999). Bilateral donors in particular have used their political influence within Bangladesh to carve out a protected space for NGO activities, and donors may have helped sustain the focus on gender equity in NGO programmes.

THE EDUCATION SECTOR: CENTRALIZED PLANNING, DIVERSE PROVISION

The primary school system in Bangladesh expanded under the umbrella of the education sector's unique administrative structure: a marriage of highly centralized planning and administration with education provision by a diverse range of state and non-state schools. The government thus has been at once hands-on and hands-off. While not without its critics, this unusual arrangement has maximized resources and helped rapidly broaden education access to include underenrolled populations. Groups of students not reached by the main system have been drawn in by more specialized providers, and from there some have been able to enter the mainstream system.

Centralized Administrative Structure

The centralized administrative structure of the education sector in Bangladesh dates back to the nationalization of community schools following independence. Before liberation, primary schooling had been an entirely local effort, funded primarily through private charity and contributions in kind. The nationalization of the 36,000 largely community-based primary schools in 1973 gave the central government direct control over school assets and management and instantly swelled the rolls of government employees. Overnight, teachers became members of the civil bureaucracy, expected to assume a variety of administrative duties such as data collection, election administration, and brokering between subdistrict and village administrations. By 1999, a quarter million teachers were being trained, disciplined, and compensated directly from Dhaka, while control of financial and personnel management remained concentrated at the centre (Muhith 1999). Centrally recruited and remunerated, teachers respond to lines of authority and accountability that connect to the government in Dhaka rather than to the village community. They are, in effect, 'a multitude of centrally supervised permanent functionaries of the government' (Mahmud 2002: 21–22).

Educational planning and policy making have also been centralized and are led by a directorate responsible for all primary education. This central control over education combined with the strong commitment to mass education at the centre proved a powerful combination and helped translate the strong political will into an ambitious expansion effort. The political impetus to expand schooling in Bangladesh depended in part on acceptance of this centralized control, since political and administrative champions of educational reform wielding considerable power at the top of the system implemented expansion based on a centrally designed curriculum.

Despite its role in enabling a rapid expansion, the centralized structure of education administration has drawn widespread criticism for improving the *quantity* of school placements but not the *quality* of education. The system is plagued by weak management and the inhibition of initiative at the district, subdistrict, and individual school levels. There is limited transparency in the allocation and use of resources, compounded by an ineffective system of accountability—of teachers to students, guardians, and head teachers; of head teachers to supervisors and school management committees; and of school management to the government. Furthermore, ineffective monitoring and evaluation provide little empirical basis for policy formulation and planning.

The Government of Bangladesh recognizes these challenges and has made attempts to address them. At the primary level, the Ministry of Primary and Mass Education is implementing a six-year programme of support known as the Primary Education Development Programme, aimed at strengthening educational access, quality, and efficiency. For secondary education, the Ministry of Education has finalized a medium-term framework that lays out targets for quality improvements as well as policy measures and specific actions needed to achieve these targets.

Diverse School Providers

Despite its tight central control over school administration and education policy, the government has allowed the provision of school services by an unusually diverse array of providers. In fact, only about half of all the officially recognized 79,000 primary schools are managed and resourced directly by the central government. The remaining half are run by communities, NGOs, charities, religious groups, and private providers. Their variety is striking: in 2005 there were no fewer than 11 officially recognized types of primary schools, and even more when unregistered schools are counted. Registered NGO schools constitute 24 per cent of enrolment, and madrassah (religious) schools have another 5 per cent (World Bank 2000, vol. 2).

The advantages of the plural provider system are numerous. The variety has fostered innovative school design, facilitated learning across systems, and increased competition. It has also allowed the government to maximize resources by tapping into strong community support for local schools. Critics have pointed out, though, that the diversity of school providers has not resulted in an effective choice of provider for most families.

The proliferation of non-state schools has been welcomed, or at least not obstructed, by the government on the grounds that these schools help with cost sharing and the contracting out of services. By providing sizable financial resources, the government has encouraged the development and operation of registered schools, many of which follow the national curriculum closely. For example, when community schools experienced a revival and construction boom in the 1980s, with many located in poorer areas, the government paid teachers' salaries in full or in part, provided grants, built facilities, boosted enrolment through food or cash subsidies to households, and supplied teaching materials. Overall, by the late 1990s, almost 10 per cent of primary education spending went to pay teachers' salaries in non-state schools (World Bank 2000, vol. 1). The proportion of non-state-school teachers' salaries being paid by the state has continued to rise, from 50 per cent in 1986 to 70 per cent in the early 1990s and finally to 80–90 per cent, plus benefits, by the end of the decade (ADB 1986; Alam 1992, 1994; Masum 2001; World Bank 2000, vol. 2).

This subsidy to private institutions has stirred little controversy, although analysts note that subsidies to private schools are not an especially equitable or effective means of contracting out as the schools tend to be set up in more affluent areas and are often of lower quality than the state schools (World Bank 2000, vol. 2: 63–71). Nevertheless, political capital can be gained by increasing state contributions to the salaries of teachers in nonstate schools. Election manifestos for 2001, for example, advocated increasing the state contribution levels to 100 per cent.

The relationship between the government and the non-state schools has been more or less harmonious, albeit fragile at times. The government has permitted religious entities and foreign-funded NGOs to operate schools on a large scale. Although it has on occasion demonstrated its willingness to intervene in such institutions, recent policy towards the madrassahs in particular has been tempered by sensitivities about appearing anti-Islamic. NGOs have also operated with a great deal of autonomy. While the government has faced some political pressure to assume greater control of the NGO schools, as illustrated by the often-repeated declaration of intent to nationalize these schools, in practice the state has supported a variety of partnerships with NGOs. A review of the Department of Non-formal Education (DNFE), a department responsible for facilitating government-NGO collaboration, revealed that four-fifths of NGOs involved in education in Bangladesh were implementing programmes for the DNFE (World Bank 2000, vol. 2). This level indicated that the directorate had built a close relationship with NGOs (Miwa 2003), although the closure of the DNFE in 2003, amid reports of corruption and mismanagement, highlight the fragility of that relationship.

Reaching the Poor: Non-formal NGO Schools

Non-formal NGO schools have occupied an important space in the education landscape of Bangladesh, playing an instrumental role in the expansion of school services to the poor and to girls. Some 1.5 million children, or 8 per cent of total enrolment, attend non-formal NGO schools that are not registered with the government. The vast majority of these schools do not adopt the national curriculum and have received few resources from the government. BRAC, the largest Bangladeshi NGO, presently educates 1.2 million of these children.[6] Thanks to a school expansion programme in the late 1980s, BRAC already had over 1 million students enrolled in 34,000 non-formal schools by the early 1990s, and employed almost 33,000 teachers (BRAC 1996).

Through innovative schooling techniques, the non-formal NGO schools have been markedly successful in reaching girls and the poor, two groups that have historically been underenrolled in schools. With a mandate to work on behalf of the poor, BRAC and other NGOs such as Proshika have made direct efforts to enrol girls from poor families and have been effective in signalling the value of education in poor rural communities. These non-formal schools have served as a feeder to the official schools, as many of the poor female students that enter the NGO schools later graduate into the formal system (Nath 2002).

The relationship between non-formal NGO schools and the government has been complex, as the government has vacillated between granting the NGOs latitude and support and trying to control them or deny them a legitimate role. To some degree, this fluctuation reflects the divisions within the large NGO community that make a consistent relationship with government difficult. By and large, however, the central government has rarely acted to obstruct the education programmes of NGOs. BRAC, in particular, has been able to function rather freely, in large part because of its tactful stress on its role as providing schools that are complementary to the state system. It has successfully portrayed itself as a positive model that can demonstrate to the government the possibility of reaching girls and the poor through innovative schooling.

The influence of the NGOs extends beyond their immediate impact on the students enrolled in their schools. Competitive pressure from the mainly foreign-funded NGO schools that are present in a high proportion of villages has served as a catalyst for the government to expand its own efforts, particularly among underenrolled populations. In particular, the government has been motivated by unfavourable contrasts made between the state efforts and BRAC's successful efforts to provide primary school services to poor families. The competition from BRAC schools also provided a stimulus for the demand-side programmes, discussed in the next section, that the government implemented in the 1990s to entice students to enrol in school. Civil servants tended to believe that BRAC had an unhealthy hold over the rural poor population because of its microcredit programmes, and some claimed that BRAC lured students from state schools by offering credit to families conditional on BRAC school enrolment. Regardless of the validity of such claims, their currency among civil servants reveals the extent to which the NGOs helped the administration recognize the need for additional support and incentives for the poorest.[7]

Demand-Side Interventions: Eliminating the Gender Gap

Boosting overall enrolment rates required a dual effort, requiring government to increase the capacity of schools while at the same time attracting new students to fill the seats. Expanding access to girls and the poor was critical to the goal of universal education and entailed a special emphasis on overcoming gender and poverty obstacles to their enrolment. A series of demand-side programmes implemented in the 1990s accelerated the rise in demand among girls for schooling, an interest that had been growing in the changing economic and social climate of the 1980s and 1990s.

The impact of these efforts on gender equity has been remarkable. After narrowing very slowly until the 1990s, the gender gap at the primary level narrowed swiftly and was completely eliminated by the end of that decade (Figure 11.3). Enrolment of girls also rose rapidly at the secondary level, from about 600,000 in 1980 to over 4 million by 2000. Girls now constitute about 55 per cent of total lower secondary enrolment, up from just a third at the beginning of the 1990s.

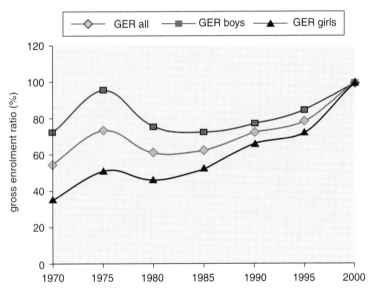

Sources: Year 2000: UNESCO Institute of Statistics (http://stats.uis.unesco.org). All other years: UNESCO 2001.

Note: Primary enrolments exclude unregistered nonformal NGO schools.

FIGURE 11.3 Gross Enrolment Ratios by Gender at Primary Level, 1970–2000

Growing Demand for Girls' Education

Initially, girls were left out of the spike in demand for schooling that followed independence in 1971. During the 1970s, expanding employment opportunities in the public sector encouraged families to invest in higher education for their sons. At the same time, increasing landlessness and declining farm size, sparked by population growth and mounting pressures on the land, were further motivation for households to invest in the education of their children, most often their sons. A gender-segmented labour market and constraints on women's employment meant that the changing economic opportunities in Bangladesh had far less impact on the demand for girls' education than on the demand for education of boys. As a result, the gender gap between girls' enrolment and boys' remained wide.

Social and economic changes in Bangladesh during the 1980s and 1990s, notably new economic opportunities for women, served to increase the demand for education of girls. As women engaged in new patterns of public employment during the economic crisis period of the 1970s, attitudes towards women's work began to shift (Chen and Ghuznavi 1977). Beginning in the 1980s, the expansion of microcredit programmes gave poor women more resources and consequently more influence on decision-making about education (Hashemi and Schuler 1996). During the same period, the export-oriented garment industry emerged as an important source of jobs for women. The fact that a minimum primary school education was needed to take advantage of these openings was an additional incentive for families to educate their daughters (Kabeer 1997; Siddiqui et al. 1990; Kibria 1995). Furthermore, a marked rise in the average cost of dowries and in rates of divorce and desertion among the poor in the 1980s may have altered perceptions of marriage as a guarantee of economic security for women.

Strong positive signals about girls' education from business, social, and political leaders have impacted public discourse and have helped shift attitudes in favour of sending girls to school. Successive political leaders, including the two female prime ministers who held office during the 1990s, took a personal interest in primary education for girls. A UNICEF public education campaign that used the cartoon character Meena also helped foster a change in attitudes. Women's microcredit groups supported by NGOs may have had an indirect influence by exposing people to new norms reinforcing the value of girls' education (Drèze and Kingdon 2001).

In part, the expansion of the educational system itself helped to generate demand. Studies have repeatedly shown that long distances to school or the absence of a school in the village deters many rural households from sending their children. In the first half of the 1990s, large-scale classroom construction, teacher recruitment, and efforts to encourage community provision in underserved areas under the General Education Project brought schools to villages, so that many households were now able to exercise effective demand for education. Also, from 1981 through the 1990s, teacher recruitment included efforts to increase the proportion of female teachers as a means of attracting more girl students (Rahman 1993). Women now constitute almost a third of all primary school teachers in the formal system and more than 90 per cent of all teachers in the BRAC schools (Hossain and Kabeer 2004).

Incentives for Girls' Education

To increase enrolment of girls and the poor, the government took specific steps to provide incentives and overcome barriers to enrolment. These included measures aimed at reducing households' reliance on the labour of children that had prevented many very poor families from keeping their children in school. The massive Food for Education (FFE) programme was the first in a series of demand-side interventions implemented by the government in the 1990s. FFE provided grain rations to disadvantaged families that sent their children to primary school, reaching more than 2 million students by 1999 (CAMPE 1999). The programme was replaced in 2002 by the Primary Education Stipend Project (PESP), a targeted, direct cash-subsidy programme that is expected to reach 5 million students a year. The other major demand-side intervention is the Female Secondary Stipends (FSS) programme, which provides stipends and tuition waivers to girls in non-municipal areas attending grades 6 through 10. Close to 4 million girls a year are receiving stipends under this programme. Both programmes were modified in 2002 to introduce school- and student-based criteria related to attendance and performance as requirements for access to the subsidies. Efforts were also made to streamline and clarify the procedures in an apparent effort to reduce the problems of leakages associated with the earlier FFE programme.[8]

Notwithstanding these leakages, the programmes have proven effective in enhancing access. There is considerable evidence that the subsidies under FFE have improved the educational prospects of many girls and poor children (Ravallion and Wodon 1999; Ahmed and del Ninno 2002). The FSS programme of female secondary-level scholarships indirectly gave parents incentives to educate girls at the primary level, since they could anticipate lower costs ahead if their daughters remained in school. Each additional year of the FSS is estimated to have increased female secondary enrolment by as much as 8 per cent. The FSS programme is also thought to help delay girls' marriage by providing an incentive for them to continue their studies (Arends-Kuenning and Amin 2000).

Specific policies have also been implemented to empower women and provide incentives for girls to enrol in school. For example, the government provided the PESP stipend payments directly to students' mothers, who were required to open bank accounts in order to receive the cash. The policy was designed to give more control to mothers over educational spending while also increasing their mobility and public interaction.

LESSONS LEARNED AND CHALLENGES AHEAD

The rapid expansion of primary education in Bangladesh and the elimination of the gender gap in schooling is a clear development success story. Today, access to basic education is nearly universal in the country. As more and more children enrol in school, the potential of millions of poor children and girls will be unleashed, holding out the promise of advances for the entire country.

A number of factors underpinned Bangladesh's successful primary education expansion. First and foremost, political will at the centre was a crucial ingredient. The strong support of high-ranking government leaders, civil servants, members of the elite, and political parties was essential to the implementation of ambitious expansion efforts in the 1990s. But it was not elite support alone that fuelled success, but rather the convergence of elite support and the aspirations and needs of the masses. With such a fit between top-down and bottom-up perspectives, it was possible for the government to capitalize on strong community demand and support for primary schools.

The success also turned on effective partnerships between the government and NGOs and other non-state providers. Successive governments have largely declined to intervene in the mainly foreign-funded education programmes. Given the highly political nature of primary education, this shows remarkable restraint and is a testament to officials' consistent political commitment to expanding education access.

A number of surprises emerge in the Bangladesh experience. The case refutes the common assumption that centralized authority over policy and planning necessarily impedes the expansion of primary education. It also demonstrates the potential for national ownership of key reform agendas despite significant input of external aid resources.

Nonetheless, problems remain. The government now faces the challenge of ensuring that improvements in the quality of education catch up with the improvements in access. Equally important, excluded groups must be brought into the system in even larger numbers. In particular, efforts are needed to expand access to groups that are geographically, ethnically, and socially marginalized, such as *chor* inhabitants, tribal minorities, and urban slum children (CAMPE 1999; Masum 2001).

Progress has already begun. The government is taking measures to address quality issues at both the primary and secondary levels, with particular attention to improving the quality of teaching and learning. It is moving towards decentralized systems of management and establishing effective monitoring and evaluation systems. Further demand-side interventions are targeting the families who are hardest to reach.

References

ADB (Asian Development Bank), 1986, 'Bangladesh: Sector Study on Education,' Education Division, Infrastructure Department, Asian Development Bank, Manila.

Alam, M., 1992, 'Secondary and Higher Secondary Education in Bangladesh: Its Growth and State Expenditures. A Time-Series Analysis of 1981–90,' Development Research and Action Programme, Chr. Michelsen Institute, Bergen, Norway.

———, 1994, 'Performance of Secondary Education Sub-sector in Bangladesh: 1981–1990,' *Bangladesh Development Studies* 22 (1): 105–16.

Archer, M., 1979, 'Introduction: Theorizing about the Expansion of Educational Systems,' in M. Archer (ed.), *The Sociology of Educational Expansion: Take-off, Growth and Inflation in Educational Systems*, Beverly Hills, CA: Sage.

Arends-Kuenning, M. and S. Amin, 2000, 'The Effects of Schooling Incentive Programs on Household Resource Allocation in Bangladesh,' Policy Research Division Working Paper 133, Population Council, New York.

Arens, J. and J. Van Beurden, 1980, *Jhagrapur: Poor Peasants and Women in a Village in Bangladesh*, New Delhi: Orient Longman.

BBS (Bangladesh Bureau of Statistics). Various years. *Statistical Yearbook of Bangladesh*. Dhaka: Government of Bangladesh, Ministry of Planning.

Bennell, P. and D. Furlong, 1998, 'Has Jomtien Made Any Difference? Trends in Donor Funding for Education and Basic Education Since the Late 1980s,' *World Development* 26 (1): 45–59.

BRAC, 1996, *Annual Report 1996*, Dhaka: BRAC Prokashona.

CAMPE (Campaign for Popular Education), 1999, *Hope Not Complacency: State of Primary Education in Bangladesh, 1999*, Dhaka: University Press Limited.

———, 2001, *A Question of Quality: State of Primary Education in Bangladesh*. Vol. 1, Dhaka: University Press Limited.

Chen, M. and R. Ghuznavi, 1977, 'Women in Food-for-Work: The Bangladesh Experience,' World Food Programme, Rome.

Cooksey, B., D. Court and B. Makau, 1994, 'Education for Self-Reliance and Harambee,' in J.D. Barkan (ed.), *Beyond Capitalism vs. Socialism in Kenya and Tanzania*, Boulder, CO: Lynne Rienner.

Corrales, J., 1999, 'The Politics of Education Reform: Bolstering the Supply and Demand; Overcoming Institutional Blocks,' Education Reform and Management Series 2 (1), Washington, DC: World Bank.

Court, D., 1976, 'The Educational System as a Response to Inequality in Tanzania and Kenya,' *Journal of Modern African Studies* 14 (4): 661–90.

Drèze, J. and G.G. Kingdon, 2001, 'School Participation in Rural India,' *Review of Development Economics* 5 (1): 1–24.

Government of Bangladesh, 2001, 'Primary Education Statistics in Bangladesh (as of June 2000),' Directorate of Primary Education, Primary and Mass Education Division, Dhaka.

Gustavsson, S., 1990, *Primary Education in Bangladesh: For Whom?* Dhaka: University Press Limited.

Hartmann, B. and J. Boyce, 1983, *A Quiet Violence: View from a Bangladesh Village*. New Delhi: Oxford University Press.

Hashemi, S., 1996, 'State, Politics and Civil Society in the Context of Donor Hegemony: Bangladesh at 25,' Paper presented at the International Conference on Bangladesh at 25, Columbia University, New York, 5–7 December.

Hashemi, S. and M. Hassan, 1999, 'Building NGO Legitimacy in Bangladesh: The Contested Domain,' in D. Lewis (ed.), *International Perspectives on Voluntary Action: Reshaping the Third Sector*, 124–31. London: Earthscan.

Hashemi, S. and S. Schuler, 1996, 'Rural Credit Programs and Women's Empowerment in Bangladesh,' *World Development* 24 (4): 635–53.

Hossain, N., 2005, *Elite Perceptions of Poverty in Bangladesh*, Dhaka: University Press Limited.

Hossain, N. and N. Kabeer, 2004, 'Achieving Universal Primary Education and Eliminating Gender Disparity in Bangladesh,' *Economic and Political Weekly* (Mumbai), 4–10 September, 4093.

Hossain, N., R. Subrahmanian and N. Kabeer, 2002, 'The Politics of Educational Expansion in Bangladesh,' Working Paper 167, Institute of Development Studies, University of Sussex, Brighton, UK.

Kabeer, N., 1997, 'Women, Wages and Intra-household Power Relations in Urban Bangladesh,' *Development and Change* 28 (2): 261–302.

Kibria, N., 1995, 'Culture, Social Class and Income Control in the Lives of Women Garment Workers in Bangladesh,' *Gender and Society* 9 (3): 289–309.

Mahmud, W., 2002, 'National Budgets, Social Spending and Public Choice: The Case of Bangladesh,' Working Paper 162, Institute of Development Studies, University of Sussex, Brighton, UK.

Maniruzzaman, T., 1975, *Radical Politics and the Emergence of Bangladesh*, Dhaka: Bangladesh Books International/World University Press.

———, 1980, *The Bangladesh Revolution and Its Aftermath*, Dhaka: University Press Limited.

Masum, M., 2001, 'Education Sector in Bangladesh: A Review,' Background paper prepared for the Pre-Election Policy Brief Task Force on Education, Centre for Policy Dialogue, Dhaka.

Miwa, K., 2003, 'Operationalizing Children's Rights to Education: A Case of Government-NGO Partnership in Bangladesh,' in N. Kabeer, G.B. Nambissan, and R. Subrahmanian (eds), *Child Labour and the Right to Education in South Asia: Needs Versus Rights*, New Delhi: Sage.

Muhith, A.M.A., 1999, *Bangladesh in the Twenty-first Century: Towards an Industrial Society*, Dhaka: University Press Limited.

Nath, S.R., 2002, 'The Transition from Non-formal to Formal Education: The Case of BRAC, Bangladesh,' *International Review of Education* 48 (6): 517–24.

Rahman, K.F., 1993, 'Primary and Mass Education: Management and Accountability,' *Daily Star* (Dhaka), 18–20 September.

Ravallion, M. and Q. Wodon, 1999, 'Does Child Labor Displace Schooling? Evidence on Behavioral Responses to an Enrolment Subsidy,' Policy Research Working Paper 2116, World Bank, Washington, DC.

Sanyal, B., 1991, 'Antagonistic Cooperation: A Case Study of Nongovernmental Organizations, Government and Donors' Relationships in Income-Generating Projects in Bangladesh,' *World Development* 19 (10): 1367–79.

Sattar, E., 1982, *Universal Primary Education in Bangladesh*, Dhaka: University Press Limited.

Sedere, U., 2000, 'Rethinking Educational Aid: Sector Support Approach to Financing Basic Education: Lessons from Bangladesh,' *Prospects* 30 (4): 451–60.

Siddiqui, K., S.R. Qadir, S. Alamgir and S. Huq, 1990, *Social Formation in Dhaka City: A Study in Third World Urban Sociology*, Dhaka: University Press Limited.

UNESCO, 2001, 'Education Counts: Key Statistics of National Education Systems,' CD ROM. UNESCO Institute of Statistics, Paris.

Unterhalter, E., J. Ross and M. Alam, 2003, 'A Fragile Dialogue? Research and Primary Education Policy Formation in Bangladesh, 1971–2001,' *Compare* 33 (1): 85–99.

White, S.C., 1999, 'NGOs, Civil Society and the State in Bangladesh: The Politics of Representing the Poor,' *Development and Change* 30: 307–26.

World Bank, 1999, 'Education in Bangladesh: A Country Sector Review,' Report 19548, Operations Evaluation Department, World Bank, Washington, DC.

———, 2000, *Bangladesh Education Sector Review*. 2 vols, Dhaka: University Press Limited; Washington, DC: World Bank.

———, 2003, *Poverty in Bangladesh: Building on Progress*, Washington, DC: World Bank.

Notes

1 These official statistics do not include the more than 2 million children enrolled in unregistered NGO schools (CAMPE 2001).

2 The gross enrolment ratio (GER) is the ratio of total enrolment, regardless of age, to the population of the age group that officially corresponds to the level of education shown. The GER can be over 100 per cent due to the inclusion of overage and underage students. The net enrolment ratio is the ratio of the number of children of official school age (as defined by the education system) enrolled in school to the number of children of official school age in the population.

3 See Court (1976) and Cooksey, Court, and Makau (1994) for a discussion of similar experiences in Tanzania and Kenya.

4 The belief that education breeds social transformation regardless of its quality has some support in anecdotal evidence that schooling has an impact on people's attitudes and behaviour, independently of their literacy and numeracy achievements (World Bank 2000, vol. 1, p. 49).

5 See Unterhalter, Ross, and Alam (2003) and Hossain, Subrahmanian, and Kabeer (2002) for a more detailed version of this argument.

6 Now known by its acronym, BRAC was the Bangladesh Rural Advancement Committee when it was founded in 1972. BRAC's 34,000 single-cohort schools, like other non-formal NGO schools, are not registered with the government and do not receive the support enjoyed by registered NGO primary schools. In 2004, however, the BRAC students became eligible to take the public scholarship examinations to enter the formal secondary system, a policy shift towards greater acceptance of NGO nonformal schools.

7 Such competitive pressures are similar to the 'corporate competition' between state and non-state schools that had expansionary effects in France and England (Archer 1979).

8 The replacement of the FFE programme with the cash stipend programme in 2002 was done in part to reduce leakage.

12

Addressing Urban Infrastructure Needs of the Poor

Public–Private Partnerships in Tamil Nadu, India

Sameer Vyas

The sprawling cities of India are home to 285 million people, about 27 per cent of the country's population. The urban areas are engines of growth, generating about two-thirds of India's gross domestic product. But the urban sector also encompasses harsh poverty, vividly symbolized by the spread of slums. Such settlements reflect persistent inequities in the distribution of wealth and welfare. Despite their contributions to urban growth, slum dwellers endure a miserable quality of life, with inadequate access to basic services such as water and sanitation that are essential to health and well-being.

The issues in providing urban infrastructure services are largely structural. The urban local bodies responsible for such services in Indian cities face severe financial and managerial constraints, with investments normally funded from tax revenues or debt. As service charges are insufficient to cover recurrent costs, the quality and maintenance of services have declined, and service networks cannot expand. Meanwhile, financial risks and policy and regulatory uncertainties stifle private funding. As a result, the promising role of greater private sector investment in urban infrastructure has gone largely unrealized.

One state in India has overcome these obstacles and is at the forefront of the move towards public–private provision of urban services. Tamil Nadu, one of India's most urbanized states, mobilized private investments of nearly $261 million through early 2004 for urban service provision. The state succeeded in attracting $220 million for the country's first-ever joint-venture, public–private institution to provide water and sanitation services. Sewerage, road, and bridge projects have also been funded in Tamil Nadu with sizable inflows of private investment. The projects have been implemented through joint ventures between the state government and one or more private companies. This approach to using public–private partnerships to provide better urban infrastructure services is inspiring investor confidence and creating new options for future expansion.

Tamil Nadu's successful experience in public–private service provision brings to light the policies and necessary preconditions that facilitate private investment. Both foreign and domestic investors have been attracted by the state's suitable macroeconomic environment, which is backed by good social performance in areas like health and education. Most importantly, the projects are highly demand-driven; in some cases, the beneficiaries are themselves equity holders and participate in the governance structures of the projects. Furthermore, the public–private partnership framework has led to a viable allocation of risk between government and the private sector; regulatory and policy risks have been assumed by the government, while commercial risks are borne in general by the private entity.

This chapter examines the first stages of three umbrella institutions in Tamil Nadu that have undertaken a wide range of infrastructure projects under the public–private partnership model: the Tamil Nadu Water Investment Company, the Tamil Nadu Urban Infrastructure Financial Services, and the Tamil Nadu Road Development Company. This chapter documents the impact and outcomes of the projects and the key elements that contributed to their success, concluding with a discussion of the prospects for expansion and scaling up.

THE CHALLENGE OF URBAN SERVICE PROVISION

The scale and pace of urbanization in India and across the globe is striking. Between 1970 and 2000, the number of metropolitan areas around the world with at least 1 million people more than doubled, from 163 to 350. Twenty-five years ago, less than 40 per cent of the world's population lived in urban areas; 25 years in the future, this share could reach nearly 60 per cent (World Bank 2000: 9). In India, the urban share of the population rose from 18 per cent four decades ago to 27 per cent in 2001, according to that year's national census. The country's urban population is expected to reach 50 per cent of the total by 2025.

The fast-growing urban areas in India are engines of growth, generating approximately two-thirds of the country's gross domestic product (GDP). Compared to their rural counterparts, urbanites on average enjoy higher standards of service and a better quality of life. Urban welfare gains, however, mask stark inequalities and widespread poverty, particularly in slum settlements.

Thus, rapid urbanization has resulted in a formidable urban development challenge: to provide adequate housing, infrastructure, and services to the cities' poor residents. The task of providing these services on the scale necessary to promote economic growth and improve the quality of life is daunting. *World Development Report 1999/2000* sounded a warning: 'Absorbing the 2.4 billion new urban residents expected over the next 30 years will require further investments in housing, water and sanitation, transportation, power, and telecommunications. The need for these new infrastructure investments comes on top of the backlog that already plagues the world's cities. Providing universal coverage for water and sanitation alone in the cities of developing countries will cost nearly 5 per cent of those countries' GDP' (World Bank 2000: 132).

Indeed, cities worldwide have already been overwhelmed by population growth, leaving them unable to provide sufficient basic services. In 1994, 220 million urban dwellers (13 per cent of the urban population in developing countries) lacked access to clean drinking water, and almost twice as many lacked sanitation facilities. Roughly half of solid waste went uncollected, while domestic and industrial effluent was being released into waterways with little or no treatment, affecting the quality of water far beyond the cities (World Bank 2000: 140). There has been little improvement in the situation since then. In India, serious problems exist in the quality, reliability, and sustainability of water services.

Lack of basic services imposes a high toll on human health, and the poor bear the greatest burden. At any given time, according to *World Development Report*, close to half the urban population in developing countries is suffering from one or more waterborne diseases. Epidemiological studies show that improving access to clean water and sanitation can reduce the incidence of diarrhoeal diseases by more than 20 per cent (World Bank 2000: 141). In India, it is estimated that nearly 70 per cent of health problems are in some way water-related. Airborne illnesses such as acute respiratory infections and tuberculosis also spread faster in overcrowded urban housing with poor ventilation.

The manner in which cities manage their development has significant effects on the rate of growth. Urban governments can foster economic growth or they can slow it down; this in turn affects their capacity to improve the quality of life for the urban poor. Institutional and governance weaknesses can distort the allocation of investments and compromise efforts at poverty reduction. The rapid pace of urbanization has led to demand for services that has outstripped traditional supply capacities. It is becoming increasingly evident that the decline in availability of services is impeding not only improvements in the quality of life but also economic growth itself.

A Promising Role for the Private Sector

The failure in provision of urban services is largely a structural problem. Since the 1950s, the infrastructure market in developing countries has been dominated by the public sector. Governments have had the responsibility to make initial investments and then to provide and maintain all the services that fall within the scope of infrastructure, ranging from water and sanitation to ports and airports. Vertically integrated government agencies have been created to undertake these complex functions.

However, governments on their own simply do not have the capacity to fund the high level of investment that will be required to meet future infrastructure needs. For instance, for the water and sanitation sector alone, 'developing countries will need to invest around $60 billion per year, or $1.2 billion every week during the next ten years. This will mean increasing water supply and sanitation investments from less than 0.4 per cent to about 1.0 per cent of their combined GDP in the next decade' (Rivera 1996: 49). In India, the Central Public Health and Environmental Engineering Organization estimates that under the Tenth Five-Year Plan (2002–07), Rs 282,400 million will be required for water and Rs 231,570 million for sanitation—approximately $6.6 billion and $5.2 billion respectively (Sethuraman 2004). Overall, for the full range of urban services like water, sanitation, solid waste collection, roads, and so forth, $90 billion will be required over the next 10 years.

It is impossible for governments faced with budgetary pressures and fiscal constraints to provide such resources without crowding out other social and economic programs that are also priorities. Therefore, the current trend is away from such exclusive government responsibility and towards a greater role for the private sector. Participation by private entities in the financing, operation, maintenance, and ownership of infrastructure and services is now viewed as a viable supplement to public sector investments, one that can help to meet the rising tide of demand. While the private sector cannot completely replace the state in service provision, it can share a substantial part of the burden, thus relieving pressure on government budgets. The challenge faced by governments in providing adequate and efficient services has, in effect, become a source of opportunity for private business.

The push towards a greater role for the private service is further driven by the objective of greater efficiency. In the context of fiscal stringency, there is greater demand for efficiency and accountability in public expenditure. When infrastructure facilities are developed by public agencies, there is typically little connection between the cost of funds and the returns on investment. Furthermore, services provided by public agencies have often been of poor quality and unreliable. It is expected that private sector involvement will be able to infuse greater efficiency into the working of the sector as a whole.

Obstacles to Private Sector Involvement

The experience with private participation, though promising, has thus far been mixed. While there are several factors driving the new approach, there are also difficulties in implementation that have hampered the effort. Policy and regulatory uncertainties and financial risks are among the principal reasons that private financing of infrastructure still falls well short of the potential, despite significant increases in recent years.

From the perspective of investors, a stable economic environment, along with a transparent and predictable regulatory regime, are essential though not sufficient elements to attract private savings and investments. This is particularly true of investments in the infrastructure sector, which is capital-intensive and requires long-term planning. Investors are particularly interested in the policy framework for the specific subsector in which they are considering becoming involved. Thus, sector-specific policies, complementing the overall effort of privatization, are important in attracting private capital for projects. This has led to what are commonly referred to as 'sectoral reforms', measures that address policy and regulatory issues within a particular industry sector. However, while regulatory reforms may be easy to prescribe, they have proved difficult to implement.

Even when the policy environment is deemed favourable, risks associated with urban infrastructure projects are generally perceived to be high. Such investments are vulnerable because of the inherent complexities of the sector and because they are highly leveraged with long-term debt. Many projects do not reach financial closure or incur high development costs. Investors therefore seek returns commensurate with the high risks they expect to take.

Against this backdrop, the impact of successful public–private partnerships in service provision extends beyond improved service and increased capacity in the specific case. Successful projects give policy makers experience, attract more investors, and build constituencies for further reforms.

INDIA OPENS THE DOOR TO PRIVATE SECTOR PROVISION

Since independence, India has implemented the standard model of public provision and funding of services. Indeed, the country's record of public investment in infrastructure has been impressive. Large projects, including many that could be described as megaprojects, were undertaken and completed by the government, and extensive networks of services were constructed. Coverage and access expanded significantly.

This march towards modernization, however, came up against major limitations and eventually stalled. From the late 1970s onward, lack of finance, capacity constraints, inefficiencies in operation, deterioration of assets, and consumer dissatisfaction increasingly took their toll on the infrastructure industries. In 2003, the Ministry of Urban Development and Poverty Alleviation estimated that 52 per cent of urban India lacked sanitation facilities and that 30–50 per cent of solid waste was not being collected (Khanna 2003). While the network of city roads expanded by 5 per cent between the mid-1990s and 2003, traffic increased 80 times over the same period (Ramakrishna 2003).

With half of India's population expected to be urban by 2025, the challenges facing the urban sector are complex and wide-ranging. The water sector illustrates both the achievements and the demands that lie ahead. Almost all urban centres have some public water supply scheme. State-level data show average coverage of 88 per cent of households, in some cases exceeding 90 per cent. However, these impressive coverage figures mask serious issues related to quality, reliability, and sustainability. For instance, household coverage figures give no indication of the hours during which water is actually supplied. Similarly, there are no accurate figures for indicators such as water unaccounted for, unauthorized connections, and contamination levels of water supplied. In fact, it is typical in most urban centres that residents who can afford to do so will supplement unreliable public supplies with expensive and unregulated private sources.

Urban Reform in India

In India, given the federal framework of the polity, the constitutional responsibility for providing urban services lies with the respective state governments. Within the states, responsibility for providing municipal services lies with urban local bodies (ULBs), assisted by the respective state governments. Investments in urban infrastructure have largely been funded on the basis of debt financing. Debt servicing and operations and maintenance costs in turn are met by ULBs from general tax revenues and user charges.

Fiscal, managerial, and other capacity constraints, along with the rapid pace of urbanization, have led to a situation in which ULBs and state governments have not been able to cope with rising demand for services. Furthermore, inadequate cost recovery and distortions in policy and in the institutional framework have compromised the long-term sustainability of even the existing levels of investments. Municipal governments are viewed as unattractive borrowers by the markets because they lack the autonomy to raise revenues or reduce spending, particularly on personnel and administration. The perception is that their commitments to long-term financial obligations are not credible.

Under these conditions, borrowing from the market without state or central government support is difficult. As a result, the Government of India and state governments have initiated a number of steps to improve the general environment for local government functioning.

The 74th Constitutional Amendment of 1992 heralded the process of urban reform with greater local empowerment. Based on the principle of deepening decentralization, its provisions included measures such as appointment of an independent electoral commission in each state and mandatory elections for ULBs, with a proportion of the seats reserved for women and other disadvantaged sections of society. It also required a finance commission to be set up in each state to make recommendations on the transfer of resources from state to local bodies.

Examples of other measures introduced by the Government of India to encourage urban reforms include the following, announced in the Union Budget for 2002–03:

- The Urban Reform Incentive Fund, to promote state-level reforms in areas such as property tax, urban land ceiling laws, rent control laws, and user charges.

- The City Challenge Fund, to provide grants to help cities meet the transition cost of reforms and become more creditworthy through restructuring.
- The Pooled Finance Development Fund, to enable smaller ULBs to jointly raise funds from the market on a pooled basis.

In recognition of the constraints on the development of urban infrastructure, the central government has also put in place a policy framework that addresses the difficulties faced in increasing the level of investments. Under this framework, current policy initiatives encourage the private sector to play a full role in the provision of services, ranging from funding to operations and maintenance. Legislative changes have been made to enable private entry in the development of the urban infrastructure sector. The sector has also been opened to foreign direct investment and has received a number of fiscal incentives in the form of tax and tariff concessions.

PUBLIC–PRIVATE SERVICE PROVISION IN TAMIL NADU

One Indian state has been at the forefront of the country's move towards public–private service provision. Tamil Nadu, with a reputation as one of the 'progressive' states in the country, is noted for efficient governance, healthy economic growth, good social indicators, and an enabling regime for infrastructure investment. It is also one of the most highly urbanized states in India, with 42 per cent of the state's total population of 62 million living in urban areas, according to the 2001 census. Tamil Nadu ranks fourth among the major states in terms of per capita income and has its share of urban poverty. Thirty per cent of the population of Chennai, the state capital, live in slums. For the state as a whole, 16.5 per cent of the urban population live in slums.

Tamil Nadu, like other states, faces the challenge of providing adequate and efficient urban services. According to the state government's human development report, 64 per cent of the state's urban population has access to safe drinking water, but only half of the supply is up to standards. Moreover, less than 40 per cent of households in municipalities and about 24 per cent of households in smaller towns have household water connections. About 35 per cent of the water is unaccounted for, in comparison to the world norm of 10–15 per cent (Government of Tamil Nadu 2002: 58).

Only 16 per cent of ULB jurisdictions have sewerage systems. But even in these cases, the systems cover only part of the population (TWAD Board 2001: 34). Although the bulk of solid waste is collected by municipal authorities, most local bodies do not have organized disposal facilities. Less than half of the roads in the state are equipped with stormwater drains.

Tamil Nadu passed legislation to bring the state into conformity with the 74th Amendment in 1994; implementation of the reform process began two years later, in 1996. Since then, the state has been in the forefront within the country of changes in urban governance, including facilitating investments through financial and administrative reforms. The first notable step was to hold elections to all ULBs in October 1996. These elections put 14,000 councillors and 750 chairpersons in office, including 3,500 women and 1,000 persons belonging to disadvantaged sections of society.

The decentralization process also included setting up a Finance Commission to formulate measures for resource sharing and allocation between the state and ULBs. The recommendations of this commission have been implemented since 1998. Subsequently, in a step taken by no other state to date, a second Finance Commission was set up to further detail the devolution formula. Additional measures included increasing the percentage of the state's own tax revenues transferred to ULBs from 3.6 per cent to 8.0 per cent, in addition to discretionary grants. The recommendations also detailed the allocation among the various classes of ULBs by size, as well as by population segments, using weightages of 40 per cent for overall population, 40 per cent for women, and 20 per cent for socially weaker segments of the population. An equalization-cum-incentive fund amounting to 13 per cent of total funds was created to reward performance and aid weaker ULBs through funding of areas such as ULB elections, debt-for-water projects, and sewerage projects based on public–private partnerships.

The Tamil Nadu state government has been innovative and dynamic in introducing new approaches to meet the demand for services. While gaps remain, these new demand-driven initiatives, structured along commercial lines, have been successful in taking advantage of market opportunities and attracting interest from the private sector. They provide promising local examples for scaling up.

At the core of these initiatives are umbrella institutions set up in the state in partnership with the private sector. Three of these, focusing on specific sectors, are the Tamil Nadu Water Investment Company, the Tamil Nadu Urban Infrastructure Financial Services, and the Tamil Nadu Road Development Company. Each of these institutions has been innovatively structured with wide-ranging mandates that allows it to conceive and develop an array of projects with private sector participation.

Improving Water and Sanitation Services

The Tamil Nadu Water Investment Company Limited (TWIC) was the first-ever joint-venture institution established in India for the development and implementation of water sector projects on a public–private partnership basis. It was set up in 2001 by the government of Tamil Nadu and Infrastructure Leasing & Financial Services Limited (IL&FS), a private financial institution, with IL&FS as the majority shareholder. The company has the mandate to develop and promote infrastructure projects in the state, with emphasis on water for households and industry and on sanitation. This mandate includes finding and obtaining financing for the projects from sources outside government, entering into concession agreements with the state government and local bodies, and setting up 'special purpose vehicles' for specific projects. The first such venture promoted by TWIC was the $220 million Tirupur water and sanitation project in the western part of Tamil Nadu state.

New Tirupur Area Development Corporation

The New Tirupur Area Development Corporation Limited (NTADCL) was established under the Indian Companies Act as a special purpose vehicle, with the primary objective of implementing the Tirupur Area Development Project. It was the first water sector project developed under the public–private partnership framework in the country. The Tirupur area is a growth centre and the principal hub of India's knitwear industry. Currently, apparel exports from the area are over $1 billion a year. The industry plans to increase output significantly in coming years and is simultaneously gearing itself to meet the competitive challenge of the emerging World Trade Organization (WTO) regime. The Tirupur Area Development Project therefore was developed to improve local infrastructure by addressing bottlenecks, mainly water supply and sewerage. The project covers Tirupur municipality, adjacent village areas, and industries located in the Tirupur Local Planning Area that covers over 220 square kilometres.

The uncertain availability and poor quality of water has been the leading constraint for local industry in Tirupur. This is particularly so for the textile dying and bleaching units. There is very limited availability of groundwater in the immediate vicinity, so water is being sourced and transported from an expanding area, beyond a radius of 50 kilometres. Since the water is being obtained from agricultural lands, there are rising social tensions around the competing demands of industry and agriculture. In addition to problems with supply, the water is of poor quality, and heavy costs are incurred for treatment before use. Estimates place the current cost of water for industry in the range of Rs 75–80 per kilolitre (1,000 litres), which makes this input extremely expensive. Compared to this cost in Tirupur, the water charge for industry in the state capital, Chennai, is Rs 62/kilolitre. In neighbouring Bangalore, it is Rs 60/kilolitre.

Households in Tirupur pay for water on a flat-rate basis and provision is unmetered. But the municipal supply is erratic. Residents may receive water only once in three or four days, and only for a few hours at a time. The supply falls far short of the accepted daily supply of 110 litres per capita, as residents receive on average only 50 litres per capita per day. Households that can afford to do so supplement their municipal water with private unregulated water. This is expensive: it is estimated that the cost of private water can be as high as Rs 1,000/kilolitre, not including the cost of storage and treatment in the house. There are also indirect costs such as the effects on health of drinking poor-quality water and the time spent waiting in distribution lines.

Under the new system being developed by NTADCL, the cost of water will be as low as Rs 45/kilolitre for industrial use, Rs 5/kilolitre for households in Tirupur, and Rs 3.50/kilolitre for rural households. NTADCL has set an initial target of processing 185 million litres of water per day and will increase this to 250 million litres per day once demand increases in the service area. The water supplied will be very clean and of a quality far superior to what is now available.

The company also plans to set up a secondary treatment facility for domestic sewage and to provide onsite sanitation facilities for slums and poor tenement areas within the municipal jurisdiction, where residents currently do not have access to such facilities. In all, the project will cover four urban towns with a combined population of 450,000 and 792 rural habitations with an equivalent population. The sanitation component will provide coverage initially for 22,300 households. Eventually the project will cover 60 per cent of Tirupur households, including low-cost sanitation for slums.

The project is estimated to cost Rs 10,230 million in total and is financed on a non-recourse basis. It is the largest single private investment in urban infrastructure in the country and has a projected 20 per cent return on investment. The project was in the construction phase in 2004. Phase one was completed in May 2005 and phase two is scheduled for completion by October 2005. The contracts are on a lump-sum turnkey basis, meaning that the entire contract for design, procurement, and construction is awarded to the contractor, who in turn is responsible for the cost, time schedule, and quality parameters of his or her services.

Financing Urban Infrastructure Projects

Tamil Nadu Urban Infrastructure Financial Services Limited (TNUIFSL), an asset management company, is structured as a joint venture between the government of Tamil Nadu and three leading domestic private financial institutions. The latter are the majority equity partners. The company was set up in the context of the second Tamil Nadu Urban Development Project (TNUDP), which is being implemented with the assistance of an $80 million line of credit from the World Bank. The project focuses on reforms, institutional development, and capacity building for urban local bodies across the state, along with investment financing for urban infrastructure projects. TNUIFSL manages the investment financing, provided through the Tamil Nadu Urban Development Fund (TNUDF). The fund also provides project development support and strategic advice to local governments, focusing on developing and implementing commercially structured infrastructure projects and accessing capital markets.

So far, the experience with this initiative has been encouraging, particularly in terms of capacity building for stronger urban management. ULBs are increasingly formulating and developing projects on their own. Most of the ULBs in the state have moved to computerized, accrual-based accounting systems. By instituting accounting, auditing, and disclosure practices that are compatible with market standards, local governments are improving their attractiveness to lenders. This is the first such effort in the country that is comprehensive, in that it covers the full range of ULB functions. TNUDF has a broad mandate to link urban civic needs to the capital market and to promote innovative methods of funding urban infrastructure.

TNUDF has organized market issues for three large projects, described below, all of which obtained full funding including co-financing from institutions and service users. In addition, the fund has focused on normal loan funding for ULBs on a non-guarantee basis. TNUDF has the distinction of being the first financial intermediary in India to raise bonds from the capital market on this basis. The bond issue, totalling Rs 1,100 million, was raised at a competitive rate of 11.85 per cent and was oversubscribed.

As part of the same initiative, the government of Tamil Nadu has created a pooled entity in the form of a trust called the Water and Sanitation Pooled Fund (WSPF). This entity identifies viable projects and funds them from concept to commissioning on a commercial basis. The main objective of the fund is to make ULBs a part of the active debt markets, giving them access to the best interest rates available. In this pioneering effort for market access, 13 ULBs and projects have been financed or refinanced by the proceeds of WSPF bond issue amounting to Rs 304.1 million. The bonds carry a guarantee from the US Agency for International Development to the extent of 50 per cent of the principal. This is the first issue of its kind in India made by a pooled fund on the US bank bond model.

Three innovative projects illustrating the potential for private sector participation include the Alandur Underground Sewerage Project, the Madurai Inner Ring Road, and the Karur Toll Bridge.

Alandur Underground Sewerage Project

TNUIFSL structured the first municipal 'build, operate, and transfer' (BOT) wastewater project in India, at Alandur south of Chennai, at a total project cost of Rs 340 million. The scheme was designed eventually to cover a population of 300,000. The collection and pumping systems were financed by debt of Rs 200 million and a grant of Rs 30 million. The sewage treatment plant was financed by the private sector operator with a concession period of 14 years. Sixteen thousand residents of Alandur were assessed for the project, and almost 98 per cent of these households had already paid towards deposits by 2004, mobilizing Rs 79.5 million. In adjoining areas also to be covered by the scheme, 65 per cent of households have paid a one-time deposit, also contributing to the equity financing of the project.

Project implementation involved both construction and BOT contracts. An engineering, procurement, and construction contractor was used to build the underground sewerage system. The same contractor designed and financed the sewage treatment plant, with an agreement to transfer it after the concession period of 14 years.

Madurai Inner Ring Road

Madurai is the second-largest city in Tamil Nadu. Located in the southern part of the state, it is a major commercial, religious, and tourist centre, linking important trade and tourist flows. The Madurai Inner Ring Road, a 27.2 kilometre two-lane road, is the first toll road constructed by an urban local body in India based on user charges. The project, completed at a total cost of Rs 430 million, has been open to traffic since November 2000. Because toll collections were encouraging, after construction was completed the Corporation of Madurai restructured its financial commitments to reduce stress on the project cash flows. A private placement of bonds was made, with an independent credit rating. This was the first revenue bond in India issued by a medium-size ULB that linked its liability to revenue generation from an asset without recourse to general revenues.

Karur Toll Bridge

Karur is one of the fastest-growing towns in Tamil Nadu. The Light House Bridge over a local river, constructed in the early part of the twentieth century, served as the main link between the eastern and western parts of the town. In order to mitigate the hardship caused by congestion on this bridge, Karur municipality, on the basis of a feasibility study done by TNUIFSL, entered into a concession agreement in 1998 for construction of a new bridge. The scheme was the first BOT arrangement between an urban local body and a private sector operator in India for financing, construction, operation, and ultimate transfer of a toll bridge without any traffic guarantees. The Rs 154.5 million project was completed in 2000.

Private Financing for Road Construction

The Tamil Nadu Road Development Company Limited (TNRDC) was established by the state government as a 50:50 joint venture of the Tamil Nadu Industrial Development Corporation (a state government undertaking) and IL&FS. It was aimed at developing road sector initiatives under the public–private partnership format by leveraging state resources and catalyzing private sector participation and investment. Its first major project was the 113-kilometre East Coast Road. The project was entrusted to TNRDC and the concession agreement signed in December 2000 for developing the project on a 'rehabilitate, improve, maintain, operate, and transfer' basis. The project was completed in record time at a cost of Rs 600 million and the road became operational in March 2002.

IMPACT AND OUTCOMES

The ultimate objective in upgrading urban infrastructure is to enhance the quality and dignity of people's lives. With affordable, reliable water service, city dwellers, particularly women and girls, need not spend valuable time waiting on the street at odd hours for water. With private sanitation facilities and regular collection of household wastes, the family's dignity is preserved and their health is protected. With steady electrical service, students do not have to sit below streetlights to study, but can do so in the comfort of their homes. Adequate power, water, telecommunications, and transportation services allow businesses to be efficient and productive. Thus, good infrastructure and services provide the foundation on which individuals and firms can realize their true potential.

In economic terms, quality infrastructure implies efficient use of resources and higher output, leading to growth, employment, and reduced poverty. In recent years much research has been devoted to estimating the productivity of infrastructure investments. The link between aggregate infrastructure spending and GDP growth is strong, with studies showing very high returns in time-series analyses. According to the Indian Ministry of Finance, 'Research indicates that while total infrastructure stocks increase by 1 per cent with each 1 per cent increment in per capita GDP, household access to safe water increases by 0.03 per cent, paved roads by 0.8 per cent, power 1.5 per cent and telecommunications 1.7 per cent. Infrastructure productivity will determine how India will cope with the increasing pace of urbanization, globalization and technological innovations in manufacturing and logistics. Environmental issues and poverty reduction, too, depend heavily on the productivity of the infrastructure sector' (Government of India 1996: 2).

The positive spin-offs of infrastructure are indeed multidimensional, with an eventual benign impact on poverty. While it is too soon for impact measurements to be available, the projects discussed in this chapter are well placed to have such effects.

The Tirupur water project, for example, is expected to have a profound impact in the project area and beyond in tangible economic terms. At one level, it will lead to an immediate increase in economic output by supplying the critical input of water to local industry, particularly the textile industry's dying and bleaching units. Local industry will be bolstered in its efforts to meet the competitive global challenges of the emerging WTO regime, and is expected to increase its export earnings from the current level of $1 billion per year to $5 billion per year by 2007. With an assured supply of high-quality water, local industry can concentrate on productivity, move up the value chain, and expand production. The indirect effects should be more employment opportunities, higher wages, an improved standard of living, and a reduction in poverty.

Successful implementation of the water project is also expected to bring improvements in local living conditions by providing convenient access to clean water. There should be a particularly marked impact on the lives of women and girls. Gone will be the days of standing in long lines for hours to obtain scanty amounts of poor-quality or untreated water. With water available on tap 24 hours a day, seven days a week, women will be able to perform household chores more efficiently. This in turn should allow them to enjoy more leisure time or take advantage of emerging employment opportunities (currently almost half the workforce consists of women). It is also hoped that freeing girls from water-fetching chores will remove one of the barriers to school attendance.

Moreover, both the Tirupur water project and the Alandur sewerage project are expected to have large positive impacts on the health of the local population. With a constant supply of clean water and access to new sanitation facilities, a significant reduction can be expected in the prevalence of illnesses spread by dirty water and poor sanitation. Given that the sanitation facilities will also cover the poorer households and slums, the projects promise to have a beneficial impact on the health and hygiene conditions of marginalized and otherwise neglected sections of society.

Finally, these projects can be expected to have a long-term impact on the local and even regional environment. Currently, for instance, the residents and industries of Tirupur draw large quantities of water from subsoil sources, even though discharge of industrial effluents has polluted the underground water. Once the water project is operational, it is expected that there will be no further need to draw water from wells. This will allow the recharging of the groundwater over time. The availability of clean water for use by industry will also reduce the level of pollutants in industrial effluents.

The three transport sector projects—the Madurai Inner Ring Road, Karur Toll Bridge, and East Coast Road—are also expected to provide multiple benefits. Clearly, in economic terms, improvement in traffic flows will reduce transaction costs and abate congestion; this in turn should have effects on almost all other sectors of the economy. At the national level, for instance, about 5,846 kilometres of national highways are being upgraded under the Golden Quadrilateral project. The World Bank estimates that this will lead to savings in fuel and vehicle operating costs of about Rs 14 million per kilometre per year. Proportional direct savings can be expected from the Tamil Nadu transport projects. Furthermore, the projects are expected to have spin-off economic benefits. The East Coast Road, completed in 2002, has already helped spawn new tourism, entertainment, and eatery businesses in its vicinity. The increased economic activity, employment, and development in the area are expected eventually to lower local poverty levels. Finally, transport projects affect the quality of life for everyone by making road travel a safer and more pleasant experience.

KEYS TO TAMIL NADU'S SUCCESS

What factors have made it possible for Tamil Nadu to successfully attract private investment for these urban infrastructure partnerships? In part it is the favourable economic, social, and political climate of the state, but sector- and project-level factors have also been fundamental. The successful projects have been ones that respond to user demands. And the framework for public–private partnerships has been carefully worked out to apportion both responsibility and risk among the partners in a sustainable way.

Tamil Nadu has long been one of the top destinations for investors in India. It has been among the frontrunners in industrial growth since independence. In the current period, following liberalization, it has also become one of the preferred destinations for flows of foreign direct investment, largely as a result of its sound economy and good macroeconomic parameters. This economic performance is matched by achievements in social development. The state's indicators in the fields of health and education, for example, are well above national averages. Both foreign and domestic investors have been attracted by this suitable economic environment backed by good social performance.

This is reinforced by the reputation of Tamil Nadu residents as industrious and enterprising. The workforce is disciplined and productive, with a strong cadre of educated and technically qualified people. Industrial strife is conspicuous by its absence. A commitment to economic growth is balanced by concerns for equity and social welfare and by a strong administrative ethos on the part of the state.

To this general setting one can add an urban infrastructure extensive enough to offer attractive prospects for investment. Tamil Nadu, with a population that is 42 per cent urban (as of the 2001 census), has 26 large cities with populations over 100,000 and 806 small and medium towns. While urban growth and sprawl have led to unmet demands for services, the same growth also creates large markets and economies of scale that make it feasible to supply urban services on a commercial basis. Assuming the appropriate institutional partnerships and planning, there can be both opportunities for profit and internal subsidies to cover the poorer sections of the population. Finally, the regulatory and policy reforms detailed earlier have further bolstered investor confidence.

Tamil Nadu thus has largely favourable conditions for attracting private investment. But this by itself is not sufficient. Investors scrutinize individual projects closely: each infrastructure project is a discrete investment, tailored to the specifics of a particular location. For investors, the critical question is the balance between risk and reward. From the government's point of view, on the other hand, conceding a very high rate of return would create pressure for high tariffs. And given the natural monopoly characteristics of infrastructure projects, there is always the potential for profiteering by the private sector, making governments wary of private entry. For projects to be sustainable, these disparate concerns must be addressed in a way that inspires confidence and comfort. If sustainability can be ensured, then scaling up and replication of the model on the same basic parameters becomes feasible.

Probably the most important project-level factor contributing to success has been the demand-driven nature of the projects. The high degree of local ownership can be measured by the extent of direct community participation in the development of the various projects. In the Tirupur project, not only does the company's board of directors include two representatives from local industry, but local industry also provides equity funding, thus making the clients part owners of the company itself. The Alandur project was made possible by the initial financial contribution of the households in the project area. Municipal council members took full responsibility for developing and promoting the project and bringing it to successful fruition. Projects such as Alandur, Madurai, and Karur have shown other ULBs that asset creation is a possibility well within the grasp of local bodies in partnership with the private sector.

The other favourable factor at the project level has been the public–private partnership framework, which has led to a viable allocation of risk between government and the private sector. While regulatory and policy risks have been assumed by the government, commercial risks are borne in general by the private entity. In addition to the normal liability, the government has also assumed contingent liabilities for events of force majeure. These contractual requirements have been clearly spelled out in project documents that are open to public inspection. The concession agreement, memorandum and articles of association, and shareholders' agreement clearly specify the rights, responsibilities, and roles of each participating party. The engineering, procurement, construction, and financing documents also spell out detailed expectations for all parties. All these documents are drafted after detailed discussions and reviews to ensure that the concerns of all the participants and stakeholders will be adequately and transparently addressed. With appropriate allocation of risks and the transparency of contractual agreements, the level of comfort, security, and mutual trust has risen, giving greater confidence to investors.

Such details as the commercial formatting of projects, appropriate risk sharing, and clarity of contracts and documentation vastly improve the attractiveness of a project as an investment opportunity. But the long-term character of infrastructure projects also requires that the commitment and ownership of all parties remain strong for the entire life cycle of a project. This is particularly so for the government, since the social aspects of infrastructure will keep the government continuously engaged with the project to some extent. Conceivably, such projects will always require the support of government in one form or another.

Yet it is also necessary to maintain a certain distance between the government and the entity directly responsible for the project. In Tamil Nadu, such a position that is not too close yet not too far has been facilitated by the governance structure of some projects. In the cases of the Tirupur water project and the East Coast Road, for instance, the government did not provide any direct funding of project costs. Government financial support was instead provided indirectly as equity contributions through the institutions directly involved, that is, the Tamil Nadu Water Investment Company and the Tamil Nadu Road Development Company. Both these holding companies are joint ventures between the government and the private sector. In each case, private investors hold the majority of the equity, making the joint ventures more private than public entities. As a result of this arrangement, there is more than an arm's-length distance between the projects and the government.

Similarly, while the boards of directors of East Coast Road and New Tirupur Area Development Corporation include government represen-tatives, they also have representatives of all the other interested parties including lenders, investors, consumers, and independent individuals. This provides a balanced governance structure that protects all the interests involved as well as the integrity of the project itself.

In sum, the sustainability of these projects and their suitability as a basis for scaling up the infrastructure initiative in Tamil Nadu rests on the demand-driven nature of the projects and their structure as public–private partnerships. Experiences with implementation have shown this model to be vibrant, robust, and dynamic, with an effective risk-sharing contractual structure that balances risk and rewards and is governed on a highly participatory basis. Within the context of a stable and growing national economy, coupled with sector-specific reforms in the state, this project model has served to attract private investments to an otherwise difficult sector.

PROSPECTS FOR SCALING UP

Beyond the specific outcomes expected from each of the projects, the demonstration effect of these investments is also significant. These projects have shown that the private sector can participate in urban infrastructure services and have unambiguously confirmed that 'it works'. This modelling effect takes place in several different ways.

First, these projects have helped the government fulfil its own mandates and expectations. These include creating quality infrastructure assets, stimulating economic growth, increasing local competitiveness, and improving social welfare and the quality of life. For the private sector, participation has confirmed that returns can be commensurate with perceived risks and that it is possible to allocate these risks appropriately between the parties. This risk sharing is the underlying principle responsible for the success of the public–private partnership model. The government assumes the risk associated with the local regulatory regime, while the private entities take on the commercial risks.

Second, the joint venture model as adopted in Tamil Nadu has shown its robustness and efficacy in meeting objectives while allaying concerns about equity, consumer interests, and social welfare. Such concerns arise because of the natural monopoly status of the projects as providers of basic services. However, the regulatory and governance structure of the agencies responsible for these projects serves to safeguard social and consumer interests as well as the commercial interests of the private partners. For instance, the boards of directors of NTADCL and TNRDC include representatives of the government, private investors, and independent individuals, a structure that serves as a means of check and balance.

Third, the projects demonstrate that cash-strapped governments can achieve leverage for additional investment by bringing in capital and operational commitments from the private sector. This serves to compensate for the fiscal constraints of governments and free up scarce government finance for other social investments. The Tirupur and East Coast Road projects illustrate this advantage. In the latter case, with a contribution of Rs 50 million from the government, a total investment of Rs 600 million was mobilized, thus leveraging the funds 12 times. In the Tirupur case, the comparable ratio was over 20 times, as a government contribution of Rs 500 million brought in a total investment of Rs 10,230 million. Similarly, in the TNUDF projects, in the case of Alandur a capital grant of Rs 30 million from the state government helped realize an investment of Rs 340 million, for a leverage ratio of 11. In Madurai, the ratio was four times. At Karur, the investment was on a BOT basis, with no government funding contribution at all. In all these projects together, the state government, with a contribution of $15 million, has been able to bring in private investments for urban infrastructure totalling $261 million.

These advantages already apparent in the projects now being implemented have led to plans for substantial expansion in Tamil Nadu along similar lines in the coming years. The next set of projects, to be undertaken by the same umbrella organizations, include water and wastewater recycling projects by TWIC at a cost of $115 million, sanitation systems for 11 urban jurisdictions to be implemented by TNUDP at a cost of $95 million, and six road-related projects through TNRDC at a cost of $180 million. The estimated total cost of this second round will be about $400 million, bringing the total private investments mobilized for urban services to about $650 million.

References

Government of India, 1996, *The India Infrastructure Report: Policy Imperatives for Growth and Welfare*, vol. 2. Report of the Expert Group on the Commercialization of Infrastructure Projects, Ministry of Finance, New Delhi: Thomson Press.

Government of Tamil Nadu, 2002, *Tamil Nadu Human Development Report*. New Delhi: Social Science Press.

Khanna, N.N., 2003, Presentation at Indo-German Business Conference, Berlin, 17 September.

Ramakrishna, A., 2003, Presentation at Indo-German Business Conference, Berlin, 17 September.

Rivera, D., 1996, *Private Sector Participation in the Water Supply and Wastewater Sector: Lessons from Six Developing Countries*, Washington, DC: World Bank.

Sethuraman, S.R., 2004, Presentation at Regional Conference on Universality of Infrastructure Services, New Delhi, 6–7 December.

TWAD Board, 2001, 'Activities of Tamil Nadu Water Supply and Drainage Board,' Chennai.

World Bank, 2000, *World Development Report 1999/2000: Entering the 21st Century*, New York: Oxford University Press.

13

Citizen Report Cards in Bangalore, India

A Case Study in Accountability

Samuel Paul

In most developing countries, the provision of essential public services to the people is the responsibility of government. Monopoly in services often results in inefficiency and non-responsiveness. When the quality of services deteriorates, consumers suffer without recourse to market alternatives. As citizens, however, they can demand better performance from government agencies. One effective tool in making such demands is the 'citizen report card'. A civil society initiative undertaken over the past decade in Bangalore, a large city in southern India, shows the potential impact of report cards as a monitoring and accountability tool.

A report card grades a service provider based on feedback from the users of its services. Services can be rated on different dimensions and the ratings compared across agencies. The dissemination of the ratings can then be used to stimulate agency leaders to improve their services, thus substituting for pressures from a competitive market for services. Report cards, reinforced by advocacy campaigns carried out by civil society groups and the media, provide a tool for increasing and targeting pressures for reform.

The Bangalore experience, with three successive report card surveys in 1994, 1999, and 2003, shows that success can take time. The first report card, in 1994, gave very low ratings to all the major service providers of the city, creating a sense of shame through public exposure of the problems. But it did not make an immediate impact on service improvement, as only a few of the providers acknowledged their problems and took corrective action. The second report card, in 1999, showed that limited improvement had occurred in some services. The third report card, in 2003, revealed substantial improvement in almost all the service providers. There was not only a significant increase in citizen satisfaction with the services, but also some decline in corruption.

Underpinning the success of the citizens' initiative was the effective *demand-side* pressure from media and civil society followed by an adequate *supply-side* response from the government. On the demand side, the report cards and attendant media publicity led to public 'glare', or heightened attention to service problems. This triggered a response on the supply side, as the state government set up a new public–private partnership forum to help the service providers upgrade their services and improve responsiveness. The political support and commitment of the chief minister of Karnataka state, of which Bangalore is the capital, was an important factor. The innovative practices introduced by the partnership forum, the proactive role of external catalysts such as civil society groups and donors, and the learning that came from the experiments initiated by the different players all contributed to the improved performance of the city's service providers.

This chapter explores the effectiveness of citizen report cards in harnessing the power of civil society to make government accountable and responsive to citizens. It describes the evolution of the citizens' initiative in Bangalore, explains the design and results of the report cards, and documents the impact on public service provision. The chapter concludes with a discussion of the factors contributing to the initiative's success and the lessons learned.

Calling for Improvements in Bangalore's Public Services

During 1993–94, a small group of citizens in Bangalore prepared a report card on the public services in their city, based on feedback from the users of these services. The reason for this unusual initiative was the dismal state of essential services in the city and the public perception that government was on the whole indifferent to this problem. The report card entrepreneurs hoped that their effort would stimulate citizens to demand greater public accountability from the service providers, or, at a minimum, give wider publicity to the problem.

Bangalore in 1993 was a growing industrial city with a population of over 4 million, already becoming a hub of information technology. Yet a quarter of its population was poor, living mainly in slums spread throughout the city. As in other Indian cities, residents depended on several public agencies established by the state government for their essential services. Thus, the city's municipal corporation provided roads, street lights, and garbage removal, while another agency supplied electricity. Water, transport, telecommunications, health care, and urban land and housing were the responsibility of other large public service providers.

A common feature of all these services was that they were provided by monopolistic or dominant-supply sources, leaving people with little choice in terms of alternative suppliers. This was a particular problem for the poor, as they could not afford the high-cost alternatives that richer people could sometimes tap in the event that public service providers failed. If the power went out, the rich could turn on their generators; if transportation failed, they might use private vehicles. But such options were seldom feasible for the poor. Poor people suffered from yet another handicap, namely their lack of influence and voice to get their problems solved at the agency level. Collective action by citizens to address these problems was difficult to organize and costly in time and resources.

A Citizens' Initiative

In response to these problems, the small citizens' group in Bangalore, of which I was part, decided to launch a survey to gather feedback on public services. The survey was carried out by a supportive market research firm, Marketing and Business Associates, with survey costs met through local donations.

Survey development began with an assessment of service-related problems through focus group discussions. Structured questionnaires were then designed and pre-tested to ensure their relevance and suitability for field-level interviews. The survey covered nearly 1,200 households, with one questionnaire for general households (mainly middle-class) and another for slum households (mainly low-income). In both cases the objectives were to determine (a) how satisfactory were the public services from the users' perspective, (b) which aspects of the services were satisfactory and which were not, and (c) the direct and indirect costs incurred by users for these services. Satisfaction was measured on a scale of 1 to 7, and ratings for the different dimensions of services were aggregated to yield averages. Trained investigators conducted the field interviews. The results obtained from analysis of the data were used to rate the different service providers in terms of quality of service, corruption, and overall user satisfaction. A structured summary of these ratings for all agencies involved was called the 'citizen report card on public services'.

The report card survey was designed to reflect people's actual experiences with the specific services they use. It thus provided much more specific and targeted data than a standard opinion poll. Users possess fairly authentic information on whether they actually receive services, whether their transactions with the agencies produce positive outcomes, and whether they have to pay bribes in the process. They know how long it takes to solve their problems and how well they are treated by agency staff. The survey covered only those households that had direct experience with the services and interactions with the agencies so that they could provide answers to specific questions. The representative nature of the sample, the professionalism and neutrality in conduct of the survey, and the large number of respondents ensured the credibility of the findings.

The initiative sought to fill critical gaps in information about the existing problems with government services. While governments and service providers have a wealth of data on the services they provide, they rarely gather the kinds of information and insights that a report card yields. As a result, these agencies are not always aware of the problems that ordinary people face in the course of using the services. If services are to be effective and efficient, these problems must be brought to light so that solutions can be found. It is this gap that a report card has the potential to fill. Obviously, a report card is only a diagnostic tool; it does not provide answers. But it can stimulate the first step: the search for answers or, at a minimum, a deeper probe into the problems being highlighted.

A report card can help to improve public services in three ways, all of which came into play in the Bangalore experience. First, efforts to track service delivery from a user perspective can help compensate for weak or incomplete government monitoring. A report card can thus serve as a benchmarking exercise. When it is repeated after a year or two, both the government and citizens can see whether things are improving or not, and take action accordingly. Second, a report card can create a 'glare effect'. In other words, when the results are publicized, the performance of service providers becomes widely known to one and all, bringing shame to an agency whose ratings are bad and, ideally, motivating that agency to perform better. This effect, of course, will work only in settings where there is freedom of the press and a relatively open society. Third, report cards can motivate organized civic groups to be proactive in demanding greater accountability from service providers. They may, for example, engage in dialogue with the agencies on ways to improve services, propose reform options, and promote public awareness about the needed remedies.

Rating Bangalore: The First Report Card

Bangalore's first report card in 1994 revealed widespread dissatisfaction with public services (Paul 1995). In the set of middle-income households, satisfaction levels did not exceed 25 per cent for any of the seven service providers covered. Dissatisfaction levels were very high among these respondents, reaching 65 per cent in the case of the Bangalore Development Authority. Satisfaction with staff behaviour in the seven agencies averaged only 25 per cent. More than a quarter of the respondents had made three or more visits to agencies to solve their problems, and the average rate of problem resolution for all agencies was just 57 per cent. Half of middle-income respondents claimed that agency staff demanded bribes, and 14 per cent of the sample said they had paid such bribes. Many households incurred additional costs because of investments they had to make to compensate for the unreliability of services (for example, buying generators to cope with power outages).

Likewise, feedback from the sample of low-income households also showed high levels of dissatisfaction. Over 70 per cent of low-income households had to make three or more visits to the agencies to solve their problems, and nearly a third had to pay bribes. Their problem resolution rate was much lower than that of the middle-class households. Overall, however, their satisfaction with service providers was not as low as in the middle-income sample, perhaps because of lower expectations.

Thus, the 1994 report card results from both middle-income and low-income households presented a picture of highly unsatisfactory and non-responsive service providers in the city. The findings were widely publicized in the Bangalore and national press. Newspapers played a particularly important role in raising public awareness of the findings; a leading paper, the *Times of India*, published weekly features highlighting the findings about individual agencies over a period of months. The full report card was provided to the state government and to the service providers themselves. Citizen groups were invited to debate the findings and propose ways to deal with the problems highlighted by the report card.

The group of citizens responsible for the initiative did not initially plan for follow-up beyond publication of the report card itself. But enquiries began to reach us on how this work, along with advocacy for reform, could be scaled up. This growing public interest persuaded us to establish a new non-profit organization, the Public Affairs Centre (PAC), in Bangalore in 1994. Early activities included responding to requests for advice from three of the seven service providers covered by the report. In particular, the worst-rated agency asked PAC to assist in further investigating its problems and finding remedies (Paul 2002).

Although the providers did not take immediate action to improve their services, a process of reform had been set in motion. In addition to the dialogue between three agencies and PAC, the municipal commissioner also decided to create a joint forum for service providers and civil society. This served not only as an opportunity for dialogue on services, but also as an instrument to generate new reform ideas and experiments.

A Second Report Card: Limited Progress

Five years later, PAC prepared a second report card on Bangalore's public services. The survey methodology in 1999 was essentially the same as that used in 1994, but the sample size was increased to 2,000 households. Two additional agencies were covered, raising the total to nine. The results showed some improvement in public satisfaction with most of the seven agencies that had also been rated in 1994 (Paul and Sekhar 2000). The average satisfaction level, however, was still below 50 per cent, even for the better-performing agencies. One disturbing finding was that corruption levels had increased in several agencies. The report card also indicated a clear link between petty corruption and inefficient service provision. Low-income people continued to have to make more visits to agencies to solve their problems than did their middle-income counterparts.

Despite the limited progress made since the first report card and the backsliding on corruption, the sequence of two report cards demonstrated how such phenomena could be tracked and highlighted through credible methods, bringing the agencies under a 'public scanner'. Moreover, it was clear that several of the service providers had taken action to improve service quality and to respond to specific issues raised by the first report card. Several agencies, for example, had improved their billing procedures. In addition, most had started joint forums with users, intended to improve responsiveness by staff.

The dissemination and follow-up actions in 1999 differed significantly from those in 1994. Well before public release of the results, PAC presented mini report cards individually to each of the major service providers in the city. This was followed by a seminar for management teams from selected agencies to exchange their experiences with reforms since the first report card. These deliberations, involving agencies that had sought PAC's help as well as those that had not, showed that all the agencies were engaged in efforts to improve their services in different ways. Finally, a public meeting was held in which the second report card's findings were presented to both leaders and staff of all the service providers, with citizen groups and media also present. Leaders of the agencies addressed the gathering and explained to the public their plans to deal with the problems highlighted in the report card. This event and the report card findings were widely covered by the news media.

Within a few months of the second report card, the potential for greater impact increased dramatically when the new chief minister of Karnataka state announced the creation of a Bangalore Agenda Task Force (BATF) to improve the services and infrastructure of the city, with greater public participation. BATF was established as a public–private partnership involving several non-official and eminent citizens along with the heads of all service providers. In contrast to the more limited agency responses, this move by the chief minister ensured systemic responses across agencies. It was the first time that a chief minister in India had launched an initiative to improve services for a large city in response to citizen feedback.

BATF became a forum in which all stakeholders could come together both to solve the city's problems and to tap ideas and funds from the private sector. The task force began its work in earnest in 2000 and catalysed reforms in several agencies. One important advance was a property tax reform that resulted in increased revenues and fewer hassles for citizens. Other areas of visible improvement included solid waste management, sanitation, and roads. BATF prepared its own simpler version of the report card to monitor the progress of the different city agencies more regularly. Over a three-year period, the BATF report cards (based on public feedback through interviews) showed a positive public response to the reforms and some improvements in most of the city's public agencies.

THE THIRD REPORT CARD SHOWS IMPROVEMENTS

Measurement of performance in public services, in terms of quality, regularity, and other features, can be a complex and costly task. Each agency has its own internal requirements for data collection, and many agencies provide multiple services, each requiring separate evaluation. However, the advantage of a summary report card, based on user feedback and repeated at periodic intervals, is that it can provide a comparable evaluation framework that can be understood and used by the public, media, government, and service providers alike. The findings from the third report card in 2003, when compared with earlier findings, thus provide a valuable measure of changes since the beginning of the report card initiative in 1994.

The findings presented in the text and figures below include both general satisfaction, reflecting a person's overall assessment of the services provided by each agency, and measures for particular dimensions of quality of service. The four dimensions presented are the incidence of problems, staff behaviour, time taken to attend to problems, and bribes paid or demanded. These measures reflect different aspects of quality and responsiveness as experienced by users of the services. An increase in the proportion of users who are satisfied with a service or agency is an indirect indicator of an improvement in that service or agency.

The findings are divided into two parts. The first presents the results from the survey of general households (mainly middle-income), and the second presents the results from the survey of slum households (mainly low-income). Nine agencies were covered by the 1999 and 2003 report cards:

- Bangalore Development Authority (BDA)
- Bangalore Electricity Company (BESCOM)
- Bangalore Metropolitan Transport Corporation (BMTC)
- Bangalore Municipal Corporation (BMP)
- Bangalore police
- Bangalore Water Supply and Sewerage Board (BWSSB)
- Bharat Sanchar Nigam Limited (BSNL) (telecommunications)
- Government hospitals
- Road Transport Authority (RTO)

Results from the General Household Survey

By 2003, as shown in Figure 13.1, user satisfaction levels among middle-income citizens of Bangalore ranged from a low of 73 per cent to a high of 97 per cent across the nine agencies, including respondents who said they were either completely or partially satisfied with the agency's services. BMTC had the highest rating for overall user satisfaction among general households, while BMP, BWSSB, and government hospitals had the lowest. The ranking appears different, however, when one considers only the proportions of people rating themselves 'completely satisfied' with services. While the BMTC had the largest proportion of satisfied users overall, BESCOM had the largest proportion of users expressing complete satisfaction. The fact that most agencies have significant segments of users who are only partially satisfied suggests that there is still much scope for improvement.

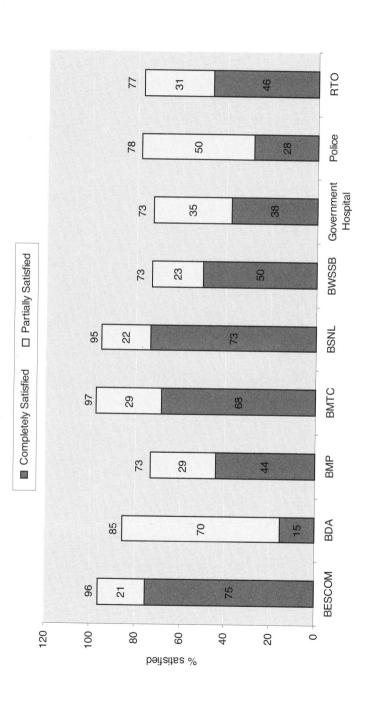

FIGURE 13.1 Overall Satisfaction, 2003: General Households

Nonetheless, a comparison of the performance of seven agencies over the preceding 10 years (Figure 13.2) reveals that there has already been significant improvement in user satisfaction. Data limitations and fine-tuning of the rating scale make it necessary to break the comparison into two parts. Comparison of satisfaction in 1994 and 1999 is based on ratings given by users who have interacted with the agencies.

The comparison of satisfaction in 1999 and 2003 is based on the extent to which users are completely satisfied with a service or a given dimension of the service (Figure 13.3).[1] This measure is especially pertinent because it sets a goal for the service providers to achieve, namely, giving full satisfaction to the user. It tells the agencies that it is important to increase the proportion of completely (rather than partially) satisfied customers.

The general pattern of across-the-board improvement in satisfaction with all the agencies over the course of a decade raises a number of questions. Does the improvement reflect real changes in the quality of services, responsiveness of the service providers, and efficiency of service delivery? Do users experience fewer problems with services and therefore have less need to visit or interact with the agencies? What actions led to such positive outcomes? Comparative ratings on more specific indicators confirm the general impression of significant improvements and give some indication of how they happened.

The first specific indicator, shown in Figure 13.4, compares the incidence of problems with the service agencies, using data from 1999 and 2003.[2] People obviously are more likely to be satisfied when they have fewer problems in getting a service. In addition, reduction in the frequency of routine problems can translate into fewer agency interactions with citizens, thereby reducing the scope for delay, harassment, and corruption. The incidence of problems, that is, the proportion of users who reported having had a problem with an agency, decreased for all agencies except BMP. This included both problems of a routine nature, such as billing errors, and more complex problems in connection with special services such as getting a building sanction or a water supply connection. Reduction in the number of problems can therefore be seen as an important reason for the improvement in levels of satisfaction.

The highest incidence of problems reported in the 2003 survey (20 per cent) is with the Bangalore police. Nevertheless, it is much below the 1999 level for that agency. The rate of decline was sharpest in the case of BESCOM, where only 5 per cent reported encountering problems in 2003 compared to 29 per cent in 1999. The general reduction in problems reflects investments to augment capacity, introduction of services using information

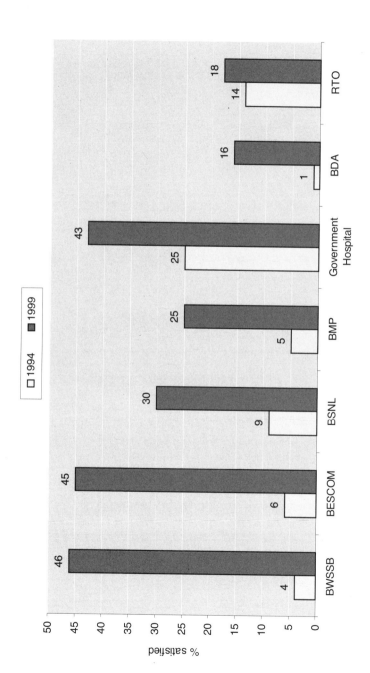

FIGURE 13.2 Overall Satisfaction, 1994 and 1999: General Households

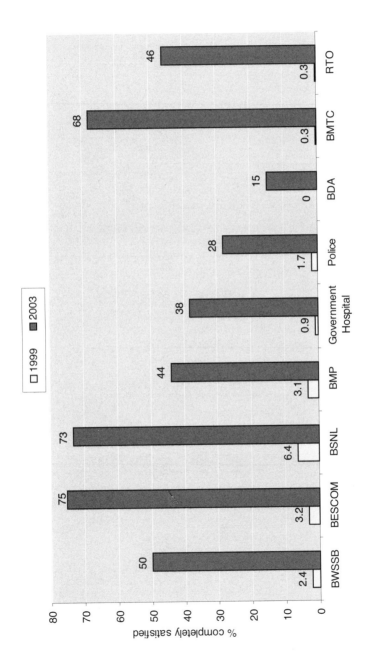

FIGURE 13.3 Complete Satisfaction, 1999 and 2003: General Households

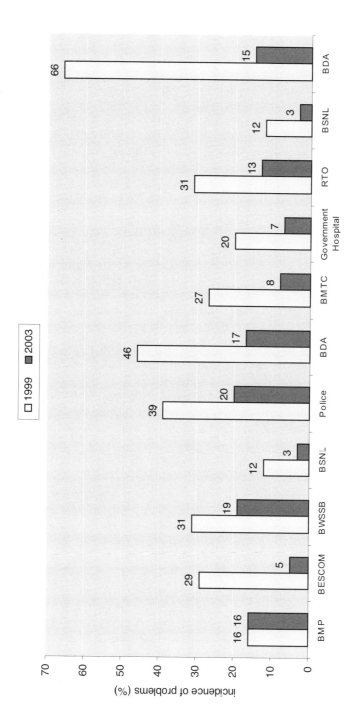

FIGURE 13.4 Incidence of Problems, 1999 and 2003: General Households

technology, and other initiatives to improve efficiency of service delivery by the agencies since 1999.

Even in the case of agencies without significant reduction in problems overall, users reported improvements in the regularity and reliability of specific services. Satisfaction with regularity of garbage clearance by BMP, for example, rose from 16 per cent in 1999 to 75 per cent in 2003. Satisfaction with accuracy of billing by BWSSB went from 32 per cent to 90 per cent over the same period.

Satisfaction with staff behaviour, a specific indicator relevant to all agencies, also showed significant improvement, most consistently between 1999 and 2003 (Figure 13.5).[3] Full satisfaction with staff behaviour was highest in the case of the BESCOM, at 74 per cent. While agencies varied in the extent of improvement, there was an unmistakably positive general trend that almost certainly reflects actual changes in behaviour. It is difficult to imagine that people who gave low ratings to an agency's staff in the past would applaud them subsequently without valid reason. Indeed, most agencies have both improved procedures to reduce opportunities for abuse of discretion and invested heavily in staff training.

In 2003, in contrast to 1999, the report card even showed significant signs of perceived reduction in corruption (Figure 13.6). Between 1994 and 1999, the percentage of respondents in general households saying that they had paid bribes increased from 14 per cent to 22 per cent. By 2003, however, it had dropped to only 9 per cent. This result, applying to transactions with service agencies in general, may not apply to specialized areas such as requests for building permits. It does not imply that all pockets of corruption have been eliminated. But it does indicate a general reduction in the corruption previously prevalent in routine transactions.

This achievement is probably the result of simpler procedures and improved efficiencies in routine operations. Reforms such as BMP's procedure for self-assessment of property tax and BDA's one-time sale deed have served to reduce the opportunities for harassment and extortion that citizens faced in the late 1990s.

Results from the Slum Household Survey

As in 1999, a large proportion of slum dwellers surveyed in 2003 were at least partially satisfied with most services. But their 2003 ratings are significantly lower than those of the general household sample. The poor do not use the entire range of services shown for general households, so only six of the nine agencies appeared in the report card for slum households.

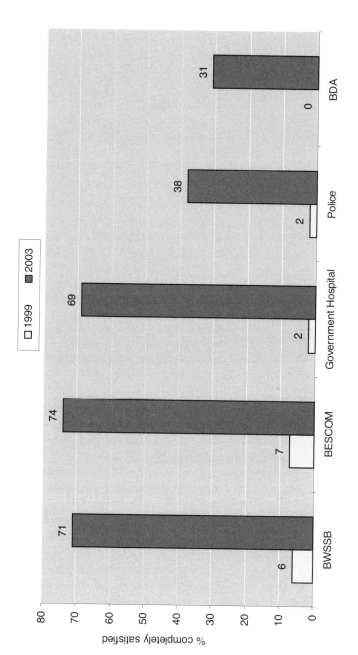

FIGURE 13.5 Complete Satisfaction with Staff Behaviour, 1999 and 2003: General Households

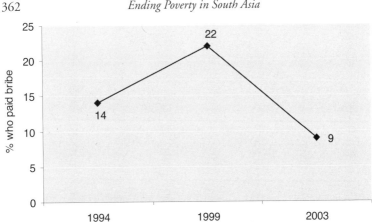

FIGURE 13.6   Incidence of Corruption in 1994, 1999, and 2003: General
               Households

Of these six, four received satisfaction ratings above 70 per cent (Figure 13.7). The satisfaction ratings given by slum dwellers ranged from 93 per cent for BMTC down to 64 per cent for the Bangalore police.

This is not to suggest that quality of services in the slums has not improved. Poor households responding in 2003 indicated substantial improvement in satisfaction with services. In particular, feedback from slum dwellers indicated that availability of water in public toilets and regularity of garbage clearance had improved substantially.

The incidence of problems also declined across the six agencies, comparing well with similar declines reported by general households (Figure 13.8). Slum dwellers in 2003 most often encountered problems in dealing with the Bangalore police and with BWSSB, as was also the case in 1999. For the water and sewerage agency there was only a small decline in reported problems, reflecting a number of institutional issues that affected its service provision in the slums. The fewest problems were reported in relation to the municipal transport agency.

For most agencies, satisfaction with staff behaviour was higher among slum households than among general households (Figure 13.9). In spite of the relatively higher frequency of problems with BWSSB, users who interacted with that agency gave its staff the highest ratings. Although Bangalore police received the lowest ratings on staff behaviour in 2003, there was still significant improvement over 1999. Even in the case of BMP, where overall satisfaction was comparatively low, satisfaction of slum households with staff behaviour turned out to be surprisingly high.

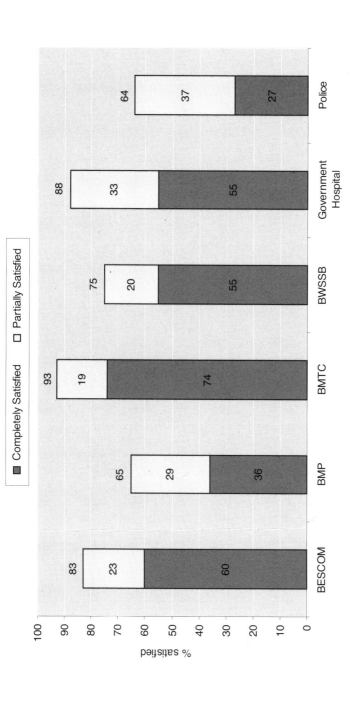

FIGURE 13.7 Overall Satisfaction, 2003: Slum Households

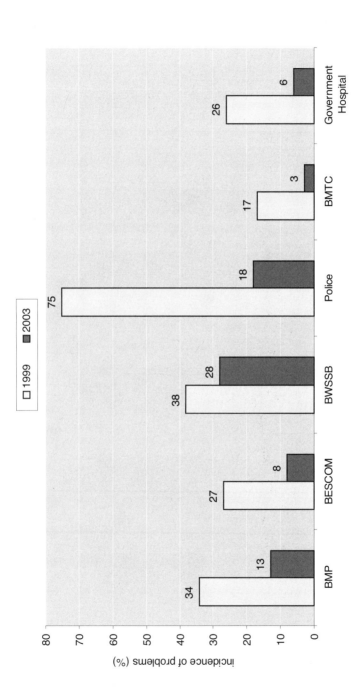

FIGURE 13.8 Incidence of Problems, 1999 and 2003: Slum Households

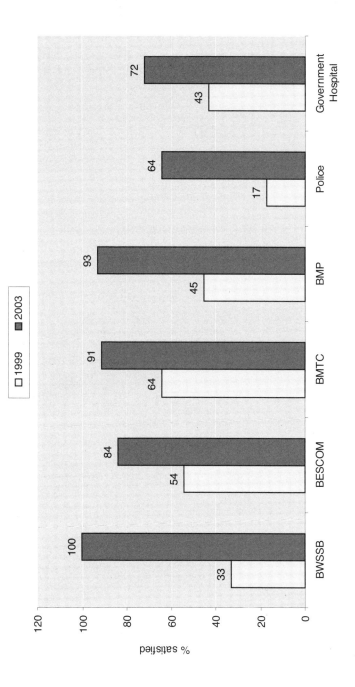

FIGURE 13.9   Satisfaction with Staff Behaviour, 1999 and 2003: Slum Households

The 2003 survey of slum households also showed a decline in the proportion of people who said they had paid bribes, from 25 per cent in 1999 to 19 per cent in 2003. In this regard, the experience of the poor is similar to that of the middle class. Nevertheless, the proportions reporting corruption are consistently higher for the low-income sample than for middle-class households, suggesting that the poor face a higher incidence of corruption than the rest of the population.

A Significant Turnaround

In summary, the most recent report card findings show that a significant turnaround has taken place in Bangalore's public services over a 10-year period. The improvement in public satisfaction levels cuts across all the major service providers, and is reflected in feedback from both middle-income and low-income households. Positive changes in specific indicators, while showing some variation, are consistent with the higher overall satisfaction ratings of the different agencies.

There is a surprising degree of internal consistency in the findings. The results seem to indicate that various reforms and streamlining within agencies have reduced the problems or hassles that people encounter during their interactions with agency staff, which in turn has diminished the scope for petty corruption. This finding has important implications for corruption control strategies. Reducing the incidence of problems has also served to ease overload on agency staff, which in turn has allowed better service to all customers. This may explain the higher ratings for staff behaviour in 2003 for most agencies.

These results took time and represent the cumulative impact of a series of actions that began with the first report card in 1994. The initial spotlight on public services set in motion actions by different stakeholders, including remedial steps by agencies to improve their services. How these and other factors interacted and cumulated to achieve a more comprehensive turnaround in Bangalore is not easy to measure and explain, nor is it possible to pinpoint the precise contribution of each of the factors. And it is unclear which components are most essential for replicating such a success in other settings.

Nevertheless, the drivers of change in Bangalore can be divided into two categories. On the one hand, demand-side factors such as citizen and media pressure sparked and sustained the initiative. This required the context of an open democratic society with institutionalized tolerance of dissent and debate. On the other hand, supply-side factors, in the form of government action to implement reforms, were also indispensable. The government response made possible the interaction between citizens and agencies that led to positive outcomes in improvement of services.

DEMAND FACTORS CONTRIBUTING TO SUCCESS

In the decade-long report card experience in Bangalore, it is possible to identify four factors on the demand side that worked together to sustain pressure for change. Most important were the report cards themselves and advocacy by a diverse network of civil society groups. These were reinforced by media attention and by behind-the-scenes support from international donor agencies. These factors operated both in sequence and interactively. Thus the first report card stimulated media publicity as well as civil society activism. By the time of the second report card, civic groups and the Public Affairs Centre were working together to maximize their joint impact.

The Glare Effect of Citizen Report Cards

The Bangalore report cards exerted pressure on the city's service providers in three ways. First, by providing focused information on performance from the perspective of citizens, the reports put the agencies under a public scanner. Such information was new to them, and as much of it was negative, it had the effect of shaming the poor performers. Evidence from the corporate world shows that measuring and quantifying work and outputs tends to make organizations pay more attention to what is being measured. Something similar seems to have happened in the Bangalore service agencies. The chairman of the Bangalore Development Authority (BDA) recalled his reaction after the first report card gave his agency a low rating: 'For the first time, there was a feedback from the public on the performance of agencies. My curiosity was triggered by the fact that in the rankings the report card assigned to the various agencies, I found the BDA had got the first rank from the bottom. I thought I should do something about this.'[4] A similar motivation is evident in the initiative some agencies took after the first report card to contact PAC for its advice and assistance to improve services. Public agencies tend to be sensitive to adverse publicity, especially in a democracy.

Second, interagency comparisons seem to have worked as a surrogate for market competition.[5] Although each service provider is a monopoly within its distinctive area of activity, the report card sets up a competitive arena by permitting interagency comparison of common attributes. Users, the media, and civil society groups see delays, bribery, and non-responsiveness as negative features in any service provider. The fact that the chairmen of some of the agencies called PAC to find out where they stood in the second report card before its findings were released shows that organizations do pay attention to how the public views them. They wanted to know not only whether their ratings had improved, but also whether they ranked higher or lower than others. This was the case despite objections by the same officials to public release of the interagency comparisons.

Third, it appears that some agency chairmen, at least, saw the report card as an aid in their efforts to reform their agencies. Although the feedback on their agencies was initially negative, these leaders took a positive view of the exercise. They used the findings to goad their colleagues to take action to improve services. This shows that a report card, when prepared impartially and professionally, can encourage the more proactive among public leaders to move ahead on the reform front. A recent assessment of the Bangalore initiative states that several agencies characterized the report cards as a 'catalyst' (Ravindra 2004). The same report quotes one agency leader as saying that PAC's work on satisfaction levels and on quality of services had a profound effect on him as a public manager. Some agencies subsequently adopted the practice of preparing their own report cards, thus affirming the value of user feedback as an internal management tool.

It is important to note that the report card was not a one-time initiative ending with the dissemination of findings. Rather, the first report card was followed up by two more within 10 years, and by ongoing advocacy for more responsive and efficient agencies.

Demand Pressure through Civil Society Groups

The report cards helped stimulate complementary public advocacy work, with the two factors together having a cumulative impact on the government and citizens of Bangalore. This advocacy, spearheaded by PAC, was carried out through a network of civic groups and non-governmental organizations (NGOs) in the city. The number of such groups increased significantly in the period following the first report card. Only about 20 were active in 1994; by 2000, their number exceeded 200. Not all of them were dynamic groups. Even so, many did participate in the campaigns and meetings organized by PAC, adding to the public pressure on service providers.

The network included two types of organizations. Neighbourhood groups called residents' associations focus on one part of the city but have a direct interest in the performance of all the service providers. Citywide

NGOs focus on specific civic or service-related issues. Both kinds of organizations participated in public meetings and seminars where report cards or other civic issues were discussed. These meetings engaged the service providers in active public dialogues, in contrast to the closed personal meetings with officials that previously were customary in all agencies. Some service providers, such as the electricity board, the water and sanitation board, and even the police, subsequently organized their own forums, inviting civil society groups for dialogue. As a result, interactions between organized civic groups and the service providers grew significantly.

Civic advocacy increased the stimulus for reform and responsiveness on the part of the service providers. This was already evident in 1999. After a public meeting held in Bangalore in connection with the second report card, a leading newspaper, the *Times of India*, said in an editorial: 'PAC, in creating this forum, has opened doors, even windows, for a healthy tête-à-tête with our service providers. The honesty on display was remarkable ... this is the spirit of democracy in action. Civil society working in tandem with government for the greater good of all' (8 November 1999).

In addition to such meetings, several NGOs have made distinctive contributions by carrying out citywide campaigns on specific issues. These campaigns, in most cases assisted by partnership with PAC, have served to strengthen the city's 'social capital.' One NGO undertook advocacy work linked to property tax reform. Another examined the municipal budget and engaged the city corporation in a debate on service efficiency and public expenditure. A third worked on the improvement of solid waste management.[6] These diverse interventions all signalled to the service providers that their activities were being watched and assessed in a systematic fashion. In different ways, all these civil society groups were demanding better services and accountability from the government and its agencies.

Reinforcement of Pressure by the Media

The print media in Bangalore played an unusual role by adding their weight to the pressure for better services. In 1994, the newspapers did little more than publicise the negative findings of the report card or other similar critical assessments. Investigative reports on civic issues were few and far between. Subsequently, however, the newspapers began to take a much more proactive role.

After deciding to devote more space to public service problems and related civic issues, several newspapers sought PAC's advice and technical support for special features. One newspaper began a series of reports on the different wards of the city, highlighting their problems and focusing on their elected council members. Another leading newspaper even took the initiative to organize meetings in different parts of the city at which citizens were invited to voice their local problems in the presence of senior officials from a selected group of public agencies. A large number of public officials thus were exposed to the issues of the localities and pressed to respond with answers. These meetings received much publicity in the newspaper, as did the remedial actions taken subsequently. This public process clearly put increased pressure on the agencies to be more transparent and accountable and to deliver on their promises.

The Role of International Donors

While international donors work most visibly on the supply side of problems by providing loans, grants, and technical assistance, there is some evidence that in Bangalore donor involvement also added to the pressure on the demand side. Since such contacts happened mainly behind closed doors, it is difficult to document their contribution. But in personal communications, World Bank officials, for example, have confirmed that in their dialogues with the government they stressed the importance of user feedback and the need to view civil society pressure as an aid to accountability. These signals may well have reinforced the demand pressure on the agencies from the other sources discussed above.

SUPPLY FACTORS CONTRIBUTING TO SUCCESS

In addition to the responsiveness shown initially by agency leaders themselves, the most decisive supply-side factor was establishment of the Bangalore Agenda Task Force in 2000, one year after the second report card. This step, an initiative of the new chief minister of Karnataka state, was reinforced by additional resource mobilization within the agencies, by an active state ombudsman, and by the ongoing political commitment of the state government.

The Bangalore Agenda Task Force

Until 1999, the modest improvements in services that occurred in Bangalore and that were reflected in the second report card resulted from actions taken by the agency leaders on their own initiative. The constraints within which they operated limited the scope of the reforms they could attempt.

The scene changed for the better in 2000 when the new chief minister (the elected head of the Karnataka state government) created the Bangalore Agenda Task Force to work in partnership with the major service providers. This step, coming only a few months after the release of the second report card, showed the government's determination to deal with the problems being experienced by the public. BATF was made up of several prominent persons from the private and professional sectors along with the chairpersons of seven service agencies.[7] This public–private partnership was authorized to mobilize funds and expertise to assist and stimulate change in the functioning of these agencies, and to involve the public in appropriate ways in the process. It provided a forum for the service providers to test and experiment with reform ideas, seek assistance, and give an account of their actions.

BATF launched a series of six monthly summits where service providers made statements on their plans, outcomes, and commitments, and citizens were invited to listen and respond. These summits were also attended by the chief minister, who personally questioned the heads of agencies on their plans and achievements. BATF thus became a forum for accountability and for monitoring by the public, creating greater openness and a sense of public participation. The task force also brought out report cards on the progress of its own work.

The private donations mobilized by BATF enabled the service providers to experiment with new systems, practices, and infrastructural options. Government funds would not have given them the degree of flexibility that private funds did. The speedy introduction of the fund-based accounting system in BMP, for example, would not have occurred without the money provided through BATF.

The professional expertise that BATF made available allowed the service providers to explore new options they might not otherwise have considered. The private funds raised by BATF were used in part to finance such selective technical assistance. Some projects, such as road building, had no need of technical support from BATF. The property tax reform, on the other hand, required the fine-tuning of criteria, preparation of a manual, workshops for citizen orientation, and other steps that needed careful planning and attention to detail. These tasks benefited much from BATF's input. The involvement of BATF experts speeded up the process and goaded BMP staff to move forward faster.

BATF had no legal or administrative authority over the public agencies with which it worked. It did not approve their budgets or oversee their programmes or projects. Its influence stemmed from its partnership and catalytic mode of operation, reinforced by direct political support from the chief minister. His participation in the summits was a testimony to his commitment and made it possible for BATF to solve tricky problems of coordination between some of the service providers in the course of these meetings. Agency leaders found the strategic inputs and assistance provided by BATF to be valuable and timely.

Resource Mobilization by the Agencies

A parallel development, encouraged by but independent of the BATF, was a significant increase in resources available to the seven service provider agencies included in the task force. New projects and expansion of infrastructure required more resources, which the agency leaders were able to mobilize from a variety of sources. The expanded BMP roads and related infrastructure programme was financed by a loan from the Housing and Urban Development Corporation. BMTC, BWSSB, and BESCOM were able to get similar long-term loans from other sources. BDA was a unique case in that it was able to raise most of the funds required for new infrastructure projects from its own internal surpluses. Overall, the budgets of these agencies increased by 50 to 100 per cent over the three-year period from 2000 to 2003. Upgrading of services and infrastructure through increased borrowing might have happened in earlier years. But it took the proactive support of the state government and the catalytic role of BATF to make this happen in a short period of time (Nilekani 2003).

Role of the Lok Ayukta

The Karnataka state ombudsman, or *lok ayukta*, played an indirect role in enhancing accountability in the agencies. This official has powers not only to investigate grievances from the public about public agencies but also to initiate investigations into agency operations. The ombudsman appointed in 2000 was active on both fronts. His raids on offices and subsequent actions to penalize public officials guilty of corruption produced much adverse publicity for many agencies and departments of the state government. His integrity and courage were lauded by civil society, the media, and political leaders. Many observers believe that these actions also had a deterrent effect, even on agencies that were not investigated by the ombudsman. Strong support from the chief minister was a major factor that made it possible for the ombudsman to function fearlessly. While BATF provided positive impetus for public agencies to perform better, political support for the ombudsman sent the agencies a warning that corruption and sloth would not be tolerated. These two approaches were thus mutually reinforcing.

Political Commitment and Support

The common thread that runs through the different supply-side interventions discussed above is the political commitment and support of the chief minister of the state. The lack of such commitment was a significant factor during 1994–99, and the political change in 1999 made a decisive difference. The new chief minister, committed to improving public services and infrastructure, was determined to find effective responses to citizens' dissatisfaction with essential services and industry's dissatisfaction with infrastructure. After setting up the BATF, he called on public agencies to mobilize more resources and facilitated their efforts. He appointed a new ombudsman known for his integrity and willingness to deal with corruption and other abuses of power. With a strong majority in the legislature, the chief minister could implement his vision without fear of political instability.

Such political will, of course, can vary with changes in leaders and governments, and this does raise questions about the sustainability of the reforms. It underscores the critical role of civil society institutions as monitors of governance and catalysts for reform. Civil society initiatives and demand for accountability are essential for coping with the vagaries of political commitment.

REPLICATING THE INITIATIVE

The foregoing discussion highlights the contributions made by a variety of interventions that reinforced one another in the Bangalore context. It is their joint influence that is reflected in the report card results for 2003 summarized above. As noted, the contribution of each of the factors is difficult to quantify. An agency head, for example, can legitimately take credit for the turnaround in his or her services. But it is also true that without the support or pressure from the other actors mentioned above, the agency head might not have taken the necessary actions.

In the absence of political commitment, civil society organizations can still serve as monitors of governance and catalysts for reform. And, in the absence of civil society demand, it is possible that political leaders and agency heads would still have some interest in reforms. It is nevertheless clear, however, that such substantial improvements in public services are likely to require both the pressure of civil society demand and political commitment facilitating a response from state agencies. In principle, such conditions should be replicable in other contexts.

The Bangalore report cards were the first to be initiated by PAC. But there have been many other applications of this tool in Bangalore as well as in other parts of India and in other countries (Paul 2002; Balakrishnan and Iyer 1998). One case of special relevance to the poor was PAC's report card on the maternity hospitals for poor women in Bangalore. Its findings led to systematic advocacy work by several NGOs and ultimately to the adoption of important reforms in the management of these hospitals, which have benefited low-income mothers and children (Paul 2002).

Another initiative that had substantial impact, despite an initial negative reaction, was PAC's report card on the investment climate in Karnataka state (Paul 2000). This showed that despite the great publicity given by the state government to rising investments in Karnataka, prospective investors faced major hurdles in implementing projects. There was clear evidence that the volume of actual investment in the state was significantly below the total of approved project investments. Based on a sample survey of investors, the report card showed that corruption, infrastructure, taxation, and interface with government, in that order, were serious barriers. The report card also rated regulatory agencies with which investors had to deal, focusing on variables such as time taken for processing, number of visits made, complexity of procedures, and bribes demanded.

The report card was released and the findings were published in the press. PAC's chairperson received a call from the industry minister the very next day, seeking an urgent meeting with the PAC team. In a lengthy conversation, the minister recounted his progressive policies and the actions his ministry had taken to improve the investment climate. He stressed the potential damage to the state from adverse publicity generated by the study findings. The PAC response was that the report card, reflecting the experiences of investors in the state, had to be taken seriously. There was no consensus at the end of the meeting, and the PAC team had the distinct impression that the minister was unhappy with the outcome.

Nevertheless, six months later PAC received another call from the minister's office, inviting the chairperson to a forum to present the report card findings and highlight the steps necessary to remedy investor problems. In addition to the minister and his senior officials, the meeting was attended by representatives of industry associations and other organized groups. The minister acknowledged the role played by PAC's report card and announced that his department was working on a reform package to respond to the problems of investors. Once the reform package was developed, senior officials of the department requested PAC to prepare a new report card as part of a benchmarking exercise to assess progress in the investment climate after implementation of the reforms. The reform package has been passed by the legislature and is now being implemented.

LESSONS LEARNED

Governments are responsible for the provision of essential public services in most developing countries. In this context, the Bangalore report card initiative has shown that there is much that service providers and their supervising authorities can do to improve services by paying attention to citizen feedback. Citizen report cards offer a valuable tool to gather such feedback from the users of services, providing diagnostic information that is more systematic and usable than individual complaints and protests against public agencies. Report cards can be a useful aid for policy makers and managers, filling gaps left by incomplete or weak monitoring by the agencies themselves.

Such a tool has particular relevance for poor people, who find it difficult and costly to make their voices heard in large and powerful public agencies. And leaders of poor people's groups or mediating organizations may not always accurately convey poor people's points of view. The survey methods used to produce the report cards permit the poor to make their voices heard directly and with minimal bias. Report card findings can empower the poor by giving them independent information that they can use in their interactions with service providers (Goetz and Gaventa 2001).

When a government and its service providers are non-responsive or perform poorly, civil society has the responsibility to demand greater accountability. Report cards in conjunction with advocacy can then become a tool to stimulate government and its service agencies to respond to the systemic problems being experienced by the people. Although there is no guarantee of effective responses, since that also depends on agency responsiveness and on the political commitment of government authorities, the Bangalore report cards show the potential for stimulating dramatic improvements. The diagnostic value of this tool for agency leaders themselves, combined with the glare effect of public attention, can create strong pressures for greater responsiveness.

The dissemination of findings and the follow-up advocacy work are likely to be more effective when concerned civil society institutions are involved from the start. In Bangalore, early consultations with NGOs working with the poor helped sharpen the survey's focus on the problems of poor households. Once the government also takes a positive stance on such changes, public–private partnerships, including ongoing forums for dialogue, have the potential to make the process more sustainable.

An important prerequisite for effective implementation of a report card initiative is the credibility of those who use the tool and engage in advocacy. The report card exercise must be seen as impartial and independent, so the conduct of the survey and the interpretation of its findings should be done with utmost integrity. In general, competent and professionally managed organizations need to act as intermediaries. These conditions apply irrespective of whether the initiative comes from civil society or from the government.

Finally, an essential requirement for effectiveness of the report card tool is a society that is relatively open and democratic, with respect for dissent. In non-democratic settings such an instrument can still be used to expose shortcomings. But sustainable campaigns resulting in real improvement in services are unlikely without commitment by political leaders to listen to public feedback, based on an understanding that the findings can and should be used to improve public services or other aspects of governance.

References

Balakrishnan, S. and A. Iyer, 1998, *Bangalore Hospitals and the Urban Poor: A Report Card*, Bangalore: Public Affairs Centre.

Goetz, A.M. and J. Gaventa, 2001, 'Bringing Citizen Voice and Client Focus into Service Delivery,' IDS Working Paper 138, University of Sussex, Brighton, UK: Institute of Development Studies.

Nilekani, N., 2003, 'Bangalore Agenda Task Force: A Partnership With Promise?' Bangalore: Public Affairs Centre.

Paul, S., 1995, 'A Report Card on Public Services in Indian Cities: A View from Below.' Bangalore: Public Affairs Centre.

_____, 2000, 'Wanted: An Enabling Industrial Environment in Karnataka,' Bangalore: Public Affairs Centre.

_____, 2002, *Holding the State to Account: Citizen Monitoring in Action*, Bangalore: Books for Change.

Paul, S. and S. Sekhar, 2000, 'Benchmarking Urban Services: The Second Report Card on Bangalore,' Bangalore: Public Affairs Centre.

Ravindra, A. 2004. 'An Assessment of the Impact of the Bangalore Citizen Report Cards on the Performance of Public Agencies.' ECD Working Paper 12, Operations Evaluation Department, Washington, DC: World Bank.

Notes

1 This measure is the most appropriate for comparisons between 1999 and 2003, as the rating scale was modified somewhat in 2003. The highest rating a user could give a service was 'very satisfied' in 1999 and 'completely satisfied' in 2003. These two categories are comparable.

2 Problem incidence was not an item in the report card survey of 1994.

3 Comparable data were available for only five agencies.

4 The BDA chairman was interviewed in a video documentary titled *State of India's Public Services: Benchmarks for the Millennium* (Bangalore: Public Affairs Centre, 2003).

5 Market competition has so far affected only one service provider, the Bangalore telecommunications agency (BSNL). Cell phones had begun to make inroads by the late 1990s.

6 These and similar initiatives are discussed in Paul (2002).

7 The seven agencies in BATF were picked by the chief minister. The roads authority and hospitals were not included as they serve areas outside Bangalore.

14

Commentary

A Framework for
Scaling Up Poverty Reduction

Shantayanan Devarajan and *Ravi Kanbur*

Poor people are poor because markets fail them and governments fail them. Failures in capital markets, for instance, prevent poor people from getting adequate education. When government steps in to 'correct' these market failures, it often introduces new problems, such as the capture of public resources by the non-poor or the inability to monitor service providers. These government failures leave the poor still poor.

To be sure, there are many excellent examples of government interventions that have helped the poor in different ways. And civil society has mobilized non-governmental projects and activities that have improved the lives of the affected populations. But these cases point to a basic paradox in the discourse on poverty reduction. Despite well-known examples of government and non-governmental projects that have reduced poverty, poverty at the aggregate level persists, or decreases only slowly. And attempts to replicate small-scale successes manifold do not necessarily succeed.

This paradox naturally raises the question of whether and how small interventions that work well for the poor locally can be 'scaled up' to achieve wider impact, perhaps at the regional or national level. This is the sense in which we will use the term 'scaling up poverty reduction' in this essay. There is a second sense of the term used in the discourse and that is simply to mean 'more poverty reduction'. Scaling up in the first sense contributes to scaling up in the second sense, but in this essay our focus will be not on poverty reduction in general but on the potential to achieve poverty reduction by expanding interventions that are known to work well on a small scale.

There are two possible approaches to studying the issue of scaling up, so defined. One is to examine real-life cases of interventions, especially where an attempt has been made to scale up successful small activities, and to assess the conditions of success. Another is to take a more conceptual approach, asking what might be needed for success, or what might explain failure, in a range of circumstances.

More than 100 case studies were prepared for the conference on Scaling Up Poverty Reduction held in Shanghai in May 2004 (http://www.worldbank.org/wbi/reducingpoverty/). These case studies contribute greatly to building up knowledge based on specific experiences in which successful activities have begun the process of expansion. A dozen of these studies dealing with South Asia are presented in this volume, thus following the first approach outlined above. This essay takes the complementary approach by developing a framework for thinking about scaling up. The framework derives from the understandings that emerge from the case studies but also helps to better interpret their findings, individually and collectively. Although it is based on the South Asia case studies in this volume, we believe the framework has broad applicability.

The section below sets out the framework in outline form, then illustrates and fleshes out the concepts with reference to the case studies in this volume. The next section looks ahead and discusses policy recommendations for governments and donors who want to promote successful scaling up. The essay concludes with a discussion of outstanding issues on which more research and policy debate will be useful.

THE FRAMEWORK IN OUTLINE

Our proposed framework is built on three key concepts: market failure, government failure, and civil society failure. The first two are well known, but the third perhaps needs some elaboration. We use these concepts to identify the gaps that scaling up must fill, as well as the constraints that such efforts will face.

When markets work well, the economic system generates outcomes that are efficient although not necessarily equitable. When markets do not work well, the economic system generates outcomes that are not efficient, nor necessarily equitable. This is market failure. A market system that does not work well can be improved upon in theory to generate both a bigger pie and a better distribution of that pie. If the interventions that are needed to improve the market system can be implemented by a benevolent, informed, and competent government, market failure can be overcome. Of course, in reality, governments are not always fully benevolent, informed, or competent. Attempts to correct market failure by governments therefore sometimes lead to the opposite of what is intended, with outcomes that generate more inefficiency and more inequity. This is government failure.

In the lives of poor people, market failure and government failure are both pervasive. If we take basic aspects of poor people's standard of living such as education, health, and insurance against vulnerability, there are good reasons in theory why markets will not provide adequate levels of these valued goods. This is borne out in practice: a large literature documents inadequate levels of education and health and excessive levels of vulnerability among the poor. All these areas are dogged by the problem of imperfect information. Moreover, market failure in another area—imperfect capital and credit markets—exacerbates the market failure in education, health, and insurance for the poorest.

Not surprisingly, governments have attempted to address these market failures through interventions of various types, including public provision of education and health facilities and interventions in credit and other markets. These interventions have had a mixed record. While there are undoubted successes, there are many instances of government failure as well, as documented by the case studies in this volume and by many of the other case studies done for the Shanghai conference. For example, despite a national commitment to universal primary education, many children do not attend primary schools and many countries remain some distance from the goal of universal literacy. Similarly, on health, water, and sanitation, government provision lags behind ideal goals in terms of access and quality of provision.

Just because there is some market failure does not mean that all markets fail all the time. Just because there is some government failure does not mean that all governments fail all of the time. Moreover, even when markets and government both fail, perhaps especially when they both fail, civil society organizations can sometimes step in and provide services and activities to fill the gap. The case studies for the Shanghai conference give plenty of examples of such gap filling. However, the gap is never filled completely, and civil society organizations typically fall short of this by a considerable margin—otherwise the record on poverty reduction would be stronger and more widespread. This is civil society failure. One answer to this failure might be to encourage the expansion of civil society activities in providing basic services to the poor. But, as we shall see, such expansion is not without its own problems and constraints.

We are interested in implications for public policy. What actions can government take, and how can international agencies support the actions that governments take, in scaling up poverty reduction by confronting market failure, government failure, and civil society failure? Let us start with market failure, and take education as a specific case. It is generally accepted that levels of education in developing countries are too low, especially for girls. There are many reasons why a market may not arise naturally to provide an increase in education that is considered socially desirable. Returns to education are uncertain and, together with imperfect credit markets, may prevent adequate investment in human capital, given the opportunity costs involved. Or there may be significant externalities and threshold effects associated with the returns to education, leading to low-level traps where the outcome is individually rational but socially suboptimal. Or the interests of parents in educating their children, especially their female children, may not match social ideals.

Let us then take as given that there is too little education without government intervention, and that it is the role of government to 'scale up' educational attainment. What should government do? The answer depends crucially on whether the low level of education is due to a supply constraint, a demand constraint, or both. If there is a supply constraint, meaning that at current private opportunity costs the demand for education exceeds the supply, then the government has to focus on expanding supply to scale up. If, on the other hand, there is a demand constraint (parents do not want to, or cannot afford to, send their children to school), then expanding supply by building more schools, for example, will not increase the total amount of education. Resources spent on expanding education will be wasted.

For developing countries, the typical situation starts out with excess demand. At this stage, expanding supply is the right policy for scaling up. But sooner or later supply will catch up with demand. At this point, resources will have to go into expanding demand as well as expanding supply, and the two will have to proceed hand in hand. Scaling up the response to this market failure thus requires first of all a diagnosis of the nature of supply and demand in relation to each other, and then a carefully staged set of matched interventions. If this is not done, there will surely be government failure in scaling up.

Furthermore, even if expanding supply is the right thing to do, the government may not be doing enough of it, or may be doing it badly. Monitoring and overseeing of school construction may be weak. Teachers may be paid but may not turn up to teach. Or the curriculum may be wholly inappropriate. Worse, government intervention may increase inequity as public resources are used to benefit the well-off at the expense of the poor. There is evidence of all of these government failures in the case studies for the Shanghai conference, and in the broader literature on education.

While the above example deals specifically with education, it should be clear that the supply/demand way of thinking applies to a whole range of issues in public services including health, water, and sanitation. It can also apply to credit markets. There is a broad consensus in the development literature that credit constraints are pervasive—that there is excess demand for credit and that its distribution is inefficient and inequitable. The response, then, is to expand supply, but the question is how to do it. One answer is to make this the task of government, and indeed that is the route that many countries have followed. By and large, these government interventions have not been successful. Quite apart from problems of corruption and political interference, there is the basic issue of information: governments have not been able to solve the information and monitoring problems that hobble the credit market. This government failure has left a gap. It has been filled in some countries by an energetic civil society sector, the microcredit sector, providing credit to very poor households on the basis of small loans and localized monitoring and control. Microinsurance is provided in much the same way.

The market-failure gap that is left unfilled, or even widened, because of government failure is thus filled to some extent by civil society. This is true not only in microcredit and microinsurance but also in myriad other activities and sectors that are deeply important to poor people's standard of living—health, education, water, sanitation, agricultural production, and so on. But civil society does something else as well. While trying to fill the gap left by the government and the market, it also highlights this gap in the public consciousness by giving voice to the voiceless. It emphasizes the consequences of market failure and demands public action, then reveals failures of public action stemming from malevolence, lack of information, and incompetence. Civil society as a whole thus simultaneously provides information on the gap, urges government to fill the gap, and attempts to fill the gap itself.

The persistence of poverty demonstrates that civil society has not, up to now, managed to fill this gap completely. This civil society failure has many causes, and an understanding of these causes is important for making the best use of civil society in a strategy of scaling up. Members of civil society organizations are not themselves immune from malevolence, ignorance, or incompetence. Policies will surely have to address these issues, especially as these organizations grow. Moreover, even well-run organizations do not generally have the ear of policy makers and government bureaucrats. They cannot always get their message across to the authorities. We will surely have to think about instruments that better allow the voices of the poor, and the public generally, to be heard by those who deliver public services and make and implement public policy.

Beyond these problems, which are present in public and private organizations alike, there is a structural issue. Civil society organizations operate, by definition, in the interstices between market and state. They interact with both, of course: many organizations sell products made by poor people in markets or provide marketable services, and nearly all organizations come under one or another set of government regulations. But their small size effectively insulates them from the full force of markets or government. This is fine if the sector stays small, but smallness is contrary to the requirement of scaling up, of expanding activities by civil society organizations so that they fill more and more of the market failure gap that they cannot induce the government to fill.

As civil society organizations expand to scale up poverty reduction, they will come up against the market on the one hand and the state on the other. For example, as microcredit organizations expand, the weight of their transactions will become significant relative to the formal capital market. Well before they expand to fill the gap they set out to fill, they will come under the influence, perhaps the volatility, of financial conditions nationally and globally. To take another example, as a small microinsurance organization expands, it will eventually come onto the radar screen of national insurance regulators, whose rules and capital requirements are set with large formal insurance companies, perhaps even with the global market, in mind. Unless these rules are modified to accommodate the expansion of smaller-scale activities, these regulations, valid as they are on their own terms, will strangle the expansion and hence the scaling up of microinsurance. A third example: as non-governmental (and non-profit) schools expand, they may challenge the national school curriculum. Such challenges may be positive, if for example they concern the tailoring of teaching methods to rural schoolchildren, or they may be negative, if for example they concern the propagation of a fundamentalist religious ideology. In either case the challenges have to be addressed and managed.

All of the tendencies noted in the analysis above are present to different degrees in reality. They are found in the broader literature, but are especially salient in the case studies brought together in this volume. The next section takes up the task of illustrating the different facets of the framework developed in this section with actual examples from South Asia, covering topics such as: (a) market failure leading to excess supply or excess demand; (b) government failure because of expansion of demand (supply) when the constraint was supply (demand); (c) government failure because of malevolence, ignorance, or incompetence; (d) civil society attempts to fill the gap created by market failure and government failure; (e) market and government constraints to civil society expansion. The following section will then draw together the lessons for policy.

ILLUSTRATIONS OF THE FRAMEWORK

Viewed through the lens of the framework outlined in the previous section, the 12 case studies in this volume highlight both the potential for and the challenges of scaling up poverty reduction in South Asia. Almost all the cases stem from an underlying market failure; the one exception is the self-help group programme in Andhra Pradesh, which helps government fulfil its redistributive role. Some of these efforts address the market failure squarely, while others address the government failure associated with the state's response to market failure.

In the first category are three programmes in India—e-choupals, Operation Flood, and to a lesser extent SEWA—as well as Bangladesh's microfinance initiatives. The e-choupals initiative tackles the inefficiency that results when traders of agricultural products hold power over farmers because of an informational advantage. The traders have better access to information about prices and other things, giving them monopoly power and affecting the distribution of profits between trader and producer. By bringing Internet-linked computers to the village, e-choupals give farmers access to the same information as traders, enabling them to check on the traders' prices and rendering the market for soybeans, among other crops, more competitive as well as more equitable. The programme also helps mobilize the farmers, who were not organized before, so that they can withstand efforts by the traders to maintain the status quo. Similarly, Operation Flood mobilizes dairy farmers and their trading partners into cooperatives controlled by the farmers. SEWA mobilizes informal women workers into a collective that could bargain for better working conditions and pay. Finally, Bangladesh's microfinance initiatives attacks a fundamental capital market failure—asymmetric information between borrower and lender—by using peer-group monitoring as the means of correction.

In each of these cases, the initiative does more than just correct a market failure. It serves as a way of mobilizing poor people. SEWA has gone from organizing informal women textile workers to providing various livelihood and marketing services to members in a broad range of occupations. In Bangladesh, the weekly meetings of microcredit borrowers also serve as a forum for information sharing among women about family planning, child nutrition, and health. By addressing a particular market failure, these movements help to solve another collective-action problem, namely, the coordination of poor people's voices into a movement. This is one reason why these initiatives were able to scale up as much as they did—as of 2005, SEWA had over 750,000 members, and Bangladesh had extended access to microfinance to 14 million people.

But this same feature points to a potential problem for scaling up. Both India and Bangladesh are democracies, which means there are established mechanisms, such as political parties, for organizing the collective voice of the people, including poor people. As these other movements, such as SEWA and the larger microfinance institutions in Bangladesh, scale up, they approach the scale of the existing political parties. This creates the potential for a conflict between the two types of institutions.

We turn now to the initiatives that aim to correct government failures, most of which were triggered by the public sector's response to a market failure. The Bhoomi project in India addressed a common failure in the public sector's performance of its duty of land registration—bribery and corruption. Land registration is a classic function of the state, as it is part of the protection of property rights. Yet the state was failing to perform this very function because of asymmetric power relationships between farmers and bureaucrats, and imperfect monitoring. The Bhoomi project attempted to tackle the problem by computerizing the land registration system. Not only did this dramatically speed up the records retrieval process, it reduced corruption and permitted the functioning of the crop insurance market by making claims more easily verifiable. Addressing a government failure contributed to correcting a market failure—in this case, in the market for crop insurance.

Similarly, in Tamil Nadu, India, the local government was not fulfilling its responsibility to provide water, sanitation, and other municipal services to its citizens, even though these services were deemed a public responsibility, presumably because of scale economies in their provision. Meanwhile, with a growing economy, demand for these services was outstripping supply. Observing the excess demand, the private sector was interested in participating in these services, but found the risks, especially of over-regulation, too high. The problem was solved by a partnership between the government and the private sector wherein the former guaranteed not to over-regulate while the latter agreed to provide services even to poor neighbourhoods. A market failure and government failure were solved by government and the market working together.

The Education Guarantee Scheme of Madhya Pradesh, India, provides another example of a programme to address government failure. Education demand was clearly outpacing supply in the state. However, efforts to increase supply by the traditional method, in which the government builds schools and hires teachers, were not working. Teachers were often absent, and school buildings were in disrepair. So the government decided to use the source of demand—the parents who wanted to send their children to school—as a means of strengthening supply. To any community that requested a school, the government gave a justiciable guarantee to provide one in 90 days. In addition, the community could select the teacher, whom the government would train. The result was a partnership between the government and the community, mutually reinforcing each other, and a substantial improvement in education in Madhya Pradesh.

These three cases of overcoming government failure illustrate the importance of forming coalitions to resist the forces that created the government failure in the first place. In Tamil Nadu, the coalition was with the private sector; in Madhya Pradesh, it was with the communities; in the Bhoomi project, it was with the farmers, who could now be mobilized through the introduction of electronic land registration. These coalitions helped the reform champions to overcome the vested interests who benefited from the original government failure and who would undoubtedly try to stop the change. But these cases also indicate some potential dilemmas in scaling up. If a partnership with the private sector is scaled up, does the whole enterprise become a private entity? In this case, it might succumb to the original market failure that triggered the problem in the first place. Similarly, if the partnership with the community is scaled up, the community might replace the government, especially the local government, which has been entrusted with the responsibility for education.

We turn now to three cases that helped government fulfil its redistributive role, rather than its efficiency-enhancing role: the self-help groups in Andhra Pradesh, the Rural Support Programme in Pakistan, and the National Solidarity Programme in Afghanistan. In each of these, the government used community groups to monitor and implement anti-poverty programmes. The government of Andhra Pradesh embraced the self-help groups, which had formed either spontaneously or with NGO assistance, as an instrument to deliver on its poverty reduction programme. The Government of Afghanistan, knowing that subnational governments either did not exist or were subject to extreme forms of capture, decided to use community groups as a means of distributing funds for small infrastructure projects. A similar approach was taken by the Rural Support Programme in Pakistan, based on the success of the Aga Khan RSP. The common feature of these initiatives is that the government used a non-governmental institution to fulfil a government function, namely, redistribution. Once again, the dilemma of scaling up is whether these non-governmental institutions can approach a scale equal to that of the government, yet not replace the government.

A final example, which focuses only on giving voice to poor people, is that of the citizen report cards in Bangalore, India. The NGO in this case, the Public Affairs Centre, was not involved in service delivery; rather, it sought to solve the collective-action problem of information generation by providing information about the quality of public services throughout the city. The report cards played a crucial role in helping poor people keep politicians accountable—witness the significant improvement in services in Bangalore over the past five years. In this sense, they were performing a role that is suited to an NGO. This also means that the possibility of scaling up this function is quite high. With assistance from the Public Affairs Centre, report card studies have since been carried out elsewhere in India and in some other countries.

CONCLUSION

What are the implications of this application of our framework to the 12 case studies, for public policy and for donors who are interested in helping governments scale up?

For governments, at least three sets of lessons emerge. First, in addressing market failures, especially those that adversely affect the poor, governments should look for opportunities to also help the poor solve collective action problems. While addressing the technical problem associated with the market failure, such as information asymmetry, one should look for opportunities to strengthen poor people's ability to mobilize and to build coalitions that can amplify their voice in policy making.

Second, even in cases where there is massive government failure, there is hope. The same government that is responsible for the failure can form coalitions with other actors to develop successful approaches to poverty reduction. The reason for the government failure is often a coordination problem within government, or a political market failure. By forging links with the private sector or with communities, governments can overcome these failures and break out of a low-level equilibrium trap.

Third, the approach used to overcome government failure—building coalitions with the private sector or communities—could create difficulties for scaling up to the next level. Scaling up means these programmes will approach the scale of either the market or the government. Yet it was a market failure or government failure (or both) that created the need for the programme in the first place. So as the scale increases, governments need to ensure that the original failure does not get reproduced in the new scaled-up programme.

For donors who would like to support governments in their efforts to scale up poverty reduction, the implications are as follows. First, there is no single institutional arrangement that works everywhere and all the time. Successful poverty reduction efforts can take place through government-only programmes (Bhoomi); through the private sector only (Operation Flood); or through partnerships between government and NGOs (Andhra Pradesh) or government and the private sector (Tamil Nadu). The cliché that one size does not fit all applies with exceptional force in this context. If an arrangement works in one country, donors should contain their enthusiasm for advocating it in other countries.

At the same time, if a particular government is failing badly, donors should not necessarily lose hope. These same governments may build coalitions with partners and overcome some of their own deficits. Finally, donors too should be aware of the dilemmas facing countries in scaling up. The very reason why a particular innovation succeeded, say in forming a partnership with community organizations, may be the reason why it is difficult to scale up. In short, we probably need to scale up something that is in short supply in the development community, namely, patience.

Glossary

adatiya	commission agent who buys produce from farmers and resells it to large buyers
arak	country liquor
ben	sister
bhai	brother
bidi	cigarette
cal	calories
Dalit	lowest caste, formerly known as untouchable
ghee	clarified butter
Gram Mahila Haat	village women's market
gram panchayat	village-level elected council
gram sabha	village assembly comprising all adult residents of a village
guruji	teacher in an EGS school
jogan	temple prostitute
jogani	system of temple prostitution
mandal	subdistrict
mandi	government-mandated marketplace where farmers sell their crops
panchayati raj	local self-government institutions
samyojak	commission agent who works with the e-choupal system
sanchalak	farmer who runs the e-choupal computer and acts as ITC's representative in the village
shura	traditional village authority
taluk	subdistrict

| tehsildar | chief revenue officer for a taluk |
| zilla parishad | district-level elected council |

Index

ECO-AUDIT
Environmental Benefits Statement

The World Bank is committed to preserving endangered forests and natural resources. We have chosen to print *Ending Poverty in South Asia: Ideas That Work* on recycled paper with 30% post-consumer waste. The Office of the Publisher has agreed to follow the recommended standards for paper usage set by the Green Press Initiative, a nonprofit program supporting publishers in using fiber that is not sourced from endangered forests. For more information, visit www.greenpressinitiative.org.

Saved:
- 14 trees
- 10 million BTUs of energy
- 1,268 pounds of carbon dioxide (CO_2) not released into the atmosphere
- 5,263 gallons of water
- 676 pounds of waste not generated